The Corruption Of Power

AFRICAN POLITICS

Ken C. Kotecha with Robert W. Adams

UNIVERSITY
PRESS OF
AMERICA

C O N T E N T S

PREFACE

This will not be a popular book. However, it is unlikely that it will not provoke interest and some controversy because it challenges scholarly shibboleths and punctures popular myths about the quality and purpose of politics and government in many black African states since independence. The central thesis of the work is that the early promise of democratic development in the interests of all groups making up the complex mosaic of African society in all nations was aborted by the inability of most African leaders to make democracy work in a way that would preserve their power and still protect the representative forms with which their nations began independence. Faced with a choice of either self-aggrandizement or fealty to constitutionality, they chose the former--and then scrapped or re-wrote constitutions to fit the political facts of life.

Perhaps in developing societies such as those in modern Africa, it can be no other way, and constitutional government along Western lines was doomed from the start. Whatever the case, the political facts of African life in most systems do not fit either popular perceptions or the accepted dogmas of a large part of the scholarly community writing in the field of African studies. A romantic veil of illusion and rationalization obscures the facts of African political life and distorts the judgment of many Africanists. Double standards of racial justice and political rectitude are applied to analyses of South African life under the deplorable, but waning, weakening apartheid system and the equally deplorable (but always forgiveable) policies of discrimination against Asian and other non-black minorities routinely practiced north of the Limpopo River.

For too long, the ideology of negritude and black liberation and the policy of Africanization in the name of "true majority rule" has justified the personalization of power and the conversion of representative institutions into vehicles perpetuating the power monopolies of dominant elites in many black African states during the post independence period. It is our hope that this book will be understood as an indictment of racism in any form, and a rebuke of militarism and authoritarianism in any place. Those who truly seek racial equality and human rights cannot afford the luxury of selective perception and intellectual dishonesty.

CHAPTER I

SOUTH AFRICA IN THE DOGHOUSE

From Sharpeville to Soweto

On 21 March 1960, seventy-five members of the South African Police Force opened fire on a large crowd of black Africans outside the Sharpeville police station, killing sixty-nine and wounding another 128. When questioned later by higher authorities, they explained that they had had no choice. Policemen's lives were in imminent danger. All their attempts to control the crowd had failed. They had tried to disperse the demonstrators, numbering in the thousands, by ordering them through loudspeakers to go home. They had warned that force would be used if the crowd did not comply. To demonstrate their ability to use force, the commanding officers had stationed two tanks in conspicuous locations, arranged for a plane to fly over the police station, and given clearly audible orders for their men to load their rifles. These actions had no impact on the milling throng, whom police described as noisy and in an angry mood. Some demonstrators spat at the police; some shouted insults and threats like "Today you will die here!" Though apparently lacking firearms, some demonstrators carried sticks, clubs, and stones. They were trying to enter and occupy the police station.

At 1:40 p.m., the crowd surged through the gates. According to some officers, two shots were

heard coming from the crowd, followed by two more
from the left flank of the police line. Then the
whole line began shooting. The shooting did not
last more than a minute. Lt. Col. Pienaar denied
giving the order to fire, but added that under the
circumstances, he would have done so had his men
not started spontaneously. He felt he had no
alternative: telephone wires between Sharpeville
and Vereeniging had been severed (presumably by
t e demonstrators); and because demonstrations
were going on all over the country that day, the
Sharpeville police had little hope of securing
reinforcements.[1]

Policemen who had fired on the crowd gave
varying reasons. One constable testified that the
demonstrators were pelting the police with rocks.
He himself had been hit in the chest. When the
crowd began pouring through the gate, he thought
his life and the lives of his colleagues were in
danger. He had heard no order to shoot, but he
was not the first policeman to do so. Some police
officers fired because they did think they heard
an order to shoot; some inferred from the gunfire
that such orders must have been given.

Africans describe the event quite differently.
According to their leaders, the crowd was in a
good mood, singing and chanting. It was a
peaceful demonstration. The demonstrators did not
show any real hostility toward the police, did not
throw stones, nor did they rush the gates of the
police station. The demonstration had been planned
as part of a peaceful campaign, and black leaders
intended to keep it so.

The Sharpeville demonstration was in fact
part of a three-year nation-wide campaign launched
by the Pan Africanist Congress. The Pan Africanist
Congress had split off from the relatively legalistic African National Congress in 1958. The
March 21 demonstrations were expected to be a
crucial test of Pan Africanist support among the
South African black population. In their zeal to
ensure a large turnout, Pan Africanist organizers

2

sometimes resorted to intimidation to prevent people from going to work.[2] They canvassed house to house on the night of March 20, exhorting people to leave their passes at home and join the march to the police station scheduled for the next day. They were careful to cite clear and limited objectives: increased wage rates for blacks, and abolition of the odious requirement that male blacks carry passes at all times. In pamphlets and in public speeches, they had emphasized that the campaign was to be completely non-violent--though it is hard to believe that they really thought it could remain so. In any case, there is little evidence that the Sharpeville demonstrators were armed in any real sense. Perhaps the sheer number of black demonstrators closing in on the police station led white police officers to panic. In view of the conflicting testimony, it is impossible to state categorically whether the police were endangered enough to justify their deadly gunfire.

The killings were reported immediately in South Africa and around the world. Domestic and foreign newspapers impressed the carnage on readers' minds with front-page pictures. Newspaper editorials condemned the killings and the South African political system in general. The broadcast media also gave the incident considerable coverage.

Soon other countries and their governments became involved. In Norway, the flags on public buildings flew at half-mast on the day the Sharpeville victims were buried. Brazil banned a football match which the South African visiting team was to play in Rio de Janeiro, and even recalled its ambassador from Pretoria. The prime minister of New Zealand asked an audience to stand silently in memory of the dead. Mr. Nehru, the Indian prime minister, moved a resolution in parliament condemning the killings; and Mr. Diefenbaker, prime minister of Canada, made a public statement deploring the loss of life and expressing his government's opposition to policies of racial

3

discrimination. The British House of Commons
adopted a resolution similar to that of the
Indian parliament.

The South African government was quite
irritated by this outcry. It felt its international critics lacked or ignored important
facts about the incident; in any case, the protest
would only encourage disregard for law and order
within South Africa, thereby making further repressive measures inevitable. In the following
weeks, the government declared a state of emergency, mobilized police, army, navy, and militia
units to maintain internal security, and arrested
over 30,000 Africans for continuing their demonstrations. Those arrested included some of the
best-known African leaders. Both the African
National Congress and the Pan Africanist Congress
were banned as subversive organizations.

The Sharpeville events reinforced the ruling
National Party in its commitment to apartheid, or
strict separation of the races. Since winning
their first parliamentary majority, in 1948, the
Nationalists had enacted much apartheid legislation. Among these laws were the Group Areas Act
of 1950, and the even more controversial Bantu
Education Act of 1953.[3] Party leaders anticipated
that over the years, Africa would become increasingly chaotic: strife in the Congo (now Zaire)
would continue, Rhodesia, Kenya, and perhaps the
whole of East Africa would be in turmoil, Ghana
would turn communist, and Nigeria would be bogged
down in an internecine civil war. As a result, the
world would be so heartily sick of black Africa
that South Africa, with its policy of separate
development, would win respect as an island of
stability.[4]

In retrospect, it is obvious that while the
National Party leaders may have been accurate in
assessing the course of events in black Africa,
their expectation that the Republic of South
Africa would be left alone to pursue its preferred
policies was mistaken. The world has not

forgotten Sharpeville. The United Nations has
appealed to all governments and international
organizations to observe March 21 as a day of
opposition to racial discrimination. Each year,
many governments and private groups invoke the
Sharpeville incident in a manner most unflat-
tering to the South African regime to support
their demands for majority rule in South Africa.

One illustration is a 1976 U.N. statement
entitled "The Sharpeville Massacre of 21 March,
1960 - Its Historic Significance in the Struggle
Against Apartheid." It describes the events of
that day in the following terms:

> ....the fatal gunning down of some eight
> score peaceful African demonstrators and
> the maiming of several hundred others,
> in a callous and live re-enactment of the
> wild west, rightfully brought international
> public opinion against apartheid in South
> Africa to a boil.... Without warning, the
> police facing the crowd opened fire and in
> two minutes hundreds of bodies lay sprawling
> on the ground like debris. The joyful sing-
> ing had given way to murderous gunfire, and
> the gunfire was followed by an authentic
> deadly silence, and then screams, wild
> screams and cries of the wounded....[5]

While the events at Sharpeville continue to
be recalled, often in thinly disguised appeals to
emotion, racial strife in South Africa gives rise
to new incidents. In June 1976, for example, the
same scenes were repeated on a larger scale. In
the town of Soweto, a few miles southwest of
Johannesburg, about 10,000 blacks were demonstrating against the new government policy of making
Afrikaans a required subject in black schools.
Henceforth, all black university students would
have to take courses in this language. As in
Sharpeville, this demonstration focused on an
issue that was fairly specific, but symptomatic
of the general climate of discrimination and
repression that prevails in the country.

The Africans shouted extremist slogans, threw stones, and created a situation which, in the eyes of the white police, threatened to explode. The police fired. The African crowd broke into a frenzy, rampaging through the streets. Two whites died; they had been dragged from their automobiles, and beaten and hacked to death with clubs and knives. It is ironic that one of the whites killed, Dr. Melville Edelstein, was a humanist Jew who had dedicated his life to the quest for justice and equality in South Africa. African casualties included 140 dead and 2,000 injured.

International reactions were predictable. The United Nations immediately adopted a resolution condemning the use of violence against the demonstrators, and black African governments vowed that Africans would "oppose violence with violence, if such is the method adopted by the retrograde Pretoria regime."[6] The South African prime minister, Mr. John Vorster, retorted that his government would be intimidated neither by the African demonstrators in South Africa nor by threats emanating from independent African States.

In view of what transpired in South Africa between 1960 and 1976 - from Sharpeville to Soweto - the June 1976 events were not likely to improve prospects for black majority rule in South Africa. There was little sign that white South Africans would yield to internal or external pressures. The South African foreign minister, Mr. Hilgard Muller, made his government's position abundantly clear on November 10, 1976. The United Nations had adopted a set of resolutions encouraging South Africa's blacks to seize power by any means necessary, including the use of violence. Muller characterized the resolutions as having "absolutely no regard for reality, and abounding in willful distortions, wild exaggeration and the Assembly's well-known double standards." His government would never yield to international pressure, he maintained, even if it were forced into complete diplomatic isolation. "What the world should realize," he added, "is that even if South Africa should have to stand alone, we have the capacity and determination to fight for our rights..."[7] The pressure in question has been fairly intense and unrelenting, as we shall see.

The Organized Conscience of Mankind

During this period of nearly seventeen years and thereafter, movements urging racial equality and black majority rule in South Africa (nearly seventy percent of South Africa's population is black and ten percent colored) have sprung up all over the world. Among these movements are the British Anti-Apartheid Movement, the Comite Francais Contre l'Apartheid, and organizations with similar names in Italy, the United States, India, and several other countries. These movements have established permanent offices and staffs, and built communication links among themselves and with the mass media.[8] They have pursued three major objectives: to "educate" world public opinion against the existing government in South Africa; to isolate the South African government and white population completely from the international community; and to provide moral and material support for African liberation movements. Some actions taken by the anti-apartheid movements to achieve each objective are discussed in the next few pages. These descriptions are merely illustrative; they do not constitute an exhaustive survey.

Educating World Opinion

To educate implies some commitment to objectivity. Most anti-apartheid movements have shed any such pretentions, over time, and now try simply to organize public opinion as effectively as possible against the South African government. They do this either through their own publications or by securing coverage by national and inter-

7

national broadcast and print media. They cultivate individuals in the news media assiduously
and supply them with material. The <u>Anti-Apart-
heid News</u>, published by the British Anti-Apartheid Movement, has a circulation of over 10,000.
It contains articles, interviews, pictures, and
cartoons condemning racism in South Africa. The
Irish Anti-Apartheid Movement published a short
book entitled <u>Ireland</u> <u>and</u> <u>South</u> <u>Africa</u>: <u>The</u> <u>Case</u>
<u>Against</u> <u>Apartheid</u>. It has also distributed thou-
sands of pamphlets to Irish school children,
condemning the political and racial situation in
South Africa. The Dutch trade union movement has
conducted a consciousness-raising program to increase Dutch workers' opposition to apartheid.
The Comite Francais Contre l'Apartheid, the Swiss
group called the Mouvement Anti-Apartheid de
Suisse, and similar organizations in other
countries also carry on a wide range of activities
to discredit South African racism.

At the international level, groups like the
International Students' Movement have distributed
thousands of "South Africa Kits" to their
affiliates. But surely most important at this
level are the activities of the United Nations.
Among its other endeavors, the United Nations has
been trying to arouse the conscience of mankind
against the South African government and the
whites it represents. The U.N. secretary general
has been directed repeatedly by the General
Assembly to produce pamphlets, other printed
materials, and films on South Africa; to promote
their widest possible distribution by producing
them in a variety of languages; to produce
special versions of this material for audiences
like trade union members, students, and women;
and to award grants to nongovernmental organizations to reprint and distribute U.N. documents
relating to the South Africa question. The U.N.'s
official position shows up clearly in the titles
of its reports. Two United Nations publications
for example, bear the titles <u>Crimes</u> <u>Against</u>
<u>Humanity</u>: <u>Questions</u> <u>and</u> <u>Answers</u> <u>on</u> <u>Apartheid</u> <u>in</u>
South Africa and South Africa: Apartheid in pract-
ice.

8

General Assembly resolutions also constitute an important source of primary material. These resolutions habitually condemn the South African regime for its frank racism, for persistent and flagrant violations of principles enshrined in the U.N. Charter, and for its defiance of resolutions previously adopted by the world body. These resolutions, and the debates preceding them, are widely reported and quoted in various publications designed to "educate" world opinion. The very fact that they have been adopted by the world assembly gives such resolutions a plausible claim to reflect the conscience of the world. The representatives of first, second, and third world countries all condemn apartheid roundly. In just one debate in the General Assembly, apartheid was described as "abhorrent" (Great Britain), "toxic" (the United States), "thoroughly repugnant" (Belgium), "shameful" (the Soviet Union), "a cancer" (Algeria), and "a catalyst of violence" (Tanzania).[9]

To ensure adequate dissemination, the United Nations has set up a Special Committee on Apartheid. This committee, whose expenses are paid out of the U.N. operating budget, holds sessions in different parts of the world. Together and individually, its members participate in international conferences on apartheid; consult with and coordinate the activities of nongovernmental anti-apartheid movements; and visit various countries to give speeches, appear on radio and television programs, and, if possible, address national legislatures. While emphasizing humanitarian objections to apartheid, they make no bones about linking the question of racial discrimination in South Africa with that of majority rule. According to them, the two problems go hand in hand. This view shows up in speeches made by chairmen of the Special Committee on various occasions:

> The struggle in South Africa is a very simple and straightforward struggle between the people on one side and the racist oppressors on the other. We have a proverb in Africa

that you do not get counted as two persons because you are fat - or as half a person because you are lean. That is the essential principle of the African struggle for emancipation - human dignity and human equality. The racists in South Africa who have become fat by appropriating the fruits of the labor of the African people, have denied any representation for the African people in parliament.[10]

The problem is not merely some overt and superficial manifestations of apartheid - such as racial segregation in theatres and hotels - but racist domination in South Africa. Since the government of South Africa was handed over to the white minority sixty-six years ago, and since a so-called "republic" was established by whites in 1961, the black South African majority has been entirely excluded from participation in the determination of the destiny of the country. That is the main issue. All the people - black and white - must be allowed to exercise the right of self determination on the basis of human equality.[11]

Implicit in such statements are two basic assumptions: first, that all interpersonal relations should be made to reflect a presumption of human equality; and second, that any government which is not based on the concept of "one man, one vote" is necessarily illegitimate. It is easy to agree with these propositions, especially in the abstract. Perhaps this, more than anything else, accounts for the success of the anti-apartheid movements in organizing world public opinion against the white South African regime.

Isolation from the International Community

Anti-apartheid forces have tried, with some success, to shut the Republic of South Africa out of bilateral and multilateral relations with other countries. A few months after Sharpeville, a conference of all independent African states decided that all states, African and non-African, should sever diplomatic relations with South Africa and/or should refrain from establishing such relations. As a result, South Africa was forced to close its diplomatic and consular missions in at least three black African countries. Since then, with rare exceptions, it has been unable to establish diplomatic relations with countries on the African continent. South Africa's quest for detente with the black African states made little difference in this respect.

In the world as a whole, the situation is not much different. Constant pressure from the African and other third world countries, plus United Nations resolutions calling for severance of diplomatic relations with South Africa, have been highly successful. In 1980, South Africa maintained diplomatic relations with only thirty-seven nations.

Moving on to the multilateral level, South Africa has been excluded successfully from almost all regional and global international organizations. Its withdrawal from the British Commonwealth of Nations, in 1961, was not entirely voluntary.[12] South Africa has been excluded completely from the Organization of African Unity and all other continent-wide organizations. It has been either expelled or obliged to withdraw from several specialized agencies of the United Nations, including the United Nations Economic, Scientific, and Cultural Organization (UNESCO), the International Labor Organization (ILO), and the Food and Agricultural Organization (FAO). A few other agencies have allowed it to retain nominal membership, while denying its delegations the right to participate in conference deliberations. Among these are the Universal Postal Union, and the International Tele-communications Union, and the International Civil Aviation Organization.

Some of these organizations have even joined actively in the effort to isolate South Africa.

11

The UNESCO has published a book highly critical of South Africa for use in schools all over the world. The ILO has encouraged trade union actions against South Africa. The FAO has investigated and publicized the land tenure problems of blacks in South Africa; and the WHO (World Health Organization) has published a study indicating the evil effects of apartheid on the mental health and well-being of black Africans.

It is common knowledge that South Africa has also been prevented, on occasion, from participating in the deliberations of the General Assembly. Representatives of the Pan Africanist Congress and the African National Congress have been invited in effect to take South Africa's place in meetings of the Special Political Committee of the General Assembly. In 1974, the Assembly recommended to the Security Council that South Africa be expelled from the world body because of its continual violation of provisions contained in the United Nations Charter and in the Universal Declaration of Human Rights. Only vetoes by France, Britain, and the United States prevented South Africa's ejection from the U.N.

In December, 1975, the National Anti-Imperialist Movement in Solidarity with African Liberation (NAIMSAL) presented a petition to the U.S. Department of State and to the U.N., calling for South Africa's expulsion from the United Nations. The petition had been signed by more than 100,000 American citizens. Such action by anti-South African lobbies may gradually bring Western vetoes on South Africa's behalf into general discredit.

Military isolation of South Africa has been one of the major objectives of almost all anti-apartheid groups. One aspect of this effort is to reduce South Africa's access to modern military equipment. Given their numerical weakness, white South Africans rely on sophisticated weaponry to control the domestic black population and to deter black African states from taking military action or giving overt support to the guerrilla groups operating on the South African borders. Recognizing this, the anti-apartheid groups have intensified their agitation for world arms embargo against the Republic of South Africa. Over time, their demands have also become increasingly specific. This is demonstrated well by the series of resolutions on this subject passed by the General Assembly, usually at the behest of anti-apartheid groups. Within a year of the Sharpeville incident, the General Assembly requested that all states refrain from exporting arms and ammunition to South Africa. A resolution of 1963 was more detailed: states were asked "to cease forthwith the sale and shipment of arms, ammunition of all types, and military vehicles to South Africa." Later that same year, they were asked to stop selling and shipping any equipment that could be used to manufacture or maintain arms and ammunition in South Africa. In 1969, all states were called upon to cut off any technical or military assistance to South Africa that might boost production of arms, ammunition, or military vehicles. The 1970 resolutions exhorted all states to stop supplying vehicles and equipment that could be used by South African paramilitary organizations, and to halt the supply of spare parts for vehicles and military equipment used by the South African armed forces and paramilitary organizations. All licences and military patents granted to South Africans were to be revoked, and no state should grant such rights to South Africa in the future. All corporations were to be prohibited by their national governments from investing in the manufacture of arms and ammunition in South Africa. The General Assembly resolved to ban the import of South African armaments as well, reasoning that this would reduce the opportunity for South African plants to benefit from economies of scale. Finally, states were to refrain from training members of the South African armed forces, even on their own sovereign territory, and to discontinue all other forms of military cooperation with South Africa.

By 1971, the General Assembly was demanding that mutual defense pacts with South Africa be reviewed. In 1973, Great Britain was directed to terminate unilaterally its military agreements and arrangements with South Africa. One year later, all states were requested to do the same; they were to end all exchanges of military attachés with South Africa, to prohibit visits by South African defense personnel to their countries, and to cease all cooperation with South Africa in technological research, especially nuclear research, that might have military applications. The obvious point of each such measure was to make it more difficult for South Africa to deter attacks from "up north," and to control domestic riots, demonstrations, and sabotage.

The anti-apartheid groups and their supporters have acted as self-appointed watchdogs, to ensure compliance. Though they have not succeeded in preventing the supply of arms to South Africa altogether, they have made a point of publicizing violations whenever these came to their attention. They have also initiated new resolutions which, in their view, were needed to plug the loopholes which some states were using.

The anti-apartheid groups are able to draw on a broad range of expertise. Anti-apartheid conferences and research are, moreover, often funded by the United Nations. One example is the seminar held from April 28 to May 2, 1975, at the headquarters of UNESCO in Paris. Representatives from various anti-South African groups had been invited to work out a strategy for "a final assault on the citadel of apartheid in South Africa and...to help South African people bury racism."[13] The meeting turned out to be a brain-storming session, bringing together persons in a position to help isolate South Africa militarily. The seminar concluded by recommending that the U.N. adopt without delay a mandatory arms embargo against South Africa. The embargoed items should include all radar and other electronic equipment, as well as aircraft, helicopters, and other

14

vehicles which could be used for military purposes or be converted easily for such use. The seminar also urged an appeal to all major trade union movements to prevent the production and shipment of military equipment destined for South Africa. Some of these recommendations were in fact incorporated in the General Assembly resolutions of 1976, which were mentioned earlier.

Attempts to isolate South Africa economically have been persistent but less successful. South Africa enjoys the most advanced economy on the African continent. Because of government encouragement, and the national drive for self-sufficiency, manufacturing now contributes the largest share to the South African gross national product. Mining and agriculture continue to be vitally important, if only because these sectors earn substantial amounts in foreign exchange; this, in turn, helps finance vital imports.

In this interdependent world no modern state, including South Africa, can attain complete self-sufficiency. With this in mind, anti-apartheid groups have sought to persuade states to stop trading with or investing in South Africa; if the white population is subjected to enough economic hardship, they assume, the system will be forced to change. States have been exhorted, in the United Nations and elsewhere, to break off economic relations with South Africa. A number of states have in fact done so. Others have been nudged in the same direction, one step at a time. The General Assembly has adopted increasingly specific resolutions on this topic. Beginning with the November, 1962 resolution asking all states to boycott South African goods and embargo exports to that country, the U.N. has moved on to resolutions aimed at one or two of South Africa's trading partners at a time. Particular states have been urged to close down their trade promotion offices in South Africa; to deny South Africa permission and facilities to open offices in their countries; to terminate or deny tariff preferences

15

to South African goods; to deny guarantees against expropriation for investments in South Africa; to prohibit government lending agencies from granting credits for trade with, or investments in, South Africa; and to withhold strategic raw materials from South Africa, especially petroleum products. (Petroleum is the only crucial mineral resource that South Africa lacks.)

Despite these efforts, many states continue to trade with South Africa. These include not only western countries, but some Asian states like Japan, and at least nineteen African states as well. Unwilling to wait for the citizens of those countries to force a stop to such trade, anti-apartheid groups have taken matters into their own hands. Several techniques have been developed. To exert pressure directly upon corporations trading with South Africa, the British Anti-Apartheid Movement published a book entitled The Collaborators; it lists all British companies that play key roles in the South African economy. The British movement also publishes a series of Anti-Reports, similar in appearance to the annual reports issued by corporations. These spell out the details of various companies' involvement in South Africa, including an enumeration of their products. The Swiss Anti-Apartheid Movement and representatives of the World Council of Churches in the United States have also published reports on companies of their respective nationalities that do business with South Africa. Such reports prompt concerned shareholders to raise questions at annual stockholders' meetings, to remind management that the company's very presence in South Africa helps to support the present regime, and to demand that the company cease trade and investment in South Africa altogether. This happened to General Motors in 1971. A group of Episcopalian stockholders called upon the corporation to close its automobile and refrigerator plants in South Africa. This demand was backed by the Episcopal Church itself. One of General Motors' own directors, a black appointed to demonstrate corporate responsiveness to social issues, vocally supported the cause. He suggested that the corporation move its South African operations "somewhere else on the African continent, where people are treated like human beings rather than dogs."14

Within a short period of time, techniques for forcing the hand of corporations doing business in South Africa have been refined and employed with considerable organizational skill. In 1973, seven religious denominations and an independent organization of Episcopal churchmen formed a group called the Church Project on United States Investments in Southern Africa. The project officials filed resolutions with International Business Machines, the First National City Corporation, General Electric Corporation, and Carter Tractor Corporation, to be placed on the annual meeting agenda in accordance with the companies' respective articles of incorporation. The resolutions called for a full disclosure of the corporations' involvement in or with South Africa, and required them to mail out the details of such involvement to all shareholders, within four months of the annual meeting. The accounting was to include lists of all employees in South Africa, broken down by race, with the wages and benefits paid to each; and of all products sold by the company to South Africa since 1962. The Project also issued its own proxy statement, which affirmed that shareholders had the right to call for such disclosures, and that this was one means of forcing all concerned to face the moral issues that business dealings with South Africa entail. The proxy statement challenged the corporate argument that their South African operations benefited the black population, demanding hard evidence. Governor Jerry Brown of California, a 1976 and 1980 candidate for the Democratic Party presidential nomination, has tried unsuccessfully to persuade the Regents of the University of California to curtail investment in American corporations with South African interests. In recent years most American corporations doing business in South Africa have agreed to abide by

17

the Sullivan Code of employment practices designed
to desegregate plant facilities and to equalize
pay and other economic conditions of labor between
white and non-white workers. The Sullivan Code
is named after its author, the Reverend Leon F.
Sullivan, a black Philadelphia clergyman, civil
rights leader, and member of General Motors Board
of Directors. Major stockholders of some corporations have threatened to sell their holdings at
one swoop (thereby reducing the stock's market
value artificially) if the corporations insisted
on continuing their accustomed practices. Churches
and universities have been in the forefront of
divestment campaigns.

Efforts like these have forced corporations,
in the interest of avoiding bad publicity, to
increase the wages paid to black employees in
South Africa, to train blacks for skilled jobs,
to contribute to charities that serve the black
population, and even to discontinue investment
- and trade in South Africa. Some churches and
universities have also lent support to the resolution passed by the Organization of African Unity
in July 1975, which exhorted independent African
states to "take particularly strong measures
against international companies which have business
interests in South Africa and Southern Rhodesia
as well as in independent Africa."[15] The object
was to force companies to choose between South
Africa and black Africa; they should no longer
be allowed to do business with both.

There have also been attempts in several
countries to force corporations indirectly to
stop trading with South Africa. Anti-apartheid
groups have appealed to the public to stop buying
South African goods imported by those companies.
This, of course, would make it increasingly difficult for South Africa to earn needed foreign exchange. The Citizens' Association for Racial
Equality in Australia published a list of South
African products on sale in Australia and New
Zealand, and of the corporations that import
these products. The Irish Anti-Apartheid Move-

18

ment has provided housewives with long lists of
South African goods sold in Ireland, asking them
to stop buying these products. The Irish have
gone even farther. They have picketed stores that
carry South African merchandise, forced schools
and hospitals not to buy goods of South African
origin, and taken other actions to make the boycott effective. In the Netherlands, about 800
groups became involved in the boycott of South
African oranges and caused almost all of the
country's supermarkets to stop purchasing this
fruit.

Some attempts have also been made to boycott
the corporations themselves. In the United States
for example, the Washington D.C. City Council has
put four large American corporations (Control Data,
I.B.M., I.T.T., and Motorola) under a "selective
purchasing system." These corporations supply
South Africa with computers, sophisticated communication and technical equipment, and electronic
systems. They also do a substantial business
with the city of Washington,D.C. supplying it
with typewriters, radios, etc. Under the new
system, city officials must refrain from purchasing supplies from companies trading with or
having investments in South Africa except when
such supplies are needed urgently and cannot be
obtained from other companies. If implemented
effectively, the selective purchasing policy
could cost the offending corporations millions of
dollars of business with the city, possibly forcing them to make their own choice between the
forces of evil and the forces of good.

Even if corporations continue trading with
and investing in South Africa, and consumers refuse to boycott South African goods, the self-
appointed forces of good have at least one other
economic weapon. With the cooperation of workers
who load and unload goods at airports and seaports,
the anti-apartheid groups could make it impossible
for importers to bring South African goods to the
consumer. The Organization of African Trade Unity

has, on several occasions, urged trade union movements in other countries to refuse to load or unload vessels carrying goods to or from South Africa. Most African states do not allow South African planes to fly over their territory, let
alone land and refuel there. Their ports are
closed to South African shipping. Attempts to
boycott ships of other nationalities carrying
South African cargo, or to prevent them from using
port facilities, are likely to increase in the
future.

During the last two decades, South Africa
has tried to increase its small white population
by recruiting skilled white immigrants from several countries. Aside from simply increasing the
proportion of whites in the country, immigrants
are needed to fill key positions in South Africa's
modern economy. Anti-apartheid groups have,
therefore, mounted a campaign to curb white migration to South Africa. The U.N. General
Assembly has asked all states to help in stopping
such migration. The Central Committee of the
World Council of Churches has made a similar request of all its members, as has the International Confederation of Free Trade Unions. In
Britain, the Trades Union Congress has promoted a
publicity drive to discourage workers from going
to South Africa. The Transport and General Workers' Union, the National Union of Mineworkers,
and the Draughtsmen's and Allied Technicians'
Association have been especially active in this
effort. The Irish Anti-Apartheid Movement has
succeeded in having the Irish government prohibit
the establishment of a South African immigration
office in Dublin. Members of this group have also
campaigned against South African recruitment at
Irish universities. When South African representatives have organized meetings to promote migration, members of the Irish Anti-Apartheid
Movement have attended the meetings in order to
disrupt them. In the United States, the American
Committee on Africa and other anti-apartheid
groups have condemned local newspapers for accepting South African advertisements for immigrants.

Some have even filed suits against newspapers for accepting advertisements which, they claimed, were explicitly or implicitly discriminatory toward non-whites.

There have been attempts to isolate South Africa in other realms as well. Year in and year out, the General Assembly has passed resolutions asking states to bar cultural, educational, scientific, or other contacts between their citizens and South Africa. It is in the field of sports that the campaign to isolate South Africa socially has been waged with the greatest fervor--and success. Sports is an area where South Africans are especially vulnerable. South African whites participate enthusiastically in sports, and take considerable pride in the international records set by their athletes. Thanks to the anti-apartheid groups, South African sports organizations have been expelled, suspended, or otherwise barred from a number of international sporting events and organizations. These include tournaments held under the auspices of the International Table Tennis Federation, the International Football Federation, the World Fencing Federation, the International Olympic Committee, the International Amateur Boxing Association, the International Judo Federation, the International Amateur Athletics Federation, and the International Swimming Federation.

In cases where the sports organizations have not agreed to bar the South African teams, the states on whose territory the games were to be played often acted unilaterally. In 1973, for example, Brazil refused to authorize a sailing race from Cape Town to Rio de Janeiro, and prohibited the use of any Brazilian port as a terminal or stopover for such a race. The same year, New Zealand rejected a visit by the South African rugby team. Matches between South African and New Zealand teams were forbidden until such time as there is "clear and irrefutable evidence that sport in South Africa (is) no longer organized on a racial basis."[17]

21

Individual South African athletes have been denied visas to enter a country where games were taking place. Mexico refused to allow South African tennis players into the country for the Davis Cup competition. In 1973, Peru refused to grant visas to members of the South African polo team, who were scheduled to play a series of matches in Lima. A number of states have also forbidden their citizens to play against South Africans. The Argentine government prohibited the Argentine Rugby Union and the Argentine Sports Federation from competing directly against South African sportsmen, regardless of where the meets take place. Some states, like the Philippines, refuse to let their citizens take part in tournaments to which South African teams are admitted, even if their team is not scheduled to play against South Africa.

Some have gone even further. In June, 1970, the Pakistani government cancelled a scheduled visit of its cricket team to England in protest against the visit of an all-white South African team in England a few months earlier. Kenya has announced that its athletes will not be allowed to play any individual or team which has ever participated in a sporting event in which South Africans competed. In 1979, the Supreme Council for Sport in Africa demanded that African states break all bilateral sports contacts with Britain and work towards having Britain barred from the 1980 Moscow Olympic Games if it insisted upon allowing the British Lions Rugby team to play South Africa. And, during the same year, the Rev. Jesse Jackson, an important American black leader, while on a visit to South Africa, vociferously expressed his determination to stop a heavyweight boxing match in Pretoria, South Africa between a white South African, Gerrie Coetzee and a black American named John Tate.

It is no wonder that many individual athletes have refused, "for reasons of conscience," to play against South African whites inside or outside South Africa. They know that to do so might jeopardize their chances of playing in international tournaments in the future. In the comparatively rare instances when South African teams have played abroad, the matches have usually been marred by the anti-apartheid demonstrations. This makes it hard for the host country to guarantee the security of South African players, and thus furnishes a plausible excuse for refusing them entry into the country in the first place. The chairman of the U.N. Special Committee on Apartheid also keeps a watchful eye on sports events, quickly protesting when any state allows its territory to be used for an event which includes South Africans. His protests often have a great impact, as in the case of Ecuador in 1974.

In the realm of fine arts, too, white South Africans suffer for their racial policies. Of course, they deliberately deny themselves many cultural opportunities. For many years, it has been illegal for blacks to perform before white audiences. More recently, it has become common for white musicians and artists to refuse to visit South Africa. Irish playwrights have denied permission for their works to be performed before segregated audiences in South Africa.

South Africans must use considerable caution in travelling abroad to enjoy cultural opportunities denied them at home. Under the International Convention on the Suppression and Punishment of the Crime of Apartheid, not only the official representatives of South Africa but its citizens individually are responsible for the crime of apartheid, and are liable to be tried and punished by the courts of any state which is a party to the Convention. At least sixteen states including Guinea, Chad, and Somalia have ratified this Convention. South Africans who find themselves in the territory of one of these states could have the unenviable task of defending their country's racial policies and serving rather long prison terms, if not worse.

Socially ostracized and isolated diplomatic-

ally, militarily, economically, and culturally,
South African whites find the world forming an
increasingly solid front against them. The world
has, in a sense, put them in the doghouse until
they mend their ways.

Aid to Liberation Movements

The anti-apartheid groups have not limited
their efforts to mobilizing public opinion against
South Africa and to reducing its contacts with the
rest of the international community. They have
also aided black Africans seeking, by means including violence, to overthrow the existing regime.
Supporters of the liberation movements can be
divided into two broad categories--those who, in
principle, oppose the use of violent and illegal
means and those who have no such compunction.
Those in the first group have usually limited
their support to acts such as the following:
demands that persons arrested by the South African
government for violating apartheid laws be released immediately and unconditionally; provision
of funds, on humanitarian grounds, for the treatment of wounded demonstrators; and raising money
for legal aid and financial assistance to families
of prisoners in South Africa.

It is, of course, much easier to obtain general agreement on projects of this nature. The
United Nations General Assembly has had little
difficulty in obtaining majorities for resolutions
that appeal to states or individuals to contribute
annually to help people persecuted under the
"repressive and discriminatory" laws of South
Africa.[18] The International Defense and Aid
Fund, created specifically for the purpose, provides funds for legal defense and aid to the families of political prisoners in South Africa.
The United Nations Educational and Training Pro-
gramme for Southern Africa, funded by charitable
contributions, and the United Nations Trust Fund
for South Africa provide substantial assistance
for educating South African blacks, especially
those with leadership potential. Thousands of

fellowships and training awards have been awarded
by these funds to South African blacks, with preferences given to those who have been persecuted
for opposing the existing regime. Great Britain,
Denmark, Norway, and France have been the major
contributors to the trust fund.[19]

Private charitable organizations make their
own policies. In their cases, the distinction
between funds for humanitarian purposes and money
that can be used for guerrilla or terrorist activities has become increasingly blurred. Some
groups have abandoned all pretense of limiting
their support to humanitarian projects, and now
contribute directly to various guerrilla groups.[20]
Their aid takes the form of cash, blankets, medical supplies, and even small arms and equipment.
Private organizations in Sweden, Denmark, Finland,
and Norway have persuaded their governments to
follow suit. The Soviet Union, the People's
Republic of China, Cuba, and some Eastern European states never have had any qualms about
supporting liberation struggles involving the
use of force. They have provided--though with
variable generosity--arms, equipment, and training to help black revolutionaries liberate their
countries from white rule.

South Africa's Own Position

The South African reaction to activity of
this kind appears to have changed little since
1960. Through improvements in its internal security and defense forces, the National Party government has sought to make prospects for guerrilla
and terrorist groups seem hopeless. Domestically,
black political organizations remain outlawed.
Students, youth leaders, trade unionists, and
budding political leaders have been detained,
driven into exile, co-opted, or, at least,
silenced. The internal security and intelligence
systems have been refined to the extent that the
civil liberties and privacy even of white citizens
are seriously compromised. Externally, the defense policy has been directed toward dissuading

the black African states from giving any large scale or active assistance to the liberation movements. The South African defense budget increased from a mere 44 million Rands in 1960-1961 to over a billion with little chance of any reduction in the future. The total size of the South African armed forces has increased considerably. Emphasis has shifted toward re- c uiting white women and training commandos as a home guard which can be mobilized on a moment's notice. The South African government has ex- panded and improved the Simonstown Naval Base and other ports, installing sophisticated naval communication and surveillance equipment. It has also begun producing its own fighter planes, missiles, and rockets, as well as a wide range of arms and ammunition. Some suspect that South Africa either possesses or will soon have a variety of nerve gases and short range nuclear weapons. In September, 1979, a U.S. Defense De- partment Satellite detected an intense flash of light while passing over a remote area of about 4500 square miles, including South Africa. Though the evidence was inconclusive, it is poss- ible that the flash resulted from the secret test of a South African nuclear device.

Even while building up its defense capabil- ities, the South African government has sought to break out of its isolation on the African contin- ent by improving relations with some of the black African states. Some gains have been made, al- though mostly by giving economic and technical assistance to any black government possessing the nerve to accept help from black Africa's common enemy. Thus South Africa has aided emperors and autocrats like former Emperor Bokassa of the Cen- tral African Empire and Dr. Kamazu Banda of Malawi. But its efforts to woo internationally respected African leaders like Dr. Houphouet- Boigny of the Ivory Coast have met with minimal success.

At home, the South African government has accelerated its program of granting independence

to "Bantustans." Bantustans, or geographically
separate "homelands" for various African tribes,
are intended to defuse racial tension by giving
blacks an opportunity to manage their own affairs,
and by reducing contact between the races still
further. It is also hoped that the creation of a
separate "homeland" for each tribe will impede
the development of a common national identity
among South African blacks. In 1979, South
Africa's new Prime Minister, Mr. Pieter Willem
Botha ordered a review of the law which set aside
only 14 percent of the country's land for the
Homelands with a view to enlarging these areas.
He also indicated his intention to allow some
form of autonomy to urban areas like Soweto in
which large numbers of blacks are concentrated.

The prime minister and members of his cabinet
have also made a practice of meeting with leaders
of the less privileged racial communities to resolve misunderstandings. Some Asian and Colored
representation has been allowed on certain statutory bodies. But neither the South African
government nor the dominant white population
have shown any willingness to share real power
with non-whites, let alone accede to majority
rule. In November, 1979, in a heated debate with
a colored delegation, Mr. Botha made it abundantly
clear that he was willing to divide power in a way
which would leave sovereignty in the hands of the
whites, but not to share it. He totally rejected
the delegation's demands for a one-man, one-vote
approach.

In the economic sphere, too, there have been
some concessions. Financial allocations to the
Bantustans have increased. Wages paid to African
workers and miners have increased substantially,
although blacks still receive nothing close to
equal pay for equal work. Certain job categories
which had long been reserved for whites have now
been opened to non-whites. In 1979, Mr. Botha
relaxed restrictions on the right of the blacks
to form trade unions. He also allowed formation
of business partnerships between whites and blacks

27

in which the majority shares are held by the blacks. In fact, there are enough other opportunities for South African blacks today that mining firms must recruit many of their workers from other countries, like Malawi and Lesotho. But the contrast between black and white standards of living in South Africa remains very great.

Socially, apartheid still reaches into the workplace, recreation and leisure, and even into the bedroom. The Immorality Act forbids sexual relations between whites and non-whites, while interracial marriages are outlawed by the Prohibition of Mixed Marriages Act. Nevertheless, there have been subtle changes even in this area. Black Africans are now allowed to participate in certain sporting events, both in and outside South Africa. Some elements of "petty apartheid' have been eliminated. Admission to the Nico Malan Theatre, for instance, is now open to persons of all races. Park benches, museums, and libraries in Johannesburg have been desegregated. Kruger National Park, the noted game preserve, has dropped some of its racial barriers. Some luxury hotels have begun admitting non-whites as well as whites; and so on. In 1979, Mr. Botha authorized restauranteurs to apply for permits to serve blacks and indicated that such applications would receive favorable consideration. He announced that laws prohibiting sexual relations and marriage between people of different races would be reviewed in the near future. He has also begun to finance large-scale improvements in black housing, transportation, and other amenities. Staple foods and transportation--two items most needed by the blacks--are receiving increased government subsidies, and the government is attempting to tackle black unemployment, housing, education, and welfare - problems that are believed by Prime Minister Botha to underlie black discontent. He has promised that his government will look at the interests of all population groups, not just the whites, and he has made repeated references to his desire to end all "unnecessary and offensive" racial discrimination.

28

He speaks of "differentiation" and not "discrimination"; of "decentralization" and not "separate
development"; and of a "total national strategy of
uniting black and white moderates in a socio-
economic assault on a common enemy – Marxism."
His advice to the whites is to "adapt or die," to
be willing to make economic sacrifices so that the
quality of black life may be improved.

Mr. Botha's new strategy cannot be interpreted to mean total abandoning of the concept of
apartheid; though his actions do represent, for
South Africa, an important step forward. The
Group Areas Act which designates where people of
different races must live or maintain their businesses still remains intact. So does the law requiring non-whites to carry permits or passes
whenever they visit white areas. The concept of
"Homelands," though not its configuration, is also
regarded as immutable. The long-range goal of
maintaining white sovereignty and of making the
white dominated political system head of the
"constellation of states" still remains unchanged.
Mr. Botha staunchly refuses to allow whites to
become a minority in a government dominated by
blacks. There is not a single white political
party in the country which is ready to declare
itself openly in favor of majority rule. Even
the most liberal party, the Progressive Federal
Party, with approximately twenty seats out of
165 in the national legislature, while calling for
one voting roll for all races, believes that the
voting rights should be restricted to those who
have reached a certain educational and social
level. Within his own party, Mr. Botha's
realistic or pragmatic approach has met with
fierce criticisms, especially from the rightist
Afrikaners resulting in loss of support for his
party in the local elections. They resent even
these relatively modest concessions to the blacks.

On the other hand, the African reaction has
been skeptical, regarding the new policy as simply
a more humane way of pursuing an inhumane policy.
They claim that there has been little meaningful

change. Black political parties are still banned.
In late 1979, 11 members of the banned African
National Congress were sentenced to long prison
terms on charges of treason. One, James Daniel
Mange, was sentenced to death.

Anti-apartheid groups and leaders of independent black African states have generally recognized
South Africa's apparent concessions for what they
probably are. They view South Africa's policy of
detente as an attempt to divide the African states,
as well as the international community, and to
disrupt the world-wide campaign against apartheid.
They also suspect that these maneuvers are encouraged by foreign governments and economic
interests which profit from the present system.
They assume that South Africa's conciliatory
moves are calculated to gain time in which South
Africa can build up a military arsenal including
nuclear weapons.[21]

The domestic changes meet with equal disdain.
The creation of Bantustans, nominally independent
but closely linked with the South African government, is viewed as an attempt to balkanize Africa,
and to impose archaic tribal institutions on
blacks. The Bantustans, they recognize, are used
as dumping grounds for the dependents of migrant
workers in white areas, and as "labor and buffer
zones as well as Trojan horses in the United
Nations."[22] Given these assumptions, no black
African state has recognized any of the Bantustans
or established any working relations with their
new governments; nor, due to overwhelming black
African opposition, have they been admitted to
the United Nations.

Economic reforms in South Africa have been
discounted as expedient adjustments to uncontroll-
able economic pressures, including a shortage of
manpower. The social changes mentioned earlier
are castigated as "manoeuvers of the racist
regime, designed primarily to perpetuate and obtain acquiescence in its abhorrent apartheid
policies, to deceive world opinion, to counter

international isolation, to hinder assistance to the national liberations movements by the international community, and to consolidate white minority rule in South Africa."[23] The Declaration on Southern Africa, adopted by the foreign ministers of the black states on July 10, 1975, provides a typical example of the non-white view of the situation. According to the Declaration, "the aim of the (South African) government in this exercise of whitewashing apartheid is clear: to deceive world public opinion into believing that some radical changes are taking place and thus reduce the regime's international isolation."[24]

Black Africans who live in South Africa and who have cooprated with the government in implementing the reforms have also come under attack. They are regarded as stooges of the whites, with no legitimate claim to represent the black peoples of South Africa. In fact, the leaders of the national liberation movements have won almost general recognition as the sole authentic representatives of the black population. Black South Africans who cooperate with the regime are often criticized as opportunists. The chairman of the United Nations Special Committee on Apartheid expressed this view in typical fashion:

> What South Africa is trying to do is to make some concessions to the so-called leaders of the black people, whom it likes, in return for their acceptance of apartheid. We have a name for such people. We cannot but reject these manoeuvers, and we have no doubt that they will not succeed.[25]

At this rate, race relations in South Africa can only get worse. If every black willing to carry on a dialog with the government is automatically suspect, there is little hope for building bridges between the races. Moreover, black South African leaders have set their sights increasingly on complete liberation, rather than on finding some modus vivendi with the whites.

31

Hopes for black independence have been encouraged
by the end of Portuguese rule in Mozambique and
Angola, and of Ian Smith's regime in Rhodesia, now
known as Zimbabwe, as well as by moves toward a
negotiated transfer of power in South West Africa,
or Namibia. The Cuban intervention in Angola led
liberation leaders to anticipate effective military aid from outside. Finally, since January,
1977, American policy toward South Africa has been
notably tougher, particularly due to the influence
of former United States Ambassador to the United
Nations, Andrew Young.[26]

In short, the South African situation today
is marked by a clash of wills. Blacks, on the one
hand, are becoming increasingly confident and
radicalized. The white government, on the other
hand, mixes tactical concessions and public relations gestures with ever more stringent security
measures. At a time in world history when the
idea of racial equality has gained general acceptance, the continued intransigence of South Africa
on the racial issue and its rejection of majority
rule makes no sense to most outside observers.
Why, they ask, do South African whites simply
ignore their growing isolation in the world. Can
they not understand the futility of their position
and their eventual defeat? There is no easy
answer. The correct answer does not lie in the
specious justifications for apartheid provided by
the South African government and its agents. And
vitriolic condemnations of liberals with no
knowledge of life in Africa also miss important
aspects of the problem. Among possible explanations for white intransigence in South Africa,
we need to consider the following interrelated
ideas and cultural traits.

Religion

Many Afrikaners, or descendants of Dutch
settlers, defend both apartheid and the subordinate position of blacks by quoting from the
Bible. In his second epistle to the Corinthians,
St. Paul admonishes, "Be ye not unequally yoked

together with the unbelievers: for what fellow-
ship hath righteousness with unrighteousness (6:14)
....Wherefore come out from among them and be ye
separate, saith the Lord, and touch not the unclean
thing and I will receive you" (6:17). The Book
of Leviticus even endorses slavery, as long as
the "bondmen" are drawn from outside the Chosen
People (25: 44-46).

The Afrikaners, who make up about sixty
percent of the white population, are largely Cal-
vinists. Over ninety percent of them belong to
one or the other of the three Dutch Reformed
Churches. Their long history of relative isolation combines with the Calvinist doctrine of pre-
destination to give them the firm conviction that
they are a "Chosen People."

Paternalism

Whites of British and Dutch descent have
shared a paternalistic attitude toward black
Africans. Many believe in all sincerity that
their domination of the blacks is actually in the
latter's own interest. Thanks to the ministration
of whites, the Africans have access to more education, better health standards, and even a higher
standard of living than they would enjoy otherwise. And the fact that the blacks did live in
rather primitive fashion, when left to their own
devices, proves their need of tutelage. The
Chosen People, as Cecil Rhodes used to say, must
act as guardians for the blacks; they have a
sacred trust to advance and uplift backward
peoples.[27] The survival of this attitude shows up
in references to high-ranking officers of the
Department of Bantu Administration as "fathers
of the Bantu," their acceptance of tribal honors,
and their dispensation of government favors as if
the Africans were children.

Afrikaner Nationalism

Over some three centuries, the Afrikaners were
involved in a long series of skirmishes and battles

33

against Hottentots, Bushmen, and the Bantu. When
British rule began to threaten their way of life
in the 1830's the Afrikaners migrated north,
establishing their own republics in Transvaal and
the Orange Free State. They fought and lost the
Boer War (1899-1902), in an attempt to stay independent of Great Britain. Given these challenges and the paucity of reinforcements from Europe,
the Afrikaners developed their own language, a
fierce sense of group identity, and a strong
network of cultural and social institutions. The
sheer size of the black majority makes the Afri-
caners all the more conscious of their group iden-
tity--and the possibility of being submerged in
an alien mass. To preserve their own nationality,
say the Afrikaners, they must retain firm and
exclusive control of the South African political
system.

Racism

     "God in His wisdom made people different,"
argue the Afrikaners. They tend to interpret the
very fact of racial differences as a divine man-
date to maintain those distinctions. Moreover,
they argue, forcing members of different races to
live together leads to unfortunate social conse-
quences--miscegenation, moral deterioration on
all sides, social ill-will, friction, and conflict.
People of different races and cultures simply
cannot be completely separated territorially; they
must be separated by law as much as possible.
The Mixed Marriages Act, the Immorality Act, the
Pass Laws, the Separate Universities Act, and
other laws are designed to minimize contact
between racial groups.

Separate Development

     Each racial subgoup is a nation in itself.
Nations, in turn, are the social matrices which
channel and give meaning to the lives of individuals. The customs, values, and daily lives of
each nation must be preserved without adulteration.
The subgroups should live and work as independently

as possible, so that each may develop to its full potential, along its own lines, and at its own pace. The African tribes must be allowed to shape their own destiny, and not become poor imitations of another culture, especially white culture. Otherwise, black Africans will degenerate into a rootless, urbanized, semi-westernized mass, with no firm identity.

It will not be possible to deal with each of these elements of Afrikaner thought within the framework of this book. In any case, none of them provides a completely satisfactory explanation of apartheid. The religious argument is only partly relevant today. It is true that, initially, the Afrikaner churches considered apartheid a Christian solution to preserving the Afrikaner nation without detriment to other nations, i.e. black and Coloured peoples. But as the social and psychological effects of apartheid and its enforcement became more widely known, some Afrikaner churchmen became suspicious. In the 1980's, the South African government can no longer rely on automatic support from the churches. Indeed, according to Leopold Marquard, "the year 1960 may well be regarded as marking the close of a period of unquestioning cooperation between the Afrikaans churches and the Nationalist Party as then constituted."28

Other religious organizations, especially Jewish and Catholic bodies, have strongly condemned apartheid. The British Council of Churches has declared apartheid "a blasphemy against the Holy Spirit." It is difficult, therefore, to regard religion as the main factor behind white support of apartheid.

The same applies to paternalism, especially when we limit our attention to the period since 1960. Paternalism, as a philosophy and as a pattern of behaviour, was becoming obsolete as early as the 1920's. As Leopold Marquard pointed out, "By the 1920's, the (African) 'child' was adolescent and showing every sign of growing to

35

lusty manhood,"29 and it was no longer possible
to deal with him on the basis of benevolent
tutelage. He expected rights of his own. Today,
African leaders maintain that it is better to be
ruled tyrannically by fellow blacks than to be
governed however well and benevolently by others.
White South Africans are by no means unintelligent;
this change in the expectations of black Africans
has not escaped them.

The third suggested explanation, Afrikaner
nationalism, is also inadequate taken alone. In
the first place, the Afrikaners of today do not
share one uniform ideology. Denis J. Worrall
maintains that "Afrikaner public opinion (today)
spreads more widely across the white political
spectrum than does the English-speaking opinion,
and within Afrikanerdom the ideological preemin-
ance of the politicians has been challenged by
editors and academicians."30 Secondly, not only
the Afrikaners, but also other whites (who comprise
forty percent of the white population) support the
present system. Few English-speaking whites cher-
ish the idea of black majority rule either. And
they have not had to go through the centuries of
hardships that is said to have created solidarity
among the Afrikaners.

The last two complexes of ideas, racism and
the ideology of separate development, are hardly
more satisfactory explanations. They may be convenient rationalizations for apartheid policies,
or bases for opposing them with all the force at
one's disposal. But they are not really central
to the thinking of white South Africans. Perhaps
God did make the races different; but this does
not prevent South African whites from mixing and
dealing cordially with non-whites when outside
South Africa. Even in South Africa itself,
Japanese are given the status of honorary whites,
for political and economic reasons; and visiting
black dignitaries, including black Americans,
have been treated as distinguished visitors and
given access to white amenities, including hotels
and restaurants normally reserved for whites.

36

More importantly, the government itself is now moving in the direction of reducing "petty apartheid" restrictions.

The ideal of separate development is widely recognized as impracticable in the South African context. Complete separation of the races would entail almost total disruption of the political, economic, and social fabric of the country. The Africans are needed in the urban areas to man factories and do other manual work. The mines could not operate without black labor. And the millions of blacks cannot all be relegated to the fourteen percent of South African land that has been set aside for the Homelands or Bantustans. It is impossible to prevent them from being influenced by white culture. Most of the Coloreds, and many blacks as well, speak Afrikaans.

In practice, some of the laws designed to separate the races are ignored. Several hundred persons of all races, but mainly white males, are convicted every year of crimes involving "immoral" association with a person of a different race. Centers of prostitution just outside South African borders, in Botswana and Lesotho, enjoy a flourishing business. They are patronized mainly by South African whites. Employers circumvent legislation reserving certain jobs for whites by changing the job description and reducing the pay.

In short, the doctrine of separate development appears to be only a means by which the South African government seeks to rationalize its policies to the outside world. But policies are less and less shaped by the doctrine.

In recent years, students of African politics have been increasingly concerned about white South Africans' domination and the denial to blacks of all political rights. They cannot vote in national or provincial elections; they cannot be elected to parliament; and they cannot protest existing policy or advocate social or political change without fear of prosecution. But these scholars completely discount the fact that although disfranchised, South African blacks and surrounding black African states do exercise indirect influence on the South African political process. Much of this indirect influence, of course, takes the form of white backlash. Soon after the end of the Boer War, in 1902, South Africa suffered severe droughts, forcing many white farmers to migrate to the cities. Many of them had no skills that were relevant to the urban, industrial job market. It is mainly at this point that the lower class "poor white" began to resent non-whites; he found himself having to compete with Coloureds, Indians, and blacks for unskilled and semiskilled jobs. Some discriminatory labor legislation was introduced as a result of poor white demands for protection against black competition. Since whites also disliked the idea of working under non-whites or holding jobs lower in prestige than those occupied by non-whites, many types of jobs were restricted by law to whites only.

A similar situation arose after the First World War. Under the prevailing electoral laws, non-whites with specified educational and income qualifications were entitled to vote on the same basis as whites. With currency inflation and increasing literacy among non-whites, some whites began to fear that non-whites would be able, eventually, to outvote them, especially in Cape Province. A solution occurred to certain politicians in 1926: separate electoral lists. No longer would the names of Coloureds and other non-whites appear alongside those of whites on the voting register; and in fact, members of different races would no longer vote for the same candidates in the same constituencies. The question of non-white voting, dramatized by a document known as the Black Manifesto, became the main issue of the 1929 election campaign. It was a committee appointed to consider this issue which first proposed a policy called apartheid. The first elections after World War II also were fought on the non-white voting issue, with many politicians raising the specter of ultimate black dom-

ination if non-white political participation
were not drastically curtailed. The 1948 elect-
tion was won by the most adamant proponents of
political apartheid--the National Party. The
Nationalists have controlled the South African
government ever since.

Thus, we come to the main thesis of the book.
The rationalizations for apartheid and white rule
are believed, in varying combinations and degrees,
by many South African whites. But the most basic
reason for white resistance to equal treatment
for blacks is fear of being overwhelmed by the
black majority--a majority which might well choose
to make continued life in South Africa impossible
for whites. The Afrikaners, in particular, have
no place to go, no "mother country" to which they
have clear links, offering at least the hope of
refuge.

The whites living in South Africa today include not only the Afrikaners and the English,
but also a large number of comparatively recent
immigrants from newly independent countries of
black Africa. They include Portuguese from Mozambique and Angola; British from Zambia, Kenya,
Tanzania, Zimbabwe and Uganda; Belgians from
Zaire; and even a few French from the former French
colonies. They, too, are afraid of black rule.
They left their former homes either because the
new regime made life very difficult for them, or
because they anticipated that it would soon do so.

Whether long time residents or recent immigrants, white South Africans see their future under black rule as a reflection of events "up north"
since 1960. Based on their perceptions, black
majority rule would leave them with only two
bleak alternatives; serfdom or exile. These two
prospects--continuing to live in South Africa on
conditions set by the blacks, or leaving the
country altogether, perhaps without their assets--
are equally unacceptable to most whites.

It would be heartening if we could demonstrate that their fears are unfounded or grossly exaggerated. Unfortunately, this is not the case. As succeeding chapters will show, South African whites have good reason to fear black rule, in large part but not solely as retribution for their deplorable treatment of blacks. This fear leaves South African whites little apparent choice but to continue the repressive policies that keep them in the doghouse of world opinion.

FOOTNOTES: CHAPTER I

[1]A precis of the Reports of the Commissions appointed to inquire into the events occurring on March 21, 1960, at Sharpeville and Langa. A Fact Paper published by the South-African Institute of Race Relations, Johannesburg, No. 10, 1961, et seq.

[2]Ibid.

[3]William Redman Duggan, A Socioeconomic Profile of South Africa (New York: Praeger Publishers, 1973), p. 32.

[4]Africa Confidential, March 30, 1961, p. 2.

[5]Statement by David M. Sibeko in United Nations Centre Against Apartheid, Notes and Documents, No. 8, p. 7.

[6]Newsweek, June 28, 1976, p. 32.

[7]John F. Burns, "South Africa Dismisses Vote in U.N." New York Times, November 11, 1976.

[8]United Nations, Unit on Apartheid, Notes and Documents , No. 4/74, March 1974, "Anti Apartheid Movements in Western Europe," p. 1.

[9]United Nations, General Assembly Debates, October, 1963, cited in Colin and Margaret Legum, South Africa: Crisis for the West (New York: Praeger, 1964), p. 235.

[10]Statement by His Excellency Mr. Ogebe Ogbu (Nigeria), Chairman, Mission of the United Nations Special Committee Against Apartheid to Moscow and Kiev, May 7, 1975.

[11]Statement by Chairperson Mme Jeanne Martine-Cisse (Guinea), Special Committee Against Apartheid at the House of Commons, London, England, January 28, 1976. United Nations Unit on Apartheid, Notes

41

and _Documents_, No. 10, 1976, p. 10.

[12]George Woodcock, _Who Killed the British Empire_ (New York: Quadrangle/New York Times Book Co., 1974), pp. 320-321.

[13]United Nations Unit on Apartheid, _Notes and Documents_, No. 28, 1975, (August, 1975), pp. 1-2.

[14]Statement by the Rev. Leon Sullivan, United Nations Unit on Apartheid, _Notes and Documents_, No. 10, 1971 (March, 1971), p. 13.

[15]Resolution adopted by the Council of Ministers of the Organization of African Unity at a meeting held in Kampala, Uganda, July 18-25, 1975.

[16]United Nations Unit on Apartheid, _Notes and Documents_, No. 4, 1974, March, 1974, p. 12.

[17]For details, see United Nations Unit on Apartheid, _Notes and Documents_, No. 29, 1975.

[18]For example, see United Nations General Assembly Resolutions, 3411c, XXX, and 3411d, XXX, Thirtieth Session, 1975.

[19]See United Nations Centre Against Apartheid, _Notes and Documents_, Special Issue, February, 1976.

[20]For full details, see United Nations Unit on Apartheid, Special Report entitled "Anti-Apartheid Movement in Western Europe," _Notes and Documents_, March, 1974, No. 4/74, pp. 6-10.

[21]For a typical example of African skepticism, see Resolution on South Africa adopted by the Council of Ministers of the Organization of African Unity at a meeting in Daressalaam, Tanzania, April 7-10, 1975. Prime Minister Botha's recent concessions have done little to change this.

[22] See Resolution on South Africa adopted by the Conference of Ministers for Foreign Affairs of Non-Aligned Countries held in Lima, Peru, August 25-30, 1975.

[23]United Nations, Official Records of the General Assembly, General Assembly Resolution 3411g, Thirtieth Session, para. 2.

[24]Declaration on Southern Africa adopted by the Ninth Extraordinary Session of the Organization of African United Council of Ministers, meeting in Daressalaam, Tanzania, April 7-10, 1975.

[25]Statement by the Chairperson Mme Jeanne Martine-Cisse, (Guinea), Special Committee Against Apartheid, United Nations Unit on Apartheid, Issue No. 30/74, p. 5.

[26]Andrew Young, "Human Rights," Department of State Bulletin, 79: 59-60, February, 1979. Also, see Anthony Lake, "U.S. Policy Toward South Africa," Department of State Bulletin, 79: 18-20, January, 1979.

[27]See J.C. Smuts, The Basis of Trusteeship in African Natives Policy, p. 7.

[28]Leopold Marquard, The Peoples and Policies of South Africa (New York: Oxford University Press, 1962), p. 248.

[29]Ibid., p. 169.

[30]Jenis J. Worrall, "Afrikaner Nationalism: A Contemporary Analysis" in Christian P. Potholm and Richard Dale (Eds.), Southern Africa in Perspective: Essays in Regional Politics (New York: The Free Press, 1972), p. 29.

CHAPTER II

THE POLITICS OF BLACK AFRICA

Despite the diversity of the countries they
rule, the black governments of Africa share many
features. After describing the geographic,
ethnic, and historical context briefly, we shall
develop a model of African politics. Some regimes
fit the model better than others do, but we perceive
at most three exceptions to the basic pattern of
clientelism[1] and authoritarian rule. The model
will help explain the illiberal policies which
white minorities in Africa associate with black
rule.

Geographic and Ethnic Diversity

With an area of about 11.7 million square
miles, Africa is the world's second largest
continent. It extends some 5,000 miles from
north to south, and 4,500 miles from east to west.
The area of the United States is only about one-
third as great. The Nile, the River Zaire (the
Congo), and the River Niger are three of the world's
longest rivers. Africa has the greatest variety
of wildlife on earth. It is also comparatively
rich in mineral wealth, although this is distributed very unevenly. Many African countries--
Tanzania, Malawi, and the Ivory Coast, among them--
can rely very little on mineral resources to
finance economic development. Africa has less
than its share of rich farmland. This is a serious

problem on a continent where two-thirds of the
people depend on subsistence agriculture. Much
of Africa is desert.

It is impossible to provide an exact population figure for Africa. Estimates range from
345 million to over 400 million. But even if the
larger number is accepted, Africa's population
density is only about thirty-four per square mile.
The only continent with a lower population density
is Australia. Occupying about twenty percent of
the world's land surface, Africa accounts for
only ten percent of global population.

The African population is quite diverse--a
fact that has several political consequences.
There is no general agreement among ethnographers
on how to classify peoples living in Africa. For
our purposes, it is sufficient to distinguish
three broad categories: immigrants from Europe,
Asia, and the Middle East; Semites and Hamites;
and Negroid or black Africans. In 1958, some
5.7 million persons of European descent, and 1.4
million of Asian descent lived in Africa.
Because so many members of these racial minorities
have had to emigrate in the last several years,
there must be substantially fewer of them in
Africa today. Accurate figures are not available.

The largest contingent of Europeans live in
the Republic of South Africa and Zimbabwe. Most
of these people trace their ancestry to the Netherlands, England, Scotland, and the Huguenots of
seventeenth century France. France is also represented by several thousands of whites in the Ivory
Coast and Senegal. There used to be large settle-
ments of French in Algeria, Portuguese in Angola
and Mozambique, Britons in Zambia, and Belgians and
Greeks in Zaire. These have dwindled in recent
years. European businessmen, missionaries, technicians, or administrators enter Africa, but most
remain in Africa fewer than five years, returning to
their homelands when business or tour of duty is
finished.

The Asians in Africa are mainly Indians,
Pakistanis, Malays, and Polynesians. Their families settled in South Africa, Kenya, Tanzania,
etc., decades ago, when these countries and their
own countries of origin were British colonies.

People from the Middle East settled, in significant numbers, in countries along the east and
west coasts of the continent. Lebanese and
Syrians came to play an important role in the
economies of Sierra Leone, Ghana (the former Gold
Coast), and Gambia. Arabs from present-day Saudi
Arabia and Oman established communities in eastern Africa, particularly on the island of Zanzibar.

The African countries bordering the Mediterranean are often regarded as Arab. This is true
only to a degree. Arabs are dark but not black,
and tend to have wavy hair. Their facial characteristics resemble those of Italians or Greeks,
rather than the features of Ghanaians or Zambians.
Ethnologists classify pure Arabs, notably those in
the Middle East, as Semites, and the peoples of
North Africa as Hamites. Such distinctions are
often blurred on the African continent, especially
south of the Sahara. There, the term Arab is
used to refer to anyone who looks somewhat like an
Arab and displays Arab and/or Islamic cultural
traits, even if ethnologically he is more akin to
the Hamites or Negroes.

Black Africa proper begins at the southern
fringe of the Sahara. Of course, no precise
boundary exists. The peoples of the Eastern Horn
countries (Somalia, Ethiopia, and parts of the
Sudan and Kenya) are often regarded as Hamitic.
Yet their fuzzy hair and dark skin attest to a
substantial admixture of Negroid blood. Some
ethnologists place these peoples in a separate,
fourth racial category, referring to them as
Hamito-Negroid or Nilo-Hamites.

The black or Negroid peoples themselves
differ greatly. The contrast between the tall
Tutsi of Rwanda and the Pygmies of Zaire shows

47

the range of physical differentiation. Most black
Africans speak languages belonging to the Congo-
Kordofanian family. Many of these languages even
belong to the same subfamily, Bantu. This in itself does not facilitate communication. The several hundred Bantu languages and dialects tend to
be as distinct from each other as English is from
Dutch or German. Most importantly, Africans are
divided into many hundreds of tribes. Tribes may
be defined as groups of people with a common way
of life and a sense of group identity and distinctiveness. Tribes within a single African country
differ in their level of technology (from hunting
and gathering to nomadic herding to farming), in
their religious beliefs, and in their traditional
political structures.

Increasing numbers of black Africans have
become more or less permanent city dwellers.
Though it is common to regard them as detribal-
ized, westernized, or "modernized," most have
not cut themselves off completely from the old
order. They visit their tribal villages, and
stay in touch with relatives there. They often
play host to a complete stranger who has come
to the city, simply because he belongs to their
tribe. If a man succeeds in the city, he is
expected to aid less fortunate tribesmen and
help them find jobs. Urban blacks often continue
to practice tribal customs and rituals (perhaps
in combination with other religions). In
cities from Abidjan to the townships of South
Africa, one finds neighborhoods settled exclusively
by members of a single tribe.

Formal Independence

European encroachment in black Africa dates
from the fifteenth century. The Portuguese
rounded Cape Bajdour in 1434, and the Cape of
Good Hope in 1497. Their primary concerns were
trade and a safe route to India. They also
professed religious goals, like helping the
Christian king of Ethiopia fight off Moslem
attackers. Eventually, their involvement in

Africa increased. They made commerce there more lucrative by entering the slave trade, and established political dominion over parts of the continent. In the eighteenth century, the British and the French followed suit. By 1900, almost the entire continent was divided among the European powers--Britain, France, Belgium, Italy, the Netherlands, Spain, Germany, and, of course, Portugal.

The last thirty years have seen the complete transformation of Africa, from a continent of colonies to one of independent states. In early 1980, only South West Africa, or Namibia, was not self-governing. Although the transformation grew out of earlier developments, especially in the decade following World War II, most African states did not actually gain independence until the 1960's. No less than sixteen of them became independent in the year 1960 alone. (See the accompanying Table.) The more former colonies won independence, the harder it became for European powers to hold their remaining dependencies. Even the Portuguese, who claimed to have had incorporated their colonies as "overseas provinces" of Portugal, were finally obliged to grant independence to Angola, Mozambique, and Guinea-Bissau.

African nationalism or national consciousness was mainly a reaction against foreign domination. African opponents of colonialism clothed their demands in concepts borrowed from western liberal ideology, like self-determination, democracy, and equality. Kwame Nkrumah declared that "...the peoples of the colonies know precisely what they want. They wish to be free and independent...and to work out their own destiny."[2] As Kenneth Kaunda agitated for Zambian independence, he denounced the British colonial regime as "undemocratic, unethical, and entirely unChristian." His party was "organizing to bring into being here a government of the people, by the people, and indeed for the people."[3]

BASIC DATA ON SUB-SAHARAN AFRICA
December, 1979

Taken from Special Report No. 61
United States Department of State
Bureau of Public Affairs

COUNTRY	POPULATION TOTAL (mil)	DATE OF INDEPENDENCE
Angola	6.35	Nov. 11, 1975
Benin	3.4	Aug. 1, 1960
Botswana	.72	Sept. 30, 1966
Burundi	3.9	July 1, 1962
Cameroon	8.16	Jan. 1, 1960
Cape Verde	.33	July 5, 1975
Central African Republic	·2.2	Aug. 13, 1960
Chad	4.2	Aug. 11, 1960
Comoros	.37	July 6, 1975
Congo	1.78	Aug. 15, 1960
Djibouti	.25	June 27, 1977
Equatorial Guinea	.31	Oct. 12, 1968
Ethiopia	30.0	Since ancient times
Gabon	.58	Aug. 17, 1960
Gambia (The)	.56	Feb. 18, 1965
Ghana	10.6	Mar. 6, 1957
Guinea	4.5	Oct. 2, 1958
Guinea-Bissau	.92	Sept. 24, 1973
Ivory Coast	7.3	Aug. 7, 1960
Kenya	15.8	Dec. 12, 1963
Lesotho	1.2	Oct. 4, 1966
Liberia	1.73	1847
Madagascar	9.1	June 29, 1960
Malawi	5.9	July 6, 1964
Mali	6.5	Sept. 22, 1960
Mauritania	1.42	Nov. 28, 1960
Mauritius	.9	Mar. 12, 1968
Mozambique	9.6-10.4	June 25, 1975
Namibia	.92	Pending
Niger	5.6	Aug. 3, 1960
Nigeria	79.8	Oct. 1, 1960

Data on Sub-Saharan Africa
Continued

Country	Population Total	Date of Independence		
Rwanda	4.2	July	1,	1962
Sao Tome and Principe	.08	July	12,	1975
Senegal	5.38	Apr.	4,	1960
Seychelles	.06	June	29,	1976
Sierra Leone	3.22	Apr.	27,	1961
Somalia	3.2	July	1,	1960
South Africa	27.39	May	31,	1910
Southern Rhodesia	7.2	Pending		
Sudan	16.8	Jan.	1,	1956
Swaziland	.49	Sept.	6,	1968
Tanzania	17.4	Tan		1961
		Zan		1963
		Union		1964
Togo	2.3	Apr.	27,	1960
Uganda	13.2	Oct.	9,	1962
Upper Volta	6.5	Aug.	5,	1960
Zaire	27.	June	30,	1960
Zambia	5.4	Oct.	24,	1964

The immediate objectives of African leaders
varied. Some, like the distinguished barrister
Dr. J. B. Danquah, favored phased devolution of
authority, in cooperation with the colonial power.
Some joined Nkrumah in advocating "positive action"
--mass protests and civil disobedience. Others
believed, with Frantz Fanon, that decolonization
was and should be a violent process. But these
were differences over tactics. All nationalist
leaders shared the ultimate objective of bringing an end to colonial rule.

Sooner or later, the colonial powers recog-
nizedthe apparent strength of African nationalism
and set their policies accordingly. In some cases,
the African leaders themselves must have been
surprised at the speed with which the colonial
rulers agreed to grant independence. After divest-
ing itself of India, Burma, and Ceylon in the
late 1940's, Britain soon began to groom the Gold
Coast (Ghana) for independence. And what it gave
Ghana, "it could hardly deny to Nigeria, the other
model colony of West Africa...."[4] When Guinea won
independence in 1958, the French colonies too began receiving independence one after the other.
The gestation period for an independent Belgian
Congo (now Zaire) was little more than six months!

The British and French made some effort to
provide their colonies with functioning political
institutions, before independence. They tried to
convert governors' advisory councils into full-
fledged parliaments, manned by duly elected representatives. They also tried to entrench western-
style legal systems and safeguards for civil rights.
Even though Great Britain has no written constitution, it helped draw up independence constitutions for its colonies. In particular, the
British made much of the concept of multiracialism. They said they were helping to build societies in which individual rights were protected,
and individual merit was the sole criterion for
economic and political advancement. As stated by
the British foreign secretary in 1960,

We reject the idea of any inherent super-
iority of one race over another. Our policy
is therefore non-racial. It offers a future
in which Africans, Europeans, Asians, the
peoples of the Pacific, and others with which
we are concerned, will all play their full
part as citizens in the countries where
they live, and in which feelings of race
will be submerged in loyalty to the new
nations.[5]

This position was not entirely unselfish.
Britain wanted to calm the fears of white and
Asian settlers in Kenya, the Rhodesias, now Zambia
and Zimbabwe, and elsewhere, in order to overcome
their resistance to independence. Also, the British hoped to continue their close ties with the
African countries after independence. They spoke
of continued interdependence: economic, diplomatic, and cultural interaction would continue,
for the mutual benefit of Britain and its former
colonies.

The French, too, tried to organize a continuing community of nations. Reflecting confidence
in the French mission civilisatrice, they emphasized how the various colonial peoples had come
to share certain features of French culture,
above and beyond distinctions of race or ethnicity.

There were other reasons for expecting
interdependence to continue. The former colonies
had done much of their trading with the European
powers; it is usually impractical to change
trading partners over night. Economic ties
would be strengthened further by economic and
technical assistance, which the new states needed
badly. African state bureaucracies would probably
need the services of European officials for some
time to come, since they lacked enough trained
officials of their own. And between missionary
activity and schools established by the colonial
governments, the more articulate members of the
African societies had in fact been exposed exten-
sively to western culture and ways of thinking.

53

In retrospect, it is clear that the aims and expectations of most African nationalists were quite different. To them, acquisition of sovereignty under international law did not mark the end of European domination. Instead, it was but a first step toward "genuine," "total," or "complete" independence.

The Quest for Self-Determination

The African understanding of the term "self-determination," and their departure from the ordinary use of that word, illustrates more than one important characteristic of the black African regimes. When Woodrow Wilson proclaimed the right of all peoples to self-determination, he meant the right of ethnic communities or nationalities, defined mainly by language and culture, to form their own state. Since then, both the meaning and the implementation of the concept have become controversial. There are two major anomalies in the invocation of self-determination by black African officials.

Absence of National Community

First, the concept of self-determination presupposed a self-aware national community. But no former colony in Africa constituted such a community.

As soon as representatives of new African states had the right to be heard in international forums, they spared no effort in demanding independence for the remaining colonies. A characteristic speech was given by the Ghanaian representative to the U.N. General Assembly, Mr. Adjei, almost immediately after his country became independent.

> ...There is a growing body of opinion, in one part of Africa, that Ghana is becoming the centre of anti-colonial forces and political agitation for independence. The enemies of freedom and independence for the African

people view this nationalistic development
with alarm. Ghana has no apologies to
render in this regard... Ghana has made
no secret of the fact that it rejects
colonial status for any part of Africa,
and that we desire to see all Africa free
and independent.[6]

Triumphantly flaunting the self-determination
provisions of the U.N.Charter and the draft
Universal Declaration of Human Rights before
world bodies, they claimed that the peoples
living under alien rule in colonies were being
denied the right to determine their own national
destinies. Ergo, colonial powers had a legal and
moral obligation to allow their dependencies to
become independent states.

    Implicit in this argument was the assumption
that the peoples living within any given colony
had some sense of community and common identity--
that they considered themselves a nation.
Actually, this was far from true in most cases.
Colonial boundaries, which now were to define the
borders of the new states, had been set quite
arbitrarily by the European powers. European
negotiators of the nineteenth century lacked
detailed knowledge of African physical and cultural
geography, especially of the areas in the interior,
and tended to draw boundaries in terms of parallels
and meridians, straight lines, arcs of circles
or by reference to topographical features like
rivers and valleys.

    Some African leaders and intellectuals had
criticized these boundaries even before independence as artificial, arbitrary, and totally lacking
in moral validity. They cut across ethnic,
tribal, and linguistic areas. Some tribes were
divided among two or more countries (e.g. the
Fulani, the Bakongo, and Luo), and the population
of any one colony included several different
tribes. Yet the tribes were the social and
political units with which most Africans identified. In the same African circles, however, the

optimistic view prevailed that after independence, the boundaries would be revised in a spirit of African unity. A resolution passed at the All African People's Conference, held in Ghana in 1958, denounced "artificial frontiers drawn by imperialist powers to divide the peoples of Africa," and called for the "abolition or adjustment of such frontiers at an early date."[7] African leaders soon discovered that it was very hard to implement such resolutions.

The colonial boundaries had been in operation for most of the twentieth century, if not longer. Any political, administrative, or economic advances made under colonial rule took place in the context of these borders. These included the development of a cash crop economy, the building of railways and roads, and the organization of rudimentary public services. Any large-scale alteration of borders was bound to generate a series of claims and counter-claims among the new states. In any case, it would require major changes in the existing administrative and economic machinery of the countries involved. It was also recognized that complete abolition of colonial boundaries would require a political union of African states. Ghanaian rhetoric to the contrary, a United States of Africa seemed patently out of reach for the foreseeable future.

Although African spokesmen continued condemning the borders as imperialist impositions, most African governments tacitly accepted them. They have tended to discourage secessionist movements, or claims for self-determination by groups within their state boundaries. In fact, the Charter of the Organization of African Unity, written in 1963, endorses the concepts of sovereignty, territorial integrity, and respect for each state's colonially defined boundaries without qualification (Article III).

The literature on nationalism suggests another major impediment to the development of national

consciousness among Africans. Nationalism is
thought to presuppose some contact with members
and non-members of the prospective national
community, and leisure to reflect on the differences. Therefore, nationalism flowered in Europe
only after the rise of an educated middle class,
in the late eighteenth and early nineteenth
centuries.[8] Karl Deutsch has insisted that, at
minimum, the growth of national self-conscious-
ness presupposes an exchange economy, as opposed
to subsistence agriculture.[9] Yet many, if not
most, Africans remain outside the money economy.
If economic exchange is limited, other kinds of
contacts are sparse indeed. Without question,
this limits interest in "national" politics.
One indication is the consistently small voter
turnout in elections immediately before and after
independence.[10]

An alternative route to national consciousness was suggested by theorists like Frantz Fanon:
colonial peoples could develop a common sense of
identity and pride through armed conflict with
the oppressors.[11] The long guerrilla war
against the Portuguese in Mozambique does seem
to bear this out.[12] But in most African countries,
independence came without armed struggle. Nigerians, the Togolese, Tanzanians, and so on, did not
become nations by this means either.

Thus African invocations of self-determination are ambiguous. In effect, the spokesmen of
black governments take the following position:
the right to self-determination becomes operative
when African people are subjected to white rule
and exploitation. As soon as a colony obtains
independence, though, the doctrine of territorial
integrity of existing states takes precedence over
claims to self-determination by peoples within
that state. Any attempt to disrupt the unity
and solidarity of the peoples of the new states is
ipso facto illegitimate.

Rejection of Interdependence
Black African leaders have also construed the

57

concept of self-determination much more broadly
than is customary. At least until World War II,
national self-determination meant formal, political independence. This gave a state the right to
enter freely into agreements with other states,
form alliances, establish diplomatic and commercial relations, and operate in the international
arena without interference from other states.
In current African usage, however, self-determination is not simply a matter of formal independence. Essential aspects of "true" self-determination include the right to determine one's own
future, secure from external pressures or allegiance to any foreign powers or interests; and
full control over one's own political, economic,
and social systems. Some African leaders have
been willing to accept very high costs in their
quest for complete freedom of action. Sekou
Toure preferred to do without badly needed
economic aid from France rather than accept
membership in the French Community. Tanzanian
President Nyerere also refuses to accept aid with
any political strings attached.

     Some leaders also invoke self-determination
in refusing to regard certain widely accepted
norms as binding within their territory. Idi Amin
insisted that it was no concern of anyone outside
Uganda if he executed thousands of Acholis and
Langis to eliminate possible political opponents.
President Macias, of Equatorial Guinea, took a
similar position in his pogrom against his
country's educated minority. Most African governments insist on their right to ignore international
law on citizenship and the treatment of resident
aliens in setting their own policies on these
subjects. (See the extended discussion of this in
Chapter IV.)

     With the support of other new states and the
communist world, African delegates have managed to
persuade the United Nations to recognize this
broad definition of self-determination, at least
implicitly. In a General Assembly resolution
adopted in 1965, every state is said to have "an

inalienable right to choose its political, economic, social, and cultural systems, without interference in any form by another state."[13] The resolution denies "the right of any state to intervene, directly or indirectly, in the internal or external affairs of any other state, or to use economic, political, or any other type of measures in order to secure advantages of any kind from another state, or to subordinate the exercise of the latter's sovereign status."[14]

The United Nations does recognize one exception to this rule: intervention is permissible if directed against a regime that practices apartheid or similar policies that benefit a racial minority. However, if racial discrimination is practiced by a majority against one or more minorities, intervention by other states is not considered justified. Such discrimination may be condemned, but it is not deemed a sufficiently serious evil as to override the right of all "peoples" to independence and territorial integrity. Thus, here too, black African governments can have their cake and eat it too. They can intervene freely in South Africa, while claiming the right to do as they please within their own borders. Whenever actions taken within their own territory draw criticism at the international level, they denounce this as violation of U.N. resolutions and interference in their internal affairs by imperialists and neocolonialists. Self-determination has thus been expanded--or reduced--to an ideological justification for any dictator who belongs to the majority race of his country.

"Majority Rule" in Black Africa: a Model

In this section, we shall develop a model of African politics. A brief look at the single parties and civilian and military styles of government will lead to a discussion of client-elism. This crucial concept is the cornerstone of the model. Policy choices made by African political leaders can be explained largely by the

59

exigencies of maintaining personal clienteles
and coalitions, and the social/political context
that makes this necessary.

Western scholars tried, for a long time, to
portray African politics as essentially democratic.
As the years went by, this became increasingly
difficult. Botswana and Gambia were the only
black African states, as of early 1980, which
had allowed opposition parties to function continuously since independence. Of the remaining black
regimes, most were either military dictatorships
or civialian governments without institutionalized
controls.[15] We shall argue that there is little
real difference between the two types of regime.

Most former British and French colonies began their independent existence with a parliamentary form of government. The chief executives
of Ghana, Nigeria, the Ivory Coast, etc., were
prime ministers responsible to duly-elected
- parliamentary majorities. Independent judiciaries
were established to apply impartially a mixture
of English or French and traditional African law.
Public service commissions and other mechanisms
were devised to safeguard the political neutral-
ity of the civil service. But constitutions
were soon altered, if not scrapped outright, to
remove all checks on the executive. The late
Kwame Nkrumah, of Ghana, Felix Houphouet-Boigny,
of the Ivory Coast, and several other independence
leaders became presidents with the power to des-
ignate many or all members of parliament personally. Political loyalty became the most important criterion for judicial and civil service
appointments.

That the trappings of European democracy
were discarded is not surprising. They had not
been used long enough to acquire an aura of
legitimacy and tradition. The colonial governments themselves appeared to Africans as more or
less partisan bureaucratic dictatorships for
most of their duration. Attempts to encourage
democratic participation in politics, to recruit

and promote black civil servants on the basis of merit, and so on, were only a hasty prelude to independence. Also, the lack of a sense of national community was crucial. The political elites had a vision of national unity, but often felt they could not trust their opponents to rise above tribal particularism. Indeed, much as they might regret it in some instances, the new rulers felt obliged to give special favors to their own supporters, and thus could not abide by western notions of political propriety very long.

One salient feature of African politics is the single-party system. In almost all states ruled by civilians, and in many of the military dictatorships as well (Zaire, Tanzania, and Benin, among others), there is a single legal party. The move toward single parties appears to have gone hand in hand with the establishment of presidential autocracy.

The fact that a country has only one political party does not mean, necessarily, that other major parties have been suppressed. Some of today's single parties were already preeminent at the time of independence. For example, Aristide Zolberg has noted that marginally superior organization gave Nkrumah's Convention People's Party and the Bloc Populaire Senegalais electoral victories. Though their structural coherence was often overestimated, these parties managed to reach a larger fraction of the electorate than did their opponents.[16] And once the French or British recognized them as valid representatives of the indigenous people, the parties in question gained additional prestige by "winning" independence. Opposition parties were weakened further when ambitious members defected to the ruling party.

Nevertheless, African political leaders have felt the need to eliminate organized opposition entirely. Although Zambia's United National Independence Party (UNIP), won large majorities in the 1964 and 1968 parliamentary elections, President Kenneth Kaunda banned all parties but UNIP in 1972. The Tanganyika African National Union (TANU) was made the sole legal political party in mainland Tanzania, even though it never faced any serious opposition. It goes without saying that opposition parties have been banned or harrassed out of existence in countries where they did pose some electoral threat, as in Kenya and Sierra Leone.

Leaders of African single party systems often claim their parties are both a unifying, mobilizing force and genuinely democratic. A single party system makes it possible to "harness the Party organization, and the enthusiasm of our people, for new tasks of fighting poverty."[17] The single party is "a national movement which is open to all, which is identified with the whole nation, and which has nothing to fear from the discontent of any excluded section of the society, for there is then no such section."[18] Much has been made of the African institution of palaver, as allegedly embodied in these parties. That is, the single party is described as a forum in which everyone can speak his mind, and where decisions reflect a consensus rather than a partisan view. However, African single parties could possess these attractive characteristics only if, in fact, they provided opportunities for all citizens to participate in the political process on a regular and meaningful basis. This is simply not the case.

The Tanganyika African National Union is often held up as the model of single party democracy. It can boast over 7,000 rural branch organizations, and it does hold elections in which voters may choose between contending TANU candidates. Yet, as Norman N. Miller discovered, village party officials are left to exercise their authority almost as they please. Not only does the party fail to prevent petty tyranny at the local level; it also fails to communicate grass-roots concerns to the higher echelons.[19] It is estimated that ten percent of all TANU members joined under coercion.[20] And, as explained in Chapter V, the rank and file has little to say about the selection of the much-vaunted alternative candidates for parliament.

Other single parties have, if anything, a less convincing record of internal democracy. It is often noted that several African single parties absorbed rival parties instead of suppressing them with naked force. Yet the circumstances of these mergers require further examination. In Kenya, the opposition leader Oginga Odinga joined former President Kenyatta's Kenya African National Union, saying this was warranted by a "revived and revitalized KANU." But he reached this conclusion only after spending eighteen months in preventive detention. Since then, the ruling party has denied him, on one excuse or another, permission to run for election. In the 1979 elections, his local KANU party branch at Kisii simply refused to accept his nomination papers. Similarly coercive methods have been used to eliminate opposition in Ghana, Malawi, and Guinea, among other countries.[21] Furthermore, it is hard to find any means by which average citizens are represented in decision making councils. Not only do constituents have little or no choice of parliamentary candidates; parliaments have at one time or other been abolished or eviscerated in all black African countries except Gambia and Botswana. Neither do decision making organs of the parties themselves provide systematic representation of constituencies. The leadership stratum of African states (like that of most other countries) is definitely not a cross-section of the population; the leaders cannot be said to represent their people in that sense, either.

One other piece of evidence that African single parties are not firmly rooted in the populace is their tendency to disintegrate immediately when their leaders are thrown out of office. This happened to the Convention People's Party when Kwame Nkrumah was ousted. When Idi Amin overthrew Milton Obote, in Uganda, Obote's Uganda People's Congress disappeared without a

whimper. The coup against Modibo Keita, in Mali,
also caused the immediate end of the Union Soudanaise. And when the military revolted against
Julius Nyerere, in 1964, TANU did not rally to
his defense. He had to ask for British troops to
regain control of the Tanzanian government.

Thus far, we have been discussing civilian
governments. But stable civilian oligarchies are
becoming the exception rather than the rule in
Africa. Of the states which gained independence
in the 1960's, less than a third have had civilian regimes continuously since independence.
Military coups have become so frequent and widespread as to constitute a routine means of transferring political leadership. Over three-quarters
of the independent African states have had to
contend, at one time or another, with attempted
or successful military coups.

Several countries have experienced more
than one coup, sometimes interspersed with civilian regimes. Madagascar, Ghana, and Nigeria all
saw three military coups within a decade. But
Benin (formerly Dahomey) holds the record. When
Dahomey became independent in 1960, it possessed
a comparatively large number of university graduates and experienced administrators. Many observers expected this to minimize the danger of
political instability. Contrary to their expectations, Benin had gone through at least seven
successful military coups and several more
attempted coups by 1979. There is no end in sight.

What accounts for African military coups?
Anyone seeking to stage a coup in Africa does not
have to look far for reasons. After assuming
power, the officers typically cite the corruption,
inefficiency, tribalism, arbitrary use of power,
and general moral bankruptcy of the preceding
regime as evils obliging them to intervene.
Their accusations are usually not unfounded. But
whether the officers' primary motive is to rescue
the body politic from these evils is highly

questionable.

Nevertheless, all but a handful of Africanists have accepted the official explanations of
military takeovers at face value. They have developed two broad interpretations of the high
incidence of military coups.

In the first interpretation, military intervention in the political realm is viewed as a
function of chronic systemic disequilibrium.
This disequilibrium may include any of the
following elements: economic collapse resulting
from politically or ideologically inspired development programs; overly ambitious programs of social
mobilization, which tear the people away from
their traditional moorings and create disruption
and unrest; political and administrative paralysis
caused by ethnic and interelite strife within
government; loss of legitimacy through corruption,
nepotism, inefficiency and tribal favoritism; and
threats to the automony of the army (through
alteration of chains of command, changes in
criteria for promotion, and similar measures).
In short, military intervention comes about because of serious failings on the part of the
regimes they displace.[22]

The second type of explanation focuses on
military officers' professionalism. African
armies are described as possessing professional
qualities that are otherwise in short supply in
African societies. They are organized hier-
archically, and are said to be disciplined, austere,
nationalistic, educated, and westernized. These
characteristics and the values that go with them
make it hard for military officers to tolerate
rule by corrupt and more or less incompetent
politicians.[23]

Most of these analysts seemed not to view the
wave of military takeovers with alarm, but to
consider them at worst a necessary evil. They
believed the African armed forces would foster
modernity, stability, and economic development.

The military seemed to be less traditional, less parochial, and certainly more familiar with modern technology than other sectors of society. Officers were considered skilled in making decisions and in getting jobs done.[24] Given their hierarchical organization and the imputation of western norms, the armed forces were, in Marion J. Levy's words, "the most efficient type of organization for combining maximum rates of modernization with maximum levels of stability and control."[25]

In the last three years or so, a small but growing number of Africanists have taken a more skeptical view. Samuel Decalo is one of them. After an exhaustive examination of the circumstances surrounding eleven military coups in Africa, he found that in almost all cases, "military intervention was directly or indirectly linked to the personal ambitions or fears of specific key officers, though societal tensions may have abetted and other civilian groups may have supported the destruction of civilian authority."[26] Empirical research into civil-military relations elsewhere in Africa also supports this conclusion. "It is both simplistic and empirically erroneous" to regard coups as "a function of the political weakness and structural fragility of African states, and the failings of African civilian elites," according to Decalo.[27] He finds the second set of conventional explanations, those that emphasize military officers' professional qualities, even more faulty.

African armies have rarely been cohesive, nontribal, Westernized, or even complex organizational structures. Neat hierarchical command charts camouflage deep cleavages....Differential recruitment and promotion patterns cause tensions that reinforce other lines of division based on rank, age, tribe, and education....

At independence many of the current top officers were rapidly promoted from the ranks

or the officer corps in the drive to achieve
Africanization of army commands. Their relative youth and spotty formal education, coupled with the limited number of senior positions in Africa's miniscule armies, created
promotion bottle-necks for junior officers
anxious to imitate their meteoric rise.
Personal animosities and ambitions have also
been rife in the officer corps. And whatever fragile organizational unity African
armies may have originally possessed has
usually been rapidly eroded by the politicization of their internal cleavages after
independence and the sharpening of personal
jealousies and power struggles.[28]

Civilian and military regimes do not appear
to differ in their impact on economic and social
development. Eric A. Nordlinger found that in the
least developed countries of the world (including
most black African states), military rule was
associated with economic growth.[29] More recently,
Robert W. Jackman subjected Nordlinger's data and
a more recent data set to an analysis of covariance,
and found that military rule made no difference in
the rate of social/economic change. This held
for countries at each level of economic development, and for African countries taken as a group.[30]

This brings us to the crucial role of clientelism in African politics. The major contenders
for power in African states are not large, impersonal organizations like the Pentagon, the Teamsters' Union, and General Motors. Rather, they
are personal alliances--informal groups of
acquaintances, or leaders with smallish groups of
followers. These groups are held together largely
by the expectation of joint rewards. The pattern
seems to hold in both the established one-party
systems and in the many successful and attempted
military coups, from the one that killed Togolese
president Sylvanus Olympio to Mengistu Haile
Mariam's coup in Ethiopia.

Clientelism, as defined by Rene Lemarchand,

67

is "a more or less personalized relationship between actors (i.e. patrons and clients), or sets
of actors, commanding unequal wealth, status, or
influence, based on conditional loyalties and involving mutually beneficial transactions."[31]
This sort of relationship arises in many different
cultures, ranging from rural Japan through Southern Italy to Northern Nigeria and Northeastern
Brazil. Clientelism is likely to be common where-
ever personal insecurity prevails, kinship units
are unable to meet important needs for their
members, social control outside such relationships is lacking, and it is not customary to pay
for each service individually.[32] In some countries,
there is sort of a pyramid of patrons and clienteles reminiscent of the fabled big city machine
of the late nineteenth and early twentieth centuries. Examples include the Parti Democratique du
Cote d'Ivoire, of the Ivory Coast, and the single
parties of Liberia and pre-1968 Mali. But in
most cases, there is no such articulated organization below the top level.

Politically significant personal alliances
are much more likely to form in some sectors of
the population than in others. These are three
major categories of participants in African
politics: 1) professional politicians; 2) the
army and police; and 3) bureaucrats. Taken
together, these people comprise less than five
percent of the population. The vast majority of
them live in the cities and have had some exposure
to western-style education; some have even
studied abroad.

The life-style and outlook of this political
elite differ markedly from those of most Africans.
The benefits of political independence, of
expropriation of foreign-owned assets, of improved health facilities, and of opportunities
afforded by foreign aid, have accrued disproportionately to them. This has a number of
consequences. In the first place, as David
Hapgood emphasizes, the elite are out of touch
with--indeed, alienated from--the people in

whose name they rule.[33] They do not share the concerns of the masses, and tend to be contemptuous of those who lack their veneer of westernization. On the other hand, government-related jobs are coveted as the most obvious means of assuring a high standard of living. Third, if members of the political-military-bureaucratic elite control most material and status resources, they are in a good position to build clienteles.

Almost every person in these groups has, or soon secures, a clientele or base of support. Usually, the clientele includes members of one's extended family, kinship group, village, or tribe. In some cases (but less frequently), a man recruits his subordinates and/or members of his church or union as clients. Sekou Toure, of course, parlayed prominence in the Guinean labor union movement into long tenure as president of Guinea. The relative size and placement of a clientele depends on the patron's prestige, the importance of his position, his ability to provide material and status gratifications, and the perceived security of his position. If he occupies a high office securely, he may continue to enjoy the support of many clients even if his aid is perfunctory. If his hold on office appears precarious, however, he will have to provide more largesse to retain his following. He may have to compete with other members of the bureaucracy, military, and politicians for clients. Largesse takes many forms, of course; a patron may reward his clients with jobs, scholarships, loans, licenses, and government contracts. He may expedite handling of their applications for building or trade permits. He may allow them access to elite facilities like exclusive clubs and residential areas. But resources for distribution to clients are in short supply, relative to patrons' needs. This leads to friction, rivalry, and even hostility within the political elite groups. This, in turn, makes for greater insecurity among the politically ambitious, reinforcing their need for large, well-placed clienteles.

The first political elite group--professional politicians--literally lives off politics. It is one of the most profitable professions in Africa, though not the safest. One African writer has explained that for politicians,

> ...the greatest misfortune that can befall them is to lose an election or to fall out of favour with those who control and wield power. For, unlike the professional or skilled man or woman, or the businessman with an independent source of income, the politician's dependence on politics for his livelihood is almost total and complete. Not only must he advertise the fact of his changed status by the acquisition of wealth and conspicuous spending; he must also insure himself against opponents who might wish to deprive him of both his acquired status and the means of his livelihood.[34]

As suggested before, there is practically no middle class in Africa except the bourgeoisie de la fonction publique. There is no native class of large land owners. Industry is still very limited; what heavy industry there is belongs largely to European or American multinationals or the government. Commerce, similarly, is passing from control by non-black minorities to control by black governments. Ambitious young men see few desirable alternatives to government-related jobs.

The professional politician's career consists of obtaining some European-style education, taking whatever party or public office he can get, and trying to move up to higher ones. In this context, a seat in parliament is a highly desirable position, even though it affords little influence on government policy. It provides the aspiring politician with a high income, improved social status, and a better chance to gain the favor of a powerful patron. The seat in parliament may become a springboard to an even better position, like that of a minister or director of a state corporation.

An African politician is usually unwilling to jeopardize his career by criticizing the government or the party. He acquiesces in, or even encourages, politicization of the judiciary, the bureaucracy, and the military; if one or more alleged opponents of the regime are to be purged, he may find it expedient to jump on the bandwagon and denounce them.

Available evidence suggests that political power is coveted not so much for its own sake as for the wealth, status, and "pull" it brings. There are few examples of professional politicians taking a cut in their real income in order to ease the burden on the national budget. Julius Nyerere does live comparatively simply, but he cannot hold the rest of the Tanzanian elite to his lifestyle. Sylvanua Olympio was assassinated by disgruntled sinecure-seekers, and the new Togolese government promptly reversed his cuts in elite pay and privileges. The fear of an impending coup is an additional factor that encourages politicians to make hay while the sun shines. Any personnel changes by the incumbent president may have the same effect: personal insecurity and ambition dictate redoubled efforts to build up one's material resources and one's clientele.

The second elite category is the military and police. Civilian governments have tended to pamper the security forces, increasing their salaries and fringe benefits, while seeking to keep them under control. Among the tactics used to control the military and the police are reorganizations, replacement of key personnel, political indoctrination, and the appointment of political commissars to enforce loyalty from within the security forces. These control measures, of course, tend to make officers feel insecure. Insecurity has the same behavioral consequences among them as it does among politicians. When the military is in power, it is suspicious of the professional politicians and fearful of counter-coups. Therefore, military regimes tend to look after their own while they have the opportunity.

In 1974, thirty percent of the Nigerian national budget went to the military. Dahomey's one-brigade army absorbed one-fifth of the budget in 1970. Sierra Leone's military regime was preaching the need for sacrifice, in 1967, but announced long lists of military promotions and raises nonetheless. In the austerity budget framed by Ghana's military government in 1967-1968, there were very sharp cuts in funds for agriculture, industry, communications, and trade; but military appropriations increased by 41.4 percent, including a five percent rise in military salaries.

The armies and police forces left by the colonial powers were relatively small, compared with the African population. The post-war Pax Americana relieved the European powers of much of the burden of providing for their own defense. An external attack on their African colonies seemed unlikely in any case. And if large numbers of troops were needed to maintain domestic order, they could be flown in quickly from the metropolis or other colonies. It made little sense to train many Africans for a local army. Those who were recruited formed infantry units, rather than navies, air forces, signal corps, or other specialized or technical services. Even so, almost all the officers were European, until the imminence of independence forced a crash program to recruit and promote black officers.

The colonial armed forces did not reflect the ethnic diversity of the African states. African officers were usually recruited from those ethnic groups known for their ability to absorb western education. In most cases, they had been converted to Christianity, and lived in or near the main cities. The rank and file, on the other hand, were largely illiterate and from the interior. They were recruited from ethnic groups which the colonial authorities considered aggressive, courageous, obedient, and likely to make good foot soldiers. Selective recruitment on whatever basis exacerbated intertribal tensions, because in the African context, the army is a privileged class.

Even under colonial governments, soldiers were relatively well paid. The government provided them with food and lodging, which, if not luxurious, was better than that available to most Africans. Army equipment, including uniforms and sturdy shoes, was also conspicuously better than typical civilian gear. (A revealing passage in Major-General Ocran's account of the 1966 coup in Ghana shows the psychological importance of good equipment; the general was appalled that President Nkrumah failed to maintain British standards in provisioning the army.)[35] Much the same can be said of African police forces.

Army and police jobs continue to be a source of patronage, and of ethnic strife. Rivalry between Mende and Temne officers accounted for two successive coups in Sierra Leone. Personnel policies in the Nigerian army set the stage for that country's tragic civil war. At independence, 75 percent of all black officers were Ibo. Special efforts to recruit more men from other tribes could not eliminate the imbalance quickly. Thus, when Ibo officers led a coup in 1966, the Hausas and Yorubas feared that the federal government would be used for Ibo tribal interests, at their expense. They retaliated. In Uganda, Idi Amin stayed in power partly by giving army and secret police appointments to members of groups which formerly enjoyed little access to such jobs. Among these groups was his own small Kakwa tribe. The traditional backbone of the Ugandan army, the Ancholis and the Langis, have been decimated.

Bureaucrats are the third elite group. While career civil servants have never mounted a successful coup, they are indispensable to military and civilian governments alike. African government bureaucracies include some job categories that normally would not be covered by civil service in the United States. Not only customs officials, postal clerks, public health and trade officials, and so on, but also many managers and teachers are civil servants. The status of African judges is the same, for all practical purposes. Many of

these positions combine some power with a relatively high income. They are among the few jobs in
the economy which, in principle, provide a pension
upon retirement.

However crucial they are as a group, African
bureaucrats are vulnerable as individuals. Merit
systems and tenure have been junked in favor of
distributing government jobs as patronage. Once
a person has become a bureaucrat, he cannot afford
to lose his job. There is usually no other way
he can maintain his standard of living. African
bureaucrats perceive little choice but to engage
in political opportunism, while feeding nest eggs
and clienteles through the corrupt use of office.

There are other groups or aggregations of
people who count politically, though not as much
as do the politicians, military officers, or
bureaucrats. An African government often finds
it wise to seek the favor of the urban masses.
- They constitute a small part of the population,
but an uprooted and potentially disgruntled part,
close to the seat of government. University
students may get more than their share of attention (not all of it benevolent) for these reasons
and because they will ultimately join the elite.
In some cases, most notably that of the Marabouts
in Senegal, religious authorities must be pla-
cated because of their hold on many thousands of
followers. But, as will be explored in Chapter
III, the single most important kind of group
entity is the tribe. However much African spokesmen may deny it, tribes are the main force to be
reckoned with, apart from the elite circles themselves, in almost every black African country.

Now that we have spelled out the essential
ideas at some length, we can state our model a
bit more formally:

1) Political organization and institutional-
   ization in black Africa are minimal.

   a) There is no direct representation of

74

popular majorities in government
decision making.

b) Popular and institutional resistance
to coups is relatively limited.

c) On the other hand, no African government has sufficient control over its
population to qualify as totalitarian.

2) Leaders build personal coalitions to
seize and hold power.

a) The coalitions resemble sets of con-
centric circles. Innermost is a
circle of personal associates of the
leader; then come their clienteles
(kinsmen, subordinates, etc., who may
occupy key positions). Around them
are arrayed client group entities,
like tribes, the lower echelons of
the party, unions, and religious
groups.

b) Leaders tend to build coalitions just
large enough to maintain themselves
in power. Their behavior recalls
William Riker's theory of the minimum
winning coalition. That is, assuming
perfect information, a coalition will
be only as large as needed to win, so
that the fruits of victory need be
divided among as few claimants as
possible.[36]

3) Clienteles, and the coalitions of which
they form a part, are held together by
payoffs.

a) Payoffs may take many forms, including that of symbolic gratifications
(public honors, humiliation of groups
which one dislikes, and so on).

b) Payoffs derive from control of government or other political offices.

    c)   Payoffs are a scarce resource, especially in the poor, minimally organized societies of Africa.

    d)   Common ways of increasing the supply of payoffs include expanding the public sector, at the expense of the rest of the economy, and outright plunder of the unpopular but relatively affluent non-black minorities.

4)   Given the supreme importance of staying in office, incumbents use any means at their disposal to thwart possible opposition.

    a)   Opposition parties are forced out of existence.

    b)   Parliaments are deprived of the means to oversee the executive.

    c)   Bills of rights are abolished or amended opportunely.

    d)   The judiciary is politicized and/or supplanted.

How does political organization in Africa compare, then, with the classic American machine model? A number of Africanists--Bretton,[37] Bienen,[38] and Leys,[39] among them--have found important similarities. American machines have been characterized as parties that rely on material rewards rather than on enthusiasm for political principles.[40] A machine exists primarily to maintain itself in power. To this end, it seeks to monopolize access to public office, and to channel citizen participation in politics. Typically, such a party does not develop cleavages over policy issues. Wherever possible, issues are treated on the pork barrel model: each politically important group receives some gratification.

A machine uses both material and symbolic payoffs to maintain loyalty. Depending on their relevance to a given machine's political context, these may include favors and services to a large number of (potential) voters; a patronage or spoils system; selection of candidates according to ethnic affiliation; corruption, including special treatment for selected businesses; and coercion (ranging from refusal to provide normal public services through harrassment to the use of thugs).[41] These features appear in African political organization, too.

There are at least two important differences, however. In the first place, American machines tend to be organized more formally, and to seek support among more social groups than their African counterparts do. Second, the decentralizing tendencies inherent in clientelism impair cohesion more in African countries than in the more compact American machines.

The word "machine" brings to mind a neat pyramid, in which an army of precinct committeemen report to aldermen, who in turn answer to the boss (who is usually the mayor). The machine takes for granted the importance of ethnicity, but tries to appeal to many different groups simultaneously, in order to insure electoral victory for all of its candidates. The African leader does not need so much active support. One reason is that a large part of the population is relatively indifferent to politics outside their village. Most people expect little from the central government. Second, in the absence of competition, African politicians do not need to worry about winning elections. Third, even if there is considerable dissatisfaction, it is hard for scattered, illiterate citizens to challenge the incumbents in any other way. Thus Presidents Mobutu, Eyadema, Malloum, and colleagues do not need to satisfy a majority of their countrymen. They need strong support only from crucial elite groups and a few tribes who can fill government manpower requirements. Hence, favoritism for certain tribes can be blatant. Adapting a key term from Edward Banfield's

The <u>Moral</u> <u>Basis</u> <u>of</u> a <u>Backward</u> <u>Society</u>,[42] we might speak of "amoral tribalism," as opposed to the ethnic arithmetic of American city machines.

Another difference relates to the scale on which a machine-like organization is built. The very fact that material or status payoffs are the major incentive for participation militates for decentralization. The local or regional chieftain need be concerned about the central organization only to the extent that it supplies him with patronage and other payoffs. He controls distribution within his own bailiwick; this tends to make his clients loyal to him personally, rather than to the large organization. The boss can exert some control at the grass-roots level only if there are few intermediary patrons. This criterion is easier to meet in a city or county than in a country covering many thousands of square miles. It appears that the only way to build an organization on this scale, with the cohesiveness and inclusiveness of the classic American machine, is to concede local and ethnic leaders virtual autonomy within their own jurisdictions. This pattern seems to apply to the Parti Democratique du Cote d'Ivoire, as well as to the now-defunct regional parties of Nigeria-- particularly the Northern People's Congress. As we shall see in Chapter VI, most African heads of government are not willing to delegate so much authority.

In sum, black rule cannot look very appealing to South Africans. Because black political leaders cannot rely on institutional sources of support and legitimacy, they must rely upon precarious personal coalitions and clienteles to attain power. There are almost no occupations outside government that would permit them to maintain the life style they develop in office; so they seek to retain power at all costs. The result is that however dedicated they are, in principle, to humanistic ideals, these leaders must devote considerable effort to providing their clienteles with payoffs. Resources badly

needed for economic development are diverted
into administrative overhead. And prosperous but
unpopular racial minorities are milked of money
and property, deprived of civil rights, and
usually lose their citizenship as well. (This will
be discussed in chapter IV.)

FOOTNOTES: CHAPTER II

[1]The concept of clientelism is developed by
René Lemarchand in "Political Clientelism and
Ethnicity in Tropical Africa: Competing Solidar-
ities in Nation-Building," American Political
Science Review vol. LXVI, no. 1 (March, 1972),
pp. 68-90.   Its relevance to our model will be
spelled out later in this chapter.

[2]Kwame Nkrumah, Towards Colonial Freedom:
Africa Against Imperialism in the World in Martin
Minogue and Judith Molloy (Eds.), African Aims and
Attitudes, Selected Documents (New York: Cambridge
University Press, 1974), p. 23.

[3]Kenneth Kaunda, Zambia Shall Be Free in Martin
Minogue and Judith Molloy (Eds.), African Aims and
Attitudes, Selected Documents, op. cit., pp. 36-37.

[4]George Woodcock, Who Killed the British
Empire (New York: New York Times Book Co., 1974),
p. 318.

[5]Speech by the British Foreign Secretary
Mr. Selwyn Lloyd at the United Nations General
Assembly meeting, September 17, 1959.   See also
Peter Calvocoressi, South Africa and World Opinion
(New York: Oxford University Press), p. 51.

[6]United Nations, Official Records of the
General Assembly, Thirtieth Session, September 24,
1958, p. 131.

[7]Colin Legum, Pan Africanism (New York:
Frederick A. Praeger, 1962), pp. 247-248.

[8]Joseph R. Strayer, "The Historical Experience
of Nation-Building in Europe," in Karl W. Deutsch
and William J. Foltz, eds., Nation-Building (New
York: Atherton Press, 1963).

[9]Karl W. Deutsch, "The Growth of Nations: Some Recurrent Patterns of Political and Social Integration," World Politics vol. 5, no. 2 (January, 1953), pp. 168-195.

[10]Aristide Zolberg, Creating Political Order: The Party-States of West Africa (Chicago: Rand McNally, 1966). With nearly universal suffrage, the turnout in the 1956 elections of the Gold Coast and the Ivory Coast was substantially less than half the eligible adults. "(T)he CCP...after many years of effort and in spite of all the advantages discussed, could mobilize, to the extent of having them register and vote, only about one out of six or seven adult Ghanaians" (p. 24). This example is particularly significant in that Nkrumah's Convention People's Party is commonly thought to have been one of the most effective political organizations in Africa.

[11]Frantz Fanon, Les Damnés de la Terre (Paris: Maspero Cahiers Libres, 1961).

[12]See in particular Tony Hodges, "Mozambique: The Politics of Liberation," in Gwendolen M. Carter and Patrick O'Meara, eds., Southern Africa in Crisis (Bloomington, Indiana: Indiana University Press, 1977).

[13]United Nations, Official Records of the General Assembly, General Assembly Resolution 2131, XX, December 11, 1965, entitled "Declaration on the Inadmissibility of Intervention in the Domestic Affairs of States and the Protection of Their Independence and Sovereignty," para. 5.

[14]Ibid., para. 1 and 2.

[15]This categorization is based on the individual country descriptions in Arthur S. Banks, ed., Political Handbook of the World: 1976 (New York: McGraw-Hill, 1976).

[16]Zolberg, op. cit., pp. 22-27.

[17]Lionel Cliffe, ed., One Party Democracy, The 1965 Tanzania General Election (Nairobi: East African Publishing House, 1967), p. 12.

[18]B. O. Nwabueze, Presidentialism in Commonwealth Africa (New York: St. Martin's Press, 1975), p. 231.

[19]Norman N. Miller, "The Rural African Party: Political Participation in Tanzania," American Political Science Review vol. 64, no. 2 (June, 1970), pp. 548-571.

[20]Ibid.

[21]See especially Jean-Paul Alata, Prison d'Afrique (Paris: Editions du Seuil, 1976).

[22]For further details of this view, see Fred Greene "Toward Understanding Military Coups," Africa Report, February, 1966, p. 10. See also Samuel Huntingdon, Political Order in Changing Societies, (New Haven, Conn.: Yale University Press, 1969), et seq., and Samuel Finer, The Man on Horseback (London: Pall Mall Press, 1962).

[23]For further details of this position, see L. W. Pye, "Armies in the Process of Political Modernization" in C. E. Welch, Jr., ed., Political Modernization: A Reader in Comparative Political Change (Belmont, California, Wadsworth, 1969, p. 292.

[24]E. A. Shils, "The Military in the Political Development of the New States" in J. J. Johnson, ed., The Role of the Military in Underdeveloped Countries (Princeton, New Jersey: Princeton University Press, 1962), p. 17.

[25]Marion J. Levy, Modernization and the Structure of Societies (Princeton, New Jersey: Princeton University Press, 1966), Vol. 2, p. 603.

[26] Samuel Decalo, _Coups and Army Rule in Africa: Studies in Military Style_ (New Haven, Connecticut: Yale University Press, 1976), p. 231.

[27] _Ibid._, p. 232.

[28] _Ibid._, pp. 14-15.

[29] Eric A. Nordlinger, "Soldiers in Mufti: The Impact of Military Rule Upon Economic and Social Change in the Non-Western States," _American Political Science Review_ vol. 64, no. 4 (December, 1970), pp. 1131-1148.

[30] Robert W. Jackman, "Politicians in Uniform: Military Governments and Social Change in the Third World," _American Political Science Review_ vol. 70, no. 4 (December, 1976), pp. 1078-1097.

[31] René Lemarchand and Keith Legg, "Political Clientelism and Development: A Preliminary Analysis," _Comparative Politics_ vol. 4, no. 2 (January, 1972), pp. 149-178.

[32] Ronald Cohen, "The Dynamics of Feudalism in Bornu," _Boston University Papers on Africa_ vol. II (Boston: Boston University Press, 1966), p. 91.

[33] David Hapgood, _Africa: From Independence to Tomorrow_ (New York: Atheneum, 1970), ch. 4 "The Elite in Power."

[34] A.Y.S. Andoh, "Background to Government and Politics in Africa," _Presence Africaine_, no. 74, 1970, p. 33.

[35] A. K. Ocran, quoted in Robert M. Price, "Military Officers and Political Leadership: The Ghanaian Case," _Comparative Politics_, vol. 3, no. 3 (April, 1971), p. 366.

[36]William H. Riker, The Theory of Political Coalitions (New Haven: Yale University Press, 1962) p. 32.

[37]Henry Bretton, The Rise and Fall of Kwame Nkrumah (New York: Frederick A. Praeger, 1966).

[38]Henry Bienen, "One-Party Systems in Africa," in Samuel P. Huntington and Clement H. Moore, Authoritarian Politics in Modern Society: The Dynamics of Established One-Party Systems (New York: Basic Books, 1970), pp. 99-127.

[39]Colin Leys, Politicians and Policies (Nairobi: East African Publishing House, 1967).

[40]Edward C. Banfield, Political Influence (New York: The Free Press, 1961), p. 237.

[41]Among the more essential works on American machine politics are Edward Banfield and James Q. Wilson, City Politics (Cambridge: Harvard University Press, 1963); V. O. Key, Southern Politics (New York: Alfred A. Knopf, 1949); and Dayton McKean, The Boss: The Hague Machine in Action (Boston: Houghton Mifflin, 1940). Another instructive old chestnut is W. L. Riordan, Plunkitt of Tammany Hall (McClure, Phillips, 1905).

[42]Edward C. Banfield, The Moral Basis of a Backward Society (Glencoe, Ill.: Free Press, 1958).

CHAPTER III

CEMENTING PERSONAL POWER

The black African political elites appear
schizophrenic. While loudly proclaiming concern
for the public interest and the plight of the
rural poor, they have acted single-mindedly to
entrench themselves in power. They have used the
authority of their offices to extract maximum
benefits for themselves and their clienteles.
This chapter will focus on practices that would
normally be considered corrupt in western
societies. Bribery, extortion, and embezzlement
are apparently common practice in all the regimes
in question (that is, all the black regimes of
Africa except perhaps Gambia and Botswana). So
are measures of physical coercion against possible
political opponents, especially those whose assets
can be redistributed to one's own clientele.
These tactics are partly buttressed and justified
by ideological appeals like Mobutu's cultural
nationalism and that pliable shibboleth, African
socialism. We shall conclude the chapter with a
discussion of intervention in the economy,
Africanization of business, and related issues.

Corruption and Tribalism

Corruption and tribalism are so intertwined,
in black Africa, that we must deal with them
simultaneously. Corruption is a means of consoli-

dating incumbents' personal clienteles and coalitions. It occurs at the expense of the public for
the benefit of one's kinsmen and tribe. Indeed,
Stanislav Andreski applied the term "kleptocracy"
to African political systems as a class, and declared: "In relations between non-kinsmen power
normally occasions uninhibited spoliation."[1]

When we speak of corruption, we use the term
not as a moral brickbat, but as a synonym for
certain specific types of behavior. The British
scholar, M. McMullan, proposed one of the more
straightforward definitions:

> A public official is corrupt if he accepts
> money or money's worth for doing something
> that he is under duty to do anyway, that he
> is under duty not to do, or to exercise a
> legitimate discretion for improper reasons.[2]

This encompasses the acceptance of bribes and
kickbacks, as well as extortion by public officials. The last phrase of the definition includes
the wide variety of ways in which an official may
use discretionary powers for his own political or
economic benefit. "Honest graft" a la Plunkitt,
i.e. exploitation of privileged information about
future government purchases,[3] is an obviously
related type of behavior. So is embezzlement.
McMullan's definition fails to include one very
important form of corruption, however. That is
nepotism, or the practice of putting one's kin
on the public payroll. The common denominator of
such behavior is that an incumbent uses the
powers of office to serve his own purely personal
ends.

Corruption has been much more prevalent in
some countries and eras than in others. Bribery
and nepotism were common in Great Britain during
the eighteenth century, but declined dramatically
during the nineteenth. American city politics
was notoriously corrupt from the mid-nineteenth
century through Prohibition, but is considered
relatively clean now.[4] It is well to keep these

developments in mind when analyzing African politics, so that similar cause and effect relationships are not overlooked.

What are some reasons for corruption? McMullan put much emphasis on divergence between government and society. Citizens may find government threatening and incalculable either because government norms and work methods are alien to them or because certain laws conflict with popular attitudes.[5] The peasant cannot be sure what the law demands, and may seek to buy general benevolence and absolution. A brothel owner or bookie, who knows perfectly well that he is breaking the law, may try to buy the right to continue a lucrative business. The discrepancy thesis fits the American case in at least two respects. The major clientele of city machines were politically disoriented and economically vulnerable immigrants. And prohibition, vice, and illegal gambling have been associated with a good deal of police corruption. Given this thesis--that government/societal divergence fosters bribery and official extortion--McMullan expected corruption to be especially common in third-world countries with western-style institutions, and in countries whose governments introduce substantial social or economic change.

The exigencies of organizing power without ideologically committed cadres, obviously, also can lead to corruption. In the days of George III, the British monarch was still the head of government. But to keep the House of Commons tractable, the king had to rely on electoral manipulation and rotton boroughs, and on buying and rebuying legislators once elected. The rise of a mass electorate and popular parties provided a new means of organizing government, and crowded the monarch to the political sidelines. We have already explained that black African political leaders--soldiers, politicians, and bureaucrats--must rely on clientelistic relationships to hold power, and these relationships are held together by payoffs.

87

Other partial explanations of corruption focus
on the needs and attitudes of officials, including
elective officials. A lack of real identification with a nation makes corruption more
likely. If officials have little commitment to
the polity or people as a whole, the concept of
public interest will have little meaning for them.
In Africa, this lack is not compensated for by
professional ethos or _esprit de corps_. The
African official is much more an entrepreneur
than a self-effacing, Weberian functionary. It
is also worth noting that, completely apart
from clientelistic calculations, family obligations weigh very heavily on well-to-do Africans.
If a man has the means, he also has the obligation
to give presents to scores of kinsmen, find jobs
for them as needed, and house them and feed them
when they come to seek work in the city.

There are also strong cultural attitudes
that encourage conspicuous consumption. If a
man has rank and a good income, he must demonstrate
this continuously or he loses face (and clients).
So, once having attained public office, the African
official adopts a life style manifestly different
from that of an average person. If possible,
he buys an automobile, preferably a Mercedes-Benz.
Indeed, the governments of several African
countries make a practice of advancing loans
to fairly junior officials to help them buy cars.
He buys or builds a mansion, and has it furnished
with imported carpets and furniture. He learns
to smoke (preferably Benson & Hedges), and to
drink (Scotch or French cognac). He and his
family wear tailor-made clothes. To make it bear-
able to keep his tie and suit jacket on at all
times, the official has air conditioning installed.
And he entertains lavishly, spending a great deal
of money on his parties.

One source of examples is the spate of showy
presidential palaces. It is true that Tanzanian
President Julius Nyerere chose not to live in the
former colonial governor's palace, but in a small
white house of his own. He appears, however, to

be a minority of one. Dr. Hastings Banda of
Malawi lives in a luxurious $5 million edifice
on a hillside overlooking the capital city of
Blantyre. He had it built right after independence,
at a time when his small country could ill aford
such a large expenditure on a project that would
produce no income. Despite strong verbal commitments to sacrifice and economic development,
Guinea's Sekou Toure has allowed mansions to be
built in various parts of the country for his use
during infrequent visits. When Benin established
a three-man rotating presidency, it had little
difficulty in finding suitable accommodations.
All three officials were former presidents, and
each had built himself a palace while in office.
Even so, a palace built in 1961 at the cost of
$3 million was thought to require substantial re-
novation before it could serve again as a presidential residence. Huge palaces have also been
built in recent years for the presidents of
Liberia and the Ivory Coast. For his palace,
Houphouet-Boigny had hundreds of tons of mala-
chite flown in from the Soviet Union.

The same ostentation is prevalent in means
of transportation. A Rolls Royce is considered
necessary even by leaders of very small states
like the Seychelles. In Benin, though, each co-
president had to settle for two Mercedes, one 300
and one 200. In 1971, President Ahmadou Ahidjo
of Cameroon bought a personal jet (Grumman Gulf-
stream) for $2.8 million. The plane's main
cabin (called the Throne Room) was reportedly
so spectacular as to make Hugh Hefner's black
DC9 look like a military transport craft. Other
examples could be cited.

The Ghanaian Commission of Inquiry on Corruption has noted that when a politician, military
officer, or bureaucrat cannot afford to pay for
his catapulted standard of living, he usually

resorts to dishonest means and manners to
make ends meet. He either goes to steal,
takes bribes, or corrupts to achieve his

aim. He refuses to cut his coat according
to his cloth. He cannot discipline himself
and as a result falls victim to bribery and
corruption.[6]

Worries about one's job security are another powerful incentive to seek extra income.

Here, too, the heads of government set the
example. Many of them are known to have amassed
considerable personal wealth, often kept in
foreign lands. In most cases, this wealth can
only have been acquired by improper means. Jomo
Kenyatta and members of his family acquired vast
real estate holdings in London and Mexico City, as
well as Mombasa and Nairobi. They also made huge
profits through illegal exports of ivory and
charcoal to Hongkong and the Middle East. (Meanwhile, Kenya professed official concern about the
effects of deforestation. The former president's
daughter Margaret represented Kenya in the U.N.
Environmental Protection Program.) Mobutu Sese
Seko, of Zaire, is one of the richest heads of
state in the world; he owns villas in Paris,
Brussels, and Lausanne, among other places.
Former Emperor Haille Selassie of Ethiopia de-
posited millions of dollars in secret bank accounts
in Switzerland. Dr. Albert Margai, the former
prime minister of Sierra Leone, resides in London.
Despite lavish spending, he has never been short
of funds. Sierra Leone's current president,
Siaka Stevens, is known to have accumulated a
considerable fortune, largely by extorting payments of various kinds from the Lebanese trading
community. And Maurice Yameogo, former president
of Upper Volta, was convicted (admittedly, by a
politicized judiciary) of embezzling $3 million
from the national treasury. As we shall see in the
following pages, conditions are depressingly similar at lower levels.

Thus far, our examples have been individuals
and their personal enrichment through public
office. The larger point we wish to explore,
however, is the relationship between corruption

and tribalism in Africa. To do this, we must examine the phenomenon of tribalism in more detail.

The term "tribalism" is not easy to define. The undisguised African annoyance with the use of the term by non-Africans has not made the task any easier. In <u>Nigeria: Background to Nationalism</u>, James Coleman distinguished between "nationality" and "tribe."[7] He reserved the term "tribe" for relatively small groups of people who share a common culture and who trace their descent to a common ancestor (e.g. the Tiv, Kanuri, Bini, Urhobo). He used the term "nationality" to refer to numerically larger peoples like the Ibo, Hausa, and Yoruba. This amounts to saying that feelings of solidarity and cultural distinctiveness constitute tribalism or nationalism, depending solely on the size of the group involved. Considering the largely positive connotations of "nationalism" in the current social science literature, and the somewhat pejorative ring of "tribalism," this sort of definition seems neither fair nor very useful.

Other writers have introduced new terms in order to avoid the word "tribalism" altogether. Melson and Wolpe use the term "communalism." However, they define it in such a way that it could include state-wide bonds of "common culture, identity, (and) complementarity of communications" as well as more exclusive ones.[8] "Ethnicity" is another term sometimes substituted for tribalism. But Immanuel Wallerstein insisted on distinguishing between ethnicity and tribalism, as urban versus rural phenomena, respectively.[9] Christian Potholm has coined the term "segmented societies" to refer to what most writers used to call tribes.[10] The terminological squabble is an unfortunate distraction from a central feature of African politics.

The crucial point is simply that the vast majority of black Africans do not give their primary loyalty to the state in which they reside.

91

They do not necessarily consider themselves part of the same community as another man simply because they both live in Nigeria or Zambia. Rather, in every black state except Somalia, Swaziland, and Lesotho, there are a number of groups which share sentiments, customs, and feelings of solidarity and which regard themselves as culturally different from other such groups. The most straightforward designation for these groups is the traditional one--tribes. In the African context, the term "nationalism" might be reserved most usefully for identification and loyalty of the same sort to the state and the whole body of people who inhabit it.

Tribalism is not a mere holdover from the past, soon to be superseded by nationalism. As Smock and Bentsi-Enchill note, education and increased contact between tribes have exacerbated intertribal competition and animosities. In the context of a "politics of scarcity," one group's gain appears to be another group's loss. Education often makes for increased ambition and awareness of gains made by one's competitors.[11]

Almost invariably, African politicians, military officers, and bureaucrats reject any discussion of tribalism with or by non-Africans. Several well-known American Africanists caution their graduate students that to avoid alienating their African contacts they must be careful never to use the word tribalism or to pursue any line of questioning that refers to or implies the prevalence of tribalism. At a discussion on African politics in Cambridge, Massachusetts in 1965, a Nigerian consul denied emphatically that there were any tribal differences among the people of Nigeria. All the people of Nigeria, he maintained, were loyal totally and exclusively to the state of Nigeria. One year later, the Nigerian civil war broke out, pitting the rest of the country against the Ibos. Zambian political leaders also claim on occasion that no tribal differences exist within their country, and any talk of tribalism as a factor in Zambian politics is neo-colonialist plot to divide and rule.

Some African leaders have taken steps to
reduce the significance of tribal loyalties
within their states. Generally, however, their
efforts have been perfunctory. When Nkrumah was
president of Ghana, he prevented the Ashanti tribe
from using their famous golden stool. Instead, he
created his own Presidential Stool, complete with
black star and magical symbols, and always used it
when making important announcements to the Ghanian
people. He hoped that creation of national symbols would foster the development of national
loyalties and counteract tribalism. Some other
black governments, notably those of Tanzania and
the Cameroons, have promoted languages not associated with any particular tribe as a means of
building a national community. Tanzania has
adopted Swahili, a sort of lingua franca of the
African east coast, as its national language. The
Cameroons is striving for bilingualism in English
and French. Efforts to teach a national language
are limited, of course, by the school system's
responsiveness to central government directives,
its effectiveness, and the proportion of young
people actually attending school. Several other
governments have declared tribalism dead, apparently hoping that sufficiently emphatic declarations would make it true. After Colonel Juxon-
Smith took power in Sierra Leone, in 1967, he
announced, "Right now I kill tribalism, both its
body and soul. It dies a perpetual death."[12] And
after crushing Ibo attempts at secession and re-
conquering Biafra, General Gowon declared that
Nigeria would henceforth be free of tribal rivalries. When Milton Obote introduced a one-party
state in Uganda, he claimed he had done so to
save the country from the scourge of tribalism.

Such actions have not eradicated or reduced
tribalism in any of these countries. It still
flourishes. Neither one-man charismatic, single-
party rule, nor military regimes has made any
difference. Neither has increased urbanization,

93

commercialization, or the development of the professions. We have noted that African cities have
become microcosms of the state--divided into tri-
bally segregated neighborhoods and/or tribal
associations. Genuine trade unions and other
economically based interest groups have either
failed or not been allowed to emerge. Parties are
either firmly associated with the dominant tribe(s)
or use what amounts to quota systems for distributing offices among the tribes in the coalition.

Inconsistent though it may seem, the same
African politicians, military officers, and
bureaucrats who disparage or deny tribalism in
public cultivate their own tribes behind the
scenes. They realize that in a society where an
outsider is considered a potential enemy, their
own tribes are the only reliable source of support
available to them. And for heads of state and
minor officials alike, it is hard or impossible to
contract out of the obligations imposed by even
very distant kinship. As R. S. Jackson remarked
(while carefully avoiding the word "tribalism"):

> The African ruling class may be isolated
> from the larger "society" governed by it, but
> members within it are hardly out of touch with
> friends and supporters belonging to their own
> communal group or subgroups which together
> comprise society. Most politicians, civil
> servants, parastatal officials, military
> officers, university professors, and the
> like maintain ties with communal fellows
> and kinsmen, if only because it is difficult
> to evade such obligations and still retain
> high social standing within their kinship
> or communal group. Access to public office
> probably increases the intensity and scope
> of these relationships as a growing number
> of persons present themselves as potential
> clients of public patrons by claiming con-
> sanguinity or by invoking the principle of
> mutual aid held to bind all clan and some-
> times even ethnic fellows.[13]

If one were to spend a week watching the actions of almost any African politician, military officer, or bureaucrat, one would observe interactions of this sort. The official may try to restrict such exchanges to certain times and places in the interest of discretion; one cannot assume they do not exist merely because they do not take place during office hours. Thus, members of the African political elites corrupt themselves not only for personal gain but also for their immediate families and for those who belong to the same kinship group or tribe and make up their clienteles. In fact, payoffs are often of such a nature that any distinction between personal and collective gain is academic. One has strong obligations to one's own group, but none to any others. The politics of tribalism, corruption, the sense of insecurity prevailing among members of the elites, and their mutual distrust exacerbate and reinforce each other. This can be observed with special clarity in two areas--in the making of government appointments, and in the use of discretionary powers.

Jobs for the Boys

In a political system where the economic base is relatively small and where government is the biggest employer, it is obvious to the political elites that the authority to fill government positions is very useful and potentially rewarding. For this reason if nothing else, African heads of state have sought to monopolize appointment power as much as possible. The departing colonial regimes established merit systems for civil service appointment and promotion, and impartial public service commissions to administer them. However, these have been set aside in favor of making appointments on an ad hoc basis. The appointee feels obligated to the person who appointed him and remains so for the duration of his employment, especially since he can also be fired without cause. Appointment power can be used to satisfy personal material needs (e.g. by demanding a straight bribe or a percentage of wages), or to reward members of one's clientele. The higher the position and the greater the perquisites of office, the greater an asset is the authority to fill it.

Virtually all African chief executives seek to retain personal control over cabinet appointments. Almost invariably, these positions carry with them a high salary, free government housing, and an official automobile--in addition to the title, social status, and power that usually go with heading a government department. Appointments to the cabinet are the most potent means of cementing a coalition of important political figures and their clienteles. One uses cabinet posts to reward one's own most important vassals and, in many cases, to coopt potential rivals.

One consequence of this appointment policy is that African cabinets are very large. Cabinets of less than thirty members are the exception rather than the rule. In April, 1965, Nigeria's cabinet had no fewer than eighty ministers, ministers of state, and parliamentary secretaries. In August, 1976, Sierra Leone had as many as forty-six ministers, despite a de facto single party system.

Real power may be restricted to a small inner circle; but once appointed, cabinet members can be removed only at the risk of antagonizing them and their clienteles. Removal from the cabinet would mean a considerable loss to the individual and his dependents and retainers. It could not be taken lightly. For example, in several African states, ministers rent their own houses to foreign embassies at exorbitant rents, while they themselves reside in government houses. An ouster from the cabinet would dry up this source of income. (So, of course, would any attempt by the head of state to forbid such practices, or deprive the ministers of government housing, or introduce rent control. Any measure of this sort would bring the chief executive much grief and little benefit.)

In most African states, the composition of the cabinet (which may be called the Cabinet, the Supreme Military Council, or by one of several other names) is shaped to a large degree by tribal considerations. Some posts are more sensitive than others. The minister of home affairs has jurisdiction over the police and prisons; the minister of defense has control or significant influence over the armed forces. These positions are usually entrusted to members of the president's or prime minister's own tribe. Most other cabinet positions as well are allocated to the dominant tribe or coalition of tribes. In Kenya, for example, cabinet seats are filled mainly by Kikuyu, (former) President Kenyatta's tribe. Luos and other tribes enjoy token representation at best, with little chance of promotion to the more important posts.

In Zambia, despite Dr. Kaunda's claim to the contrary, the cabinet reflects a delicate balance of tribal divisions. This was true, despite official denials, of the first post-independence cabinet. And during the United National Independence Party's 1967 convention, tribal interests were manifesting themselves openly. It had been agreed before the convention that certain party posts would entitle their incumbents to parallel government offices: the president of the party would also be president of the Zambian state, party and state vice presidencies would be held by the same individual, and so on. Given the double significance of party office, elections at the convention followed straight tribal lines. When the votes were in, it turned out that all Bemba and Tongo delegates had voted for their own candidates. So had the Lozi and the Nyanja. The party was divided, but the government was firmly in Bemba hands—with token representation of the other tribes. Kenneth Kaunda continued to emphasize non-tribalism in his speeches. But his actions often failed to coincide with his rhetoric. Between independence and 1967, his government neglected completely the areas inhabited by the Lozi; when he visited these districts, he was confronted with demonstrations denouncing him as an "interpreter" of Bemba interests.

The same sort of situation prevails in most other black African states. Despite his Marxian ideas (including the belief that economic class interests are the only ones that count), Guinea's president Sekou Toure takes tribal arithmetic into account in making top government and party appointments. In Chad, the late president Francois Tombalaye's blatant favoritism for the Saras proved to be his undoing. The government of Brig. General Felix Malloum carefully included members of most major tribes. Even so, Moslems in northern Chad have been sufficiently dissatisfied with their share of offices and influence to carry on an extended rebellion (under Hissene Habre). And in the Ivory Coast, the PDCI is organized on explicitly tribal lines. All tribal associations are incorporated within the Party. Representation in the national legislature is no longer based on geographical districts; tribal considerations play a significant role in nominations to the Assembly. Even in Abidjan, the capital, where people from all tribes live, the PDCI is organized on tribal lines, rather than by streets or districts. And the Cabinet membership reflects the delicate game of tribal arithmetic played with considerable astuteness by President Boigny.

Appointments to the foreign service come second only to ministerial positions in terms of their political value. They provide travel opportunities for one's family and proteges, the capacity to influence selections of persons to be sent on cultural and exchange visits, access to foreign exchange, and improved chances of securing a scholarship for overseas studies for family members or for members of one's clientele. Appointments to the foreign service are useful not only as rewards but as a convenient way of removing from the local political scene a troublesome minister, commanding officer, or other leader whom the head of state or government would rather not alienate. The appointments of Malawi's minister of local government, Mr. R. B. Chidzanja, as ambassador to France, of the Nigerian brigadier Ogundipe as the Nigerian high commissioner in London, and of Ghana's Major General Aferi as an ambassador to Mexico are all examples of such appointments.

Although the powers of African legislators have declined considerably since independence, the sizes of African legislatures have not. In fact, their numbers have almost invariably increased. Under the prevalent single party system, legislatures are in session for many hours fewer each year than they were in the pre-independence period. The legislators, knowing that opposition to the government bills is futile or unexpected, have little incentive to read the documentation and become conversant with all aspects of a particular issue. Being a member of parliament is therefore an undemanding job. But it is an important position in terms of the system of rewards. All the former perquisites of the office of a legislator have remained or even increased. Members still receive large salaries and allowances for themselves and for their families, including, in several countries, the use of an official automobile. And although a legislator may not have much impact on government legislation, he does enjoy a vantage point from which to exercise influence on behalf of his supporters in the various government departments and offices. Nominations to the single party legislatures are therefore an important process in which tribal and other considerations are carefully taken into account.

Once individuals have been elevated to the position of legislators their removal entails either alienating them totally or providing them with satisfactory alternative positions. In Tanzania, for example, those legislators who lose their bid for re-election have almost always been found other jobs by the government. In Zaire, when provincial legislatures were abolished in a bid for centralization, retiring members collected up to one million francs for loss of office. And even then many of them were provided with other public offices.

In all countries, whether under military or civilian rule, jobs in the police or armed forces are a fruitful avenue for personal gain or for doing favors. These groups are always pampered and enjoy high salaries and other fringe benefits, including residence in newly built barracks with all the modern conveniences, availability of means of transportation, and other services. Even the provision of a new uniform and new pairs of solidly made shoes are of significance in the African context. There is also little likelihood of retrenchment or reduction in the amount of appropriations. No African government in power lightly refuses a request for additional funds made by the police or the army. And only the best is good enough for those who defend the nation against external aggression and internal subversion. Naipaul seems to have captured the situation correctly in the following remark in one of his novels:

"....the low, sprawling modern building, glass and coloured concrete, as bright as beads, that the Americans had built in the bush as a gift to the new country. It had been intended as a school, and symbolically it stood....it had been visited but never used; there had been neither pupils nor teachers; it had remained empty. It had a use today. The cleared space in front, partly bushed over again, was full of lorries (trucks). And in the shade of the lorries, there were groups of _fat_ soldiers."[14]

The word "fat" is perhaps an apt description of the African military today; and the ability to provide a person with an opportunity to become "fat" is a great political asset. Under the circumstances, tribalism acquires a new significance. In Kenya, for example, during the colonial period, the Kikuyu were conspicuously disinterested

in joining the police or the army. There were
hardly any Kikuyu in the Kenya African Regiment
which fought so valiantly during the first and
second world wars. When Kenya became independent,
over 60 per cent of its police force was composed
of people from the Kalenji tribe. There were
hardly any Kikuyus in the police or in the armed
forces. Today, they can be found in large numbers
not only in the lower ranks (as one might have
expected) but also as officers and in other high
positions. The main qualifications for appointments to commanding positions in these two sensitive bodies have, since independence, been political loyalty and belonging to the right tribe,
rather than experience, merit, or efficiency, or
even education. The whole exercise, at least in
the initial phase, was portrayed as an attempt to
bring about "balance" in the composition of the
army and the police forces. Similarly, in Zambia,
the Bemba, who were equally under-represented in
the army, now seem to dominate the officer corps.

In virtually all African states, the government is the largest single employer, and it has
grown considerably since independence. In Senegal,
for example, there are about 50,000 civil servants
to administer a total population of about four
million. The situation in Benin is even worse.
The payment of salaries to these civil servants
and the cost of their liberal fringe benefits,
usually including free government housing, loans
for purchases of automobiles, and free medical
and health services, are a sizable drain on the
budgets of many African states. It is a huge
burden and it continues to grow. A job with the
government is relatively secure and worth striving
for. At any point in time the majority of African
politicians, bureaucrats, and military in any
country are likely to be looking for ways and
means of having their relatives, kinsmen, or tribesmen appointed to one government position or another.
It is entirely common for those entrusted with the
task of recruiting personnel for government departments and state enterprises to extort gifts,
percentage of salary, and other favors from the

applicants. And this also applies to promotions and transfers after initial appointments to the service.

A large number of influential people are heavily involved in the structure, composition, and privileges of the civil service and have a lot at stake. Attempts to reorganize the civil service or reduce its size or privileges are therefore quite likely to be opposed strenuously, if not killed altogether. In 1971 President Busia of Ghana announced rents paid by civil servants occupying government owned houses would be increased considerably and that the increases would become effective forthwith. There was so much resentment against the measure that it was never implemented. And Busia, realizing that insistence upon its implementation would hurt his own clientele, preferred to drop the issue. In Nigeria, the Udoji Commission on the operation of the civil service awarded substantial raises to civil servants in 1974, although it was clear that injection of such large sums of money into the country's economy at that time would only aggravate the already serious problem of inflation.

Certainly, one might expect a military government to avoid such a pay increase. Military governments are generally thought not to have to worry much about public opinion, and to be able to afford to take actions which are in national interest, however painful they may be in the short run. In Nigeria, however, this was not the case. The raises were approved, at least partly because the action would have adversely affected the clienteles of the military rulers themselves.

Drastic political changes do not bring in their wake equally drastic and permanent changes in the bureaucracy. A large number of bureaucrats may be dismissed following a military take-over, but the size of the bureaucracy is likely to creep up again soon. The new leaders need, quite as much as their predecessors did, to use government jobs as patronage. In June, 1975, for example, following a military coup, the Chad Military Council announced that it had undertaken the task of uncovering irregularities, unjustified promotions, irresponsible recruitment, and arbitrary payment of pensions. At the same time, the country was almost bankrupt and did not even have enough funds to pay minimum contributions to international organizations to which it belonged. In the short run, some savings were made by reducing the expenditure on the civil service. Now the government payroll is back to its original size. The drivers have changed, but the trucks are the same.

Undoubtedly, tribalism plays a significant role in this syndrome, though African leaders continuously seek to deny or minimize its importance. In 1967, in Zambia a resolution moved at a UNIP's convention clearly implied that there was tribal influence in the selection of civil servants. Public discussion of this resolution was curtailed. President Kaunda himself was responsible for suppressing it, reportedly because it included the emotionally charged word "tribalism." In Kenya, there are complex regulations and procedures for recruitment and promotion in the civil service. Upon reading these, one would be impressed with the independence and impartiality that are required of the Public Service Commission, which must approve most senior appointments and promotions. In practice, however, the selections are made by a small group of politicians and bureaucrats even before the various applicants are interviewed by the Public Service Commission. In 1973, nepotism and tribalism had reached such serious proportions that a non-Kikuyu politician was impelled to remark that members of the same tribes seem to be getting all the jobs and dominating all government departments. He continued: "that tribe (an obvious reference to the Kikuyu) would one day be eaten up by the other forty-one tribes like the satisfied hyena is eaten up by hungry hyenas..."[15] Nothing much has come out of such daring though rare criticisms.

In Nigeria, as Ali Mazrui has noted,

"In the course of the first few years of
independence, politics became seriously
characterized by tribal nepotism and
regional favoritism. The Ibo were as
guilty as any other of the dominant ethnic
groups in Nigeria. The struggle in the
country was for the control of the center
so as to distribute resources to one's
region or tribe.... Priorities and allocation of jobs and resources among many
leading Ibo, as indeed among other groups,
were strongly influenced by considerations of
ethnic aggrandizement."[16]

It is doubtful if the advent of military rule :
brought about any genuine change in the Nigerian
methods of recruitment to the civil service. It
may indeed be noted that tribalism even affected
appointments in the universities which, if the
pronouncements of African leaders are to be
believed, must be first to ignore any such influences. This was clearly in evidence when in 1965
Dr. Eni Njoku, an Ibo, was removed from the position of the Vice-Chancellor of the University of
Lagos and replaced by Dr. Saburi Biobaku, a Yoruba.
It was a story of "hidden politics and barefaced
tribalism." Yet an official statement described
the change in the following terms:

"The Council felt that a change was desirable
in order to facilitate the smooth and harmonious running of the affairs of the university. It believed that a new Vice-Chancellor
more sympathetic to the need for easier
relationships between himself and the Council
and also between the Senate and Council, was
called for."[17]

The non-African professors, especially the famous
law professor Dr. Gower of England, who had
supported Dr. Eni Njoku because of his experience
and unquestionable merit, found themselves accused
of "neo-colonialism."

The corrupt exercise of the power to make

government appointments prevails from top to bottom, from cabinet positions to the low-ranking messenger, from a dockworker to the head of the nation's largest university. The lowliest customs or railroad official uses the jobs at his disposal to pay debts, nurture his clientele, and line his pocket.

Corrupt Exercise of Discretionary Powers

It is very common in all African states that public officials refuse to perform acts which they are legally required and paid to do until extra contributions have been paid to their personal coffers. The fact that a member of the public may be entitled under the law to a particular service or to the issue of a certain document makes little difference. Registering a birth or a death, obtaining a certified copy of an entry in the government records, obtaining a passport, having one's luggage and health certificates checked by the appropriate officers when entering or leaving the country, or even reporting a crime--tasks which in developed societies would be regarded as minor and can be speedily accomplished--would in the majority of African states lead to considerable frustration and headaches unless this additional contribution is made.

In most cases, the public officer delays action. "We cannot find your file," "the officer in charge is unavailable," "we are too busy now," or "come back tomorrow" are replies all too familiar to those who deal with African public officials. Once the contribution is made, however, the misplaced file mysteriously appears, the unavailable officer is at your service, and the once-busy clerks will engage in endless talk on any subject broached.

It often required some knowledge of the local colloquialism to determine when such a contribution is expected. However, the proper expressions are quickly acquired. In West Africa, the euphemisms are: "fill up my cheeks"; "grease my palm"; "loosen your hand"; "wet my throat"; "put something under the stool"; "let my mouth be wet"; "put your hand in your pocket"; "set me free"; "come and see me at home"; "it is up to you"; "let something talk"; "put me somewhere"; "put your hand into mine"; "tickle me" etc. This practice is prevalent among low and high echelon officers, including cabinet members whose signatures are required on many government documents. With the centralization of government offices in the capitals, the cost of transportation to and from the offices is sufficient incentive to "contribute" without waiting for the usual clues.

Regular travellers to certain countries of West Africa have learned to place money in the passport before handing it to the customs officer-- known as "adding a page." When it is returned, the gratuity has been removed and the officer ushers the traveller through customs without - inspecting his bags. Those ignorant of or refusing to accede to this local custom must suffer through the most deliberate possible baggage examination. According to a Ghanaian Commission of Inquiry on Corruption:

> "Border guards, like police officers, are reputed to use their position to enrich themselves instead of safeguarding the Ghana economy....At the Kotoka International Airport and the ports, some openly and shamelessly demand gifts from incoming passengers, completely oblivious of the discredit they bring to their uniform and the nation.
>
> . . . . .
>
> Corruption ranges from City Engineers' offices in granting building permits, collection and use of market tolls and other rates.
>
> . . . . .

Accountants, auditors, treasury officers, have all been known to practice bribery, corruption, and extortion in the performance of their duties.

. . . . .

Much revenue is lost to the government through the dishonesty of many officers at the harbours and borders.

. . . . .

The Public Works Department officers assigned to supervise the work of contractors either received bribes or sometimes extorted large sums of money from the contractors before certifying that the contract has been properly executed.

. . . . .

The list of malpractices and categories of public officers involved is infinite. Some headmasters, judicial officers (especially court registrars and bailiffs), community development officers, mortuary attendants, officers in charge of telephone and electricity installations, are all reported to indulge in corrupt practices."[18]

The situation is much the same in most of the new African states.

Even more damaging to the national economies than the acts described above is the wrongful exercise of discretionary powers. All legal systems vest discretion in the hands of those who interpret and apply the laws, and, of necessity, must restrict the rights of individuals for the sake of public welfare, order, and security. In the American legal system, the term "police power" is often employed to refer to those laws and regulations which are enacted to protect the health, safety and morals of the community. These

include housing and fire regulations, restrictions
upon prostitution, and public health and sanitation codes. It is easier to cite examples of
laws and regulations that fall within the meaning
of this term than to define the limits of police
power. By its very nature, police power precludes
precise definition valid at all times and in all
circumstances. The Unabridged Edition of The
Random House Dictionary of the English Language
defines the term simply as "the power of a nation,
within the limits of its constitution, to regulate
the conduct of its citizens in the interest of
the common good." Its exact meaning and scope
therefore necessarily vary according to changing
conditions, conceptions and constitutional provisions.

If a state takes a restrictive view of its
functions, the police power will be used to achieve limited objectives. But if it assumes a
more expanded view of its responsibilities, then
the government will increase its activities
correspondingly. It has been noted in preceding
chapters that African leaders regard "total" or
"genuine" self-determination and economic development as their major goals. Ostensibly, in order
to improve the economic welfare of their peoples
(and, consequently, in the exercise of their
police powers broadly interpreted), they have
instituted many policies almost invariably resulting in injury to non-African economic interests.
Constitutional restrictions limiting the exercise
of this power were, as discussed elsewhere in this
book, rendered inoperative in the post-independence period. Contemporary African laws leave
considerable discretionary powers in the hands of
those who administer them. Or, to put it differently, African politicians, bureaucrats, and
military leaders enjoy considerable latitude in
the way they exercise their authority.

The effect of police power laws, therefore,
depends on the attitude of those who execute them.
Applied impartially the laws promote national
interest in the public good--broadly construed.

If the police power is conceived of as an opportunity for officials to benefit themselves or their clienteles and dependents, then not only is disrespect for the laws encouraged but very tangible economic and other social costs must be borne as well. In most African states the latter is the case.

United Nations and other foreign experts who advise African governments are often disillusioned when they make recommendations aimed at the interests of the country as a whole. National economic plans and proposals for reform of the police alike are ignored if they threaten individual and group self-aggrandizement. Let us examine concrete examples of how discretionary powers have been exercised in some African states and the adverse effects of the abuse and misuse of power.

Between 1960 and 1965, Ghana, in its search for economic independence, established a number of state enterprises. As indicated elsewhere in this book, they were given certain privileges, often at the expense of non-African businesses operating in the country. The governing boards and staff of these enterprises were not appointed on the basis of merit, technical and professional knowledge, or experience. They added to overhead costs but contributed little to the success of the businesses. As a result, they rarely operated at optimum levels and often even physical plant and equipment deteriorated as a result of poor maintenance. As Dennis K. Greenstreet has noted:

"Normal qualifications for appointment and promotion were often given less weight than family and personal connections together with the ethnic group to which a person belonged. The immediate family of those holding management positions considered themselves entitled to share the facilities provided, such as the use, free of charge, of official motor cars...."[19]

The inevitable conclusion, according to him, was

that the public corporations would have been more successful "had many of those holding responsible political and administrative/management posts throughout the public services paid a little less attention to feathering their own nests at the expense of their own people and a little more attention to the public good."[20] The failure of Mali's socialist programs, especially in marketing and production of agricultural products, in the early seventies, can also be traced to their use by the bureaucrats, politicians, and others as a source of personal enrichment. In both, the root causes were the misuse or abuse of the discretionary powers of appointment and management of the state enterprises.

While Ghana was under colonial rule, Section 2 of the Public Lands Ordinance authorized the British Governor to purchase or take private land or property whenever it was required for public service. The Governor was required only to publish a notice in the Official Gazette before recording a deed vesting the property in the government for use "according to the true intent and meaning of the Public Lands Ordinance." Although this power was often exercised, in nearly all cases the colonial government specifically indicated the purpose for which the land was acquired. Usually it was to build structures thought to be in the public interest such as offices, schools, roads, hospitals, railways, harbors, markets, and cemeteries. After independence, the law was amended by the State Lands Act of 1962. The new legislation contained no definition of "public interest," and it did not require that the Government hold and use the land according to the true intent and meaning of the law. Since then there has been "an unholy taciturnity, almost a conspiracy of silence, about purposes for which lands are acquired,"[21] and little inclination, on the part of succeeding governments, to change the law. On the contrary, according to M. A. Mettle:

In its present form the terminology of the

State Lands Act, 1962 makes it possible for
the President, under the guise of land required "in the public interest" to take land
belonging to the Leader of Opposition and
give it to his girl friend to build thereon.
It should surprise no one, therefore, that
there was a rampage for land in the urban
areas both in the heyday of the Nkrumah
administration and during the short-lived
Busia government. The circumstances were
tainted with suspicion and corruption.[22]

All legal systems include an eminent domain
law. But a law which leaves the exercise of
eminent domain to the complete discretion of those
in office threatens more economic harm than any
delay which may result from a law which places
restrictions upon the exercise of this power by
those in authority.

In Uganda, lands, factories, warehouses, and
other properties of the expelled Asians were declared in November, 1972, to be "abandoned
property." A committee was established to allo-
cate and distribute the abandoned properties
among Africans. According to David Martin:

"The spoils of the economic war went to the
soldiers. The Chief Army Medical Officer,
Lieutenant-Colonel Bogere was awarded
Kampala's 45,000 pounds Speke Hotel by Amin.
Initially the business allocation committee
was run by civil servants but this was
taken over by the army when it was realized
many of the firms were going to civilians.
At least five African civilians in Kampala
awarded shops are known to have been killed
by soldiers who seized the properties and
today over half the capital's businesses
are in the hands of soldiers, almost all
Moslem Nubians. Many others found their way
into the hands of soldiers' relatives and
at least three Kampala businesses were
allocated to two of Amin's four wives.
Stocks that were taken over with the

businesses were sold by the new owners and
the money pocketed and spent. The Asians'
cars were sold at two auctions, the first
where the army had their pick at nominal
prices, and it is doubtful whether even
these were paid for."[23]

Whether the distribution was made by a committee
of bureaucrats or a group of soldiers it is doubtful that the results would have been very different. As previously described, both bureaucrats
and military leaders generally exercise discretionary powers in the interest of themselves or
their clienteles. There is every reason to think
that Ugandan bureaucrats would have acted in the
same way. There was little chance of the firms
coming under control of deserving and experienced
African businessmen.

   In Zaire, the situation was similar. The
economic fruits of the nationalization of foreign
businesses have not been equitably distributed.
Over ninety per cent of the assets left by the
non-Africans were shared by favored minority of
"honorable and gifted" men from the Political
Bureau of the ruling Party, the state or regional commissioners, the cabinet and the national
legislature.

   In the exercise of police powers, states
may introduce licensing systems. The administration of such systems requires a grant of discretionary power to those who issue licenses. Normally, however, such powers are checked by providing
a right of appeal to an independent, impartial
tribunal or to the regular courts. African states,
following their broad interpretation of the police
power, have introduced licensing for a number of
economic activities. The purpose is to place
their economies firmly under the control of
Africans.

   In Kenya, for example, a license is required
in retail business, import-export trade, the sale
or repair of radio sets, tourist enterprises,

buying and selling used automobiles, fishing in
Kenyon territorial waters, slaughtering pigs,
among many other forms of economic activities.
With the politicization of the judiciary and
expansion in the discretionary powers of government officers, such laws provide inviting opportunities to exercise these powers for personal
gain or for benefit of one's clientele.

African politicians and bureaucrats at all
levels have taken advantage of such opportunities.
In Benin, the head of state, Kerekou, was
positively implicated in a corrupt thirty-five
million franc scheme to issue fishing licences in
the country's rich territorial waters. In Ghana,
the Ollenu Report documents a number of corrupt
practices in connection with the issuance of
import licences.

Preferential treatment of favored applicants
may bring overnight riches for those so treated.
In Kenya, licences to export the most lucrative
items have been granted only to government ministers or to corporations headed by them or members of their families. In Ghana, the government
ministers themselves have accepted bribes for the
issue of licences. The situation changed very
little during the period of the military regime.

After the 1972 coup, the National Redemption
Council established a Logistics Committee (composed mainly of military officers) with power to
purchase directly many essential commodities
(sugar, soap, matches, cement, etc.) and distribute them to the people. The committee had also
the power to appoint licensed agents in various
parts of the country to control retail distribution. It was later found that people in one
region were unable to obtain these commodities.
The committee had appointed one woman trader as
the licensed agent for the whole region, and
allocated what they estimated to be the needs
of the whole region to her. However, she had
held back almost ninety percent of the allocation
for sale at much higher prices in other parts of

the country. There was a change in the personnel and the name of the Committee, but the fundamental attributes of the system remain unchanged.

At times, the misuse of such discretionary powers has been openly encouraged, rather than merely tolerated, by the heads of states themselves. In Zambia, for example, where it counted President Kaunda himself advocated partisan use of discretionary powers:

> "During this ceremony (appointing a new cabinet member) Kaunda promised unashamedly to implement the Economic Reforms to show that 'it pays to belong to UNIP'. At one point in the speech the President angrily warned Mr. Justin Chimba, the newly appointed Minister of Trade, Industry, and Mines that he would be sacked if he gave trading licences to ANC MPs elected for Barotse Province. The President said: 'If you renew these men's licences you would be sacked yourself....The ANC MPs will be taught a lesson....' Turning to other matters he said he was determined to implement Humanism. Humanism would become prime subjects at schools, colleges, and universities throughout Zambia...."[24]

The proposed action was pregnant with tribal implications.

Whether the aim of the official ideology is to promote African capitalism or African socialism, the practical results are the same. A government, like that of Malawi, may seek to encourage African businessmen by making direct loans to them or guaranteeing their credit. In such programs, decisions are made not on the basis of economic and entrepreneurial considerations but as a means of rewarding kinsmen, members of the family, tribe, or of one's clientele. Similarly, if a government assumes control of a certain trade or industry, the discretionary powers of management are exercised by the government officers with a view toward maximizing their own interests and those of their supporters. In Ghana, Mr. Asare, former Minister of Agriculture, profited to the extent of $2.5 million when the government undertook to import for re-sale to farmers agricultural machinery and equipment. In Nigeria, a military procurement officer realized one-half million naira on a single government contract made by him with an overseas corporation for the purchase of cement. (The Nigerian government ordered twenty million tons of cement costing over $100 million, a large proportion of which suffered considerable damage because it could not be unloaded within a reasonable time at the highly congested Nigerian ports.) Another military officer made a similar amount on a contract for supply of arms and equipment.

African governments have undertaken many programs and services in the name of Africanization of their economies. These measures include assisting Africans in feasibility studies, financing the operating of their businesses or industries, approving income tax relief for such enterprises, nationalizing privately owned buildings and renting them to African businesses, awarding contracts for supply of goods or services to the government (with preference being given to African contractors), building facilities in suitable locations on government land at public expense and leasing them at nominal rents to Africans, and appointing agents for distribution of goods imported by state import & export corporations. Administration of these policies implies broad discretionary authority, authority usually exercised in the interests of those endowed with the discretionary powers.

Frequently, African politicians, bureaucrats, and military directly violate the laws, especially when confident of being able to get away with it. Instances of the police accepting bribes to free a person accused of speeding or other traffic offenses, from applicants for driving licences not qualified to receive them, for

issuing certificates of road-worthiness to automobiles and trucks clearly unsafe to operate are
routine in most of Africa. Unfortunately, however,
examples of obvious illegal actions by public
officials do not end there. According to the
report of the Ghanaian Commission:

> Policemen, including those of senior rank,
> are believed to accept bribes to suppress
> investigations into crimes reported to them.
> The methods used in such cases may range from
> half-hearted investigations; refusal to ac-
> cept a case as criminal; destruction of
> important evidence, or the disappearance of
> parts or the whole of police dockets on the
> cases under investigation. A senior police
> officer testified before the Commission that
> when he took over the command of a region,
> he discovered that about 700 police dockets
> were missing! An Assistant Commissioner of
> Police in charge of a region had the repu-
> tation of "selling" cases under investi-
> gation and closing the dockets on some
> flimsy grounds.[25]

Simultaneously, the same officers often deliberately overlook widespread wrongdoing by members
of their own tribes or from whom they may be
receiving the derivative base of support,
especially when the wrong has been committed
against a member of the opposing tribe or group.

In Nigeria, senior police officers have
participated in planning and carrying out armed
robberies. In Ghana, the military officers
themselves engage in smuggling goods out of the
country. In Gambia, the headquarters of a smuggling ring was located in a government-owned
house occupied by none other than the Vice-
President of the country. In Senegal, ministers
and members of the legislature and senior diplomats,
routinely visit Gambia for shopping and return to
the country without paying import taxes claiming
protocol or service diplomatique. In Kenya,
government ministers have been involved in illegal

exports of cloves, ivory tusks, and other goods.

The above examples of misfeasance, nonfea-
sance, and malfeasance on the part of African
politicians, bureaucrats, and military are admittedly selective and somewhat imprecise. But anyone who has lived in Africa, or has watched events
on the continent closely during the post-independence period, knows that these examples are
representative of what occurs nearly everywhere
on the continent.

Instances of corruption are extremely difficult to document beyond doubt--the guilty parties
are rarely brought to trial, evidence available
is usually circumstantial, and often there is
tendency on the part of the leaders to ignore or
under-emphasize the problem. The same applies to
tribalism. In fact, the situation is comparable
to the commission of sexual offences in the
United States where the number of persons convicted of rape bears little, if any, relationship
to the actual number of sexual offences that are
in fact committed. Similarly, in Africa the
number of corrupt activities that do come to
light are almost miniscule compared to the actual
state of affairs.

In a few cases mostly unsuccessful attempts
have been made to curb the problem. One of the
best known (thanks to the publicity given to it
by the Tanzaniaphiles) was articulated by President
Nyerere. In his famous Arusha Declaration, he
prohibited Tanzanian political leaders and bureaucrats from owning more than one house each and
holding directorships of private businesses,
receiving two or more salaries, or owning shares
in a corporation. Ideologically, this was portrayed as evidence of Tanzania's seriousness
about implementing socialism and preventing the
emergence of an African bourgeoisie. What has
been left unpublicized, however, are the facts
that these requirements were forced upon the
TANU Executive Committee by the President, that
several members of the President's own Cabinet

117

were opposed to them, and perhaps more importantly, that they have been implemented only in part. Also the requirements did not apply to ownership of rural land, and, in any event, could be circumvented easily by transferring the properties or interests to members of one's family or kinship group. Tanzanian officials have made ample use of these loopholes. Tanzanian politicians, bureaucrats, and the military are by no means even relatively free of corruption today.

The situation is not much different in Zambia. The Leadership Code, issued in his Kabwe Declaration by President Kaunda in December, 1972, required that no African leader of any consequence should farm more than a small plot of land, own more than the one house he lives in, or employ more than a handful of people. If any leader did any of those things, he could not draw a salary from the state. In its application the code has been considerably watered down and it has been difficult, if not impossible, for President Kaunda to apply the Code strictly to many of the members of his own UNIP. UNIP members have obviously benefited considerably from the Mulungushi reforms introduced in 1968, imposing restrictions on the activities of "non-citizens" in an effort to ensure that a larger share of the Zambian economy comes into the hands of the indigenous people. But the same leaders, however, continue to pay lipservice to African Socialism and Humanism.

In Ghana, according to General Albert Ocran (who was instrumental in overthrowing President Nkrumah in 1966), the objectives of his colleagues in staging the coup were "to put an end to moral decline, including bribery and corruption," and to ensure "that such shameless thievery, plundering and cheating--call it what you will--should not occur in Ghana."[26] Before allowing return to civilian rule, therefore, the military had ensured that a provision was made in the new Constitution to require all members of the Cabinet to declare their assets immediately upon their appointment.

This provision, however, like many other constitutional provisions, was respected more in the breach than in its observance. In 1971, and at least fourteen months after they had taken office, none of the ministers appointed to President Busia's cabinet had declared their assets. Within a few years, the Busia government, too, fell victim to another military coup.

In such circumstances, however, the change has often provided the new government leaders with unique opportunities to indulge in crusades against corruption. New brooms sweep clean. In Nigeria, for example, following a change of government on July 29, 1975, thousands of military state governors, senior officers in the armed forces, high court judges, police chiefs, senior diplomats, bureaucrats, railway workers and others were either dismissed or forced to retire on grounds ranging from inefficiency and gross misconduct, to ill health and absenteeism. In many cases, no reason was given. In October, 1975, Brig. Murtala Muhammed, the new head of state, even announced:

> "We have set up a panel to investigate and determine the assets of certain categories of public officials who have been removed from office. At the end of this exercise officers who are found to own assets over and above what could reasonably be computed to represent their legitimate earnings would forfeit all such excess assets by confiscation."[27]

The onus was now upon the person being investigated to prove that what he owned then had been lawfully and legitimately acquired. Ironically, those who had squandered their illegitimate earnings on conspicuous consumption fared better than those who had tried to save and invest some of their ill-gotten gains. Similar commissions of inquiry have been appointed in other African states after the removal of civilian leaders, though the terms and the powers of the panels have not necessarily been so wide as they were in

Nigeria.

Periodic cleansing exercises obviously are of some value. But they cannot substitute for institutional checks on leaders exercising public authority in democratic systems. When the commissions or panels are initially established, there are insistent demands to teach the corrupt a lesson, enthusiasm for probing their activities is high, and zeal to impose stiff penalties is even higher. In time, however, when the new leaders and their own supporters indulge in similar activities (which, as the record shows, eventually occurs), the "reform" administrations fall prey to the same behavior as their predecessors. They cannot apply standards of rectitude and performance to their own supporters with the vigor and consistency employed toward those they drove from power.

The penchant of African politicians, bureaucrats and military leaders for enhancing and entrenching their own political and socio-economic positions, with the support of their respective clienteles, results at best in neglect of the interests of non-Africans and of those Africans who, by reason of their belonging to the less privileged tribes or other disaffected groups, do not share in the political pork barrel. At worst, the outgroups have been subjected to deprivation, deportation and death, at best, harrassment and humiliation. And, by and large, none has successfully opposed the policies of those in power. One reason for their impotence is that in virtually all African states, after coming into power the new rulers arm themselves with an arsenal of legal and administrative tools capable of inflicting physical violence and use them whenever they wish. Some of these tools are uniquely useful against particular groups. Others may be used indiscriminately. And, of course, the same tools are available for use against recalcitrants within their own group or groups who, for various reasons, might challenge the existing state of affairs.

Capital Punishment

Holding a precarious tenure under an arbitrary administration, no African leader can regard himself as sufficiently secure and enjoying the loyalty of his people. He therefore adopts a skeptical approach, especially towards those outside his own clientele and tribe. He is perenially suspicious of individuals or groups who might conspire against him. Because of deficiencies in his own administration, he knows that some who conspire against him may elude detection. In defense he becomes ruthless; he uses capital punishment against presumed foes he does discover in hopes that the prospect of drastic penalties will deter other, potential opposition. He becomes obsessed with the constant need to demonstrate his toughness. The death penalty has, therefore, become the answer to an increasing range of political offenses on the continent. Though such penalties are usually imposed against specific individuals, there are instances of collective guilt and punishments, too.

The substance and application of treason laws provide the best examples. In January, 1975, ten persons were executed in Somalia for this offense. They had been found guilty of "exploiting religion to create national disunity and subvert State authority." Their crime was to have opposed a decree granting equal rights to women.

In Ghana, a law enacted in 1959 introduced a comprehensive and nearly inclusive definition of treason. The new law prescribed the death penalty for this crime. Under the law, anyone who "prepares or endeavors to procure by force any alteration of the law or the policies of the government; or to carry out by force any enterprise which usurps the executive power of the state in any manner of both a public and a general nature was to be deemed to have committed an act of treason." The term "by force" was defined as including any "show of force calculated to arouse reasonable apprehension that force will be used."[28]

Any person accused of treason could also be convicted of a lesser offense called Treason-Felony which was defined as "any preparation to procure by unlawful means any alteration of the law or the policies of the Government." The law also provided that any citizen of Ghana could be tried and punished for anything done outside Ghana as if the offense had been committed within Ghanaian territory. Thus, Ghanaian citizens abroad risked prosecution upon returning home if they criticized their government while out of the country.

In 1963, Sierra Leone enacted a Treason Act, widening the definition and scope of the Government's remedies against treasonable activities and included capital punishment among sentences that could be imposed. It extended the jurisdiction of the Sierra Leone government to all treasonable offences committed by any persons ordinarily residing in Sierra Leone or in the public service of Sierra Leone, regardless of whether they were Sierra Leonean citizens or not or whether the crime was committed within or outside Sierra Leone. The result was, in effect, to make the Lebanese, Syrians, and other non-Africans residing in Sierra Leone liable to prosecution if they should dare, for example, to criticize the country's racist citizenship laws anywhere in the world.

In 1965, Guinea adopted a new Penal Code which incorporated a wide range of offences against the state. These included, among many others, attempting to demoralize the army, endangering the territorial integrity of Guinea, and communicating with any foreign power with the object of causing injury to the military or diplomatic position of Guinea. It was also an offense against the security of the state for any person, Guinean or non-Guinean, to support or advocate in a public speech or in writing the continued maintenance of any African country in a state of political, social, or economic dependence on any foreign power. The sentences prescribed for these offenses ranged from imprisonment of five to twenty years to life imprisonment or execution. It was also specifically provided that non-citizens could be found guilty of these offenses regardless of whether the offenses in question were committed inside or outside the Guinean national territory. One may cite, _ad_ _infinitum_, examples of similar treason laws enacted by the new African states, backed by the death penalty.

Armed with such laws and politicized judiciaries, it has been easy for African leaders to remove from the scene, either temporarily by imprisonment or permanently by imposition of death penalties, all serious challengers. A few examples of such exercise of power are given below. It should be understood, however, that such powers are exercised by African leaders at many levels of authority. Usually it is only when heads of states become involved that the world press or international agencies like Amnesty International publicize the circumstances. For every publicized case, there must be hundreds of individuals, poor and friendless, dead or dying in prison unnoticed by the world.

Zaire: President Mobutu has weeded out systematically those Zairians who were likely to pose an effective challenge to his political leadership. On May 30, 1966, for example, the Zairian government announced the discovery of a conspiracy to overthrow President Mobutu's government. Among those arrested were Evariste Kimbe (a former Prime Minister), Jerome Anamy (Defense Minister in Mr. Adoula's government in 1964), Alexandre Mahamba (who had held several ministerial positions in the past), and Emmanuel Bamba (a former Minister of Finance and a close friend of former President Kasavubu). On June 1 they were all brought before and tried by a military tribunal and sentenced to death. On June 2 the sentences were carried out in full view of the general public. As a British newspaper commented

"....it was bad enough that they were found guilty and sentenced to death after a trial

123

which mocked all ideas of justice. To have
hanged them before a vast crowd, whose presence at the grisly spectacle had been ensured
by declaring a public holiday was an act of
barbarism that cannot be excused even by the
bloody record of the Congo during the past
six years."[29]

President Mobutu's objective was to demonstrate
his power and his willingness to use it against
leaders of opposing tribes or groups. The strategy has succeeded. The position of Mobutu, at
least for the time being, has become entrenched.
Other political hopefuls or potential challengers
have either joined the system or abandoned their
aspirations and abandoned politics altogether.

Sierra Leone: On July 19, 1975, eight men
were executed at Pademba Road Prison in Freetown.
This was described by the government as the "final
outcome" of sentences imposed upon them at treason
trials for conspiring to overthrow the existing
government. Those convicted included at least two
former ministers--Dr. Mohamed Fornah and Mr. Ibrahim Taqi, and Brigadier John Bangura, a military
leader. Some of the accused were tried before a
military tribunal, while others were tried in the
regular courts. At one of the trials, the
Attorney General of Sierra Leone, Mr. Constance
Davies, had argued that it was unnecessary for the
government to prove all the charges against the
accused. If only one count was proved, according to the Attorney General, the rest must be
deemed to have been proved. He had also argued
that if one of the accused was proven to be
guilty, the rest, too, must be presumed to be
guilty.

Guinea: An undeterminable number of persons
have been executed in Guinea for posing threats
to the existing government of President Sékou Touré.
The executions have often been kept secret.
Following the alleged "invasion" of Guinea in
November, 1970, a number of Guinea's residents
were arrested for participating in the "invasion"

or conspiring against the existing regime. The
accused were tried by the hand-picked National
Assembly, sitting as the Supreme Revolutionary
Tribunal. During the trial, tape-recorded "con-
fessions" were put in evidence; but none of the
accused was permitted to be present or to be
represented by counsel. Sentences were announced
on January 24, 1971: ninety-two were sentenced
to death and an additional seventy-two to life
imprisonment with forced labor. The latter
included the Roman Catholic Archbishop of Conakry,
ten Lebanese, three Frenchmen, and two Germans.
The total number executed is uncertain, though
it is known that five persons, including a woman,
were hung from a bridge in Conakry in what Radio
Conakry described as a carnival atmosphere and
in which "the people spat and stoned the bodies."
Immediately following the imposition of the sentences, Ishmael Touré had declared "You have the
enemy in your hands. Get rid of the vermin....
The traitors will be sacrificed to keep the
revolution alive. A new phase begins today.
There is no room for half-measures...."[30] In
Guinea, there have obviously been times when
President Touré must have been very unsure of
the loyalty of the majority of his people; but
the major brunt of his suspicions has clearly
been borne by the people of the Fula tribe,
and especially those among them having Barry or
Diallo as their last names.

Selective Genocide

Some African states have indulged in institutionalized violence of the most brutal kind--
genocide. A policy of annihilation has been
employed against tribes of which those in power
are acutely afraid or suspicious. Uganda is by
no means the only country that has indulged in
this practice, although its case is the one that
has been most publicised.

Uganda: The total number of people who
have been killed in Uganda during the last seven
years will probably never be known. Estimates

125

range from 100,000 to 300,000. In a secret memoradum distributed by one of President Amin's own cabinet members to African heads of states in early 1973, it was estimated that about eighty to ninety thousand people were killed within two years of Amin's coup in January, 1971. And the Minister was at pains to emphasize that this was a conservative estimate. Some of these admittedly constitute arbitrary killings by undisciplined and rapacious members of the Ugandan armed forces. But there can be little doubt that the majority of the killings were pre-meditated and follow a certain pattern. After his flight to England, the former Ugandan foreign minister wrote an open letter to President Amin in which he contended that those who have "disappeared" in Uganda have in fact been "liquidated for personal, political, or factional reasons." He went on to state:

> "I want to confirm here and now that indeed you are personally responsible for the liquidation of all the people who have 'disappeared' in Uganda ever since you came to power. People have 'disappeared' either because you have specifically ordered their liquidation as individuals or as a group or because they have fallen victim to the murderous ravages of lawless elements who have thrived in the country as a result of your deliberate refusal to restrain the criminal activities of such elements, or to place any sort of discipline over them."[31]

We must note here the use of the word "faction" by one minister and of the word "group" by another. Both, of course, were referring to tribes. But old habits, especially when acquired by African ministers, die hard, and none was therefore willing to use the word "tribe." An indisputable fact is that many of these killings were directed against Ugandan Africans who belonged to the Acholi and Langi tribes. People of these tribes had provided former President Milton Obote's clientele, and presumably still favor and are working towards his return to power. Under-

126

standably, they were the main targets of Amin's suspicions. In February, 1976, for example, after an alleged attempt to overthrow President Amin, Ugandan military units searched the areas occupied by these two tribes with a list of 7,000 names. Many people on the list were summarily and brutally killed. According to a former Ugandan civil servant, President Amin was pursuing a "final solution" to the "Acholi and Langi problem."

Burundi: It would be difficult to summarize the complex evolution of events in Burundi since its independence in 1962. Suffice it to say that tribal rivalries, ambitions and fears seem to be at the center of political life there. Following an abortive attempt by the Hutu to rebel against the Tutsi-dominated government in 1972, in which about 2,000 people were killed, the government of President Micombero unleashed a reign of terror against the Hutu. The President declared martial law and proceeded, with the use of his armed forces and revolutionary youth brigades to wipe out the Hutu intelligentsia systematically. In a report written for an English organization called Minority Rights Group, Professor Rene Lemarchand and Dr. David Martin had the following to say:

"In Bururi the army attacked all Hutu more or less indiscriminately. In Bujumbura, Gitega and Ngozi all 'cadres' of Hutu origins--including not only local administrators but chauffeurs, clerks and skilled workers--were systematically rounded up, taken to jail and either shot or beaten to death with rifle butts or clubs. In Bujumbura alone an estimated 4,000 Hutu were loaded up on trucks and taken to their graves. According to one Tutsi witness 'they picked up almost all the Hutu intellectuals above the secondary school level' and many more, one might add, below that level. Some of the most gruesome scenes took place on the premises of the Université Officielle....and in secondary and technical schools. Scores of Hutu students were physically assaulted by their Tutsi confreres; many were beaten to death... groups of soldiers and jeunesses would suddenly appear in classrooms, call the Hutu students by name and take them away. Few ever returned. At the Université Officielle about one-third (120) disappeared in these circumstances. The Ecole Normale of Ngagara...lost more than 100 students out of a total of 314.... Not only the Hutu elites but nearly all potential elites were thus physically liquidated.... Twelve Hutu priests are said to have been killed, and thousands of protestant pastors, school directors, and teachers. In the Bujumbara hospital six doctors and eight nurses were arrested and are believed to be dead.... The repression took on the qualities of a 'selective genocide' directed at all the educated or semi-educated strata of Hutu society...."[32]

These are, unfortunately, not the only instances of policies that amount to genocide. In Equatorial Guinea President Francisco Macias Nguema killed about 50,000 persons, mostly educated, at least partly because of tribal jealousies. And hundreds of thousands of Ibos were killed in Nigeria both prior to and during the short existence of the secessionist state of Biafra.

Preventive Detention

Imprisonment is another form of physical violence that those in power in Africa frequently inflict upon suspected rivals or challengers. This is done by having them sentenced to a term of years, either by politicized judiciaries or by the head of state or any other authorized person, exercising powers vested in him under preventive detention laws. The argument is that it is in the public interest to keep these people out of circulation. (At a certain point, the distinction

128

between imprisonment following the imposition of
a sentence by a regular court of law and preventive detention becomes in essence meaningless.)
It is ironic that the same preventive detention
laws which were being criticized day in and day
out by African nationalist leaders during their
struggle for independence have now been made even
more stringent and are being used increasingly by
African heads of state. What is worse is that even
the few safeguards protecting individual rights
that remain in the law are, in practice, ignored.
Provisions contained in colonial preventive
detention laws for notification to the detainees
of the grounds of their arrest and detention,
periodic review of each by an independent body,
visits to prisons by voluntary humanitarian agencies, and publication in the official gazettes of
names of those placed under preventive detention
are all observed chiefly in the breach. A large
number of African states, including Malawi, Zaire,
Rwanda, Chad, Guinea, Cameroon, Tanzania, Zambia
and Gabon, make frequent use of preventive detention laws, though only a handful are willing to
disclose to the world the total number and the
circumstances in which such persons are imprisoned.
Let us look at a few examples.

Tanzania: In 1977, there were more persons
under preventive detention in Tanzania than in the
whole of South Africa. One such detainee was
Abdulrahman Mohammed Babu, a former member of the
Tanzanian Cabinet. According to him:

"As soon as I was taken in I was stripped,
searched and then thrown into an isolation
cell which I later came to know was reserved
for the leprosy cases. I had to spend the
rest of the night on a bare wet cement floor
in this cell of six feet by seven. I remained in the cell for exactly two weeks in
complete isolation without being allowed out
for fresh air...."[33]

The letter was smuggled out of the Ukongo Prison
in Daressalaam addressed to the United Nations

Commission on Human Rights. In that letter, Mr.
Babu stated that he had remained silent about his
treatment under preventive detention for over three
years because he "had no desire to embarrass our
President at a time when he was leading the struggle for human rights in Southern Africa" but felt
that the time had now come to publicize his case
because, in his view, "the political leadership is
too preoccupied with political expediency....[34]
Under Tanzanian law--the Preventive Detention Act,
1962--a detainee must be informed of reasons for
his arrest within fifteen days, and should be
afforded an opportunity to make written representations to the President. Mr. Babu was never
told why he had been imprisoned and no opportunity
was ever given him to make representations,
written or oral, to the President. His case is
not unique.

If Mr. Babu had been charged and tried before
the regular courts, it would, in all probability,
have made little difference. In 1971, Bibi Titi
Mohammed, (a founding member of TANU and a former
President of Tanzanian Women's League), Michael
Kamaliza, (a former minister of labor), and others
were convicted by the regular courts of treason and
sentenced to life imprisonment. Soon after their
arrests, however, and well before formal conviction
President Nyerere made several public statements
presupposing their guilt. Editorials appearing in
the state-controlled newspapers also treated them
as if they were convicted criminals. The government leaders and prosecutors obviously were not
afraid that the courts would dismiss the indict-
ments on the grounds that such statements seriously
prejudiced fair trial. They also knew that even
if the accused were acquitted by the courts, they
could, as was done in the case of one Mr. Joseph
Kasella-bantu, always be detained for an indefinite
period under the preventive detention laws.

Zaire has enjoyed unprecedented political
stability (thanks to President Mobutu, some claim)
over the last twelve years. However, those who
never tire singing the praises of President Mobutu

often neglect to mention that today the Zairian prisons contain hundreds of political detainees who have never been presented with legal charges and have never had their day in court or before any other tribunal. Whenever there are rumors of an impending plot or internal upheaval, people are rounded up by President Mobutu's forces and detained for an indefinite period of time. More often than not they come from tribes well-known for their non-support of President Mobutu and his political party, the MPR.

Dr. Joseph Danquah's detention and death in solitary confinement in Ghana, the lengthy house arrest of Mr. Oginga Odinga in Kenya, and the detention of Mr. Babu in Tanzania are all illustrative of the extent to which leaders of new African states have been willing to go in suppressing any challenge or opposition to their regimes. At times, such actions are taken without concern for world opinion or for the provisions of the Universal Declaration of Human Rights. In Malawi, for example, Dr. Banda has repeatedly stated that any person engaging in subversive activities would immediately be placed under preventive detention and that neither the views of Amnesty International nor of other such world agencies would matter. In 1974, when Amnesty International protested the detention of several teachers and civil servants, Dr. Banda went so far as to warn that any person whose name is even mentioned by such an organization would be detained longer than might otherwise be the case.

Nor have changes in the government made much difference in the practice of preventive detention. Only the faces change. In October, 1968, Mr. Rajat Neogy, a Ugandan citizen of Asian parentage and the editor of the highly respected scholarly journal Transition, was arrested on charges of sedition by the government of President Milton Obote. He was released by the courts on March 28, 1969, only to be placed immediately under preventive detention upon the order of the President. At the time of

131

the military coup in Uganda in January, 1971, there were about fifty political detainees in the country. One of the reasons given by General Amin for the military takeover was that the civilian regime of President Obote had been guilty of "unwarranted detention without trial and for long periods of time of a large number of people many of whom were totally innocent of any charges."[35] Within a few months of President Amin's accession to power, however, the total number of those in preventive detention rose to at least eight hundred.

Elsewhere in this book we have examined the vast scope of interference by most African states in the organization and operation of the economy. Governmental ownership and/or regulation of large segments of the economy provides those in authority with a convenient mechanism for enriching themselves and rewarding their clients. The same powers, however, can also be used to inflict economic ruin on those in disfavor. In the African context, imposition of economic sanctions on government employees is at least as serious a matter as the prospect of physical violence. The government is the principal employer in most African economies. Thus, a threat of dismissal from government service carries political weight far beyond what might be considered "normal."

Jobs in the private sector are not easy to come by, especially for people known to be in disfavor with the government. And those who become self-employed by setting up their own businesses can be made easy targets of economic violence. This occurred in Zambia, for example, when those who did not belong to President Kaunda's party were refused trading licences. Those who operate and work in factories or mines can easily be dealt a telling blow by clever use of administrative and regulatory machinery. In Zaire, several persons known to be opposed to the regime of President Mobutu, in 1969, were arrested for trying to foment strikes and creating other economic difficulties for the government. Twenty private

132

bank employees were arrested the same year for leading a strike. A government announcement asserted that "exemplary punishment awaits those grave-diggers of our economic independence."[36]

In Nigeria, under a 1968 law, workers in certain occupations are expected to submit all disputes to government appointed arbitrators. They may not go on strike. Newspapers are forbidden to publish anything that might cause "public alarm or industrial unrest." These and similar laws make it easy for those in power to inflict heavy economic sanctions, whenever it seems expedient, against those who challenge their authority or policies.

Even students cannot escape such reprisals. In Kenya, a number of students caused an article to be published in the University of Nairobi's student periodical condemning the ruling clique for maintaining itself in power by oppressing the masses, conspiring with imperialist and neo-colonialist powers, and promoting the interests of a few at the expense of the majority. President Jomo Kenyatta and his ministers had little difficulty solving the problem through use of economic sanctions. They merely revoked the scholarships of the students responsible for the article (in effect, denying them further access to education), dismissed the faculty adviser who had allowed the article to reach print (making future employment as a teacher unlikely since all universities are controlled by the government), and curtailed funds available to the University for student publications. Having taken these actions, it was relatively easy for the President to repair the damage caused to his political status by appearing on national television (controlled by the government) to charge that the article was an irresponsible action on the part of a few individuals who had failed to realize the great sacrifices that were and are being made by both their parents and the Kenya government in giving them education. Most of the students involved were Luos.

The situation was more or less the same in February, 1969, when students demonstrated against the government for not allowing Mr. Oginga Odinga, the Luo leader opposing President Jomo Kenyatta, to speak at the University College. The government simply closed down the college for two weeks, threw out the students and their belongings from the university dormitories, and reopened the college only after they had signed a pledge that they would not participate in any more "unauthorized demonstrations." In so far as non-citizens and non-Africans are concerned, the threat to revoke their trading licences, work permits, or other necessary documents is sufficient to prevent them from actively supporting those opposing the regime in power.

Once a government has armed itself with the tools of physical and economic violence and demonstrated its capacity and willingness to use them against critics and opponents, an attitudinal change takes place among the people. This change is often accelerated by government propaganda, portraying those opposing the regime as misfits, troublemongers, or even insane. Eventually, a climate of fear becomes all pervasive and those inclined to oppose the government turn inwards and find refuge in sullen silence or become co-opted. In 1974, a number of farmers belonging to the Chagga tribe resisted efforts by the Tanzanian government to force them into Ujamaa villages. They were immediately castigated as: "bourgeois reactionaries, blood-sucking capitalists, and exploiters of labor." Some were forcibly moved to unsuitable locations where, deprived of shelter, many died of pneumonia. But all the others "got the message" and moved into the villages without further resistance. In Zambia it is a common practice of President Kaunda's UNIP to encourage demonstrations against groups or individuals opposed to the government. The government's control over when and where such demonstrations take place becomes very useful in such circumstances.

The same applies to criticisms of governmental policies and practices in the national media. Radio and television are in government hands in all black African states. The same is true for newspapers in a vast majority of them. And even in those rare cases where the press is reasonably free, there are other ways the regimes in power may curb adverse publicity. In Kenya, for example, the two main newspapers in the country--The Daily Nation and The Standard--now practice self-censorship. In view of their prior experience, this is understandable. The government has often rebuked editors and owners of these newspapers, albeit privately, whenever it believed the papers had over-stepped their bounds. Often these rebukes degenerated into intimidation. The Managing Editor of The Daily Nation was once arrested and kept in custody for thirty-six hours for reporting what had been said openly in the national legislature. When The Standard once published an article critical of the Vice-Chancellor of the University of Nairobi, whose removal had been demanded by some of the students, its editor received a telephone call from a low level bureaucrat in the President's office. When he asserted his rights under the freedom of the press provisions of the Constitution, he was simply told, "you will be hearing from Special Branch (Kenya's KGB)." In less than half an hour, he received a telephone call from the Minister of Home Affairs instructing him to put an end to publication of stories on the Vice-Chancellor. The order was followed.

News media criticisms of government, especially when touching upon sensitive areas like corruption, tribalism, and nepotism, are not only rare and indirect but often almost apologetic in tone. In Nigeria, in August, 1973, a journalist reported on a threatened strike against the wishes of the authorities. His head was shaved and he was flogged at the police station for embarrassing the Governor. And nothing was done about it, either by the federal authorities or by the national press association. In Tanzania, where

the government controls the media totally, persons
imprisoned under preventive detention are so
thoroughly discredited, that those who may be
friendly with such persons or thinking in the same
terms dare not show much interest in the fate of
those under detention. Rumors of networks of
informers, the omnipresent security system, and
the overall climate of fear are sufficient to intimidate anyone inclined to oppose the regime in
power, even if his intentions are perfectly
honorable and constructive. They find it wiser
to keep their heads down than to raise them and
face the risk of retribution.

In this regard, the regimes in power find it
much easier to handle the non-Africans, many of
whom are aliens or have been stripped of their
citizenship. They can be easily silenced by
statements emanating from ministers or other
officers, while the head of the state maintains
his international image by continuing to make
moderate statements. On the island of Zanzibar,
between 1964 and 1970, President Abeid Amani
Karume had taken various drastic measures directed
against the island's Arab, Indian, and European
minorities. A number of Zanzibarians had, as a
result, left the islands or failed to return.
The rest, too, would have been only too glad to
leave if they had been allowed to take their
assets with them, even to the Tanganyikan mainland. In 1970, President Karume successfully
proposed legislation requiring all non-Africans
whose children had left Zanzibar, under threat of
imprisonment, either to recall their children or
to pay compensation to the government for expenses incurred by it in educating them since child-
hood. Similarly, if a non-African girl wished
to leave Zanzibar to marry a person resident
elsewhere, she could obtain an exit permit only
by paying the government a sum of $8,000 repre-
senting the estimated value of free education,
medical benefits, and social services received
by her while residing in Zanzibar. In a country
where the per capita income was less than $400
a year, this was a major sum and many non-African

girls were, as a result, virtual prisoners on the island. Simultaneously, Karume constantly spoke of integration--which to him meant marriage, voluntary or involuntary, of young non-African girls with Africans both young and old, while President Nyerere maintained total silence.

The threat that discriminatory legislation may be enforced against them makes non-Africans scrupulous in avoiding all statement and actions that could possibly be interpreted as a criticism of those in power. In 1971, while on a visit to the mainland, President Karume told a large crowd of Africans that only those with one African parent should be allowed to become or remain Tanzanian citizens. The statement made non-Africans residing in Tanzania shudder in utter disbelief and when there was no immediate denial of its validity from President Nyerere, many of them became suspicious of the future intentions of the Tanzanian government. In such an environment of perpetual insecurity, speaking out, openly and candidly, against the political crimes of those in power is understandably the farthest thing from the minds of non-Africans.

Hounding Into Exile

All African states reserve the right to deport non-citizens, regardless of whether they have only recently entered the country or were born and resided there all of their lives. For any government to exercise this power is a comparatively simple matter. In most cases, all that is required is the issue of an order by the President or other appropriate authority requiring a named individual to leave the country within a specified period (usually short), on the ground that his presence in the country is not conducive to national interests. The total number of such expulsions may not be large, but the mere fact that actions can and are taken against non-citizens is in itself sufficient to make all such persons think twice before opposing (or giving assistance to anyone opposing) the regime in

power. As has been observed elsewhere in this book
such expulsion orders have been made in Malawi,
Tanzania, Sierra Leone, and a number of other African countries. Kenya is known to have deported a
few non-Africans who were even its own citizens.
In Ghana, a non-African lawyer who had been
practicing there for over sixteen years was
summarily deported on the ground that his presence in the country was not "conducive to the
good of Ghana," because he had been willing to
defend those who were prosecuted by the government for criticizing leading officials. Similar
instances have also taken place in other African
countries, with the result that non-African
lawyers have had to refuse cases or refrain
from pressing a particular action lest they
themselves become the objects of government retaliation. In Kenya, for example, it is virtually
impossible to find a lawyer who would be willing
to accept citizenship cases against the government.

Such use of powers of expulsion has not been
limited to non-Africans and non-citizens. In
Malawi, for example, all members of Jehovah's
Witnesses were ordered to leave the country.
Dr. Banda even declared the property of the
Watchtower Society and the personal properties of
the leader of the Witnesses "subject to forfeiture," i.e., taken over by the government as state
property. The organization, according to Dr.
Banda, had "acted and has been acting in a manner
prejudicial to the safety of the state and subversive to the authority of the lawfully established government." The main "crimes" committed
by the Witnesses were their refusal to swear
personal allegiance to the life-time President of
Malawi, to become members of the Malawi Congress
Party, and to carry party identification cards.

What is of even greater significance in
contemporary Africa is the extent of voluntary
exile. It is never an easy decision for a person
to leave the country of his birth and residence,
especially if he has to leave all assets behind

and is uncertain of where he is going to go and
what he is going to do. And, yet thousands of
Africans and non-Africans have left their countries or have been hounded out. These were not
decisions taken by them without prolonged deliberations. They, perhaps more than others outside, were better able to judge whether it would
be worth their while to dig in and fight against
the evils being committed by those in power.
Each refugee is, in fact, a vote against and a
reflection of the way the new African states are
being governed.

The list of African countries that are
responsible for aggravating the world-wide
refugee problem is not much shorter than the list
of African countries represented in the United
Nations. There are literally thousands of
Ugandan African refugees residing in Kenya,
Tanzania, England, and the United States; of
Nigerians (mainly Ibos) residing in the United
States, Britain, and Ivory Coast; of Kenyans
(especially Luos) residing in Tanzania and the
United States. The list could be lengthened.
The total number of Africans and non-Africans
who have gone into exile voluntarily as a result
of the reign of terror and intimidation and the
political use of physical, economic, and
psychological violence during the post-independence period will never be known. But it is
not a small figure.

Cultural Nationalism

The culture of any African state can be said
to have passed through three periods--one, before
the coming of the Europeans and the establishment
of colonial rule when each tribe had its own distinct cohesive culture; two, the colonial rule
when the Africans, in varying degrees, absorbed
(or were made to absorb) Western cultural influences; and three, the post-independence era in
which leaders of many African states have, in
their search for "total" or "genuine" self-
determination, sought to develop a distinctive

139

national culture as a component of national identity or consciousness. In most, such attempts have also been tied to their search for economic independence. Invariably, the government or those in power have sought to play an active role in the creation (or discovery) and dissemination of this national culture and have even set up special governmental agencies and programs for the purpose. Before going any further, we shall briefly describe measures taken in a few new African states for developing this national identity and culture.

Zaire: In an effort to create among the people of Zaire a feeling of national pride and dignity, and to promote their economic well-being, President Mobutu has formulated and utilized the concept of "Authenticity." One of the best expositions of the concept is contained in a lengthy speech made by him before the United Nations. According to him:

It (Authenticity) is a dictate of conscience for the people of Zaire that they should return to their beginnings and search for the values of their ancestors in order to appreciate those who contribute to the country's harmonious and natural development. It is the refusal of the people of Zaire to blindly espouse imported ideologies. It is the affirmation of a man of Zaire or man himself, as he is and where he is, with the mental and social structures that are his own.... A return to authenticity is not narrow nationalism, a blind return to the past. On the contrary, it is a useful instrument for peace among nations, a condition for existence among peoples, a platform on which cooperation of states can be built. For authenticity not only implies a profound knowledge of one's own culture but also a respect for the cultural heritage of others....

To perpetuate the exploitation of the black

by the white, the colonizers set about
destroying African traditions, the African
language, African culture--in a word, bruta-
lizing the black so that he could not speak,
think, eat, dress, laugh, or breathe except
by following the teachings of the white.[37]

This statement is not mere rhetoric. When one
examines the various actions taken by President
Mobutu in the name of "Authenticity," there
emerges a fairly sophisticated pattern designed to
achieve concrete objectives.

In its initial stage, the concept was invoked
to replace European names with indigenous ones.
The name of the state itself was changed from the
Democratic Republic of the Congo to the Republic
of Zaire, a word which was believed to have its
origin in the local Bakongo language, meaning
"the river that swallows all others." The longest
river in the country, the Congo River, was renamed
the Zaire River. The highest mountain, Mount
Stanley, commemorating the historically renowned
American explorer, Henry Morton Stanley, was
renamed Mount Ngaliema. The two long lakes called
Lake Albert and Lake Edward were renamed Lake
Mobutu Sese Seko and Lake Idi Amin Dada respectively in order to "decolonize the minds of the
people of Zaire and Uganda and to restore dignity
to our countries."[38] All the provinces in the
country were given new authentic names. All
streets, squares, parks, and other public places
bearing European names or associated with European history or civilization were renamed. Those
public places or monuments that could not be
renamed without distorting the meaning were removed or destroyed, e.g. monuments erected in
honor of World War II veterans and statues of
King Leopold II and Henry Morton Stanley ("a
tractor was driven up the hill; a rope was thrown
around the neck of the statue and then the tractor
started downhill, snapping the figure off at the
ankles").[39]

In early 1972, President Mobutu de-Westernized his own name by changing it from Desire-Joseph Mobutu to Mobutu Sese Kuku Ngbendi wa za Banga, meaning "the earth, the warrior, who is peppery, who is all powerful, who blazes a trail, and who goes from conquest to conquest without anything or anyone being able to stop him." He advised all Zairians to follow his example and change their imported names as well. Almost immediately members of his cabinet and other high level government officers took his advice. For example, the Minister of Commerce, M. Jean Baptiste Alves, changed his name to Jean-Baptiste Lanza; Foreign Minister M. Marion Cardosa changed his to Batwanyele Losembe, and Minister of Agriculture M. Pierre Andre to Pierre Kaynga. A few months later, all Zairians having foreign first or last names were required by law to adopt authentic names. All mulattoes born of indigenous mothers and non-African fathers were required to adopt their mothers' last names. All government employees were informed that any employee who insisted on keeping his European name would lose his job. Indigenous priests and nuns in the country, numbering over 60,000 were required to adopt authentic names. If they failed to do so, they could be deprived of their Zairian citizenship and expelled from the country. All new born babies were to be given authentic names, and for any priest to refuse to give such names at the time of baptism was made a criminal offense. All newspapers in the country changed their names, even before they were required by the government to do so. Le Progress became Salongo, La Tribune Africaine was reborn as Elombe, Le Courrier d'Afrique as Elima, and L'Etoile as Myoto. Even the Ecumenical Calendar came under scrutiny: under a new law, Christmas was to be celebrated on June 24, the date on which the country's new and "authentic" constitution was introduced by President Mobutu.

As the campaign for "Authenticity" became more intense, mere symbolic change was regarded as insufficient. It was believed that the attitudes of the people had to be changed so that instead of frowning upon or ignoring traditional customs and practices they would look upon these with a certain degree of respect and take pride in them. For this purpose, religion, education, and even personal behavior had to be changed. It was declared that the purpose of the Catholic Church should be to "rehabilitate our ancestral belief in a supreme being" and that this function could be best performed only by authentic (meaning African) Zairians.[40] In the course of time, the President ordered Zairianization of the clergy, closed down the Pope John XXIII Seminary, expelled a number of non-African Catholic missionaries, suspended the publication, sale, distribution, and possession of thirty-one religious publications, barred a well-known Catholic weekly from entering the country, and subjected to ridicule and contempt the African Roman Catholic Archbishop of Kinshasa who had written an article critical of some aspects of the authenticity campaign.

The educational system, based mainly on what had been inherited from the former colonial power, was held inadequate. The European languages, used in the schools as media of instruction, were held incapable of "penetrating deeply into the minds of Zairians." Indigenous languages were to be used instead, even though none of these had a vocabulary adequate for teaching science and mathematics. The substantive content of courses in social sciences were revamped to emphasize Zairian history and culture. And, to assure faithful implementation of the edicts, all Catholic universities were brought under government control. In matters of personal dress and behavior, too, emphasis was placed on de-Westernization. Kissing in public, wearing miniskirts, and putting on wigs were made unlawful, as was the wearing of neckties.

The national political system had to be based on authenticity. In its name, President Mobutu managed to centralize all power in his own hands. Through a constitutional amendment, the

143

Mouvement Populaire de la Revolution (MPR),
headed by President Mobutu, was declared the
supreme political authority in the country. All
other political parties were made illegal. Every
Zairian upon birth automatically became a member
of the MPR. All interest groups, including youth
organizations, women's groups, and trade unions,
must be affiliated with and remain subordinate to
the Party. Its overwhelmingly dominant position
was justified on the basis of authenticity:

> The notion of political partisanship is
> foreign to Zaire and even to all of Africa.
> It is a system which was imported (from
> abroad) and which no doubt has justification
> for existence in other countries, but not
> in ours.[41]

On November 30, 1973 President Mobutu declared that political independence was not enough
and that time had come for "the Zaire citizen to
become owner of the grounds of his ancestors."[42]
This led to nationalization of foreign-owned
mining companies, and at least partial nationalization of those that were too large or complex for
the government to operate. A little later, the
President said, "All plantations, ranches, farms,
and quarries must rightfully revert to Zairians."[43]
This led to the expropriation of all foreign
planters and large farmers, who had provided
most of Zaire's exports of tea and coffee. Ancestral rivers, roads, and airspace must be used for
the benefit of authentic Zairians. Foreigners
(a term that was interpreted in terms of race
rather than citizenship) involved in transportation
business were forbidden to continue their operations and required to sell to authentic Zairians
(as has been observed earlier, only a small group
of Zairians actually benefited economically
from such exercises), within a specified period,
at a price fixed by the government. And, a little
later, the campaign to place foreign-owned enterprises in the hands of Zairians was extended to
industries and to all small businesses and services,
many of which were run by Italians, Greeks, Portu-

144

guese, Pakistanis, and the Lebanese.

The concept of "authenticity," left deliberately vague and flexible, has enabled President Mobutu to entrench his own position and increase his popularity, at least for the time being. Its trumpet is played almost unceasingly over the state-controlled television and radio stations. Its capacity to marshall a powerful emotive response from Zaire's diverse population is not easy to question. In fact, according to Victor D. Du Bois, to be caught up in the campaign and to be a part of it is "at once an exhilarating and unforgettable experience."

Chad: Chad's policies of Chaditude are not unlike those of Zaire. Between 1972 and 1974, the name of its capital was changed from Fort Lamy to N'Djamena meaning city at peace or calm following colonial domination. It also means "leave us alone." Street names were also changed. President Tombalbaye changed his own Christian name Francois to N'Garta and required all people having Western names to "Chadianise" their names. The whole European way of life came under heavy attack.

Not unlike President Mobutu's suppression of the church and establishment of Mobutuism as a virtual state religion, President Tombalbaye's strategy was to force people into being initiated according to Yondo rites. Historically, Yondo is an initiation ritual that gave the Sara tribe cohesion and enthusiasm in the struggle against its enemies. In the seventies, in practice it meant circumcision for all adult men (and clitoridectomy for women) followed by a period of residence in villages under primitive conditions. A number of people who refused to participate in these rituals, or who insisted on continuing to attend Western religious churches were shot, buried alive, or put to death in other excruciating ways. According to one well-authenticated report, in one area where people had refused to submit to the rites, armed men surrounded all the churches

145

in the area, broke into them during Sunday service, took out all the adult men, and killed them.

Through the use of witchcraft, hypnotism, drugs, and practices such as circumcision, African leaders can easily convert traditional religion into a profoundly anti-Western weapon, especially when directed against the Catholics who are required to live exclusively within the framework of a religion that is based on Western culture, history, and civilization and use it to divert the attention of the people from some of their real and immediate problems.

For President Tombalbaye, returning to ancestral initiation practices had another useful purpose. His regime was embroiled in a civil war against the FROLINAT in Northern Provinces (occupied mainly by Muslims) and a newly formed Democratic Movement for the Chadian Revolution in the Southern Provinces. The President himself belonged to the Sara tribe; the initiation ceremonies were intended to mobilize the Saras behind the chief of state, and also to incorporate others into this community. It was hoped that the result would be to strengthen President Tombalbaye in his position of authority by increasing his clientele and by whipping up popular enthusiasm for opposing the Muslim rebels in the north. In fact, similar oath-taking ceremonies took place among the Kikuyus in Kenya whenever the position of President Jomo Kenyatta seemed to be in some danger.

Zambia: Britain had agreed to give independence to Zambia (Northern Rhodesia) only after the African nationalist leaders had all agreed and promised that in operating the new state they would be guided by tenets of equality and non-discrimination. This was particularly important to the large number of Europeans and Asians who had settled in the country and who hoped to continue living there after independence. Within less than a decade, however, the new state embarked upon a program of cultural nationalism which, both in tone and substance, constituted an attack on Western culture and, at least indirectly, upon non-African residents in the country. It all started in October, 1966, with the drive to change the names of streets and hotels. Any name which was even remotely associated with colonialism had to be changed.

In time, this was followed by efforts to make the people take an exaggerated pride in Zambian culture. President Kaunda took to wearing a Ghanaian toga and Vice-President Kapwepwe designed a black "Chilenge Shirt." Zambians were expected to wear these new types of clothing. The government-controlled radio and television programs emphasized "Zambian" music, dance, and theatre to the virtual exclusion of all other material. Mixed marriages were frowned upon. The wearing of miniskirts, wigs, jeans, and tight trousers was condemned, as was the use of cosmetics. African womanhood and African civilization had to be protected from the degenerative influences of Western culture. Those Zambians who had married non-African wives ("toothless bulldogs") were told that "our culture in matters of dress is not to go naked."[44] Members of the UNIP's Youth Brigade took it upon themselves to force women to lengthen their dresses. There was almost a reign of terror, especially in the Copperbelt area (where most of the non-Africans lived), directed against those Africans who had straightened their hair. "They were hunted in the beerhalls, at public meetings and at football matches. Whenever and wherever they were found their hair was cut short by youths armed with scissors."[45] Those who objected to these practices, claiming that in a free society people had the right to dress as they pleased, were castigated as "reactionary revisionists of our Humanism, and a cancer or ulcer to Zambia."[46]

President Kaunda and other UNIP leaders not only allowed such practices to continue, but at times even encouraged them, because they served two useful purposes. One purpose was to strengthen

147

UNIP's base of support. Each tribe in Zambia had
its own distinct culture. And the right of each
to exist in a multi-tribal society was acknow-
ledged, at least in principle. Yet, when it
came to the question of selecting components
of a Zambian national culture, it was usually the
culture of the tribes supporting the UNIP that won
out. It was their languages, their songs, and
their folkstories that were broadcast regularly
over Zambian radio. In this new "Zambian" culture,
not only did Western elements have little place,
but neither did the culture of other tribes,
especially those that did not go along with the
regime in power. A second benefit of such
activity was that it provided a convenient out-
let for the excess zeal and energy of young
adherents of UNIP, and directed their attention
away from other government and party operations.

Tanzania: On the island of Zanzibar, the
creation of a national culture involved efforts
to bring about racial assimilation. The Arabs,
who were the largest minority there, were fairly
well integrated with the Africans in the socio-
logical sense. They spoke the same language
(in fact twenty-five per cent of Swahili words
are of Arabic origin), professed the same religion, prayed in the same mosques, and celebrated
the same religious festivals. There was even
considerable social inter-action and inter-
marriage between the two groups. The new African government leaders, however, wanted to make
the minorities assimilate completely with the
Africans. For this purpose, many minority individuals were forced to attend African folk
festivals, to go into villages and do manual
work with the Africans, to speak only Swahili,
and to wear African dress.

But to President Karume of Zanzibar this was
not enough. In 1970, he told a mass rally that
he wanted the people of Zanzibar to be "genuinely"
integrated, to him this meant racial assimilation,
especially mixed marriages or interaction between
African males and non-African females. He declared

(tantamount to law on the island) that all persons who hinder the implementation of mixed marriages on the island would be deported and their passports confiscated. Although he already had four wives, Karume approached some Iranian families with the proposal to marry one of their daughters. When rebuffed, he forced six Iranian girls to marry members of his own Afro-Shirazi Party. The marriages were celebrated against the wishes of the brides and their parents. When the parents objected, a number of them were placed in jail. The age differentials between the brides and the husbands were, in some cases, as much as fifty years.

The pictures of the brides, ranging in age from fourteen to twenty-two, were smuggled out of the country, and appeared in some London newspapers. Complaints to the United Nations, President Nyerere, and other international organizations by the relatives of the girls made little difference. Six teenage Asian girls are known to have committed suicide in circumstances which involved their being forced to "marry" African politicians. A number fled to Tanganyika in dark hours of the night in small boats, often pursued by and facing arrest, or much worse, by Zanzibar's naval patrol boats. In 1972, one author had occasion to meet a fisherman who claimed that he had helped at least thirty Arab and Asian girls escape in this manner, at considerable risk to his own life.

In mainland Tanzania, cultural nationalism has taken forms similar to those in neighboring Zambia, like the harrassment of girls wearing miniskirts or jeans, called "Operation Vijana." But what some Tanganyikan politicians had in mind was not much different from the kind of assimilation and the creation of "national" culture that President Karume had advocated. An article appearing in Daily News of Tanzania (a state-controlled newspaper) on September 13, 1972, for example, contained the following:

"It's time for 'Operation Tit for Tat'....
Some of them (the Asians) have taken out

149

token (or is it paper) citizenship to safeguard their interest and no more! This is
the time for stock-taking. ....Maybe Amin
was wrong in some ways but looked at from the
right perspective, he should be more right
than wrong.

How many Asian women are married by Africans
in East Africa: are they up to 10 (excluding the so-called forced marriages and any
other in Zanzibar)? How many Asian unmarried
women have illegitimate children from
African men? And how many African women
have illegitimate children from Asian men?
These are by-products of promiscuous friendship. They hate us yet want our women!
And how many young African men have girl
friends or finances (sic) of Asian origin
and vice versa?

I pause for an answer.....

For those who may think I am being extremist
or racialistic, here is a challenge. There
is a dance every Saturday night at Forodhani
Hotel, Dar. Let them come there next Saturday with their wives/husbands, boy or girl
friends of the opposite race (Asians or
Africans). I will be there to take stock.
Let us make a start..."[47]

Such tirades did little to enhance African culture,
but did provide some psychological satisfaction
to the Africans at having humiliated the non-
Africans. And toleration of such activities by
the regime in power helped divert the attention
of the people from some of their own problems
created, at least partly, by the government
leaders themselves.

The fact that leaders of African states
channel the quest for a national culture so as to
benefit their own clienteles and to divert the
attention of the common man from government wrongdoing is not surprising. Of course, governments

have greater potential today than ever before for shaping their citizens' perceptions. According to C. Wright Mills, men "in their everyday life do not experience a world of solid fact; their experience itself is selected by stereotyped meanings and shaped by ready-made interpretations. Their images of the world, and of themselves, are given to them by crowds of witnesses they have never met and never shall meet."[48]Every man observes, interprets and reports; but the terms of his reports "are much more likely than not the phrases and images of other people which he has taken over as his own."[49] In fact, with the expansion of the mass media, "every man is increasingly dependent upon the observation posts, the interpretation centres, and the presentation depots," or what he calls The Cultural Apparatus that is established in every society. Mills contends further that this "Cultural Apparatus, no matter how internally free, tends in every nation to become a close adjunct of national authority and a leading agency of national propaganda."[50]

Nowhere in Africa today is the Cultural Apparatus internally free. It is usually controlled by the regime in power. It is the regime that decides to promote a particular form or aspect of culture, provides the necessary funds, allows the use of government buildings or parks, and hires the artists and the musicians. It also controls the media. In national broadcasts, government newsletters, official ceremonies, and on other such occasions, those in power determine the substance of national culture and how it is to be disseminated to the public. The function of cultural nationalism in Africa is to justify the positions and policies of those who are in power.

Negritude, Pan-Africanism, and African Socialism

European colonization of virtually the whole continent and the resentments it created fostered a sense of Pan-African identity among educated

151

Africans. The economic and social practices of the colonialists resulted not only in widespread demands for self-determination but also in assertions on the part of some Africans that there exists a unique continent-wide African culture, transcending the artificial territorial boundaries.

To find elements of culture common among the peoples of such a vast and diverse continent has, of course, not been easy. But once one assumes that such a culture exists, it is not difficult to claim that all states and all peoples sharing this culture are obliged to support it actively and create conditions for its further development, dissemination, and flowering. Independent African states must help in the liberation of the rest of Africa so that those who are still in the clutches of the European colonialists, neo-colonialists, and racists can share this unique African culture. Those Africans who, voluntarily or involuntarily, have moved away from the continent must be marshalled so that they too can participate in and contribute to this culture. The newly independent states must improve political, economic, and social collaboration among themselves in order to facilitate the sharing and development of African culture; and African political leaders must be encouraged to incorporate pan-African ideals in their official ideologies.

We have neither the intention nor the space to deal with these complex objectives, each of which raises several fundamental issues. What is important, for present purposes, is that the use of Pan-African ideology can bolster the domestic political positions of incumbent political leaders. In particular, it serves to divert attention of the people of those states from some of the regimes' own misdoings and policy failures.

Although Aime Césaire formulated the concept of Negritude, its fullest elaboration came from Leopold Senghor, the President of Senegal. It was partly a reaction against the French policy of assimilation. In Senghor's own words, "We could assimilate mathematics or the French language, but we could never strip off our black skins nor root out our black souls. So we set out on a fervent quest for the Holy Grail, which was our Collective Soul. And we came upon it...."[51] According to him, "Negritude is the whole complex of civilized values--cultural, economic, social, and political-- which characterize the black peoples, or, more precisely the Negro-African world."[52] He described in general terms an Africa in which ancestors are revered, in which the extended family forms the nucleus, in which there are strong links between generations, with ties to God, and in which there is a hierarchy of family, clan, and tribe. But to him, the basic African culture was symbolized by and expressed in emotionalism and heightened sensibility of the Africans as against the rationalism of the Europeans.

The concept, at best, is ambiguous. Moreover, as Dr. K. A. Busia of Ghana has correctly pointed out, strong emotional quality and heightened sensibility are not necessarily common to all Negro Africans. Whatever the case may be, the doctrines of Négritude made leaders like Dr. Senghor very popular with educated blacks in former French Africa. Négritude emphasized the dignity of persons of Negro African descent and the intrinsic worth of African customs and ways of thinking. This was a welcome message for Africans who felt that though they had absorbed French language, culture, and civilization, they were somehow inferior to those having white skins. Négritude's implicit rejection of non-whites and of western culture was also an asset, rather than a liability, from this point of view.

By contrast, the national leaders of former British colonies, recognized that not all persons residing on the continent of Africa were Negroes (especially those in North Africa). They therefore spoke in terms of a more inclusive Pan-Africanism, or a form of continental unity which they saw as a potent weapon against the forces of neo-colonialism and imperialism. The Panafricanists, too, assumed essential unity of culture among the peoples of the African continent. Most of their writings, therefore, emphasized cooperation among all independent countries of the continent to foster their common culture. And often this too was couched in anti-Western terms. One representative writer declared that Panafricanism is:

> a question of affirming our "Africanity," that is to say our personality, without attempting to dress it up in Western or Eastern costume. What must be constructed harmoniously and rapidly is an Africa that is authentically African. Africa has her own needs, concepts, and customs. She does not seek to deck herself out in borrowed clothing that does not fit.[53]

Other African intellectuals emphasized different but related themes: "African unity is no more a goal in itself than was independence. It simply is a means of development, of a force of inter-African cooperation. It is indispensable because of the unjust nature of the relationship between the underdeveloped African nations and the economically strong nations."[54] A further argument for unity among all independent African states is that this would make possible more effective action against the white racist regimes of southern Africa.

Based on these ideas, institutions like the Organization of African Unity, the African Development Bank and others have been established to promote political, economic, and social cooperation, unity, and solidarity among the African states. In a continent bedevilled by disunity, racial diversity, existence of various linguistic groups, lack of efficient transportation and communication, and the impact of different foreign cultures on different parts of the continent (including the more recent struggle for influence by the great powers), such cooperation has rarely been easy.

Nevertheless, the organizations and the rhetoric of African unity can be used to one's domestic political advantage. Political philosophy of pan-Africanism is highly persuasive. African leaders have found it relatively easy to generate mass enthusiasm by depicting an eventual United States of Africa in utopian terms. The pan-African ideology is also a convenient mechanism for increasing dissatisfaction against non-Africans residing within a state. And, perhaps more importantly, it is a useful weapon for simple political survival. By taking a militant pan-Africanist stance and promising a rosy future, a national leader can easily brand those within his state who oppose his politics and practices as anti-pan-Africanist. Opposition to any African leader who is already in power and who makes the appropriate pan-Africanist noises is often characterized as treason not only against that particular state but also against the whole of Africa. When looked at from this perspective, declarations by President Amin of Uganda, or Emperor Bokassa of Central African Empire, or President Karume of Zanzibar of willingness to make whatever sacrifices necessary to fight white racism in Southern Africa, to be the first to volunteer to send troops and equipment to the front, or to lay their lives on the line for the liberation of every inch of the continent look suspiciously like self-serving propaganda.

The same is true with regard to the ideology of African Socialism that most African leaders claim to espouse. In their view, capitalism was unacceptable because of its association with the European colonial powers; Communism, though some of its elements did seem appealing, might mean becoming satellites of the East; acceptance of European socialism could be interpreted as continued reliance on the Europeans. What was needed, therefore, was an ideology that could be portrayed as unique to the Africans, which is or can be said to be based on African traditions,

155

and which can rationalize or justify the kind of
politics that we have described in the preceding
pages. African Socialism apparently comes nearest
to meeting these requirements. It is a flexible
term which can be given different content by
different regimes. As the accompanying extract
clearly demonstrates, there was little agreement
among the African leaders as early as 1963 on
the meaning and scope of the term African Socialism. The situation has changed little since then.

Widely different countries like Tanzania and
Kenya both claim to be following the ideology of
African Socialism. In Tanzania, African Socialism
(rooted, of course, in African traditions as
claimed by the Mwalimu himself) resulted in nationalization of foreign-owned factories and plantations and the establishment of state corporations.
Similarly, rural plantations were nationalized
and converted into "Ujamaa" villages in the name
of African Socialism. In neighboring Kenya, a
government statement issued in 1965 claimed that
Kenya had adopted the system of African Socialism.
Among the policies that were claimed to be representative of the application of African Socialism
to Kenya were these:

> (8) In promoting Africanization, citizen-
> ship guarantees as outlined in our Consti-
> tution will be recognized and maintained
> but without prejudice to correction of
> existing racial imbalances in various
> sectors of economy;....

> (10) A system of traders' licensing will
> be considered to restrict certain types
> of trade and business to citizens, with
> a deliberate bias, in the case of new
> licences, in favor of African applicants.[55]

These policies reflected racism more than
genuine socialism. But Kenyan leaders chose
nevertheless to call them African Socialism.

Government Intervention in the Economy

In reality, in most African states ideological consistence has always taken second place to economic and cultural nationalism. To most African politicians, bureaucrats, and the military, African Socialism was simply a useful tool. In most cases, if there were any persons who genuinely believed in implementing socialism and planning how such policies could benefit the people as a whole, these were expatriate advisors from either the socialist countries of the East or leftist-leaning Western Europeans and Americans. To the Africans, socialism simply provided a convenient mechanism for direct or indirect expropriation of the properties of non-Africans. In those African states that defined African Socialism in quasi-Marxist terms, this was achieved through policies and practices designed to increase state participation and control over national economies. In others, like Kenya, which eschew Marxist rhetoric, expropriation was achieved through the use of ingenious, imaginative, even devious techniques of indirect seizure.

There were differences in strategy and techniques, in timing and intensity; but with rare exceptions like Ivory Coast, the results were basically the same--depriving the non-Africans of the use and enjoyment of their properties and transferring or operating these to the benefit of those African politicians, bureaucrats, and military who were in power and/or of members of their clienteles. As R. H. Jackson has perceptively noted:

"In sofar as ideology plays any important role in African politics, it is utilized by leading sectors of the political class to define the relationship of the entire country to such external groups as foreign powers or foreign business firms. In this way the ideology of....'African Socialism' is employed by political leaders and sometimes also by intellectuals to define their entire

157

country, or even tropical Africa as a whole, as an exploited class in relation to the developed world within an international system of social stratification. In this way the political class <u>attempts to mask</u> its own very striking privileges within the society it rules....these (nationalized) assets are not collectively owned so much as they are appropriated by individuals, factions and elites within the political class to be used for their own benefit or to be allocated to their followers."[56]

The Non-Africans as an Economic Resource

All the protections and safeguards that were or could have been made available to non-African minorities through democratic political structures and processes were rendered inoperative within a few years of independence. These included fundamental rights guaranteed under the constitutions, separation of powers, an impartial and independent judiciary, a non-political bureaucracy, and freedom of the press and organization. These, coupled with the introduction of single party systems or military regimes and arbitrary, if not cavalier, application of citizenship laws, resulted in almost total exclusion of the non-Africans from the formal politics of virtually all black African states.

Their participation in the informal politics of tribalism and corruption was also limited. They did not, and indeed could not, form the kind of clientele that is so crucial in African politics. African tribes not in power at a particular time could hope, at least, for political change of benefit to them. But this was not the case with non-Africans. Their racial and cultural differences placed them permanently beyond the pale. With each change in government, a new set of African leaders came into power with their respective clienteles and proceeded to govern in the same way as their predecessors. Such changes made little difference in the status of the non-Africans.

Criticism or condemnation of non-Africans is a convenient propaganda tool with which to mask the privileges and benefits being reaped by those in power. It is also a ready explanation for all the problems of the new state. New leaders, like the old ones, are unlikely to omit taking advantage of such an excellent opportunity. Non-African support is not necessary for continued maintenance of anyone in power. On the contrary, it might mean the kiss of death.

The principal role of non-Africans in the informal politics of tribalism and corruption is to satisfy the increasing demands for material and other benefits by those in power. Every Christmas in Freetown, Sierra Leone, African members of the legislature, city council, civil service, and some cabinet members make rounds of major non-African stores to collect their Christmas "gifts." In Malawi, the Asian residents were expected to make substantial contributions to the funds of the Malawi Congress Party at frequent intervals. Refusal or even a show of reluctance to make such contributions was sufficient to invite retaliation. In Kenya, a few rich Indians are known to have been milked by the KANU and KADU leaders. In Tanzania, especially in the rural areas "donations" were extracted from non-Africans on a regular basis by the regional officers of TANU. And one can easily add a number of other such examples to this list.

Through selective enforcement of laws, considerable sums of money may be extracted from non-Africans. Each piece of restrictive legislation, in fact, serves a dual purpose. It enables the Africans to reward their own at the expense of the non-Africans. But it also enables the African politicians or bureaucrats to extract a price from the non-Africans for using their influence to have any particular regulation or restriction made inapplicable to an individual or

159

a group of non-Africans. Non-Africans may also pay an official handsomely to mitigate the impact on them of discriminatory regulations. A non-African non-citizen applying for renewal of a trading licence, for example, has to choose between closing his operations and paying a price for continuing, even for a short period. He will generally opt for the latter. In fact, he has little real alternative. On the other hand, he can never be certain that the discretionary powers will be exercised in his favor even after he has paid the demanded price. In Kenya, a number of Asian traders are known to have paid substantial sums of money only to be refused renewal of licences once the payments had been made. In Sierra Leone, certain politicians are known to have extracted large sums of money from Lebanese businessmen in return for using their influence to remove the names of these business-men from a secret list of persons to be expelled from the country. In fact, there was no such list. And in Zambia, at least two Asians are known to have paid as much as $10,000 each to have their citizenship papers processed, only to find that they were unacceptable as Zambian citizens by the new African government.

Time and again, one of the authors has heard non-African businessmen, both in East and West Africa, complaining that over time the demands being made upon them are becoming more and more onerous. As one of them put it, "their appetites have been increasing day by day, and often, they are almost insatiable." There is little sense of balance, and, as indicated earlier, each African leader has to maintain his high standard of living, cultivate his clientele, and prepare for the day when he may no longer occupy public office. As a Kenyan Luo told one author, Presi-dent Kenyatta and other Kikuyus have no compunc-tion in extracting an additional suit from an Asian retailer (whether he can afford it or not) even if they already have a thousand of their own. This businessman's dislike of the Kikuyu was ob-vious, but he could as well have been talking

160

about other countries and leaders of Africa.

Through their limited role in the politics
of corruption and nepotism, non-Africans residing
in African countries do, of course, gain some
advantages--a decision delayed, a license renewed,
a specific legal requirement waived, etc. But in
the long run they continue to remain consumable
items, sources of material and other benefits, to
be exploited by whichever tribe or groups of tribes
acquire control over the machinery of state.
Their usefulness to those in authority lasts only
as long as they can accommodate the ever-increasing
demands. Once they become poor, their usefulness
is gone, and they can be discarded with impunity.

Such a situation may be perfectly acceptable
to those who enter Africa as transients, and who
know that eventually they will return to their
homelands. But it is certainly not likely to
engender much confidence in those who have made
Africa their homes, those whose children are
growing in that environment, and those who may be
reinvesting all their savings in businesses and
other interests in the countries of their residence. Quite possibly, these people might have
been willing to cooperate in some redistribution
of wealth, if they had reason to believe that
this would serve a public need. But, as was
made clear in the preceding pages, this is not
the case. They might even have been willing to
suffer a measure of economic loss, if there were
other compensating factors. This, too, is not
the case.

To Africans "total" or "genuine" self-
determination meant not only political and economic decolonization but also cultural and psychological decolonization. As has been explained in
the preceding pages, cultural nationalism in post-
independence Africa (in states as varied as Zaire,
Tanzania, Zambia, and Chad) had two main components, both interconnected and reinforcing each
other. These were (1) emphasis on traditional
African culture, whether real or imagined; and

161

(2) the elimination by group persecution and ridicule of non-African, and especially Western, culture. Statements made by African leaders prior to independence were rife with assertions of their commitment to multiracialism and the advantages of pluralistic societies. However, soon after independence, the political rhetoric changed drastically. Within less than a decade, many African leaders began to talk about national unity and the need for non-Africans to embrace African culture and to behave and live like the majority of the Africans if they wanted to continue to live on and enjoy the fruits of the African soil.

Most non-Africans understood the need to emphasize traditional African culture, if only to redress the balance, but attempts by African leaders to promote traditional culture by ridiculing Western and other cultures were bound to insult most non-Africans. To make matters worse, while the non-Africans were consistently accused of failing to integrate with the Africans, the extent and nature of integration that was expected of these non-Africans was never made clear. Simultaneously, a new arrogance was shaping the conduct of the African professional politicians, bureaucrats, and the military. In Kenya, a number of educated Africans formed the practice of deliberately snubbing the Asians whenever the latter sought to socialize with them (though the same persons had little hesitation in approaching the Asians whenever they needed to borrow money, which, of course, was rarely repaid). In Sierra Leone, the Syrians and the Lebanese were treated in similar, if not worse, fashion.

The African tried to win status, respect, and recognition by humiliating the non-Africans. President Amin's pleasure at being carried for several miles on the shoulders of Englishmen residing in Uganda, however amusing or comical it may have sounded to readers when they first heard of it, was an obvious, if ludicrous, manifestation of this phenomenon. There have been numerous

instances when African heads of state have deliberately kept leaders of non-African communities
waiting for hours before seeing them, despite confirmed appointments, only to dismiss them in a
matter of minutes. African cabinet members have
deliberately behaved the same way toward non-
African businessmen. African bureaucrats (both
in East and West Africa) are known to engage non-
Africans in long discussions whenever they come
for the large number of licences and permits which
they must obtain at regular intervals. During
these discussions, officials make it abundantly
clear who is boss, humiliate the applicants at
every opportunity, making disparaging remarks
about their religious or other cultural practices.
The non-African, knowing he needs a licence or
permit, has little alternative but to remain
pliant, submissive, and exceedingly polite.
Through such devices, the Africans may feel
psychologically decolonized. But non-Africans
must conclude that they are no longer welcome in
countries they have considered home, even if they
are willing to make some economic sacrifices.

The overall quality of life for them deteriorated to such an extent that minimal services
expected of any government (colonial or African)
are not being provided. Africanization and
politicization of the police, the bureaucracy,
the prosecutors, and the judges have resulted in
failure to maintain law and order. Non-African
complaints to the police often go unheeded; if
the police do investigate the commission of a
crime, it is rarely complete and comprehensive.
If the case goes to court, the non-African is
often treated by the prosecutor as if he were the
criminal. In the end, even if there is a conviction, the judges impose a lenient sentence and
blame the criminal act on social conditions and on
the victim's failure to integrate with the Africans.
Increasing incidence of theft, robbery, and
murder in many parts of Africa and the growing
practice among non-Africans (who can afford it) to
hire bodyguards are all evidence of a situation in
which non-Africans feel that their very physical

security is endangered by continuing to live in an independent African state. Many fear to leave their houses at night. They can never be sure that upon returning they will find their automobiles unstolen, or their houses unburgled. Simultaneously, they dare not raise a furor about the way they are treated by the police when they report a crime. A Tanzanian lawyer, Mr. Pardhan, is known to have found himself placed in preventive detention for as long as eighteen months for having made remarks critical of the Tanzanian criminal justice system.

And finally, there is tacit or even outright reverse discrimination. In June, 1972, in a Kenyan town of Nakuru a dance was held to raise funds for the Kenyan Olympic team which was about to leave. The team included a number of field hockey players who were of Asian origin. The organizers of the dance, in an effort to increase the sale of tickets, had invited Mr. Mark Mwithaga, an African member of the Kenyan legislature representing the Nakuru constituency, to attend the dance. While attending the dance, he was asked to say a few words. He spoke for about half an hour concluding his remarks with the following:

Look at the Olympic team today. A Singh here and a Patel there. Even in the East African Car Safari it is all Singhs. I look forward to the day when there will be no more Singhs in the Olympic teams, only Africans.[57]

The net result of economic, political, cultural, and psychological deprivation and humiliation of the non-Africans has been that many of those who had settled in Africa for generations and had made the continent their homes have either fled, been forced out, or are in the process of departure. Their numbers are difficult to document, if only because some of them have been replaced by new immigrants who enter Africa for a specified period and for certain specific tasks with little intention of remaining there once their term has expired.

164

Population statistics measuring the presence of non-Africans in African states before independence and since are imprecise, at best. They understate the number of long-term non-African residents who have been forced out.

For the African common man, the results of the drive for "genuine" self-determination have been equally disappointing. One of the main problems confronted by all African states is the lack of high level and intermediate professional and skilled manpower. The sudden and unceremonious departure in many of these states of professional and semi-professional non-Africans, brought about in the name of Africanization, aggravated these problems. In Kenya, for example, despite its claims of pursuing gradual rather than precipitate Africanization, resignation and/or dismissals of a large number of non-African professionals adversely affected the provision of various services. As has been noted:

> Had Kenya's Ministers made more sincere noises about needing their services more might have stayed. As it was, antagonism drove them away along with the vets, the doctors and dentists and nurses and other professional people. Forty percent of the Government's vets left in a year; one hospital had to advertise in London for nurses; suddenly a town like Nyeri found itself with only one doctor, an Asian, and fifty years' progress dropped away as the only alternative source of medical attention became the missions, as it had been in 1910.... This decamping of professional people went right down to the secretary level.[58]

Some of their places were taken by hastily trained and recruited Africans. Inexperienced and/or unqualified to meet the demands of office, they created bottlenecks in the smooth and efficient provision of the requisite services. Long delays, painfully slow paperwork, and malfunctioning of equipment were the inevitable consequences.

165

Jobs for which no "suitable" Africans could be found were filled by persons hired abroad on contractural terms. In the hope that at least one would demonstrate some ability and acquire sufficient experience to take over from the foreigner at the end of his term, African supernumeraries were also appointed for each of these positions. In consequence the government incurred costs equal to three to four times the salary that had been paid to the former non-African resident professional in return for services which, in most cases, were of distinctly inferior quality. If a government is willing to pay the price, technicians, administrators, and professionals can always be recruited from overseas on temporary assignment. This does not necessarily mean, however, that they will be able to work at optimum efficiency immediately. They may have no experience working in a tropical climate; they may not know the local language; they will need to learn local modes of operation. Often they have little skill in working with antiquated tools and equipment. Their commitment to serving the public, however strong it may be at first, may disappear within a short period. Often, a foreign professional or technician seeks a term of service in Africa to enhance his career objectives once home again. He has little or no interest in how his work will affect others. If he has been made available by another state as part of a foreign technical aid program, his political loyalty does not, of course, lie with the African country. In some cases he may even act as an intelligence agent for his home government.

Thousands of putative expert advisers and consultants can be found today in the ministries, armed forces, education, media, health, and sanitation departments of African governments. Not all of them deserve expert status and many are of limited utility to the new states. And even if they are truly useful, they are unlikely to remain in the country for more than two to four years. Removing the resident non-Africans in the name of

Africanization and replacing them with such
"experts" can hardly lead to the best use of the
resources available to the new states.

M. O. Ijere spells out other costs of hiring
foreign technicians:

> Another problem is connected with the wage and
> salary structure of foreign personnel. The
> latter are usually better paid than their
> African counterparts. They enjoy fringe
> benefits like subsidised housing, free medi-
> cal services, car basic allowance and "bush"
> or "out-of-station" allowance. These add up
> to about one-fifth or one-fourth of the
> salary. Altogether they constitute a heavy
> drain on the economy and saddle it with
> heavy economic burdens difficult to minimize,....
>
> The consumption patterns of foreign pro-
> fessionals have a heavy import content. The
> high income class save more for economic
> development. In the situation under con-
> sideration, the foreign manpower is not
> integrated in the economy. Schemes to re-
> distribute income by-pass him because of the
> numerous "allowances" he enjoys. Savings out
> of their high income are relatively low or
> repatriated and thus their impact on capital
> accumulation is rather minimal, if not nil.[59]

In the name of economic nationalism, the vast
majority of African states have used a variety of
strategies and techniques to Africanize their
economies and have rationalized these through
varying definitions and interpretations of "African Socialism." Some have directly or indirectly
nationalized non-African businesses and replaced
them with state corporations or monopolies, at
least in key sectors of the economy. Others have
introduced licensing and other measures directed
against non-Africans with a view to encourage
African businessmen and entrepreneurs. These
measures, however, appear to have done little to
help the states or the ordinary Africans living

within their borders. Let us look briefly at the
economic impact of these measures.

Nationalization and Expansion of the Public Sector

In ideological terms, such measures can be
readily justified. They can easily be characterized and sold to the people as "a move to the
left," "the common man's charter," "control over
ancestral grounds," or simply as Africans taking
control over their own economies. It can be argued
that the government can solve problems of underdevelopment only if it controls the economy and
major resources. Judicious nationalization could,
conceivably, improve balance of payments, make
possible a broader distribution of the benefits
produced by the enterprises, and permit the government to steer production according to national
priorities. Foreign influence and neo-colonialism
would be dealt a heavy blow, and the profits made
from nationalized enterprises would be reinvested
in the country, according to the desires of national leaders, instead of being squandered or
sent abroad, etc.

The benefits that may theoretically accrue
from nationalization have simply not materialized
in Africa. Lacking the capacity to implement such
policies effectively, some African states have
been forced into joint ventures, or into concluding management contracts with the former
owners of the nationalized industries. In virtually all other cases, establishment of state
corporations has resulted in a reduced level of
production and efficiency, if only in the initial
stages, and there have been difficulties in
marketing the products, especially when foreign
banks and marketing channels were involved.

Such problems are by no means insurmountable.
They can be resolved satisfactorily and effectively provided the country can marshal the services
of dedicated, enthusiastic, efficient, and incor-
ruptible administrative and managerial personnel.

And this is exactly where lies the main problem of socialist-oriented African states. In most cases, appointments of local directors for the newly established state corporations have been made on political grounds. The main outcome has been no more than temporary profits for those placed in charge of the nationalized enterprises and their clienteles.

Ghana's experience in this respect is instructive. While Kwame Nkrumah was in office, Ghana adopted several measures establishing state corporations. In fact, very few of these state monopolies survived more than a few years as viable economic entities. In October, 1965, only ten of over thirty of Dr. Nkrumah's cherished state enterprises were making a profit. The others had accumulated losses running into millions of dollars. When Dr. Nkrumah was deposed in 1966, only three or four enterprises out of the thirty-two investigated by P. C. Garlick were even paying their way. Most had employed members of the governing party led by Dr. Nkrumah, the CPP, and were financially drained by dishonest employees. In 1967, a group of United Nations experts which had visited Ghana to advise the new military government on reorganizing these state enterprises pronounced a harsh judgment, though it made no specific references to corruption and dishonesty among the managerial and administrative personnel of these enterprises.

Historically, such judgments have had little impact. In 1976, the new head of Ghana, General Acheampong, charged that the state corporations had neither made profits for nor had they contributed to the national economy in any other way. On the contrary, according to him, they were a drain on government resources. He complained that the heads of these state corporations paid themselves and members of their staff

fat salaries, bonuses, allowances, and other fringe benefits. Some of the managers have provided for themselves expensive official

169

cars, others have acquired luxury buses
which, apart from taking the staff to
and from their place of work, stand idle
almost the whole day. Still others have
financed the formation of dance bands and
cultural troupes and have engaged generally
in financial ventures which tend to weaken
further their already precarious financial
position.[60]

Once in financial difficulties, more and more
time of those in charge must be spent covering up
their problems and explaining their failures. The
most common excuse is that such corporations perform a social purpose. They have a social responsibility to serve the community, to provide
facilities for future development, etc. and cannot
be expected to make profits.

Licencing and Other Measures to Promote African Business

In the climate of present-day African politics, it is simple to enact laws imposing business
restrictions in the name of promoting the interests
of Africans. However, the results are often
counterproductive. The laws invest the government ministers and bureaucrats with immense
powers of choice. There is no assurance that
licences will be given to those businesses that
are most productive and refused to those that are
not. On the contrary, it is more likely that the
most productive and competitive ones will be
refused, in order to reduce the competition and
ensure the success of African firms.

The same argument applies to work permits.
These are given to a specific person entitling
him to engage in a particular type of employment.
The individual is therefore tied to a particular
job. There is no incentive or opportunity for him
to move into areas where his expertise or talents
may be better utilized, or to retrain in order to
increase his productivity or marketability. Nor
is there any certainty that when a non-African is

refused a work permit, his position will be taken
by an African who will perform the same functions
effectively and efficiently. Similarly, when
a particular business or type of business is
reserved for Africans, non-African capital or
expertise will not be directed toward those
economic activities; but there is no corresponding guarantee that Africans will continue to
provide the services at the same level of efficiency and competitiveness, let alone introduce
new developments. The criteria for the issue of
licences and permits are vaguely defined and
the procedures so complex that they invite
corruption.

Again, these difficulties are by no means
insurmountable. If there existed a sufficient
pool of African businessmen possessing the
necessary education, sense of responsibility,
acumen, and entrepreneurial abilities, and if
there were an impartial administrative apparatus,
which rewarded only those Africans who possessed
these qualities, the social costs of applying
such policies would be acceptable. Unfortunately,
however, this is not the case in most African
states. Despite all the incentives--loans,
training programs, preferential treatment in the
issue of import and export licences and in the
grant of government contracts, reserved sectors,
and elimination of non-African competition--Afri-
can businessmen, by and large, have failed to
demonstrate their capacity to take full advantage
of the opportunities.

It was generally believed, especially by
leaders of the East African states, that the main
reason African businesses had not been a success
was because they had been discriminated against
in the past, solely because of their race or
color, by private financial institutions in the
grant of credits. In the post-independence
period, they were, therefore, extremely anxious
to correct the consequences of discrimination by
making it easier for the Africans to obtain
credit than would be the case if they had to

171

compete with non-African establishments. In Kenya,
for example, the government established an
Industrialization and Commercial Development
Corporation whose main function was to facilitate
the granting of loans to Africans. This was intended to help them purchase Asian and European
businesses which were being refused trading or
other licences, or to establish new enterprises,
especially in sectors that had been reserved for
Africans. In a sense, this was a credit guarantee
scheme under which the private banks granted credit
to those Africans whose applications had been
approved by the Corporation, on the understanding
that the Corporation would be responsible if any
of the African debtors defaulted in repaying the
loans or paying the interest thereon. In other
words, repayments were guaranteed by the state
and were to come out of government funds.

Most of the loans, in fact, went to professional politicians and bureaucrats or members
of their families and tribes. Some of the members
of the Corporation responsible for approving the
loans were themselves involved in business activities and obtained loans from the Corporation.
The default rates on these loans must have been
fairly high (there were some rumors that it was as
high as sixty per cent), because the Kenyan government has consistently refused to disclose the
true figures.

The Kenyan government operated a similar
scheme for giving training and credits to Africans so they could take over the retail trade
business from the non-Africans. In 1974, Malcolm
H. Harper conducted a scientific survey of small
African business in Kenya. He noted the emphasis
on obtaining credit:

Most small businessmen who attend courses in
Kenya admit that their main motive is to
qualify themselves for a loan. They may adopt
the procedures, and display a formal certificate of attendance, but this is all to satisfy a subsequent visitor that they deserve a

loan. The simple accounting procedures
have no other reason for them except to
qualify for a loan. And when a loan is
not forthcoming, the procedures are discredited, along with the institution, which
to their minds has failed to provide the
African businessmen with the opportunities
they rightly deserve.[61]

The situation is basically the same in West
Africa. As Teribe has observed in Nigeria:

...lending to Nigerian businessmen is
fraught with dangers, owing to the financial
inexperience and unreliability of many of
them. Few Nigerian businessmen keep good, if
any, financial records, and not all of them
keep scrupulously to agreements and promises
with regard to the use and repayment of
loans and advances....

...it is not unknown to find Nigerians obtaining loans from the commercial banks only
to put half of the amount into staging
outdoor parties to remember long-departed
ancestors.[62]

Buying up existing businesses from non-
Africans or starting new ones with the help of
loans obtained from the government has not meant
continuity of good management practices, despite
government efforts to provide advice, training,
and supervision. In Africa, as elsewhere, the
success of many small businesses is inextricably
tied with the ability to ensure optimum deploy-
ment and utilization of scarce resources.
Inefficient or wasteful use of capital paves the
road to bankruptcy. Keeping a close check on
inventories, managing the cash flow so that the
creditors will be paid on time, and building up
a reservoir of goodwill with customers while
simultaneously collecting outstanding credits
within a reasonable time, all require abilities
that cannot be easily learned in a crash training
program. In 1974, Malcolm H. Harper concluded

173

that "although nearly all shopkeepers believed they needed additional capital more than anything else, their main problem was poor development of the capital they did have, usually in the form of excessive stocks of slow moving goods."[63] Among the examples given by him of gross misuse of capital funds are:

A vehicle mechanic wanted more capital for a lathe, but had many thousands of shillings tied up in wrecked cars which he had bought over the years for the sake of one or two parts.

A baker had two years worth of wrapping material, far in excess of the minimum order acceptable to the printer;

A quarry had five months sales of cut blocks heaped on the ground and could not afford the capital investment necessary to start using explosives;

A tambourine manufacturer could not afford a goat skin to cover his tambourines yet had half a years worth of plywood in stock;

A butcher, who might have been thought to be protected from overstocking by the nature of his product, was unable to afford a few hundred shillings necessary to improve his storage facilities but had several weeks worth of cattle on the hoof behind his shop, which he had bought in advance of their slaughter with no possibility of profit through fattening or price changes.[64]

And yet, he found, the owners of these businesses proud of their excessive stocks. To them it was the primary index of success. In the absence of properly kept accounts, this was, in a sense, understandable. He found that only fifty-seven per cent of the shops were keeping any records at all of the movement of cash within the business.

174

By and large, African businessmen are imitative rather than innovative. An English businessman told one author in Ghana in August, 1976, that, with adequate training, education, and access to funds, Africans may be able to duplicate or take over existing industries and operate them in a reasonably effective and efficient fashion. They can certainly learn the technical requirements of operating a factory. But they lack innovativeness, or entrepreneurial qualities that involve identifying less familiar outlets and finding ways to exploit opportunities in timely fashion. This requires business acumen, initiative, and the capacity to take calculated risks. And these abilities can only be acquired gradually through time and experience.

Apart from the above problems, there are two other elements which account for the dismal record of African businesses. One is the question of trust. African partnerships and joint ventures rarely succeed, not because Africans are by nature individualists, but because of the lack of mutual trust and confidence in the honesty and integrity of the participants. If an individual is himself involved in siphoning off some of the profits of the business, understandably, he will suspect that others are doing the same. The lack of mutual trust in fact often results in competition among the partners as to who can siphon off more than the others. The ethos of the impersonal and honestly, efficiently run corporation, of keeping corporate and personal accounts separate, are yet to be rooted among most African businessmen. In the general climate of corruption and nepotism, it is also understandable that a large number of investors prefer to invest their savings in real estate rather than in corporate or partnership shares.

Second, one cannot afford to ignore the social environment in which an African businessman must operate. By nature, he may not be frugal. Even if he is, he is expected to impress others with a large house, car, and a retinue of servants,

and to entertain lavishly. His family and tribal
obligations also cut heavily into his profits. He
is obliged to hire members of his family or tribe,
regardless of his need or their qualifications,
and to pay for the education of children of the
extended family when the parents are less well
endowed. He must foot the bill for ceremonies to
be performed on birth, marriage, death, or other
festive occasions.

The result has been that in a large number of
cases, businesses begun at considerable social
cost have collapsed within a short period. And
even if they continue to operate, this is usually
at a static or lower level of productivity, with
adverse effects on the rates of employment and on
overall efficiency of production and distribution
of goods and services in the country. In most
cases, post-independence measures taken in the
name of economic nationalism and ostensibly for
the purposes of removing poverty, ignorance, and
disease have not led to any increased income for
the state as a whole or any improvement in the
average per capita income of the African common
man.

In the absence of adequate statistical data,
it is difficult to estimate real economic growth
in post-independence Africa. One may only specu-
late what growth might have occurred if African
leaders had used more conventional methods.
Suffice it to say that in 1972, after an analysis
of available figures, a Nigerian economist concluded that independence has in fact inhibited
rather than encouraged economic growth. According to him:

...the situation in Africa has not measured
up to expectations. Between 1960-66 the
real gross domestic product of developing
Africa increased at an average annual rate
of 3.4 per cent; and the corresponding increase in product per capita was about one
per cent per annum. This compares unfav-
orably with the 1950's so that instead of a

"substantial" increase in the rate of growth
as was aimed at, a decline in the rate of
growth actually occurred. The minimum rate
of growth of five per cent was achieved by
less than one-third of the African countries.

Another objective of the development decade
is the elimination of hunger. The sad fact
is that since 1960 food production per
capita actually declined in a large number
of African countries....[65]

It is possible, of course, to argue that in
the African context the important issue is distribution of income rather than growth rates as a
whole. There is no doubt that some redistribution
has indeed taken place since achievement of independence. But this redistribution has flowed
largely from the hands of non-Africans into those
of African politicians, bureaucrats, and military
with some filtering down to their clienteles.
The position of the common African worker or
peasant has remained unchanged or has even declined from what it was before independence. As
noted by a former member of Idi Amin's cabinet:

> Your "economic war" has not improved the
> condition of the masses in any way, and
> has in certain aspects worsened them, e.g.
> through the creation of permanent shortages
> of essential foodstuffs, and through the
> need to import goods which Uganda previously
> used to export. The most that the "economic
> war" has done is to enlarge and entrench the
> class of the national bourgeoisie, whose
> interests are diametrically opposed to
> those of the workers and peasants, who form
> the overwhelming majority of the population.[66]

Mutatis mutandis, this statement could have been
made about a number of other African states.

The inequalities of income that prevail in
African states today are not the result of any
palpable efficiency, frugality, hard work, sense

of responsibility, and innovative capacity on the part of those who have become well-off during the post-independence period. Rather, those who enjoy the biggest incomes do so because they have used political power in the ;manner described in the preceding pages to benefit themselves. Such a group does not deserve to be characterized as the "elite." It is not the cream of the crop; it is not composed of the finest among the Africans. It is not brimming with self-confidence and sense of security. If anything it is insecure, spend-thrift, gluttonous, corrupt, and devoid of con-science. (A number of Africans who did have some pangs of conscience have either been killed or imprisoned, or have left their own countries and are now in exile in various parts of the world.) What had taken years to build is being reduced to rubble, and nothing much can be, or has been, done about it.

The politically favored stratum in black Africa can hardly be considered a good replace-ment for the non-Africans who have so unceremo-niously been hounded out of Africa. Admittedly, some among them probably were guilty of exploiting the Africans, but many of them did possess the qualities, capacity, and the will to help Africans and African economies. In the heady days of post-independence, African leaders could think only of "genuine" or "total" self-determination, of the need to find scapegoats, and to divert attention from their own misdoings. In the process, they (with a few exceptions like Julius Nyerere) whipped up public opinion against all non-Afri-cans, making no distinctions among them. All, regardless of their backgrounds, occupations, religions, conduct, or qualifications, were por-trayed as exploiters of the innocent African.

As Dennis Hills has pointed out in his book on Uganda, "....the Kondo (the African robber) and the soldier (in Uganda) do not want to know whether you are useful or useless, charitable or uncharitable to Africans. They want loot; with the added bonus, probably, of enjoying the moment

of white humiliation."[67] To a degree, this is
true of almost all African states. In doing so,
they have, of course, also failed to appreciate
and learn from the non-Africans the qualities
which contributed to their success. President
Jomo Kenyatta, for example, is known to have
complained several times that many buildings in
the Kenyan capital city of Nairobi belong to the
Asians. And this has been interpreted as something of which the Asians ought to be ashamed.
Such an attitude, of course, completely disre-
gards the fact that instead of squandering their
money on non-productive ventures, they saved
and invested it in building residential houses,
warehouses, and factories. Their businesses
prospered not because they regularly and consistently exploited the Africans, but because they
were hard-working, frugal, kept proper accounts,
paid their debts on time, could place total trust
on their partners or employees, and, above all,
possessed the necessary entrepreneurial qualities.
As the following example given by Mamdani demonstrates, the Asians of Uganda were not unwilling
to teach these qualities to others, even when
they were about to be thrown out of the country.

> After the expulsion order the African admini-
> strators remained, as always, polite but
> indifferent. The daily ritual of having to
> wade through lengthy red tape was a tedious
> affair. One waited for hours, with the
> tropical sun above and the scorched pave-
> ment below. At the Uganda Immigration
> Office, where I had stood in line with a
> hundred others, the officials had decided
> to check people's documents before they got
> to the counter, so those with a missing doc-
> ument might be saved a number of hours of
> waiting. A very humane gesture. One of the
> officials, a rather amiable man, was briskly
> going through my part of the queue. He
> stopped to examine my neighbor's documents.
> After the usual greeting the neighbor unex-
> pectedly asked: "So you think we milked the
> cow but didn't feed it?" repeating Amin's

oft-quoted charge against Asians. The fellow
looked up and smiled. "If you think that is
the whole story, you are not only wrong but
in trouble" he continued. The official looked
up, a question on his face. My neighbor per-
sisted, "Do you know what an Asian would do
if he were in your place?" Silence. "Do
you see this queue of people?" "Yes."
"And the cruel sun?" "Yes." "And how un-
comfortable people are?" "Yes." But now
the official was becoming a bit impatient.
"If I were in your place, I would have a
stand of coca cola there, pay somebody to
sell the cokes and maybe some groundnuts,
and make myself some money." Everybody
in the queue laughed. The official smiled
good-naturedly. The next day, when I returned to the queue, I saw a stand of coca
cola, and a small queue in front of it! It
was the birth of an African businessman.[68]

Adjusted to scale, this incident illustrates the
tragedy of what "might have been" if the new
African leaders had been more concerned with
long term development than short run exploitation for limited advantage.

180

FOOTNOTES: CHAPTER III

[1]Stanislov Andreski, "Kleptocracy or Corruption as a System of Government" in Arnold J. Heidenheimer, ed., The African Political Corruption: Readings in Comparative Analysis (New York: Holt, Rinehart, and Winston, Inc., 1970), p. 354.

[2]M. McMullan, "Corruption in Public Services of British Colonies and French Colonies in West Africa," in Arnold J. Heidenheimer, loc. cit., p. 319.

[3]William L. Riordon, Plunkitt of Tammany Hall (New York: Dutton, 1963), et seq.

[4]See especially James Q. Wilson, "Corruption: The Shame of the States" in Arnold J. Heidenheimer. op. cit., pp. 298-306.

[5]McMullan, op. cit., pp. 322-326.

[6]Final Report of the Commission of Inquiry on Bribery and Corruption, (Accra: Republic of Ghana, 1975), p. 4.

[7]James S. Coleman, Nigeria: Background to Nationalism (Berkeley and Los Angeles: University of California Press, 1958), pp. 423-424.

[8]R. Nelson and H. Wolpe, "Modernization and the Politics of Communalism," American Political Science Review, December, 1970, pp. 1112-1130. See also R. Nelson and H. Wolpe, eds., Nigeria: Modernization and the Politics of Communalism (Michigan State University Press, 1971.)

[9]Immanuel Wallerstein, "Ethnicity and National Integration in West Africa," in M. E. Doro and N. M. Stultz, eds., Governing in Black Africa (New York: Prentice Hall, 1970), pp. 129-139.

[10]Christian P. Potholm, The Theory and Practice

of African Politics (Englewood Cliffs, New Jersey: Prentice Hall, Inc., 1979), pp. 14-19.

[11]David R. Smock and Kwamena Bentsi-Enchill, eds., The Search for National Integration in Africa (New York: The Free Press, 1976), p. 8.

[12]M. J. Balogun, "Military Rule and Demilitarization: The Experience of Sierra Leone, 1967-1968," The Quarterly Journal of Administration, Nigeria, October, 1974, p. 25.

[13]R. S. Jackson, "Political Stratification in Tropical Africa," Canadian Journal of African Studies, Vol. 7, no. 3, pp. 396-397.

[14]S. Naipaul, In a Free State (London: Andre Deutsch, Ltd., 1971), p. 234.

[15]Statement by Mr. Shikuku. See Africa Digest, December, 1973, p. 132.

[16]Ali A. Mazrui, Post-Imperial Fragmentation: The Legacy of Ethnic and Racial Conflict (Denver: University of Denver Press, 1969), p. 6.

[17]For further details of this incident, see Africa Confidential, August 27, 1965, pp. 6-7.

[18]Final Report of the Commission of Inquiry on Bribery and Corruption, Ghana, loc. cit., et seq.

[19]Dennis K. Greenstreet, "Public Corporations in Ghana during the Nkrumah Period, 1951-1966," The African Review, 1973, p. 23.

[20]Ibid., p. 30.

[21]M. A. Mettle, "Compulsory Acquisition of Land," Review of Ghana Law, Vol. IV, no. 2, August, 1972, p. 130.

[22]Ibid., p. 131.

[23]David Martin, General Amin (London: Faber & Faber, 1974), p. 234.

[24]Fola Sore, "The Challenge of Nation Building," Africa Quarterly, p. 182. See also B. O. Nwabueze, Presidentialism in Commonwealth Africa (New York: St. Martin's Press, 1975), p. 180.

[25]Final Report of the Commission of Inquiry on Bribery and Corruption, Ghana, loc. cit., Part II, Chapt. 5, para. 67, p. 92.

[26]"Ghana: Busia's Battles," Africa Confidential, Vol. 12, no. 11, May 28, 1971, p. 1.

[27]Radio Broadcast by Brig. Murtala Muhammed, Head of the Federal Military Government on Fifteenth Independence Anniversary of Nigeria, October 1, 1975.

[28]Treason Act, No. 73 of 1959, Laws of Ghana, Sections 2 and 3.

[29]The Guardian, Manchester, England, June 3, 1966. Also see: Africa Digest, Vol. XIV, no. 1, July 9, 1966, p. 1.

[30]"The Isolation of Sekou Toure," Spotlight on Africa, Africa, 1967, p. 72.

[31]"The Story Continues: Kibedi's Open Letter to Amin," Transition, Issue no. 49, p. 20.

[32]The Times, London, England, May 21, 1976.

[33]"Prisoner of the Month," Amnesty International October, 1977, Amnesty International Publications, London, 1977.

[34]Ibid.

[35]"Manifesto of the Ugandan Army" published in "Uganda: The Birth of the Second Republic," (Mimeo, no date) by Idi Amin Dede, Head of Uganda's Military Government.

[36] "Le Regime Presidentiel Au Zaire," Etudes Africaines du Crisp, Centre de Researche et d'Information Socio-politique, Paris, T. A. 144, December 20, 1972, p. 22.

[37] United Nations, Official Records of the General Assembly, Twenty-eight Session, October 4, 1973, p. 51.

[38] Africa Research Bulletin (Political, Social, and Cultural Series), July, 1973, p. 2914.

[39] Victor D. Dubois, "Zaire Under President Sese Seko Mobutu, Part I," American Universities Field Staff Reports, Central and South African Series, Vol. XVII, January, 1973, p. 16.

[40] Africa Recorder, May, 1972, p. 3114.

[41] Victor D. Dubois, op. cit., p. 10.

[42] New York Times, December 1, 1973, p. 18.

[43] Jean de la Gueriviere, "Zaire's Second Independence," Translations on Africa, U.S. Department of Commerce, Washington, D.C., no. 1449, March 21, 1974, p. 28.

[44] Fole Soremkun, "Zambia's Cultural Revolution," Presence Africaine, no. 73, 1970, p. 204.

[45] Ibid., p. 192.

[46] Ibid., p. 204.

[47] Daily News, Tanzania, September 13, 1972.

[48] Irving Horwitz, ed., Power, Politics and People: The Collected Essays of C. Wright Mills, p. 405.

[49] Ibid., p. 406.

[50] Ibid., p. 410.

184

[51]Leopold Senghor, "Negritude and African Socialism," Martin Minogue and Judith Molloy, African Aims and Attitudes, Selected Documents (New York: Cambridge University Press, 1974), p. 230.

[52]Ibid., p. 231. Also see: Gerhard Grohs, "Difficulties of Cultural Emancipation in Africa," The Journal of Modern African Studies, Vol 14, 1976, p. 69.

[53]Sekou Toure, "Africa's Future and the World," Martin Minogue and Judith Molloy, African Aims and Attitudes, Selected Documents, op. cit., p. 222.

[54]Ibid., See also: Allioune Diop, "The African Personality," Minogue and Molloy, pp. 234-236.

[55]"African Socialism and Its Application to Planning in Kenya," Minister for Economic Planning, Kena, Kenya Government Sessional Paper, no. 10, 1965, Nairobi, Kenya. For an interesting analysis, see Ahmed Mohiddin, "Socialism in Two Countries: The Arusha Declaration of Tanzania and the African Socialism of Kenya," Africa Quarterly, January/March, 1973, pp. 333-356.

[56]R. H. Jackson, "Political Stratification in Tropical Africa," Canadian Journal of African Studies, Vol. 7, no. 3, 1973, p. 399.

[57]Frank Furedi, "The Development of Anti-Asian Opinion Among Africans in Nakuru District, Kenya," African Affairs, 1974, p. 347.

[58]Richard Cox, Kenyatta's Country (New York: Praeger, 1965), p. 169.

[59]M. O. Ijere, "African Manpower Problems and Advanced Countries," Afrika Spectrum, Vol. 8, 1973, pp. 14-15.

[60]"Acheampong Hits Out at Losers," African Development, January, 1976, p. 83.

[61]Malcolm H. Harper, "A Prototype Experiment to Test the Possibility of a Cost Effective Extension Service for Small Scale General Retailers," Institute for Development Studies, University of Nairobi, Discussion Paper, IDS/DP 193, January, 1974, pp. 3-4.

[62]I. Teribe, "Financing Indigenization," Quarterly Journal of Administration, January, 1975, p. 165. See also: African Development, January, 1974, p. 8.

[63]Malcolm H. Harper, loc. cit., et seq.

[64]Ibid.

[65]E. C. Edozien, "The Development Decade in Africa: A Preliminary Appraisal," Nigerian Journal of Economic and Social Studies, 1972, pp. 78-92. See also: Jean M. Due, "Development Without Growth: The Case of Ghana in the 1960's," The Economic Bulletin of Ghana, 1973, Vol. 3, pp. 3-15.

[66]Open letter by former Foreign Minister Kibedi to President Idi Amin, Transition, Vol. 49, p. 28.

[67]Dennis Hills, The White Pumpkin (London: George, Allen & Unwin, Ltd., 1975), p. 194.

[68]Mahmood Mamdani, From Citizen to Refugee (London: Frances Pinter, Ltd., 1973), p. 46.

CHAPTER IV

THE QUEST FOR ECONOMIC INDEPENDENCE

Autarky is a nearly impossible condition to realize today no matter how large or well-endowed with resources a state may be. The illusory quality of autarky, however, has not dissuaded most African states from the pursuit of "total" economic independence. This preoccupation with economic self-determination has, in fact, led to a kind and degree of government intervention in African economies that probably has hampered national development. Policies rationalized in the name of economic independence have also resulted in major damage to the interests of non-African residents and investors. This much is undebatable.

Whether government economic measures have led to improvement in the standard of living for the general population is more difficult to establish. In many specific instances, such as the Africanization of commerce in Zaire and Uganda, it would be easy to argue the contrary.

This chapter will examine several policies undertaken by black African regimes in pursuit of economic independence. Although we cannot consider every instance in which a particular approach has been employed, we shall describe its application in at least one country in some detail. And, we shall indicate how widespread these policies are in black Africa.

187

The economic and social policies in question are: expulsion of "foreigners" and unwanted citizens; removal of individuals and groups from certain occupations; restrictions of retail trade to black Africans; requiring the sale of businesses in the control of certain groups to black Africans; forcing foreign businesses out of intermediate levels of distribution and small industry; reserving certain types of business activity for black Africans only and requiring that they own a minimum percentage of shares in all other enterprises; expropriation of real estate; nationalization of the professions; and deportation with forfeiture of property. This list of interventionist policies is not exhaustive. We do not examine African attempts at economic planning, for example, or import-export policies. The point is that the record in virtually all black African states in the economic realm would make a white South African feel very insecure about his economic prospects under black majority rule.

Uganda achieved political independence on 9 October 1962. From this date forward the power to expel an alien from the territories falling within its colonially defined boundaries was transferred from the British to the new black African leaders.

In August, 1972, the total population of Uganda was a little over ten million. Although most of these people were black Africans, there were among them about 80,000 people of Asian origin, mostly Hindus and Muslims. The Asians had been present in Uganda at least since the end of the nineteenth century. In 1901, in a report to his government, Britain's Special Commissioner to Uganda was impelled to refer to the territory as "the America of the Hindu."

In August, 1972, President Idi Amin announced that the 80,000 Asians residing in Uganda had ninety days within which to put their affairs in order and leave the country. The deadline coincided with Hindu and Muslim

religious festivals. The Hindu Diwali Festival of
the Lights was to be celebrated on November 6 and
the Muslim Id-El-Fitra, marking the end of the
Ramadhan, was to fall, depending on the moon, on
either November 8 or 9. In a broadcast explaining
his expulsion order, he said that the decision had
been taken to:

> ...free our people from economic domination
> by foreigners and to rescue them from the
> ruthless jaws of exploiters who are deter-
> mined to see to it that this motherland of
> ours, green and beautiful as it is, is
> milked completely white of its wealth and
> her people left poor and destitute. Indeed
> it is a decision aimed at achieving economic
> independence which our people have all along
> been wishing to achieve. We have got to
> fight for our economic independence as we
> did for our political independence--and the
> war has been declared.[1]

The expulsion was not entirely unplanned. In
October, 1971, the government had required all
Asians living in the country to travel to special
camps to be physically counted. Each Asian was
issued a green pass which he was required to
carry with him at all times. In December, 1971,
President Amin had invited several Asian leaders
to a conference where he presented them with a
long list of business malpractices and claimed
that he held the whole community responsible for
these activities.

A study made by the International Commission
of Jurists has confirmed that from the very
beginning of this expulsion period of three
months, the Asians were assaulted physically and
ill-treated in other ways by members of the
Ugandan armed forces. As the Asians prepared to
leave, soldiers visited their houses at night,
threatening and beating many, taking what they
liked. One, Mr. Darmi Ranchod Katoria, his wife
and two children were shot by the soldiers. Two
young girls aged eighteen and twenty were

189

forcibly carried away with "promises" of marriage. Several Asians had their hair and beard cut with broken beer bottles. Plundering and looting of their belongings was a common occurrence. This occurred even on their way to the now famous Entebbe Airport to leave the country for the last time. An Asian refugee stated upon arrival in England, "We took a taxi from our home to Kampala to catch a bus to the airport. We were stopped by soldiers at four road blocks. Each time they dragged my brother and me out of the car...They took our shoes and all my money, my tape recorder, my watch, and my necklace."[2]

The Asians en route to India, aboard the trains headed for the port of Mombasa, Kenya were:

> pursued by Ugandan military men up to the border of Kenya and ill-treated. The soldiers forced their entry into the trains, detained the passengers at several stations and harrassed them. Some Asian girls fleeing from Uganda had to bribe with money and jewelry for Ugandan Army soldiers who had tried to abduct them.... Four other girls were held in the barracks by army men and it was not known what happened to them. Some twenty Indians, both men and women were reported missing from the special trains carrying the expelled Asians from Kampala to Mombasa.[3]

Describing his last experience in Uganda one man said: "On the road from Jinja, where I lived, soldiers stopped me and told me, 'You Asians are the cause of all our troubles in Uganda. If you do not leave by the end of the month we will slash all your throats.'"[4]

Officially, each Asian was allowed to take out of Uganda $131 in cash, and personal effects to the value of $1,310. (The rest of their properties were confiscated as "Abandoned Property.") In reality, however, many of them were obliged to leave almost everything behind, including what the government had assured them

they would be allowed to take. According to the
report of an Indian charitable organization, endorsed by the International Commission of Jurists,
"Their belongings were searched and they were
deprived of their little cash, jewelry and other
valuable articles like wrist watches, rings,
blankets, sweaters and even shoes. The gold chains
and necklaces of women were snatched away....
They were almost penniless when they landed in
Bombay."[5]

The same situation was reported by those
Asians who went to England. Their personal
belongings were looted by the army and their
money frequently taken away as they left the
country. Some had arranged for their personal
effects to be sent as unaccompanied baggage
hoping that this way they might be comparatively
safe. Even those possessions did not all leave
Uganda. According to a report from an official
British agency:

> Tons of treasured possessions were left
> behind--piled in heaps at Entebbe airport
> to be wrecked by weather or pilferers. Of
> the baggage which did leave and arrive in
> Britain much had lost all identification.
>
> Unaccompanied baggage to be transported by
> charter flights was piled in heaps at Kampala
> and Entebbe into lorries and aircraft regard-
> less of ownership, destination or documen-
> tation. Large quantities left in the open
> air at Entebbe are now believed to have
> been destroyed.[6]

In a speech made August 19, 1972, outside the
national capital, the Ugandan President had said,
"And I will not only send away those Asians
(referring to Asians who were non-citizens) but
every Asian of Indian, Pakistani, or Bangladesh
origin, extraction, or descent whatever his
citizenship."[7] However, partly in response to
international protests, the Ugandan Representative
of the United Nations assured the members of the

organization on August 23 that all persons who had become citizens of Uganda would be allowed to reside in the country "regardless of color, provided their papers were not forged."[8] Although this assurance was accepted by the world body (which, in any case, was not too keen to discuss these issues) at face value, in retrospect it is obvious that the Uganda government honored the sanctity of its pledge more in the breach than in the observance.

In reality, not only were those Asians who had become Ugandan citizens forced out of the country; rather, it was they who suffered the greatest hardships as stateless persons, and found themselves in a most desperate situation. After it was obliged to proclaim to the world that it had no intention of expelling Asians who were Ugandan citizens, the government undertook "an elaborate operation to examine thoroughly and check all documents of citizenship in an obvious effort to deny citizenship to as many Asians as possible."[9] According to Gwen Cashmore, "it was in this check that over half (of the Asians) lost their citizenship and became stateless."[10] One major thrust of this operation was to revoke the citizenship of Asians who had become Ugandan citizens automatically. Any person born or residing in Uganda at the time of Independence (October, 1962) had acquired citizenship automatically if one of his or her parents had also been born there. Now any Asian claiming citizenship was required to produce original birth certificates of himself as well as of one of his parents. No alternative proof of birth was acceptable. This was in a country where systematic registration of births had not even begun until the 1930's. Photocopies of the original certificates were not acceptable either. It was almost impossible to obtain certified copies from the Office of the Registrar, which closed down its offices on most days. Production of Ugandan passports issued by the Ugandan government itself was regarded as insufficient evidence of Ugandan citizenship. If even one of the

required documents was not in the original, all
the documents were torn up and the individual
declared a non-citizen.

The official examining a particular set of
documents had almost complete discretion in
finding whether or not the individual concerned
was a citizen. Usually, he did not pay much
attention to the provisions of the Ugandan laws,
let alone the rules of international law. One
man tried to explain that although he did not
have the original certificate in his possession,
he was in fact a Ugandan citizen by operation of
the law; he was told, "Young boy, if you argue
like a lawyer, you would get a good hiding." He
was pushed out of the office, declared a non-
citizen, and expelled from the country. An
African lawyer nearly put himself in serious
trouble for accompanying an Asian client to
explain to the officials the status of his client.

Any number of similar cases could be cited.
One, Mr. D. R. Bhamani, had acquired Ugandan
citizenship in 1964. This fact had been accepted
by the Uganda authorities in 1972, when he was
issued a travel permit (allowing him to leave
and re-enter Uganda) which described him as a
Ugandan citizen. But during the verification
period, his papers were taken away from him and
he was declared a non-citizen. A Mr. Dattani
had acquired Ugandan citizenship by registration.
In a letter dated February 12, 1973, written from
a refugee camp in Belgium to which he had been
taken as a stateless person in November, 1972,
he said:

> I had a letter from the Ugandan authorities
> saying I am Ugandan citizen but at the time
> of approving my citizenship (during the
> verification period) that letter was torn by
> the officer and (he) told me that I am not
> Ugandan citizen, and afterwards they gave
> me another letter saying that I am not
> citizen by birth or by registration. Really,
> I came penniless from Uganda. They even

took away a wristwatch which I had on my wrist....[11]

Mr. H. J. Vyas, a Ugandan citizen since 1964, and at one time Chief of the Uganda Lint Marketing Board, stated in a letter that during the verification period he was told by General Amin's officials that he had never been a Uganda citizen, and his Uganda passport was confiscated. No reason was given.[12] Mr. L. S. Dave had registered himself as a Ugandan citizen in 1962. In August, 1972, when he presented his papers to a verification officer, his Certificate of Registration was marked "Cancelled--Not a Citizen--His name looks different." He drew the attention of the officer to the fact that the difference in name on the Certificate of Registration and on the Declaration of Renunciation of British Citizenship (which he had been required to make under Ugandan laws before he could be registered as a Ugandan citizen) was very minor. But this was to no avail. On the Certificate his name appeared as Labhshanker Shivrambhai Dave. The suffix "bhai" is commonly added to the names of elderly asians as a mark of respect, a fact which was well-known to all African officials who had come into contact with the Asians. Nor was Mr. Dave given any opportunity to have his case reviewed. These are just a few examples of the arbitrary and highhanded ways in which Asians were deprived of Ugandan citizenship and expelled from the country as stateless persons.

But even those Asians who managed to have their citizenships verified found this to be a mixed blessing. When the Ugandan president discovered that a substantial number of Asians had succeeded in proving that they were lawful Ugandan citizens and thus could not be expelled as aliens, he announced on November 2, that after November 9, the "verified Asians" could only remain in the country as farmers in the remote and arid areas of Karamoja, where land would be allocated to them by the government. They would, under no circumstances, be permitted to reside or carry out business in the cities. They were soon to be physically counted, given identity cards, and transported to these rural areas. According to the President, this was necessary to mix them with the other Ugandans and convert them into "proper Ugandan citizens." However, there was to be no guarantee of security of tenure for those willing to go and work on this almost barren land.

For the highly urbanized Asians, many of whom were born in Uganda and had lived there for generations, this meant that they would have to leave their skilled or semi-skilled jobs, vacate homes which they may have had built with their savings, sell their businesses at rock bottom prices (assuming they could find buyers), and begin a new life cultivating cassava. They would have to do this with primitive tools and live in thatch-roofed huts with no water or electricity. Even then they would have little or no assurance of being allowed to continue to live in peace. For many this was the limit. All but a couple of hundred "verified citizens" left Uganda. It was hardly a choice. One of the "verified citizens" settled in the United States with the help of the Tolstoy Foundation explained his predicament to a reporter from the Rockland County Journal News in the following terms:

> The expulsion decree was very confusing. When it was first published and posted around the country, it stated that only non-Ugandan citizens would have to leave. Because I hold Ugandan citizenship, I thought I would be allowed to remain, but then Amin in his speeches began to say that no, everyone who is not a black African must leave.
>
> Oh, if you had Ugandan citizenship, you were given a choice. You could remain in Uganda if you were willing to sell your property and go live in the bush...this was hardly an alternative because it would have necessitated giving up an urban,

middle-class existence to live as a tribes-
man....[13]

From being a prosperous community, well established
in homes they owned, driving their own cars, their
children attending schools, and solidly anchored
in a society whose language and culture they
knew, they were suddenly uprooted and despoiled.
Within a period of less than three months, they
were homeless, jobless, moneyless, and exiled to
various parts of the globe.

While the Asians bore the main brunt of the
expulsion orders, they were by no means the only
Ugandan residents forced out of the country. In
November, 1972, at least fifty-eight missionaries
were required to leave on the ground that "the
imperialists might get into the country again
through religion."[14] When the Roman Catholic
Archbishop of Kampala requested the government to
reconsider, he was accused of being an agent of
Israel and South Africa. Several long-time
British residents were also ordered to leave.
Among them were Mr. Henry Radford, who had lived
in Uganda for over twenty years; Mr. Cyril
Widgery, who was born in Uganda, lived all his
life there, and had been working for the government since 1945; Major Price, aged seventy-four,
whose tea plantation had been nationalized earlier;
and Mr. Michael Gaiger, a Barrister-at-Law, who
was working as a senior State Attorney in the
Ministry of Justice. Others saw no point in
staying on and left. Between August 1972 and
August 1973, the number of European residents in
Uganda fell from 10,000 to less than 2,000.

Both the official and unofficial processes of
depriving the non-Africans of their property began
as soon as the expulsion order was announced.
There were many cases where houses, shops and
business premises were occupied by members of the
Ugandan armed forces. The Asians could do little
about it. Although not officially sanctioned, the
practice was tolerated or even encouraged tacitly
by the government. There was no one to listen to

the complaints of the victims, let alone provide effective remedies.

Unofficially, the government had prohibited the sale of any Asian owned property, farm, or business to anyone except a Ugandan African. The fact was that very few Ugandan Africans were able or willing to make offers that approached the market price of the property. But this was of no concern to the government. All Asians were required to declare their assets and liabilities on a prescribed form and submit it to the government. They could appoint an agent to act in their name during their absence, but such an agent had no right to sell, rent, or convey the property to anyone except with the consent of an Abandoned Property Custodian Board established by the government, in whom all unsold property of the expelled Asians was vested by law. The Board was supposed to manage "property abandoned by departing Asians" and to process Asian claims for compensation. In reality, its function came to be the allocating, almost free of charge, of the buildings, farms, and businesses vacated by the Asians.

Despite several statements emanating from the government promising compensation, it is most unlikely that the vast majority of the foreigners will ever receive anything more than a nominal payment, if anything at all. Those non-Africans who were Ugandan citizens might have to forego their claims altogether, if only because the Ugandan government would raise norms of international law which require that persons whose claims a state is espousing should be its citizens.

The Board (or other persons acting in behalf of the government) thus handed over to Ugandan Africans about three to four thousand Asian businesses without requiring much by way of payment. Some of the larger Asian enterprises (e.g. sugar and textile factories) were retained by the government, to be operated as state enterprises. The total assets left by the Asians and subsequently reallocated by the government have been

197

estimated at three hundred million dollars.

Following the departure of the Asians, a number of European businesses and plantations were also taken over by the government, without payment of compensation. The Kampala Club, the traditional preserve of the Europeans in Uganda, was taken over for the exclusive use of the Ugandan President and members of the government as a place to "discuss matters of state and entertain visiting dignitaries." The search for economic independence--through the application of the devices of expulsion followed or preceded by expropriation without compensation--made it possible for Ugandan Africans to acquire almost overnight premises occupied by the non-Africans, their businesses, automobiles, farms, furniture, and even their pets.

Unfortunately for the ordinary Ugandans the effect of this economic war "to free our people from economic domination by foreigners" was far from beneficial. With ever increasing scarcity of goods, the new African businessmen (many of whom were formerly soldiers) soon became adept at hoarding and overcharging so that, in the end, the government had to institute death penalties for such activities. This only made matters worse. Many of the new proprietors, afraid that they might suffer the same fate they had meted out to others, simply sold the remaining stocks and closed down the businesses altogether. Today, the Ugandan economy is in a state of almost total collapse. And this in turn has adversely affected the lives of those few non-Africans who are still there.

In April, 1976, President Amin attended a meeting of diplomats accredited to Uganda and requested their assistance in calling upon foreigners to invest in Uganda. He said he was willing to offer them full assurance against future nationalization of their investments, and even promised that he would permit repatriation of profits made on those investments. There were few takers. The government was also forced to

198

recruit foreigners to come to Uganda on contractual terms lasting two to four years to take the place of the Asian doctors, engineers, accountants, and other professionals. It was not very easy to obtain the right kind of people with the right qualifications either. Following the involuntary departure of President Idi Amin to Libya in 1979, the new Presidents Yusufu K. Lule and Godfrey Lukongwe Binaisa (who took over from Lule a few months later) both sought to revive the largely floundering economy by seeking new foreign investments. President Binaisa even tried, without much success or enthusiasm, to invite former Asian industrialists to return to Uganda to operate sugar, steel, and other enterprises that had been nationalized during the Amin regime in partnership with the Ugandan government.

It should not be assumed that non-blacks in Uganda were allowed to operate within a non-discriminatory environment prior to Amin's dramatic moves in fall, 1972. In many ways, devices employed by the Ugandan government in the pre-1972 period, especially in the areas of public and private employment and trading, did have an adverse impact upon the economic interests of non-Africans and resulted in many of them leaving the country. These devices, however, were not much different from those adopted by Kenya; we shall turn our attention now to these.

Removal from Positions in Public and Private Enterprises

The policy of giving preference to black Africans over others equally or better qualified in the civil services of the new African states is generally referred to as "Africanization." This policy has been pursued by a number of the black African states, with varying degrees of intensity. Among these countries is Kenya. One explanation of Africanization is furnished by A. L. Adu, a senior Ghanaian civil servant, who, among other things, was also responsible for advising the Kenyan government on matters relating to the civil

199

service:

> ...in the ultimate, the real justification for
> Africanization is the natural and under-
> standable desire of every people to be able
> to manage its own internal affairs. It is
> the public service counterpart of the urge
> for political and economic independence.
> This independence is, to most people, meaning-
> less unless it is matched by the ability of
> the people, through its civil service, to
> administer, to run and control it.[15]

Or, in other words, "genuine" independence can only
be said to have been achieved when black Africans
occupy all significant civil service positions.
Moreover, such a situation must be brought about
fairly quickly. "Africanization to be effective,"
according to Mr. Adu, "requires an emergency
operation to deal with an emergency situation.
It requires the adoption of extraordinary measures
for the mobilization of manpower resources available for the civil service."[16]

Why this mania for Africanization, one may
ask. Why can't the new state continue to be
administered by former colonial civil servants
(of course, with policy directives from political
leaders) until such time as enough well-qualified
people are available? And why the emphasis on
black Africans and not Asians, or Arabs, or
Europeans who may have settled in those states?
The argument varies from state to state, depending
in particular on the extent to which non-Africans
are represented in the civil service and the pace
at which it is carrying out the Africanization
program. However, the following lines of reasoning
are typical: (a) the civil service must reflect
the general complexion of the population; (b)
black African governments cannot expect the same
loyalty and sensitivity from "alien" civil administrators as they can from a civil service which is
African in complexion; (c) African government
ministers (political leaders) prefer to work with
African advisors and bureaucrats; (d) positions

in the departments of the police, army, and, the interior are so sensitive from the point of view of national security that they must be held by Africans; (e) national pride and honor demand that only Africans represent the new state in matters of foreign policy; (f) Africans are in tune with local psychology, character, and attitudes and should therefore be more effective in the performance of their duties; (g) it is one of the best means to inculcate qualities of integrity, hard work and esprit de corps among the Africans; and (h) there is, from client groups, considerable political pressure and the need to show quick results.

Whatever the validity of these explanations, new African states have often Africanized their civil services hastily and to the detriment of non-blacks. Kenya provides a typical example. Its total population as recorded at the census of 1962 was 8.6 million, including three significant minority communities. Asians, Europeans, and Arabs comprised respectively 2.0 per cent, 0.6 per cent, and 0.4 per cent of the whole. Altogether, the non-Africans numbered 270,321. A little less than half the European population was involved in farming in the Highlands. The rest were either in business or occupying top administrative and executive positions in the civil service. Three-quarters of the Arabs lived in urban areas, and ninety-three per cent of them were living in the coastal areas, in and around the port city of Mombasa. The Asians had been living in the coastal areas for centuries, but began to move into the interior only in the nineteenth century. In 1962, ninety-three per cent were living in urban areas, partly because of the European success in reserving the fertile Highlands exclusively for themselves. Concentrated in the towns and trading centers, they filled an economic vacuum between the European farmers and administrators and the African masses. They became shopkeepers, craftsmen, and clerks and junior executives working for European banks, insurance companies, and other corporations. A large number of them also joined the civil service, performing similar functions, especially in the departments of railways, customs, treasury, and public works.

The civil service reflected the status system of Kenyan society as a whole; the Europeans occupied the highest positions, the Asians dominated in the middle strata, and the Africans were found mostly in the lower categories of jobs. Nevertheless, change had been underway since the 1950's, when a non-racial civil service commission was established to enforce a merit system of appointment and promotion without regard to race. By the time Kenya became politically independent in December, 1963, it had not only a large and efficient civil service, but also several experienced and competent Africans in top positions. Among them were Charles Njonjo, Duncan Ndegwa, and Robert Ouko. Still their numbers were relatively few, compared with the Europeans and the Asians.

Prior to independence, the colonial government had introduced a scheme to compensate those Europeans who had been recruited from Britain to join the colonial service and had been sent to Kenya. Ostensibly this was to compensate them for losing their careers as a result of the British government's decision to relinquish its colonial possession. The terms of compensation were so generous that an average young Briton would have been foolish not to take advantage of the opportunity. (Locally, the payments came to be known as "the golden handshakes.") And a number of them did so, though many also managed to remain in Kenya on a contractual basis for terms ranging from two to five years. Those who did so received salaries higher than they were getting as permanent and pensionable employees. Asians, most of whom had been recruited locally, did not qualify for compensation. They had little choice but to continue to work for the successor state.

Before further description of post-independence developments within the Kenyan civil service,
it is necessary to provide the legal background
for the citizenship status of non-Africans who
continued to live in Kenya after it received political independence. The colonial power regarded
place of birth as the main determining factor in
granting citizenship. A person born in territory
under British control was a "British Subject:
Citizen of the United Kingdom and Colonies."
However, to control migration from one part of the
empire to another, it had permitted, within certain
limits, local laws limiting the entry of British
subjects from other parts of the empire for
purposes of permanent settlement. In 1956, the
Kenyan local legislative body, with the consent
and approval of the British Governor, had placed
severe restrictions on non-Africans entering Kenya
from other British colonies, and establishing
residence there for an extended period of time.
To distinguish between those entering Kenya for a
visit of short duration and those non-Africans who
had already established residence there, the law
provided for the issuance of Residents' Certificates to those British subjects who had been in
Kenya for a period of ten years out of sixteen
immediately preceding the date of their application. Those British subjects who were born in
Kenya and whose mothers had been residing there for
an aggregate of not less than five years out of
any period of eight years were also entitled to
the issuance of such certificates. This certificate (which was usually issued in the form of
an endorsement on the last page of a person's
British passport) entitled the holder to reside
permanently in Kenya with the right to leave and
re-enter the country at any time.

When Kenya became independent in 1963, a
vast majority of Europeans, Asians, and Arabs
living there either had been issued or were
entitled to receive such certificates. The validity of this law and of the certificates issued
under it was recognized by the new African state
under an agreement concluded between it and the

British government confirming the continuity of the
legal order prevailing in Kenya at the time of independence. The new constitution adopted by Kenya
upon independence divided all persons with the
right of permanent residence in the country into
two categories: (a) those who automatically
acquired Kenya citizenship upon independence and
(b) those who were granted an option to apply for
registration as Kenya citizens within a stipulated
period (two years from the date of independence).
Everyone born in Kenya with one of his or her
parents also born there was placed in category (a);
others with the right to permanently reside in
Kenya under the laws existing at the time were
given the option of either retaining their British
citizenship or of registering themselves as Kenya
citizens on or before December 12, 1965. The
Constitution specifically provided that such
persons "shall be entitled upon making application
before the specified date in such manner as may
be prescribed by or under an Act of Parliament to
be registered as citizens of Kenya."[17] To avoid
dual citizenship, those who automatically acquired
Kenyan citizenship on independence were to simultaneously, through operation of a newly passed
British Act of Parliament, lose their British
citizenship; those registering as Kenya citizens
within the prescribed time were to simultaneously
renounce their British citizenship. About one-
third of the Asians fell under category (a), and
the rest under (b).

Almost immediately after independence, the
new African state embarked upon an ambitious
program of Africanization of the civil service.
It was argued by the new government that there was
a racial imbalance in the civil service in that
the minority racial communities occupied the
majority of the positions, especially at higher
levels, and that this imbalance, an obvious
inequity, needed to be corrected as quickly as
possible. The government declared that the policy
of giving preference to Africans was only temporary. Constitutional guarantees of and official
support for a multiracial society would be resumed

as soon as the civil service reflected as nearly as practicable the racial composition of the population.

This was to be the proper balance; non-Africans should not occupy more than 3.0 per cent of the positions at all levels. This was rule by the majority and the fact that the non-Africans constituted a much higher percentage of educated or qualified persons in the society made no difference. Other arguments referred to above were also invoked whenever it served the government's purpose. As a former member of the Kenyan Public Service Commission told one of the authors in 1970, "it was a quota system in which the non-Africans had everything to lose, and nothing to gain." Initially, the government began implementation of the program by recruiting only Africans to fill all positions that became available. Virtually all advertisements for government positions in the Official Gazette or published in the local newspapers clearly indicated that black Africans would be preferred over Asians or Europeans, regardless of citizenship. Soon afterwards, the same argument--the need to correct the imbalance--was used in approving promotions. A little later, the Asian and European senior civil servants were made to retire prematurely to make room for African graduates of institutes established by the government to train Africans through six-month crash courses. Those on contract were notified that their appointments would not be renewed. And, before long, especially those who had not been successful in registering themselves as Kenyan citizens, found themselves fired from jobs which they thought were permanent and pensionable, to make it possible for the government to provide employment for thousands of African high school graduates who soon became available to fill junior positions. From 45,000 in 1955, the size of the civil service increased to 77,000 in 1969. And, by 1969, only about a dozen Asians occupied high positions in the Kenya government headquarters in Nairobi. Although all were citizens, none felt

secure; even though each of them was not only
capable of performing satisfactorily the duties
of his own position but also that of his superiors.
And, many others had been passed over for promotion, though they were equally, if not more,
efficient than their African subordinates who
were rewarded with amazingly quick advancements.
The government explained away such situations as
the inevitable consequences of a policy which
seeks to remedy past injustices. The situation
was not much different in the army and the police.
As Richard Cox has remarked in Kenyatta's Country
published in 1965:

> There are a few Asian officers, recipients of
> Queen's commissions since 1957. But they have
> severe doubts as to whether the new Kenya
> Army holds any future for them, although
> they are not the stumbling block to African
> promotion that Asians are in the lower
> echelons of the civil service and to some
> extent in the police. One frequently sees
> Sikh police officers in Nairobi, the badge
> of the force pinned at the front of their
> immaculate white turbans. The threat to their
> livelihood is harsh--efficient and impressive
> though they may be. As soon as Africans are
> qualified for their jobs, and probably before,
> they will be cast out on pension along with
> the Customs officers and Post Office clerks,
> the railway men and Council officials.[18]

Although exact figures are unavailable, there
is abundant evidence that the new African government has been less than lenient in granting its
citizenship to non-Africans. As was observed
above, many Asians had been granted an option to
be registered as Kenya citizens; and the Kenya
government has understandably made it a point to
emphasize that few Asians took advantage of this
opportunity to become Kenyans. They were given an
opportunity, but they preferred to cling to their
British citizenship.

In the first place, it is a case of the pot

206

calling the kettle black. The Kenya government itself has failed to register over 10,000 Asians who did apply to be registered as local citizens on or before the prescribed date of December 12, 1965. Under the Constitution they were entitled to be registered and yet their applications have remained unprocessed to this day. According to a reliable and knowledgeable source:

> these applications were lying dumped in two rooms unattended and unopened. The documents were left this way and people wishing to travel had trouble even getting them back, let alone having them processed. The story is that there were instructions from higher authorities to harrass the applicants for registration as much as possible.

Most lawyers had stopped taking citizenship cases. In the words of a lawyer, known to one of the authors, "It is heartbreaking. You write letters and they remain unacknowledged for years. I am so fed up that I do not want to get involved with the citizenship cases." Although it is possible to institute court proceedings against the government for not registering those applicants who were entitled to Kenya citizenship, no attorney has taken the case, nor (in the prevailing environment) is one likely to do so. Many Asians failed to acquire local citizenship partly as a result of such frustrations, partly because of their own unwillingness to live under an African government, but mainly because of the fact, based on their experiences in the period immediately following independence, that possession of local citizenship would not necessarily be a guarantee of equality of treatment and opportunity. Asians in Kenya today, numbering less than fifty to sixty thousand, are mostly those who fell under category (a) and acquired local citizenship through operation of law.

Realizing that very few non-Africans had become local citizens by the end of 1965, (the Kenya government made it almost impossible for

207

them to naturalize later on) the African leaders began talking about "Kenyanization" or "localization" of the civil service. The official policy now it claimed was to give preference to citizens over non-citizens. Instead of references to racial or ethnic origin, government announcements of positions in the various departments now carried a proviso to the effect that preference would be given to Kenya citizens. A random, though unscientific, survey of Asian youths in Nairobi carried out in 1970 indicated that over eighty percent believed that, because they were Asians, they had little chance of being recruited for government positions, regardless of whether they were citizens or not, except on those rare occasions when the government could not find the right person and, even then, it would be only until an African was available to take over from him. Over ninety percent thought that "Kenyanization" was simply a legal guise, in practice it meant "Africanization." (At times, though, the government did fail to maintain the facade, see for example the Kenya Development Plan, 1970-74, p. 25 and p. 420).

The government has, of course, not been able to Africanize the civil service completely. However, for those positions it had to recruit non-Africans, the tendency has been to favor appointment of foreigners on a non-permanent basis. New doctors, engineers, administrators, and other professionals are hired, largely from Europe and the United States, on contract basis as consultants attached to the various ministries and departments. The consultants often perform functions that theoretically are the responsibility of the newly appointed young Africans. The contractual appointee has the obligation to train the neophytes. But, if he is interested in renewal of his own contract, the training period takes much longer than the government had planned resulting in the need to pay both the outsider as well as the African trainee. It has also been difficult for the government to recruit and keep the right kind of outsiders. Most of the

British working for the Kenya government come with
no knowledge of Africa and attitudes highly dysfunc-
tional to their successful interaction with Africans of any background. And, yet, the government
insisted on hiring them and forcing into premature
retirement Asians and Europeans who knew the
local language and customs, were accustomed to
local methods of operation, and, more importantly,
would have performed the same functions at less
than twenty-five percent of the cost. As has been
noted:

> Had Kenya's ministers made more sincere
> noises about needing their services, more
> might have stayed (the point is that they
> did want them to stay). As it was, antag-
> onism drove them away, along with the vets,
> the doctors and dentists and nurses and
> other professional people....Forty percent
> of the government's vets left in a year;
> one hospital had to advertise in London for
> nurses; suddenly a town like Nyeri found
> itself with only one doctor, an Asian, and
> fifty years' progress dropped away as the
> only alternative source of medical attention
> became the missions, as it had been in 1910.[19]

And this was repeated at all levels and in all
occupational groups. In 1964, the Kenyan national
legislature remained closed for over two weeks
simply because all the verbatim reporters had
left and none suitable could be found to perform
the work. Not only government workers but the
people who had to deal with the government,
especially private businesses, suffered through
switchboard delays, tediously slow paperwork, and
bungling of simple tasks. Part of the cost of
Africanization was borne by foreign governments.
Britain continued to pay a percentage of the
salaries of those non-Africans who had been recruited through London, other countries (United
States, Canada, West Germany) sent technical
advisors and consultants at very little cost to
the Kenya government, and of course the United
Nations could, in a pinch, be relied upon to

209

furnish the right kind of an expert. Had the
British not agreed to finance purchase of European
farms by Africans, paid part of the wages of
British advisors, consultants, and other persons
hired by the Kenyan government on contractual
terms, and given economic assistance to the new
African government in hundreds of other ways, it
is quite likely (especially if the Asians had not
been available to serve as scapegoats) that the
British in Kenya would have suffered the same
discredit the French did in Algeria. "For the
sake of international respect and the survival of
domestic economy, the ideal of a non-racial
society is paid much more than lip-service. But
the hot, deep down urge is to force this former
'White Man's Country' into a mould that is
demonstrably African dominated, or in Senator
Lupembe's phrase 'blackanized'."[20]

   The emphasis on pursuing the policy of Africanization with great urgency has, of course, had
its effects on standards of efficiency and
operation. The haphazard way in which Africans
were recruited to replace the Europeans and the
Asians, especially at middle levels, adversely
affected the civil service and will continue to do
so for a long time. More important was the effect
of such a policy on Africans who occupied high
positions in the service prior to independence--
positions which they had come to fill on the basis
of genuine merit. They observed inexperienced
Africans being appointed to high positions without
having to undergo the same kind of rigorous
training and maturity they had to go through. They
noted the decline in the overall standards
affecting their own performance and workloads,
and the injection of political and tribal considerations in the recruitment procedures. Though
disillusioned and resentful, they accepted these
conditions, but at the price of their self-
respect.

   Having done what they could to Africanize the
civil service, the police, and the army, the
leaders of the new state turned their attention to

employment in the private sector. By this time, the period of two years allowed to apply for citizenship for first and second generation non-Africans had elapsed. For reasons described previously, very few had acquired Kenyan citizenship. It was easy, therefore, for the African leaders to make citizenship status the main vehicle for their drive against the employment of non-Africans in the private sector.

Until 1967, the government had remained satisfied with exhorting private employers to increase the number of Africans in their employ. That year it decided to take matters into its own hands. It enacted a new Immigration Act which provided that the presence in Kenya of any person who was not a citizen but had been issued (or was eligible for the issue of) a certificate of permanent residence under the existing laws would be unlawful three months after publication by the Minister of Home Affairs of a notice in the Official Gazette which was applicable to him.[21] In publishing such notices, the minister did not have to refer to a person by name. He could refer to groups, e.g. all non-citizens employed by a particular employer, or engaged in a specified occupation, or trade, or profession. For policy purposes, non-citizens were classified into twelve broad categories. People in higher categories were supposed to be performing functions of more value to Kenya than those who fell into lower categories who the minister might decide at any time were expendable. The procedure was designed to bring about a phased withdrawal of non-Africans from private employment. For example, on December 4, 1967, the minister published a notice in the Gazette affecting all non-citizens engaged in the following occupations: (a) Clerical: Secretaries, Stenographers, Typists, Clerks, Bookkeepers, Cashiers, Office Machine Operators; (b) Sales: Technical Representatives, Brokers, Shop Assistants, etc. A notice published on February 3, 1969, referred to all non-citizens working for twelve named banks. One published on October 21, 1969, named those engaged in the sale, storage, or distribution of petroleum or petroleum products. Once a person or the category in which he fell had been "called up" through such a notice, it meant that, in the government's view his value to Kenya had ended. If he still wished to remain in Kenya after three months from the date of the notice, he was expected under the new law to obtain from the government an "Entry Permit."

The use of this term was misleading (perhaps deliberately so). The implication is that the person applying is outside the country when, in fact, he may have been born and living there for years. The "Entry Permit" was intrinsically tied to the right to work. Without it, it was unlawful for certain people to be engaged in any employment, occupation, trade, business, or profession, whether for profit or otherwise. Thus, a stenographer, who fell under the notice published on December 4, 1967, continuing to work after March 4, 1967, could be prosecuted for being unlawfully employed unless she had by then secured an "Entry Permit" from the appropriate government officers.

The issue of entry permits was entirely at the discretion of the government. Such permits were granted for specific periods, ranging from three months to two years. Each time an application was made for a permit or its renewal, the applicant had to pay a prescribed fee, ranging from two hundred to two thousand shillings. ($1.00 = approximately 7-9 shillings). In many cases, the fee amounted to as much as the applicant's monthly salary. Even if the applicant was willing to take a chance and risk working without such a permit, it was not easy to find an employer willing to do the same. It was a criminal offense for any person to employ someone whose presence in Kenya was unlawful, i.e. who was not a citizen and who did not have in his or her possession a valid entry permit. Part of the form used to apply for an entry permit had to be completed by the employer. He was required to state the non-citizen applicant's salary and the period for which the employment was offered. He also had to indicate steps he had taken to recruit a citizen for the same position, arrangements he had made (or proposed to make) for training a citizen for that position, and the extent to which the non-citizen applicant would assist in training a citizen to take over from him. An entry permit was issued only after the government had been satisfied that effective training programs had been (or would be) instituted by the employer making it possible for a citizen employee to displace the non-citizen within a specified period.

With each application for renewal there was, therefore, a correspondingly increased burden on the employer to prove to the government the need to retain the applicant. In addition, to enable the government to obtain a broader picture of the employers' activities and practices, all employers were required by law to submit to the government regular reports indicating the number of non-citizens in their employ, their positions, names, and races. They were also to provide for each non-citizen worker the name and race of the citizen employee being trained to replace the non-citizen. They were also to specify the dates on which the training had begun and when it was expected to end. The government kept a careful record of the progress of large corporations, and took every opportunity to remind them of their obligation to ensure that the local people (Africans) enjoyed a share of the profits they were reaping from African lands. A point was, therefore, fairly quickly reached when, as much as they may have hated it, employers stopped recruiting non-citizens and began discharging those in their employ. Some corporations laid off a large number of such persons simply to avoid the frustrations of having to answer to the government at regular intervals.

The Europeans generally fell within the higher categories since they were largely occupying managerial or professional positions. But the Asians and the Arabs also, occupying the medium level clerical, administrative, and technical positions,

213

were gravely affected. Working for private European or Asian business concerns for years, they
suddenly found themselves out of work. The employers, having seen how fruitless it would be to
oppose the policy, cooperated with the government,
especially the European corporations. The government rewarded them by being lenient in approving
entry permits for those occasional European
employees who by choice fell within the categories
that had been called up. Of course, the overall
efficiency of the business operations suffered and
overhead expenses increased because of the obligation of having to hire trainees and institute
training programs, but these were written off as
conditions of doing business in an African country.

In Kenya, the entry permits were often referred to as "Work Permits." Although it was unlawful
for a non-citizen to remain in Kenya without an
entry permit, the government was not as much concerned with expelling from the country those who
had overstayed as with making sure that they
had moved over and made room, as far as jobs were
concerned, for the Africans. If they were willing
to stay on in Kenya as unemployed and live on their
savings the government was unlikely to prosecute
them. But few could afford doing this. Most
began to leave. Only those who were automatic
citizens or those whose services were essential and
of benefit to Kenya (as interpreted by the government at different times) could continue with their
work. Those who had decided not to opt for Kenya
citizenship and had specifically retained British
citizenship were sooner or later allowed to enter
Britain, many after having lived in Kenya unemployed for at least a couple of years. But, it was
those who had simply renounced their British
citizenship since they fully expected ultimately
to be Kenya citizens who found themselves in the
most unenviable position of all. They were now
stateless, and had difficulty even to obtain travel
documents to migrate to a country where they would
at least have the right to earn their livelihoods.
The authors have a letter from one such person in
their possession.

It was almost impossible for the displaced employees to go into business on their own unless they happened to have a large amount of capital in their own name. (In that case, they probably would not have been working as civil servants or for others.) Licensing laws introduced by the new African government made it illegal for them to open their own business on a small scale.

Instead of describing in detail the restrictions on trading and other business activities imposed upon non-citizens by Kenya, we shall move to Sierra Leone in West Africa where laws similar to those in Kenya were introduced by the government discriminating against its Arab (Lebanese and Syrian) minority. But, as a concluding comment on Kenya, suffice it to say that out of over 200,000 Asians and Arabs in the country on the day of independence after only fifteen years of majority rule less than sixty to seventy thousand remained. And, although the total number of Europeans there is still around forty thousand, it is often forgotten that among them there are many who are newcomers--the old, experienced, and settled communities have opted or been forced to rebuild their lives elsewhere.

Prohibition Against Engaging in Retail Trade

With an area of 27,925 square miles and a population estimated in 1971 at 2.6 million and an annual growth rate of about 1.5 percent (one of the lowest in Africa), Sierra Leone, a small country located on the west coast of Africa, can hardly be regarded as suffering from overpopulation. Yet, some 10,000 Arabs, who only twenty years ago were solidly anchored in Sierra Leonean society, now seem to be living there only on sufferance, uncertain of their future.

The Arabs, mostly from Syria and Lebanon, began to migrate to Sierra Leone in the 1890's. Unlike the Europeans, who tended to regard Sierra Leone as a "white man's grave," the Arabs were not reluctant to bring their wives and raise their

215

families there, or even to settle in non-coastal
areas. In 1913, in Freetown alone, there were at
least twenty-five Lebanese children residing on a
permanent basis, all born in Sierra Leone.   A
number of Arabs, partly because they were too poor
to return to Lebanon or Syria to marry or to send
for prospective brides, married African women.
Children of these mixed marriages, as well as
those born out of wedlock, are generally referred
to in Sierra Leone as the Afro-Lebanese.   The
Arabs bought or built homes in the country.   A
Lebanese is on record as having purchased a
house in Freetown as early as 1920.[22] The hundreds of modern multi-storied concrete houses
found today on Kissy Street and other thorough-
fares of Freetown and Bo, many built during the
1950's, are indicative of Arab willingness to
invest in the country of their residence, and
provide adequate evidence of their intention to
reside there in the future.   Although most began
their careers as street hawkers or small shopkeepers, the Arabs gradually became involved in a
wide variety of economic pursuits. By 1960, they
were playing a significant role in the country's
economy as retailers--purchasers of locally produced palm kernels, palm oil, cocoa, and coffee,
and sellers of rice, textiles, and other imported
goods, and were even becoming involved in gold
and diamond mining, construction, small-scale
manufacturing, and agriculture.

    By the late 1950's, Britain had already made
up its mind to relinquish its colonial possessions
in West Africa and was grooming African leaders to
take over the reins of government. Not unnaturally,
Britain was concerned about the future of non-
Africans under an African regime and sought, in
the days preceding independence, to have incorporated into the Constitution under which Sierra
Leone would achieve independent status certain
guarantees and safeguards for non-African British
citizens. It was also interested in making sure
that the new state would respect basic human
rights for all persons found within its territory.
These issues were thoroughly discussed at consti-

tutional conferences at which all African political factions were fully represented. It was only after the terms of the proposed Constitution were specifically agreed upon by the various factions that Britain finally decided to grant independence to Sierra Leone on April 27, 1961.

An examination of the Constitution adopted by Sierra Leone on the day of its independence suggests that the question of the effect of transfer of sovereignty upon the inhabitants of Sierra Leone and their national status had been settled in a fashion which was both rational and sensible. Article 1, subsection 1 of the Constitution referred to those Arabs who had been in the country for at least three generations. It was agreed that these people should be considered Sierra Leoneans for all intents and purposes, and must acquire through operation of the law, citizenship of the new state. It read:

> Every person who, having been born in the former Colony or Protectorate of Sierra Leone, was on the twenty-sixth day of April, 1961, a citizen of the United Kingdom and Colonies or a British Protected Person shall become a citizen of Sierra Leone on the twenty-seventh day of April, 1961: <u>Provided</u> <u>that</u> a person shall not become a citizen of Sierra Leone by virtue of this subsection if neither of his parents nor any of his grandparents was born in the former Colony or Protectorate of Sierra Leone.[23]

Apart from Arabs of the third generation, all Africans indigenous to Sierra Leone, of course, also acquired the citizenship of the new state under the above provision, as did the Afro-Lebanese, who fell within the purview of subsection 1 because their mothers and grandmothers had been born in Sierra Leone, even if their fathers were first generation immigrants. To avoid dual nationality, Britain, as had been agreed upon earlier, amended its laws so that any British subject residing in Sierra Leone, upon being invested with local

citizenship under Article 1 (1), automatically
ceased to be a British subject.

Citizenship in the new state was not automatically conferred upon the second generation
Arabs, i.e., those born in Sierra Leone but neither
of whose parents had been born there. It was believed that those among them who might wish to
retain their British citizenship should be able
to do so. It was therefore agreed that such
persons would be given an option. They could
acquire Sierra Leonean citizenship provided they
made their desires known within two years. Otherwise, they would be regarded as having opted to
retain their British citizenship. However, if
they should take specific action to make known
their desire to acquire local citizenship by
applying for it within the prescribed period, it
was obligatory on the part of the new state to
accept them as its citizens, as provided for in
Article 2, subsection 1. Article 3, subsection 1,
gave similar option to those among the first
generation immigrants who, by virtue of their
residence in Sierra Leone had applied for and been
accepted, prior to independence, as British subjects by naturalization or registration.

No specific provisions were made affecting
the citizenship of the remaining first generation
immigrants. They were to continue to be treated
as alien residents. Article 9 of the Constitution,
however, empowered the Sierra Leone parliament
to enact laws "for the acquisition of citizenship
of Sierra Leone by persons who do not become
citizens of Sierra Leone by virtue of the provisions
of this Chapter" and it was anticipated that the
new state, whose leaders had specifically endorsed
the concept of multi-racialism, would soon after
independence enact its own naturalization laws
under which it would be possible for those among
the first generation who might wish to do so to
apply for local citizenship.

The principle of jus soli was retained in
respect to those who were born in Sierra Leone

after independence. It was also provided that parliament had no right to deprive of his Sierra Leonean citizenship any person who was born in the country after independence or who had acquired Sierra Leonean citizenship by virtue of the provisions of Article 1 (1).

The Constitution also contained elaborate provisions relating to basic rights, including a non-discrimination clause. To curb any propensity to water down these rights, the drafters of the Constitution made amendment of these provisions much more difficult than for the rest of the articles.

In retrospect, all the precautions taken by the British served little purpose, for less than a year after gaining independence the government of Sierra Leone introduced retroactive legislation which rendered inoperative those key provisions of the Constitution which governed citizenship. These provisions, which had reflected solemn commitments made during pre-independence conferences, were revoked through passage by the parliament of Sierra Leone on January 17, 1962, of two constitutional amendments, "deemed to have come into operation on the twenty-seventh day of April, 1961."[24] The first of these retroactive amendments restricted the citizenship granted under subsection (1) of Article 1 to "every person of negro African descent." The addition of these four little words to the Article had far-reaching consequences. First, in effect, they deprived the Arabs whose families had been in Sierra Leone for three or more generations of their citizenship-- or more accurately, they were considered as never having acquired local citizenship in the first place. Second generation Arabs (i.e., those born in Sierra Leone but neither of whose parents had been born there), who had been given the options of gaining Sierra Leonean citizenship within two years of independence, were no longer qualified to exercise that option, and those who had already done so were to have their certificates of citizenship revoked. This was because subsection (1) of

219

Article 2 of the Constitution, which governed the granting of citizenship to such persons, began with the words: "Any person who, but for the proviso to subsection (1) of Article 1 of this Constitution, would be a citizen of Sierra Leone...." When Article 1 was retroactively amended so as to apply only to those of negro African descent, subsection (1) automatically thereafter applied only to those persons of negro African descent, none of whose parents or grandparents had been born in Sierra Leone.

In explaining this provision to the parliament, the Prime Minister went on record as stating that one must be of negro African descent to be regarded as entitled to registration under Article 2 (1).[25] Article 3 of the Constitution, which had granted a similar option to first generation Arabs, was repealed outright by the ex post facto amendment. Second, because the phrase "of negro African descent" was defined as referring to a person "whose father and whose father's father are or were negroes of African origin," most Afro-Lebanese were now deemed never to have become Sierra Leoneans, for it was the mothers of most of the Afro-Lebanese who were Africans, not the fathers. To soften the blow on the Afro-Lebanese, the amending act permitted "any person, either of whose parents is a negro of African descent" to apply for Sierra Leonean citizenship, but it was not incumbent on the government to approve such applications. Even assuming it was granted, the citizenship held by such persons would be of second-class nature, since they were barred from becoming members either of parliament or of any local authority until "they shall have resided continuously in Sierra Leone for twenty-five years after such registration or shall have served in the civil or regular Armed Services of Sierra Leone for a continuous period of twenty-five years." Third, as noted earlier, under British law those who had acquired Sierra Leone citizenship by virtue of the original subsection (1) of Article 1 had already ceased to be British subjects.

The retroactive admendment of 1962 was unilateral and in no way binding upon the British
government which, understandably, was not inclined to readmit the Arabs and Afro-Lebanese to
their former status as British subjects. These
persons now became stateless. In an effort to
lull them into a false sense of security, it had
been provided (perhaps facetiously) in the
amending act that those deprived of their citizenship by the ex post facto legislation would be
granted the status of "Commonwealth Citizen."
But since they were no longer British subjects,
and no other nation in the Commonwealth would
accept them as citizens, the status of "Commonwealth Citizen" was legally meaningless. It took
some time before these persons realized that they
were in fact stateless and that the passports
issued by the Sierra Leone government indicating
their status as "Commonwealth Citizens" were of
no value. Article 4 of the Constitution, which
had retained the principle of jus soli for those
born in Sierra Leone after independence was also
retroactively amended to read:

> Every person of negro African descent born
> in Sierra Leone after the twenty-sixth day
> of April, 1961, shall be a citizen of Sierra
> Leone at the date of his birth if at that
> date his father is or was a citizen of
> Sierra Leone.[26]

The addition of these four familiar words barred
all children born of Arab parents between April 27,
1961, and the enactment of the ex post facto amendments from having acquired Sierra Leonean citizenship by birth.

The combined effect of the two constitutional
amendments was to preclude all Arabs, whether of
the first, second, third or future generations
from acquiring Sierra Leonean citizenship automatically (i.e., through operation of the law) or
from being entitled to opt for such citizenship.
The only exception was for the Afro-Lebanese; but
even if they were to be accepted, it would be as

second-class citizens.

The new state was apparently intent upon having absolute freedom of action in respect to granting or refusing its citizenship to those not meeting a combination of geographic and racial qualifications--i.e., those not of "negro African descent." The only avenue left for the Arabs who had thus been unceremoniously deprived of their citizenship was to apply for naturalization under a newly enacted law entitled the "Sierra Leone Nationality and Citizenship Act, 1962."[27] To qualify for naturalization under this act, the applicant was expected to satisfy the Prime Minister (the minister charged with responsibility for matters relating to citizenship) on a number of points having to do with the applicant's good character, residency in Sierra Leone, and knowledge of the language currently in use in the country. Even after he had been so satisfied, the Prime Minister was under no legal obligation to approve the application or to give the reason for this refusal to do so. Nor was such a decision subject to appeal or review by any court of law. The Prime Minister's authority did not end when he had approved an application and the applicant had renounced his previous citizenship (Sierra Leone did not allow dual nationality), taken the oath of allegiance, and been issued a Certificate of Naturalization. The naturalization could be revoked for several reasons, among them the display by the naturalized citizen, in action or speech, of disloyalty to or disaffection with the government of Sierra Leone. This put the applicant almost entirely at the mercy of the Minister, both before and after naturalization.

Even with these limitations, it was obvious that the government had no intention of being liberal in approving such applications. When the Act was being discussed in the Sierra Leone parliament, Dr. Siaka Stevens, who later became President of the Republic of Sierra Leone, but was then the leader of the opposition, expressed the view that since Sierra Leone did not stand to from the resident Arabs, they should not have the right even to apply for naturalization. In response, the Prime Minister said that it was a common practice to allow residents to apply for naturalization but that "very stringent measures would be taken before this privilege will be accorded to non-Sierra Leoneans."[28] Within a matter of weeks, it had become common knowledge among the Arabs that the government was likely to be extremely selective in granting citizenship by naturalization. A thirty-four year old Sierra Leone-born Arab businessman, whose family had settled there in 1908, when asked in August, 1976, as to why he had not applied for naturalization under the 1962 Act said:

> I would have applied if I had thought there was a chance to get it. I asked several government officers (with whom I was very friendly) on a number of different occasions. And each time they told me right away that I was not going to get it.[29]

Although the law was never rationally or uniformly applied, it seems that the government did, in the end, approve a few hundred applications. Most naturalizations took place between 1962 and 1967, but there is evidence to suggest that some Certificates of Naturalization were also issued between 1967 and 1969 when Sierra Leone was under military rule.

In 1969, Sierra Leone reverted to civilian rule under the leadership of Dr. Siaka Stevens. A new constitution was drafted enabling Sierra Leone to have its own head of state, Sierra Leone was declared a Republic (though remaining a member of the Commonwealth) on April 19, 1971, and Dr. Stevens became its first president. Unlike that of 1961, the 1971 constitution was almost totally silent on the question of citizenship. It simply provided that parliament was the supreme legislative authority for Sierra Leone and that "any bill relating to citizenship of Sierra Leone shall not be passed by parliament in any session unless at the final vote thereon in that session it is supported by the votes of not less than two-thirds of all the members of the parliament." Under the transitional provisions contained in the 1971 constitution, all existing laws and enactments made under it were to remain in force until such time as they could be amended by the new parliament and were to be "read and construed with such modifications, adaptations, qualifications and exceptions as may be necessary to bring them into conformity with this (1971) constitution." Presumably because the 1962 Citizenship Act had been enacted by parliament only by a majority vote, or because it merely supplemented the citizenship provisions contained in the 1961 constitution, or because the government had yet to determine its future policy on citizenship, all applications for naturalization under the 1962 act received between 1969 and 1973 had been left unprocessed. In 1973, the government came up with yet another law: the Sierra Leone Citizenship Act, 1973, replacing the 1962 Act. The effect of this law was to place the Arabs in an even more precarious position than the one they had held under the previous regime.

The Act was totally silent on the question of naturalization of persons of non-negro African descent. The net effect of the provisions was that while it was possible for a Guinean or Tanzanian African who had migrated to Sierra Leone in 1965 to apply for naturalization as a Sierra Leonean, the same privilege (i.e. that of even applying for naturalization) was now not to be available to Arabs born in Sierra Leone and whose families had lived there for generations. It took away from them even this limited right which they had enjoyed after the 1962 constitutional amendments. Third, the 1973 Act raised serious questions about the status of even those Arabs who had acquired Sierra Leonean citizenship by naturalization under the 1962 Act. Part VI of the 1973 law required all those who had previously had citizenship conferred upon them by naturalization or registration to apply for renewal of their citizenship "in the prescribed manner within the period of three months after the coming into operation of this Act." It is understood from reliable sources that the post-Republic government suspected a number of naturalized Arab citizens of having acquired Sierra Leonean citizenship by fraudulent means such as bribery. By forcing all to re-apply for citizenship, the government hoped to weed out these, and others regarded as "undesirable." Nonetheless, the fact remains that the effect of this provision was to deprive the legitimately naturalized person of his citizenship as well as the one who had gained his citizenship by force or fraud. All were now expected to re-apply and prove de novo to the new regime their fitness for citizenship. The form prescribed by the government for applying for renewal required a statement by the applicant of the circumstances under which he gained citizenship, plus a photostatic copy of his original Certificate of Naturalization/Registration.[30] What made matters even worse was that although the naturalized citizens were expected to apply for renewal of citizenship within three months of the Act's coming into operation (i.e. on or before August 24, 1973), the above rules were not published in the Sierra Leone Official Gazette until September 20, 1973. It was also unclear whether the Arabs qualified for renewal of citizenship under a law which, with the exception of women married to Sierra Leonean citizens, permitted only persons of negro African descent to acquire Sierra Leonean citizenship by naturalization. It is understood that, in the end, only about thirty naturalized citizens sent in letters within the prescribed period seeking renewal. It is not known how many of these were refused renewal. The rest could be presumed, under Article 14 (2), to have failed to apply for renewal and consequently must be deemed to have renounced their Sierra Leone citizenship.

In August, 1976, the parliament enacted yet another law relating to citizenship: The Sierra Leone Citizenship (Amendment) Act, 1976. It extended the right to apply for citizenship by naturalization to those falling within two more

225

categories--(a) a person only one of whose parents was of negro African descent provided he was continuously residing in Sierra Leone for a period of at least eight years; and (b) a person neither of whose parents was a person of negro African descent provided he was residing in Sierra Leone and had been continuously so for a period of at least fifteen years. The Act was portrayed as a major concession to the Arabs. In the parliament, the government claimed that "this Bill will lay to rest all criticisms levelled against us that we restrict our citizenship only to negroes."[31] The above provisions were also reproduced in the government-controlled Sierra Leone newspapers and included on government radio and television broadcasts. Admittedly, this constituted a major change in the general policy of the government in operation since 1962 of restricting Sierra Leone citizenship to persons who were of negro African descent or who were at least fifty percent negro. But, in terms of the impact of this law on the resident Arabs, one must examine the relatively unpublicized portions of the Act.

Section 13 of the Act subjects non-citizens and naturalized citizens alike to a series of discriminatory tax laws. Considerations of space oblige us to give only a very short summary account of these laws. The deceptively-titled Pay Roll Tax Act, 1972, has nothing to do with an employer's obligation to deduct from his employees' wages taxes to which the employees are liable. Instead, its crucial provision requires all employers to pay a tax on each of their employees who is either a non-citizen or naturalized. This tax, payable regardless of the length of time in the calendar year such a person was actually employed, was initially only 100 Leones per employee (1 Leone - $.89 approximately), but a little later a government minister was empowered to increase the tax by simply publishing a notice in the Official Gazette.[45] In 1973, the tax was raised to 250 Leones annually, in 1975 to 1000 Leones, and in August, 1976, it was to be increased to 2500 Leones a year. This "pay roll" tax is not deductible to arrive at the employer's taxable income, nor is it legal for the employer to pass the tax on to his employees. In a country where the starting salary of a government-employed medical doctor is less than ten thousand Leones a year, the "pay roll" tax is no small burden on private employers. No employer can afford to overlook this liability in making decisions on recruitment or retention of employees who are non-citizens or naturalized citizens. The government obviously intends that in the competition for scarce jobs, the Arabs will be perpetually at a disadvantage.

If the provisions of the <u>Non-Citizens</u> (<u>Registration</u>, <u>Immigration</u>, <u>and</u> <u>Expulsion</u>) <u>Act</u>, <u>1965</u> had been applied only to non-citizens, the law would have represented a reasonable attempt on the part of the government to ascertain the total number of resident aliens at any given time, and to have some control over their entry into and their movements within the country. But from the start, the law was specifically inapplicable to "privileged Africans," i.e., citizens of Gambia, Ghana, Ivory Coast, and Liberia, plus others which the minister was empowered to add from time to time. Although "privileged" aliens were exempt from the Act, <u>naturalized</u> <u>Sierra</u> <u>Leoneans</u> fell as much under its provisions as did unprivileged non-citizens. The Act, and the rules prescribed thereunder, required all who fell within its purview to appear before a government officer, satisfactorily to establish their identity by documentary means, pay a small registration fee, and obtain a Certificate of Registration with an affixed photograph which was expected to be carried at all times and produced on demand by the police. All changes of address had to be reported, as did any trip away from Sierra Leone of more than two months. Registration had to be renewed annually, though the fee dropped after the first year.

Although the Arabs--especially those whose families had been living in Sierra Leone for generations--felt degraded at having to register annually and report their whereabouts to the police

like aliens, most complied with the law. The fee
was nominal, carrying the certificate on them only
a minor inconvenience, and few often changed their
place of residence. The law, however, took a
different shape altogether when new rules were
issued in 1975. Under these rules, issued on
January 2, 1975, but deemed to have come into
operation on July 1, 1974, any non-citizen (or
naturalized citizen of non-negro African origin)
who had a business of his own was required to
obtain in addition to the Certificate of Registration a "Residential Commercial Permit" for a
fee of 500 Leones, and to renew this permit every
July for a renewal fee of 250 Leones. In
practice, the permit was nothing more than an
endorsement on the Certificate of Registration,
made by the appropriate officer, indicating that
the bearer had paid the fees and that he was
allowed to engage in the specified activity until
a certain date. In August, 1975, the fee for the
initial endorsement was increased from 500 to 1000
Leones, and the renewal fee from 250 to 500
Leones. Seven months later the renewal fee was
again doubled to 1000 Leones. In 1976, both the
initial and renewal fees were increased to 2500
Leones annually. It is no longer possible to
regard this as a tax charged to cover the expenses
involved in keeping track of the non-citizens in
the country, especially in view of the fact that
naturalized Sierra Leoneans who happen to be Arabs
are now also subject to the fee. Instead, it
must be thought of as one of the prices the Arabs
must pay for their lack of any negro African blood.

The Non-Citizens Registration Act and the Pay
Roll Tax Act by no means exhaust the roster of laws
bearing discriminatory provisions against the
Sierra Leonean Arabs. Although the Business
Registration Act, 1972, is in itself apparently
innocuous, the rules under which the Act is enforced
divide all business establishments owned or
operated by one person into three categories: (a)
Non-African/Non-Citizen, (b) African/Non-Citizen,
and (c) Citizen. Corporations and partnerships
were classified in a roughly analogous fashion.

228

Annual fees prescribed for those corporations, partnerships, and individually owned establishments in category (a) were highest, fees were lowest for those businesses in category (c), with the fee for category (b) falling somewhere in between. According to the citizenship (Amendment) Act, 1976, naturalized citizens are treated the same as non-citizens for purposes of the Business Registration Act and the rules enacted thereunder. Business establishments owned by individual Arabs, or corporations or partnerships in which the Arabs have a majority interest would therefore always fall under category (a), where the fee is highest. A naturalized Arab businessman born in Sierra Leone whose family has lived there for over a generation would, in fact, end up paying a larger fee under this Act than a recent immigrant from Guinea or Tanzania engaged in a similar business.

A comparable distinction among various categories of businesses is also made for income tax purposes. Business concerns owned by non-citizens or naturalized citizens pay higher income taxes than ones owned by citizens of negro African descent. Interestingly, this tax is calculated on the turnover of a business, not its profits, so that an Arab-owned establishment is liable for a certain minimum tax (3000 Leones annually, 6000 if it is a partnership) whether or not it has been operating at a profit. It is not surprising that the bulk of the income tax paid came out of the pockets of non-citizens, or naturalized citizens treated as aliens under the terms of the 1976 Citizenship Act. Arab controlled businesses apparently are destined to continue paying higher taxes than establishments owned by black Africans.

Although the Sierra Leone government obviously had no intention of allowing naturalized citizens to enjoy the same political and economic rights afforded to citizens of negro African descent, it was abundantly clear from the August, 1976, debates in the parliament that even upon these conditions, the government was unlikely to be very liberal in approving applications for naturalization as

229

Sierra Leoneans. Indicative of the government's attitude were such comments as:

"We are not saying that everybody who is a white man will be naturalized. No. The stringency of application will continue. We are only talking about qualifications."

"Naturalization is a concession. You cannot ask me for a reason. I am not obliged to give you a reason. If I am on the naturalization committee, I see you and don't like you, I can refuse."

"Citizenship is a very serious affair. It is not very easy to become a citizen of U.S.A. nor of the U.S.S.R."

"The United Nations should not make our laws." 32

Despite the limitations imposed upon the political and economic rights of naturalized citizens, some Arabs may still apply for naturalization. The reason for this (and for the government's declared intention to be very niggardly in approving these applications) is that non-citizens suffer from at least two further limitations. First, since the enactment of the Land Development (Protection) Act, 1962, they were prohibited from purchasing land in the whole of Sierra Leone. In the past, they were allowed to own land at least in the western area (areas including and adjoining the capital city of Freetown) where they had acquired substantial holdings. Thenceforth, they could neither buy new land, nor expand their holdings, nor sell or transfer their holdings to other non-citizens without government approval. Second, and, perhaps of even greater importance, are the laws prohibiting non-citizens from participating in a wide number of economic activities. As early as 1965, with the passage of "An Act to Exclude Non-Citizens from Retail Trade in Certain Areas and from Certain Other Industries and to Prevent Non-Citizens from Opening New Retail Businesses, and to Encourage Industry and Business

Promoted by Citizens of Sierra Leone," an attempt
had been made to restrict Arab participation in
the retail trade, since for purposes of the Act,
the word "citizen" was defined in such a way that
it excluded those who had acquired Sierra Leonean
citizenship under the 1962 Act.   The Afro-
Lebanese, however, were classified as "citizens"
under the 1965 legislation, and provision was
also made for the government to exempt "privileged
Africans" from the law.

     The Act empowered the government to declare
certain parts of Sierra Leone as "restricted
areas." In areas that had been so declared, non-
citizens were precluded from opening any new retail
business. Moreover, non-citizens already in
business in those areas were prohibited, effective
immediately, from retail trade in specified commodities. One of the public notices published by
the government under this law gives some idea of
how this law was implemented. It read:

          Areas listed in the first column to be
          restricted areas to non-Sierra Leoneans for
          the purpose of retail trade in commodities
          listed under the second column, and in
          quantities specified in the third column.

The specified commodities included such commonly
traded items as cigarettes, matches, sugar, milk,
and salt. The government declared the whole of the
western area and 160 small towns or villages in the
provinces as "restricted areas." Both the towns
and the commodities had been carefully selected.
There were Arab retail traders in each of the 160
areas in the provinces with the trade in the
specified items constituting a substantial portion
of their business. In addition, non-citizens were
also precluded from trading in rice, coffee, corn,
and ground nuts in the whole territory of Sierra
Leone. Considerable difficulty was encountered in
the implementation of this law, however, and the
retail prices of many important commodities soared,
while the efficiency of the distribution system
plummeted. The military regime, therefore, repealed

the Act in October, 1967, only to have the new
civilian regime replace it with a new and more
far-reaching law entitled The Non-Citizens (Trade
and Business) Act in 1969. This act did not
apply to naturalized citizens, but it did apply
to all non-citizens, including the Afro-Lebanese.
While the 1965 Act was applied to specified areas,
the 1969 Act was made applicable to the whole
territory of Sierra Leone. Under it, all non-
citizens were prohibited from engaging in (including owning or controlling, directly or
indirectly) a number of commercial, occupational,
and professional activities. Among others, these
included:

a) Participating or operating retail trade
of such goods as may be specified by the minister
in the Gazette. Thirty-eight different items were
so specified;

b) Opening any new establishment, especially
for retail trade, or expanding an existing establishment, without the government's approval in
writing;

c) Opening a supermarket or expanding an
existing one. Supermarkets already in operation
to obtain, within six months, a special license
upon payment of a fee of 1500 Leones with the
government having the right to impose terms or
conditions upon which the continued operation will
be allowed;

d) Operating or participating, after six
months from the commencement of the Act, in several small scale manufacturing and service industries. The selected activities from which the non-
citizens were barred were the very ones the Arabs
had developed and were now operating with considerable success. By thus narrowing the fields
open to non-citizens, the government hoped that
the citizens automatically would be able to take
over and operate these businesses with the same
efficiency and margins of profit.

232

The effect of the Act was to require many non-citizens to rechannel their efforts and resources to activities not prohibited to them but with the fear that if they succeeded in a new activity, that too would be included on the lists issued by the minister. In any case, the competitiveness of even those non-citizen operations which were not prohibited by the Act was also adversely affected, since they would now have to rely on obtaining necessary support from newly established, citizen-operated concerns, with the inevitability of at least some reduction in the availability of needed supplies and services.

Within fifteen years of independent African majority rule, the Arabs, many of whom were or hoped to be registered as local citizens, found themselves confronted with two equally undesirable alternatives. One, to apply for naturalization once again under the 1976 Act knowing that as naturalized citizens they would continue to be excluded from political participation and pay higher taxes than citizens of negro-African descent but, as citizens, they could participate in specified economic activities. Two, to remain in the country as non-citizens with the prospect of being excluded from virtually all economic activity, plus having to pay even higher taxes than citizens of negro-African descent. Those who selected the first alternative might enjoy an element of security in the sense that they could not be expelled from the country as easily as non-citizens. On the other hand, by renouncing their former citizenship the naturalized citizens would lose the right to migrate at a future time to the country of their citizenship or to seek that country's diplomatic protection in the event of Sierra Leone's decision to nationalize or expropriate their properties without compensation.

Whether they take the first or the second alternative, their position in Sierra Leone would remain unenviable. Eventually, the younger, more enterprising, better educated Arabs are likely to cut the Gordian knot--to leave their former home-

233

land to the demoralized remnant of a once dynamic
force in the nation's economy.

Requiring Sale of Operating Businesses to Africans

The Republic of Zaire (formerly the Belgian
Congo and until recently known as the Democratic
Republic of the Congo) achieved political independence on June 30, 1960. Living there at that time
were thirteen million Africans scattered among
more than 200 different tribal groupings, about
110,000 Europeans (mainly Belgian, Italian, Greek,
and Portuguese), and less than 10,000 Arabs (Lebanese, Syrians) and Indians and Pakistanis. As
is well-known, for the first six to seven years
of its existence as an independent state, Zaire
was almost continually embroiled in internecine
conflicts so much so that the word "Congo"
became almost synonymous with chaos and confusion.
As a result of the general breakdown of law and
order, open resentment demonstrated by various
African tribes against the whites, and an inevitable reduction in economic activities, the non-
African population had, by 1970, dwindled to
about 60,000, including those who came after 1966
when the country appeared to enjoy a semblance
of political stability. In the late nineteen
sixties, Zaire had adopted a policy of encouraging
foreign investment and in 1969 introduced a new
Investment Code which provided tax holidays for
new investors and guaranteed repatriation of
profits and capital. This coupled with the general
climate of stability prevailing in the country for
the first time had increased foreign interest and
investments. In August 1970, President Nixon,
welcoming President Mobutu to the United States,
said:

> The Congo is a good investment.... It is one
> of the richest countries in the world in
> terms of natural resources....And when we
> combine rich natural resources with a strong,
> vigorous people and a leader who is able to
> provide the stability and the vision for
> progress for that country, then that country

is a good investment: a good investment for its own people or for others who may desire to participate in its growth.33

However, this situation did not last long and today President Nixon must be glad that he neglected to follow his own advice and did not invest all his savings in that country. The leader whom he praised as having a vision for progress did indeed introduce to his country an entirely new concept-- the Return to Authenticity--but its effect on foreign investors has been much different from what President Nixon had in mind. According to President Mobutu:

> To perpetuate the exploitation of the black by the white, the colonizers set about destroying African traditions, the African language, African culture--in a word, brutalizing the black so that he could not speak, think, eat, dress, laugh or breathe except by following the teachings of the white. It (Authenticity) is a dictate of conscience for the people of Zaire that they should return to their beginnings and search for the values of their ancestors in order to appreciate those who contribute to the country's harmonious and natural development. ....It is the affirmation of a man of Zaire or man himself, as he is and where he is, with the mental and social structures that are his own....34

In practice, this concept has manifested itself not only in cultural but also in political and economic arenas. In politics it has found expression in the ideology of "Mobutism" (discussed in another chapter); in economics in the policy of "Zairianization." Though the philosophical meaning attributed by President Mobutu to his concept of Return to Authenticity might seem vague, in terms of its implementation in economic matters it has had a very clear objective--that of bringing Zairean economy almost totally under the control of the authentic Zaireans. And, more significantly, in

235

pursuit of this objective he did not allow himself
to be diverted by philosophical considerations such
as whether Zaire should have a free market or
centrally planned economy nor did he bother to
explicitly opt for a middle-of-the-road economic
policy called African Socialism or other such name.
His concerns were simple. According to him, Return
to Authenticity requires; "the Zaire citizen to
become owner of the grounds of his ancestors;"
"all plantations, ranches, farms, and quarries
must rightfully revert to authentic Zairians;"
and "all commercial and trading activities on the
ancestral grounds must be in the hands of Zairians."
In other words, almost everything found under, above,
or on the ancestral grounds must be brought, in the
name of authenticity, under Zairian ownership or
control. In short, in concept and implementation,
Return to Authenticity is virtually the same, at
least in the economic sphere, to the search for
"genuine" or "total" independence pursued by many
of the other new African states.

Before examining this in detail, it is necessary to remark at the outset that although many
of the laws putting into effect the President's
program were couched in standard legal terms, one
important difference in word usage is found. The
word "foreigner" (or "alien") denoted ethnic origin,
not place of citizenship. Any person who was
ethnically a non-African was regarded, as far as
implementation of the authenticity policy was
concerned, as an "alien" or a "foreigner," regardless of the citizenship or passport held. Anyone
who looked like a Greek, was treated as one, often
this included Italians as well as Cypriots. Anyone
who looked like an Indian was, to many government
officers, a Pakistani, (the majority of the Asians
in Zaire were Muslims), and all were aliens or
foreigners.

Following the President's declaration of November 30, 1973, that political independence was not
enough and that time had come for Zairians to take
over everything on the ancestral grounds, a broad
range of measures were announced to force the

236

"foreigners" (henceforth referred to here as non-Africans) to turn over their businesses to Zairians. Some of these were:

1) All Portuguese (about 12,000 living mainly in the center of the country and Lower Zaire) were prohibited from living in the Bas Zaire, Banduranda, Kasai and Shaba regions; and all Pakistanis (about 3,000) from living in the regions of Kivu, Haute Zaire, and Shaba. The regions had been carefully selected--over eighty percent of the Portuguese and Pakistanis living in Zaire resided and had their businesses in the very areas from which they had now been prohibited. Moreover, the law required them to "immediately transfer their businesses to Zairians under terms and conditions to be supervised and arbitrated by the government."35

2) All foreigners involved in transportation business, i.e. operating taxis, buses, or trucks were forbidden to operate such vehicles and required to sell the businesses, including the vehicles, to Zairians at a price fixed by the government.

3) By a December 1, 1973, decree all non-Africans were prohibited from trading in a wide range of basic commodities. Only Zairians could trade in these goods. These included commonly traded items like building materials, cotton and synthetic cloth, shoes, sugar, flour, tobacco, cigarettes, rice, matches, etc. (This also made it difficult for the Portuguese and the Pakistanis to re-establish themselves and develop new businesses in regions in which they were still permitted to live.)

4) On December 11, 1973, the list of goods in which non-Africans could not trade was made all-inclusive. Non-Africans could no longer trade in Zaire. They were required to cede their businesses (including the stock in trade and other assets) to authentic Zairians within three months from the date of this decree. This measure had a devastating effect upon the Italians and the

Greeks (about 15,000 established chiefly in Lumumbashi and Shaba region) as well as on the Lebanese and the Syrians, generally known in Zaire as the Levantines.

5) All non-Africans were prohibited from taking gainful employment without first obtaining a work permit from the government. This was a thinly disguised attempt to prevent displaced non-African businessmen from re-entering the ancestral economy via salaried positions.

6) Although the non-Africans were given three months to relinquish their businesses, there is ample evidence to suggest that the President really wanted transfer of their businesses to Zairians completed before the end of 1973. He required all non-Africans to complete, on or before December 31, questionnaires in which they were to give details of the nature of their business, value of stocks in hand, and the price for which they were willing to sell the operation. Failure to submit the necessary documents to the government made them liable to lose their right to the property and risk immediate expulsion from the country. A non-African hiding or modifying documents relating to the value of his assets was liable to be sentenced to imprisonment for a maximum term of five years, a fine of 5000 Zaires (approximately $2,500), and immediate confiscation of all his property. After the questionnaire was filed, the government was to inspect the operation and determine the actual price at which it must be sold to Zairians. No appeal against the price set by the government was allowed.

7) Until the business had actually been transferred to a Zairian, the non-African was required to continue normal sales and to refrain from engaging in "economic sabotage" or creating "artificial shortages." The non-Africans were understandably reluctant to incur added debts by buying or importing new stocks and yet if they did not do so, they opened themselves to accusations of sabotaging the economy by failing to

continue normal sales. The political leaders and their supporters made the situation even worse for the non-Africans. Each tried to outdo the other in demonstrating how bad the non-Africans were. In Lumumbashi, the regional committee of the political party in power called for immediate expulsion of non-Africans sabotaging the economy and propagating false rumors. In Bukavu, where a large number of Greeks and Pakistanis had settled, the committee called on people to "denounce fraud and not to accept corruption which affects the good name of Zaire and its leaders."[36]

8) Under the law, the Zairian purchaser might "invite" the non-African owner to remain as manager of the business and receive salary and compensation on an annual basis from the profits made by that business. Some non-Africans succeeded in making such arrangements with the Zairians. The alternative of selling the property outright to a Zairian was often not feasible in practice. The tense environment in which the new laws were applied, and the lack of experienced Zairians with the required capital made it impossible to obtain the price approved by the government, let alone the fair market value of their assets immediately prior to the November,1973, declaration. Many non-Africans sold their businesses at ten to fifteen percent or less of the true value. They were faced by two equally bleak alternatives--one, sell at a fraction of market value; two, work as employees in their own businesses under Zairian owners in a subordinate position in the hope of salvaging something more.

9) Under the law, a non-African could not leave the country without first obtaining from the government an Exit Permit. Issue of the permit was conditioned upon the government being satisfied that the non-African had actually ceded all his business operations in working condition to authentic Zairians and that the financial aspects of the transaction were in order.

10) Meanwhile, the laws placed severe re-

strictions upon non-African activities within Zaire. They were forbidden to hold meetings of more than three persons where actions taken by the government could be discussed. They could not withdraw more than $200 a day from their bank accounts; they could not use a language other than French or an indigenous vernacular in telephone conversations or in telegraphic messages (which, in effect, meant they could not communicate with outsiders through regular channels without the government knowing about it); railways and travel agencies had been instructed to refuse to handle as freight the personal property of the affected non-Africans; and at all custom check points, especially in the Shaba region, the persons, vehicles, baggage, and documents of non-Africans leaving the country (especially the Portuguese and Pakistanis) were thoroughly searched by suspicious, illiterate, ill-instructed, and rapacious soldiers.

11) The law empowered the president to grant individuals or classes of non-Africans specific waivers from application of the above laws. Just as Kenya pragmatically tempered the effects of non-Africans' leaving the country by phasing them out, Zaire made pragmatic concessions to selected non-Africans or groups of non-Africans by granting them waivers. Thus, all American businesses, presumably because of the ongoing negotiations for major capital investments in Zaire by Kennecot, Bethlehem Steel, Reynolds, and Kaiser, were granted waivers. So were some British corporations, incluing Unilever "one of the largest foreign enterprises in Zaire, owning a number of large plantations for the production of palm oil, rubber, tea; and owning factories and a number of sales outlets all over the country."[37]

12) In accordance with the president's declaration that "all plantations, ranches, farms and quarries must rightfully revert to Zairians," all farms and plantations owned by non-Africans, accounting for most of Zaire's exports of tea and coffee, were taken over and declared the property

240

of authentic Zairians. This was also the case with mines. The measure affected small privately owned tea and coffee plantations as well as large ones owned by multinational corporations. Most seriously affected were the Belgian settlers who, through all the years of turmoil following independence in 1960, had managed to hold on to their land, cultivating and caring for it, and contributing a large portion of Zaire's agricultural production. Small farms were distributed to individual Zairians and the larger ones were to be run, at least for awhile, as state enterprises.

The policy of forcing non-Africans to turn over operating businesses to authentic Zairians was not an unmitigated success. Some of the new owners sold the existing stocks and failed to reorder new supplies, thus effectively closing down the businesses. By 1975, agricultural production had fallen below what it was at the time of independence in 1960. International Monetary Fund officials were insisting on a stringent economic stabilization plan, including some retreat from the policy of Zairianization, before approving short-term loans by the world organization. By December, 1976, only three years after the president's November, 1973, Declaration, Zaire had defaulted on payment of its debts. The governor of its Central Bank travelled to New York, Washington, and London to renegotiate the debts owed both to foreign governments and private banks, seeking their consent to extend repayment over a period of ten to fifteen years. In 1977, President Mobutu announced a National Recovery Plan which sought to attract foreign investors by promising that they will enjoy special advantages in Zaire, including the right to transfer dividends outside the country. However, this did not materialize. By early 1980, Zaire's economy was in almost total collapse; all the farms and businesses taken over in 1973 had become largely unproductive. Over seventy-five percent of the trucks in the country were not operating because of the lack of spare parts. The railway and river transportation systems were in shambles.

Some of the hospitals had either closed down or
were desperately short of medicine. The price of
essential food products had risen over twenty
times since 1973. Over forty percent of the country's income from exports a year was necessary
simply to service foreign debts of over $3 billion.
The country had been obliged to swallow its pride
and accept stringent austerity measures "suggested"
by the International Monetary Fund in an effort
to bring its economy in order.

Of course, the drastic decrease in the world
price of copper, Zaire's largest export, had made
it difficult for the government to meet its international monetary obligations. However, it must
be believed that the Zairianization program with
its accompanying disjunctions had much to do with
the financial crisis. The government itself had
seemed to realize this when it began in 1976-77,
once again, to welcome foreign investors. But the
damage done by the policies of "Zairianization"
has so far proved irreversible. The mad dash to
economic independence carries an excessively
high price tag--as the example of Ghana makes
abundantly clear.

Displacing Non-Africans from Intermediate Level (Non-Retail) of Distributive Trade and Small Scale Manufacturing

To many people the dismal performance of the
Ghanaian economy since the country's achievement
of political independence in 1957 seems inexpli-
cable, especially in light of its abundance of
raw materials, both agricultural and non-agricultural, an excellent source of energy (not
based on oil); an adequate infrastructure for a
country its size, and a large number of educated
people in a variety of non-technical and technical fields. To understand the post-independence
economic evolution of Ghana, it is necessary to
identify two separate periods--a) 1957-1966, the
Nkrumah Period; and b) 1966-1980, the Post-
Nkrumah Period. Basically, the first period
characterized by a policy which placed emphasis

on industrializing the country through a network of public or state enterprises. It eventually led to the ouster of Dr. Nkrumah as president and virtually bankrupted the country. The second period has been marked by more attention to creating a class of indigenous entrepreneurs and has resulted in stagnation, unemployment, and inflation. Though the end result has been the same, the strategies and techniques adopted by Ghanaian leaders during the two periods have been very different, except that from 1957 until now the underlying goal has been to improve the economic position of black Africans at the expense of non-African economic interests.

As background, it is necessary to describe the attitudes of leaders during both these periods toward the legal status of non-Africans residing in the country. When Ghana became politically independent, there were several thousands of Europeans (mostly British), Arabs (Lebanese and Syrians), and Asians (Indians and Pakistanis) residing in the country. Soon after independence, the new African leaders declared that mere place of birth was insufficient to attribute local citizenship to a person. They argued for additional links with Ghana--a person should have undergone "a natural process" of belonging to Ghana and he must genuinely identify with the interests of the new state before being vested with Ghanaian citizenship.

Accordingly, the government enacted laws providing that a person resident in Ghana could not be regarded as having acquired Ghanaian citizenship by birth unless he could prove to the satisfaction of the Minister of Interior that he and one of his parents or grandparents had been born in Ghanaian territory. The system of compulsory registration had been introduced in Ghana only after 1946, and that too had operated far from perfectly, especially in areas outside the main cities. Most such applications to the minister were, therefore, bound to be supported by secondary evidence: an affidavit, a school

243

certificate, a marriage certificate, or simply a
statement from an elderly person stating that he
remembered having heard about the person a
certain number of years ago. The law gave the
minister unfettered discretionary power to approve
or disapprove any application. He was not bound
to explain his decision nor was it subject to
review by any judicial or administrative tribunal.
While it would have been almost impossible for
the minister to verify the claims with any reasonable degree of certainty, the law made it much
easier for him to base his decisions on extran-
eous grounds. It had been strongly suspected that
the law had been directed at least in part against
the Lebanese and the Syrians because many of them
had supported political parties opposed to Dr.
Nkrumah. Whatever the case may be, it had now become much more difficult, both in law as well as
in practice, for non-Africans to obtain local
citizenship than was true under British administration which followed, more or less strictly,
the _jus_ _soli_ principle. On the other hand, the
new African government went out of its way to make
the grant of local citizenship easier for Africans
from other parts of the continent.

     As an initial step to unify all Africans, Ghana
amended its laws in 1961 to give citizens of
"approved countries" continuously residing in Ghana
for a period of five years, with adequate knowledge
of one of the indigenous languages, the right to
acquire local citizenship by a simple system of
registration. The list of "approved countries"
contained names of those African states with which
Ghana was on friendly terms. But non-Africans,
though born in Ghana, were not necessarily acceptable to the new African government as local
citizens. Moreover, even though the power to
grant non-Africans local citizenship was very carefully and conservatively exercised during the
Nkrumah period, a new law introduced in the post-
Nkrumah period has made it easier for the government to deprive a naturalized citizen of his
Ghanian citizenship. It has also required all non-
citizens in Ghana to obtain and carry identity

cards which must be produced whenever demanded by the police or other authorities.

Nkrumah Period, 1957-1966: Within a year of independence, Dr. Nkrumah declared that his government, having achieved political independence, was now determined to achieve economic independence through a massive program of industrialization relying on state enterprises. Very soon, thereafter, non-Africans involved in commerce and industry began to feel the impact of the government's intrusion in the economy. In fact, Ghana's Minister of Industry openly conceded that the essence of Ghanaian socialism was "to avoid the situation where the most profitable sectors of industry were in the hands of foreigners." Some of the steps taken by the Nkrumah's government were:

1) The entire cocoa (Ghana's main agricultural export) purchasing and exporting market was reserved exclusively for the government owned and operated Ghana Cocoa Marketing Board. Similar state monopolies were created for other agricultural products, e.g., Ghana Timber Marketing Board, and Ghana Agricultural Development Corporation (which was granted a monopoly over exports of bananas, coffee, copra, palm oil, and other agricultural products.)

2) Diamond mining corporations were prohibited from continuing to export diamonds on their own initiative. They were required to market their diamonds only through the Ghana Diamond Marketing Board, thus making the government the sole exporter of Ghanaian diamonds.

3) Through the state owned and operated Industrial Development Corporation and The National Development Cooperative, or by direct legislative action, a series of state enterprises were established, including Ghana Plastics Products Corporation, The State Furniture and Joinery Corporation, Paper Conversion Corporation, The Ghana Paint Corporation, The Ghana Match Corporation, The Ghana Crafts Corporation, and Ghana Fishing Corporation.

4) The Ghana National Trading Corporation was established to engage in import and export trade.

5) All state and state-sponsored enterprises enjoyed various preferences and privileges. The Ghana National Trading Corporation had priority in the issue of import licences. The government ministers had power to (and did) exempt cooperatives and state enterprises from payment of all taxes, rates, and duties, and government buildings were often made available for use by such enterprises without payment of rent. All government purchases, with rare exceptions, were made through or from these enterprises.

6) Sooner or later the entire private sector, foreign as well as local, was expected to be brought under state control. Until this was done, however, the private sector, especially the larger and more profitable enterprises, were heavily taxed. Personal and corporate income tax laws were revised, a purchase tax was imposed on a wide variety of "luxury goods" (appliances, refrigerators, air conditioning units, automobiles, etc.) usually consumed by owners or employees of such operations, all corporations were required to purchase government bonds amounting to at least ten percent of their total annual income redeemable only after ten years and carrying an interest rate of a mere four percent a year.

The government acquired the assets of some of the larger private enterprises and converted them into state corporations. Others continued operating within an environment that included increasing restrictions upon their activities and preferences to state run enterprises. Most feared that it was only a question of time before they would be forced to leave the market altogether. Some even went bankrupt. Comments like the following were commonplace:

> "Last year 50.96 per cent was taken from us, plus compulsory savings. In the current year, we shall be mulcted of 65 per cent

246

including compulsory savings and diesel oil tax. This is an intolerable burden...."

"Statutory wage increases....we are now threatened with a statutory forty hour week, with compulsory investment in Ghana of 60 per cent of our net profits and with the obligation of giving a first option to the government if we wish to sell all or part of our equity."38

Most of the retail trade was in the hands of the Arabs. They purchased agricultural products from farmers and sold them in turn to large European exporting corporations; and sold to the farmers goods that had been imported in bulk by the European importing firms. The monopolization of agricultural trade by the government, and the state participation in import trade with accompanying restrictions on imports by foreign enterprises made it difficult for many Arab retailers to continue trading on a reasonably profitable basis. They were also affected by the increased taxes, though not as much as the large European corporations. Some of them hung on, others moved to different fields, including manufacturing consumer goods where the government had not monopolized the market, e.g. rubber shoes, shirts, biscuits, furniture, etc. They had few multi-national connections, flexibility to make decisions to switch to other enterprises by themselves, and, though afraid that the government might later take over their enterprises, they were at least not being abused almost daily, as was the case with the Europeans, as agents of neo-colonialism and imperialism. And, after all, they had been living there for a long time and considered Ghana their home.

In June, 1965, Dr. Nkrumah announced that "we are now poised upon the threshold of a major economic breakthrough, which will establish us firmly as an economic power...."39 But, in fact, most of the state corporations established by his government were, for a multitude of reasons,

operating at a loss. After his ouster from power
by a military coup in 1966, the United Nations
Economic Mission sent to Ghana to report on the
economy indicated:

> "Too many industries were created in too
> short a time without proper management 'di-
> gestion' and they have resulted in a large
> public debt and a large continuing liability
> for the import of the raw materials required.
> As things stand, most state enterprises are
> a problem rather than a help."[40]

By that time, however, it was too late to undo
the damage that had already been done to the
economic interests of the Europeans, the Arabs,
and other non-Africans who had invested in the
country.

Post-Nkrumah Period (1966-   ): With the
collapse of the Nkrumah regime, private enterprise
became respectable again. However, this did not
mean that Ghana had ended its search for economic
independence. Soon after seizing political power,
General Acheampong said, "We are almost like a
nation at war without an external enemy," and
promised to "place the economy on a war footing."[41]
And, since then, Ghana has had no compunction
about warring against its internal enemies--non-
Africans engaged in commercial and industrial
activities in the country. As soon as they had
shown signs of reviving from Nkrumah's confis-
catory taxes and state monopolistic practices,
black Ghanaian businessmen began complaining that
non-Africans• were restricting their progress and
that non-Africans should be discouraged from
participating in economic activity which could
easily be undertaken by the Africans. It did not
take the government too long to decide what it
was going to do--use its legislative and regulatory powers to Ghanainize the economy but
gradually and from bottom up. (The country was
already burdened with foreign debts, especially to
Britain and other Western powers and it was, in
any case, not an opportune time to take measures

that might be interpreted in those countries as radical.) So it was that in 1968, The Ghana Enterprises Decree was issued by the ruling military group which had named itself the National Liberation Council, designed to encourage Ghanaian businesses by imposing certain restrictions on the activities of non-citizens. It prohibited them from engaging in retail trade (unless their annual sales exceeded 500,000 Cedis--1 Cedi = approximately $.90)--or wholesale trade (unless the annual sales exceeded one million Cedis), or extractive, processing, manufacturing, or other industry (unless the business in question employed more than thirty persons and involved fixed capital investments of more than 100,000 Cedis), or representing overseas manufacturers, or operating taxi services. If a non-citizen was engaged in any business that fell within the provisions of the decree at the time it was issued, he had three alternatives--one, close down the business; two, expand it sufficiently so that it qualified for exemption from the restrictive provisions of the decree; and three, seek special dispensation from the government. Under the regulations, he could be allowed, at the sole discretion of the government, to continue for a maximum period of five years (two years in the case of manufacturers' representatives and taxi service operations), provided he agreed to a) create within three months a training program to equip Ghanaians with all the skills required to operate his business; b) ensured that within two years all his employees were Ghanaians; and c) made certain that within three years at least fifty percent of the business capital was owned by Ghanaians. If he wished to continue to remain in business in Ghana on a permanent basis, his only rational choice therefore was to expand his operations. The decree particularly affected those Arabs and Asians (the latter being by far the smaller group) who had tenaciously and perseveringly redeployed their capital and retooled themselves to perform whatever economic functions they could within the highly circumscribed socialist framework of Nkrumah's regime.

249

The new regime went even further and introduced at regular intervals other measures, the
effects of which were no less damaging to non-
Africans. In 1969, the government indulged in a
massive project to force the aliens either to
obtain Work Permits (which were subject to periodic
review and which could be refused by the government
at any time) or to leave the country within a short
period. This made it difficult for those Lebanese
and Indians who had, despite the 1968 decree,
surreptitiously continued to be engaged in, either
as owners or employees, the economic activities
that had now been reserved for the Ghanaians. In
1970, the Ghanaian Business Promotion Act was
passed. The title is a bit misleading. Its real
purpose was to control the influence of non-Africans in the Ghanaian economy by streamlining the
1968 decree and removing some of the loopholes of
which the Lebanese and the Indians were taking
advantage. While substantially reproducing the
terms of the 1968 Act, the new Act made a few
changes which had far-reaching consequences as
far as the non-Africans were concerned. For
example, the term "alien enterprise" was now
redefined so that any business enterprise operating in Ghana was deemed to be an alien enterprise "unless the entire capital or other financial interest in it was owned by citizens of
Ghana and the enterprise was controlled by
citizens of Ghana."[42] The provision that an
"alien enterprise"--the annual sales and capital
of which exceeded certain amounts would qualify
for exemption from the restrictive provisions of
the Act was now re-worded so that this would be
the case only if the income tax returns submitted
by that business for the year 1967-68 indicated
that its annual sales had in fact exceeded that
amount. Businesses that had expanded since 1968,
therefore, were now to be treated as covered by
the Act regardless of their size. The next year,
1971, saw the enactment of the Manufacturing Industries Act under which all individuals or
corporations that had established industries
prior to the life of the Act were to obtain,
within three months, a special license from the

250

Minister of Commerce and Industry. The Act
empowered the minister to review the previous
decisions of the government granting permission to
establish the industries and to impose any new
conditions that he might deem appropriate before
issuing the special license. All those who had,
during the Nkrumah period, cooperated with the
regime's emphasis on industrialization, or who,
barred from the previously lawful economic
activity in which they were initially engaged,
had switched to manufacturing now found themselves
once again under the government's hammer. In
fact, this was not at all surprising. Because by
then, it was already being claimed that ".... the
upward mobility of the smaller (Ghanaian) firms
into middle scale manufacturers...was being stifled
considerably...by the presence of large numbers of
expatriate groups in all phases of simple industrial activities which normally should have been
undertaken by the indigenous sector of the population."[43] It was argued that the Ghanaian entrepreneurs had to be protected from the Arabs and
the Asian businessmen who,

> "had seven decades of business experience
> in West Africa during which to establish
> themselves as formidable business groups...
> their movement to manufacturing was moreover
> facilitated by (their) ability to redeploy
> their accumulated profits from many years
> of trading in the country; and that further
> credit was readily extended to them by the
> commercial banking institutions."[44]

What these critics apparently had in mind (and
their eyes on) were the highly profitable small
scale manufacturing activities, mainly of consumer goods, in which the Lebanese and the Indians
were at that point engaged--the former in making
biscuits, bread, plastic wares, rubber shoes,
and light metal and wooden furniture and fixtures
and the latter in mass production of ready-to-
wear clothes, like shirts, underwear, and trousers.
The Chamber of Commerce (dominated by the Ghanaians),
the Ghana Manufacturing Association, and the Assoc-

iation of Ghanaian Businessmen had all argued
that "the government should extend the areas
presently restricted (and eventually totally
exclude aliens from the economy, except for the
larger firms in European hands)."[45] And, so it
was. In 1975 came the Investment Policy and the
Ghanaian Enterprises Development Decrees, ostensibly
to achieve self-reliance, but, in reality, extending the effort to promote Ghanaian enterprises,
through the use of legislative and administrative
devices, by excluding non-Ghanaians from specific
areas. The provisions of the decrees, which
superseded the 1970 Business Promotion Act, are
fairly detailed and complex. Basically, however,
they sought to accomplish four objectives:

1) To reserve certain commercial and
industrial activities wholly and exclusively for
Ghanaians--the list included manufacturing and
service industries, e.g., baking, printing and
publishing, making cement blocks, ordinary gar-
ments, suit cases, shopping bags, tire retreading,
as well as operating travel, advertising, and real
estate agencies, and even beauty salons. It was
possible, under the law, to exempt from this
provision those non-Ghanaians who were citizens of
one of the African countries provided that country
made similar concessions to Ghanaians operating in
their own countries. No such exemption was to be
granted to citizens of non-African countries,
even on the basis of reciprocity.

2) All wholesale and retail trade was
reserved for the Ghanaians. The only exception
was a department store or a supermarket with net
current assets of 500,000 Cedis and annual sales
of at least one million Cedis.

3) Ghanaians must own at least fifty per
cent (and in certain circumstances at least fifty
five per cent) of those enterprises producing
goods which the Ghanaians regarded as their basic
necessities--e.g., soap, detergents, textiles,
matches, beer, cement, rubber, flour, hoes, sugar,
salt, baby milk, etc.

252

4) There was a long list of other activities--over fifty of them, including distribution and servicing of motor vehicles, shipping, distribution of petroleum products, manufacture of furniture, cement, plastic, metal and paper containers, candles, ball point pens, records, biscuits, rubber products, etc. In all these, the Ghanaians must own fifty per cent of the capital (forty per cent if the capital employed was more than 500,000 Cedis and the annual sales more than one million Cedis).

5) In those enterprises engaged in the exploitation or processing of minerals (e.g., bauxite and aluminium) and of timber the state must own a certain percentage of the capital--ranging from twenty per cent to fifty-five per cent.

The first three actions listed above severely affected the economic interests of the Lebanese and the Indians. One of the authors, in his visit to Ghana in August, 1976, met an Indian who had been residing there for over thirty years and who before the decrees had been operating a textile factory employing over seventy-five people, had had to close down the factory because of this law. He had yet to find a buyer. The highest offer he had received was less than thirty per cent of the market value. Meanwhile, he was working as a waiter!

The assumption that by merely making the non-Ghanaians relinquish their operations will guarantee the effective and efficient operations of these by the Ghanaians still remains to be tested, as does the idea that such actions will create a genuine Ghanaian entrepreneurial class in the country. By 1980, the Ghanaian economy had become almost stagnant. Its real rate of inflation was one of the highest in the world--between 70 and 130 percent in the last two years. The tourist trade was almost non-existent. There was shortage of food, soap, vegetable oil, and other essential items. Water, electricity, and gasoline were often unavailable. Ghana's new leader, President

Dr. Hilla Limann has called for foreign investment and has promised to cooperate with the
International Monetary Fund and the World Bank.
The government is also preparing a new development
plan, which will encourage private investment,
especially in mining. Whether this will make any
difference in practice remains to be seen. The
Ghanaian political leaders, both during the
Nkrumah period and post-Nkrumah period, have been
quick to point out the advantages enjoyed by the
non-Africans--their access to capital, their
decades of business experience, their monopolistic
tendencies, willingness to bribe public officials,
and, even their social customs and beliefs--but
have been less than quick to recognize (or try to
emulate) their dedication to business, their
palpable efficiency, and capacity to exploit
economic opportunities.

The fourth and fifth items, requiring non-
citizens to enter into joint ventures with
Ghanaian individuals or the state of Ghana,
adversely affected the European corporations much
more than either the Arabs or the Asians. But,
instead of describing in detail how they were
affected in Ghana, we will now move to Nigeria,
where an almost identical law was introduced
creating similar difficulties for large European
corporations there.

Requiring At Least Forty Per Cent Indigenous Ownership of All Enterprises

On October 1, 1960, Nigeria began its life
as a politically independent state with several
factors in its favor. It had the largest population on the continent, a diversified economy
producing at least three different export crops
(cocoa, palm oil and kernels, ground nuts and
ground nut oil), a healthy balance in its foreign
reserve account, and a well-deserved reputation
for politically moderate leaders. All of this
provided a very favorable foreign investment
climate which the new leaders wished to preserve.

Soon after independence, Dr. Nnamdi Azikiwe, the Nigerian leader often referred to in those days as the doyen of the Pan-African leaders in West Africa, declared that Nigeria opposed arbitrary nationalization. Its Six Year Development Plan (1962-1968) specifically stated that government intervention in the economy would be limited to public utilities. The government took considerable pride in portraying Nigeria as a country which welcomed foreign investment. Western businesses venturing into Africa for the first time more often than not opted in favor of Nigeria. As a result, new investments flowed into the country from all parts of the western world, especially the United States, France, Italy, Belgium, Israel, Canada, Switzerland, and Greece. Britain, of course, was already heavily involved and continued so, especially in wholesale trade, banking and insurance; while the Lebanese and the Indians were engaged in retail trade and medium level industries, though on a much smaller scale than the British. Several new industries were also established by foreigners including textile factories, cement plants, steel mills, etc.

Historically, indigenous businessmen had been anxious since the 1950's to break foreign dominance, especially in retail trade, but, by and large, the government had been able to contain such pressures. There were some exceptions to the generally open door policy. For example, in 1966-1967 the government established an Expatriate Quota Allocation Board which sought to contain the influx of foreign manpower into the country (this was done largely to ameliorate the increased rate of unemployment among educated Nigerians) and in 1968 the government required all foreign companies carrying on business in Nigeria to incorporate locally so that the government could monitor the assets used by them in their Nigerian operations and the profits earned therefrom. But these were comparatively insignificant barriers. Then came the military coup in 1966, the counter-coups, the civil (?) war of 1967 to 1970, the demonstration effect of other African states and last but not

255

least, oil. (Today Nigeria earns at least $15 billion a year from oil alone, though it earns much less from its export of agricultural cash crops than it did before independence and imports about $500 million worth of food every year to feed its growing population of about 80 million.)

By early 1970, Nigeria had reversed its open door policy toward foreign investors. It declared in its Second National Development Plan (1970-1974):

> The government will seek to acquire, by law of necessity, equity participation in a number of strategic industries that will be specified from time to time. In order <u>to ensure that the economic destiny of Nigeria is determined</u> by Nigerians themselves, the government will seek to widen and intensify its positive participation in industrial development.[46]

The use of the phrase "strategic industries" preceded a little earlier by the term "by law of necessity" in the first sentence might lead one to think that the government (which had just gone through the wrenching experience of the Nigerian/ Biafran conflict) was concerned about economic activities which had a bearing on national security and territorial defense. In reality, however, the second sentence was, in retrospect, more important than the first. What the government had in mind was to bring not just the strategic but all economic activities under its control.

By June, 1971, it was clear that the government was bent upon assuring that Nigerians participated in the economy to a greater extent than had been the case. And in February, 1972, it declared a new law called The Nigerian Enterprises Promotion Decree, (referred to from now on as NEPD).[47] The use of the word "Promotion" in the title might lead one to believe that the government's intention was to promote Nigerians by giving them training in business operations, providing Nigerian businessmen with access to guaranteed loans, subsidies, or some other support which would enable them to compete effectively against the foreigners. In fact, the decree can be interpreted as little less than a partial take-over of selected foreign economic operations.

Before documenting this assertion, it must be noted that the word "Nigerian" as used in the decree should not be interpreted in terms of legal status. The term "Indigenisation" used by Nigerian leaders everywhere except in legal documentation, describes the objective far more clearly than the former legalistic term. And even the laws defined the term "Nigerian" as including any person of African descent who was a citizen of another African country which allowed the same privileges (i.e., to establish and operate in that country) to citizens of Nigeria. Assuming the existence of such a reciprocal agreement between Zambia and Nigeria, therefore, a Zambian citizen of English or Asian descent would not be treated in Nigeria, for the purposes of this decree, as a Nigerian but a black Zambian would. More over, as noted earlier, in 1973 the government, anticipating an increase in the number of non-Africans wanting to naturalize as Nigerian citizens, amended the citizenship laws in order to make it extremely difficult for non-Africans to acquire local citizenship, even if they were born in Nigeria and had lived there for decades.

The NEPD, officially announced in February, 1972, gave non-Nigerians (referred to from now on as non-Africans) who were engaged in economic activities specified in Schedule I, two years within which to sell their operations. Effective March, 1974, all such activities were reserved for Nigerians and, of course, other Africans who would fall under the above definition. Schedule I listed twenty-two different economic activities, including transportation, publishing, bread and cake making, hair-dressing, candle manufacturing,

257

assembling radios, etc. This list of assorted
economic activities makes sense only in the
Nigerian context--almost all these were the very
activities in which the Lebanese and Syrians were
heavily engaged. Secondly, and perhaps of greater
importance, was the Schedule II containing a list
of thirty-three different economic activities,
including boat building, bottling soft drinks,
construction industries, operating department
stores and supermarkets, furniture making, distribution and servicing of motor vehicles, wholesale
distribution, manufacture of bicycles, matches,
cement, metal containers, paints, varnishes,
soaps, detergents, suit cases, poultry farming,
screen printing on cloth, operating travel agencies,
etc. All non-Africans engaged in any of these
activities, too, were to cease operations by March,
1974. Only those who fell under Schedule II and
who had capital assets of over 400,000 Naira
(1 Naira = approximately $1.56) and annual sales
exceeding one million Naira were to be allowed to
continue operation beyond that date and only on
condition that, by then, they had transferred at
least forty per cent of their equity to Nigerians.
This last provision had a significant effect upon
large Western corporations operating in the
country, including, for example, the United Fruit
Company, the Compagnie Francaise d'Afrique Occidentale, the Societe Commerciale d'Afrique de
l'Ouest, I.C.I., Lever Brothers, Bata (Nigeria)
Ltd., Dunlop (Nigeria) Ltd., Guinness (Nigeria)
Ltd., Leventis Motors, United Trading Company of
Nigeria, and Tate & Lyle (Nigeria) Ltd. In all,
the NEPD affected about 3000 enterprises. Those
affected through Schedule I were mainly unincorporated sole proprietorships or family owned
partnerships, those through Schedule II were mainly
private or public corporations.

For the unincorporated enterprises (sole
proprietorships and partnerships), the problem
was to find Nigerian buyers with the requisite
capital. In all, they represented a total
investment of about $300 million dollars, and
individual Nigerians did not have the money. To

facilitate the process of transfer, therefore, the government required all commercial banks in the country to grant at least forty per cent of the credits to Nigerians. It also established a special fund from which loans could be made for purchasing small-scale industries. Loans were especially difficult to secure to foreclose small family businesses involved in retail trade or in the service sector. Nevertheless, towards the end of 1973, the government warned foreign owners that unless they sold out before March 31, 1974, their businesses might be forfeited. Some non-Africans managed to make a deal. The new purchasers paying for the business in installments and the non-African staying on as "advisor" or "chief executive" to assist the new owners. Under the law, however, they could not stay on in this fashion for more than two years. They could remain in the country only if they had sufficient capital to move on to a Schedule II business or some other economic activity not covered under the NEPD and could obtain the necessary licenses and residence permits from the government. Otherwise, they had no alternative but to leave unless, of course, they intended to continue living on their savings. If they decided to leave, their savings and the proceeds of their businesses could be taken out of Nigeria only by installments.

For incorporated enterprises (public and private), the problem was how to ensure that forty per cent of their equity was owned by Nigerians on or before March 31, 1974. One method, of course, for the public corporations was to issue the appropriate number of new shares for purchase exclusively by Nigerian citizens. It is here however that the government's use of its regulatory powers resulted in definite loss to the corporations. The government established, under the provisions of a newly enacted Capital Issues Decree, a Capital Issues Commission.[48] Ostensibly, this commission was responsible for investigating the assets of the corporation seeking to issue new shares, considering its record of price-earning ratios, finding out the use to which it intended to put the proceeds from the sale of new shares, and, on the basis of these and its determination of the general financial standing of the corporation, _fix the price_ (usually low) at which the new issues would be offered. In some cases, the commission could even determine and direct the type of securities to be offered.

One businessman said, "I am amazed there hasn't been more of an outcry," another said, "They talk about asset stripping in Europe, here it is just asset robbing," and a third remarked, "The only consistency I can see is that all shares must have a lower price-earnings ratio than five." [49] Of course, the Capital Issues Decree allowed for an appeal against the decisions of the commission. But there were sound political reasons for a corporation not to pursue such a course. Moreover, even if it succeeded in having a higher price fixed for its shares, the appeal would have taken at least six months. Meanwhile shares of other corporations would go on the market and the Nigerians might not have funds left to buy its shares before the due date.

For private corporations, the best method, of course, was to find Nigerians capable of raising sufficient funds to buy forty per cent of the equity. If they could not, the next best alternative was perhaps to find a Nigerian or Nigerians willing to act as "frontmen" and hold shares in trust for foreign owners. The government became very concerned about this practice. It could not subject the private corporations to the shenanigans of the Capital Issues Commission. It therefore tried its best to encourage private corporations to go public and offer their shares to Nigerians in the open; and if any private corporation insisted upon disposing of its equity in private, the Nigerian officials made it a point to question the directors of that corporation to discover their real motives. In short, they became almost automatically suspect. The Nigerian government had established the Nigerian Enterprises Promotion Board to facilitate private transfer of shares but it also had the power to step in to effect transfer if it found that the owners were not making a genuine effort to sell their businesses.

It must be added that the law also provided that the Boards of Directors of public corporations must reflect the new pattern of ownership and that at least one-third of the board members should, therefore, be Nigerians.

All of this could be interpreted as an effort by Nigeria to use its newly found oil wealth to buy out foreign businesses. But this would not be entirely true. The government has been very careful in issuing loans, and insisted upon government authorities fixing prices at which the transfers are to take place. (Its import bill is fairly high and it apparently does not feel the need to be generous to foreign corporations. The government believes, correctly or not, that because of its expanding economy foreign capital will continue to flow into Nigeria despite the restrictions.)

Because of haphazard enforcement, the very complexity of the projected transfers, changes in political leadership, and often successful attempts by foreigners to evade the decree a number of foreign businesses were unaffected by the law. This forced the Nigerian government in 1976 to promulgate another decree--harsher than the one before. It created three categories of businesses--

"the first, 100 per cent Nigerian owned, ranges from cosmetics manufacture to film distribution and covers a wide scope of businesses. The second, to be 60 per cent Nigerian owned, includes banking, insurance, mining, fertilizer production, pulp and paper mills, plantation agriculture, cement manu-facture, construction industries and large-scale department stores and supermarkets. Any foreign enterprise not in these two categories falls automatically into the third, which calls for 40 per cent Nigerian ownership. The businesses (but not the banks)

have until December, 1978, to meet the
deadline."[50]

If in 1974 foreigners thought they had obtained a
reprieve, they soon realized that it was only
temporary. Partly because of overly ambitious
plans which resulted in considerable overspending
on government imports and partly because of the
need to provide a competitive edge to local manufacturers, in 1978, the government prohibited
importation of over sixty different items--inclu-
ding footwear, furniture, matches, cameras, clothes,
etc.--and decreed that the existing stocks must be
sold off within three months. The austerity
measures almost plunged the country into a recess-
ion without any corresponding improvement in the
status of the local manufacturers. However, despite the various restrictions, including limits
on how much the subsidiaries or affiliates of
foreign corporations can pay to their parent companies in consulting fees, on how much profits
can be repatriated, and on how much can be paid
by way of salaries to foreign employees, foreign
investors in Nigeria have continued to increase
in number. Profits, in many cases, continue to
be fairly large and the foreign multinationals
are capable of withstanding some of the political
pressures, though this has not always been the
case. For example, in 1979, Nigeria nationalized
5 percent of all the major oil companies' interests
in the country and will probably increase this
figure as soon as they acquire some confidence in
their ability to operate the oil fields. They
also have proved capable of exercising their
political muscle by taking selective retaliatory
measures against those corporations (e.g. Bar-
clays Bank, British Petroleum) that flauntingly
cooperate in matters of commerce with South Africa.

But clearly, Nigeria is embarked upon indigenization to place control of its economy in the
hands of Nigerians and to ensure that Nigerians
are the main beneficiaries of the exploitation of
their country's resources. Non-Africans will be
tolerated only so long as they are needed. But

262

simply buying foreign enterprises (at whatever price and however cheaply) does not mean that the new owners will continue to operate with the same efficiency. In fact, some might disappear. After all, "it is not unknown to find Nigerians obtaining loans from the commercial banks only to put half of the amount into staging outdoor parties to remember long-departed ancestors."[51] As far as the foreigners are concerned, however, one of the virtues of the Nigerian approach is that (thanks partly to the OPEC price fixing) most foreign businessmen have at least managed to salvage something from their investments and years of work. This cannot be said about many other countries of Africa.

Expropriating Urban and Rural Land

Tanganyika and the islands of Zanzibar agreed upon a union April 26, 1964, known since October 29, 1964, as the United Republic of Tanzania. This section, however, concentrates mainly on mainland Tanzania (formerly known as Tanganyika).

No other country among Africa's new states has received such worldwide publicity for its social experimentation as has Tanzania, particularly in respect to the ideology of socialism and self-reliance espoused by its highly regarded president, Dr. Julius Nyerere. Within less than a year of majority rule, the president declared:

> God has given us the land, and it is from the land that we get the raw materials which we reshape to meet our needs....It belongs to the community.[52]

In 1967, when his government adopted a series of measures nationalizing private properties, he maintained: "our purpose was primarily a nationalistic purpose; it was an extension of the political control which the Tanzanian people secured in 1961.... Such an economic expression of nationalism is nothing new in the world."[53] Whatever the merits of Dr. Nyerere's ideology of socialism, his arguments justifying the nationalization measures were not much different from those used by other African leaders who had argued in favor of genuine or total independence. The president had added:

> "...the economic institutions of socialism, such as those we are now creating in accordance with the Arusha Declaration are intended to serve man in our society...where the majority of the people in a particular society are black, then most of those who benefit from socialism there will be black. But it has nothing to do with their blackness; only with their humanity."[54]

This oblique reference to race was designed to counter allegations that his measures had been motivated by racial considerations. The fact that over ninety-five per cent of the properties that had been taken over belonged to non-Africans was unpublicized. Next year, when these measures were being aggressively implemented, the president made it clear that in his view "capitalists were in fact robbers--daylight robbers--who should be punished more severely than the petty offenders" and that "the local capitalists should ask themselves whether the properties they hold really belong to them, and if the answer is no, they should return these to the rightful owners."[55] It was abundantly clear to those on the scene that the term "local capitalists" had been reserved for the non-Africans who had settled in Tanzania and occupied a prominent place in its economy. (In 1962 there were about 115,000 Asians, 20,000 Arabs, and 6,000 Europeans in Tanganyika, the total population of which was over nine million). At the lower level, however, African leaders were less hesitant to use terms with racial connotations; their language, too, was often more pointed than that of the president. The combined result of Dr. Nyerere's ideology and its implementation has been that non-Africans have had little alternative but to surrender their properties to the government, representing "the rightful owners;" over sixty per cent of them have also found it necessary to leave the country. How this occurred is described below. However, for the sake of brevity, its scope has been limited to issues involving nationalization of buildings and farms.

Tanzania is a vast country, roughly the same size as Nigeria, almost as large as Pakistan and Venezuela. Immediately prior to political independence, less than one per cent of its land was alienated to private individuals, largely to Europeans and Asians, by the previous regimes-- either in the form of freehold grants, sales, or leases ranging from a term of thirty-three to ninety-nine years. Seventeen per cent of the land was reserved for forests and wildlife, and the rest considered as belonging to and occupied by the various African tribes or communities according to customary laws and usage. According to the 1961 World Bank Report:

> Rules of customary usage in matters of land tenure have never been by any means uniform over a large area. Nor are these rules static. All generalizations, therefore, are subject to regional exceptions and are liable to become outdated. In much of the territory, the right to occupy land is considered irrevocable; in many areas it is the fact of cultivation, the establishment of tree crops or the construction of a house which guarantees individual use for as long as the signs of individual activity persist; in certain places individual occupancy may be terminated on grounds of misconduct. Inheritance of use rights is generally possible by either matrilinear or patrilinear tribal rules.[56]

The weight of evidence, therefore, was certainly not overwhelming in favor of the contention that under African customary laws, land belonged to the community. Nevertheless, on the ideological basis that under African traditional customary law an individual could only exercise the right to use, not to own land, the government enacted a law on February 13, 1962, converting all freehold land

into ninety-nine year government leaseholds.
Accordingly, all non-Africans who at the time of
independence thought they owned the land (on which
they may have erected a building or started a
farm) now, through operation of the law, became
mere lessees of the government (representing the
community). If this was the only change brought
about by the new law, from a practical point of
view, this conversion, at least in the short run,
would not have made much difference. But this
was not the case. The new law also required all
lessees to pay annual rent to the government as
might be assessed. Moreover, it was incumbent
upon a lessee to develop the land leased to him as
might be required by the government or risk term-
ination of the lease, or revocation of his right
of occupancy as such leases were called in
Tanzania.

If the land was located in an urban area
in respect of which the government had formulated
a development plan, the appropriate government
minister could, if he deemed it desirable, draft
certain "development covenants" which, upon
notification to the lessee, were, under the law,
to be deemed to have become part of the lease
agreement and binding upon the lessee. Should
the lessee fail to comply with the terms of
these new convenants, he risked forfeiting the
lease to the government. The new covenants might
require the lessee to erect a residential house,
an office building, a warehouse, a parking lot,
or carry out other improvement the government
provided for in its development plans within a
period considered by the government to be reasonable. If, for any reason, the lessee failed to do
so, the Minister for Lands, Forests, and Wildlife
had the power under the law to issue a certificate
to the effect that by reason of non-compliance
with the notice, the lease had become forfeit and
was terminated as from the date of the termin-
ation of the notice. The government also had the
right to require a lessee to develop the land
located in an urban area for which no development
plans had been prepared if it considered that the

land in question was, nevertheless "ripe for development."

If it was located in a rural area and the government considered it "ripe for development" on the basis of a survey report of its potentiality and the Minister of Agriculture's opinion that the proposed development was economically feasible it was, as urban land, open to the government to draft new covenants which, upon notification, became part of the lease and binding upon the lessee. If the land in question was small in acreage, it was permissible for the government to dispense with the surveyor's and minister's reports, and rely upon recommendations of the local authority. In either case, the lessee was obliged to develop the land as, and when, required by the government or risk forfeiting it. In all cases, decisions of the government could be appealed to a specially appointed tribunal, not to the regular courts.

With respect to land leased by the previous regimes to private individuals, the new African government argued that these rights were "granted" by the government of the day; they could not be "claimed;" and that the new government (which had succeeded to the powers of the previous regime) had the right, at any time, to alter the terms and conditions on which the rights were "granted." Accordingly, through enactment of new laws, it invested itself with the same powers (to require development) over leaseholds as it had acquired over the freeholds. It also asserted that the old leases had been granted on the understanding that the land would be developed; and that it was therefore justified in issuing new land regulations which would be deemed to have been incorporated in all such leases. If a lessee had any objection to the incorporation of new terms which obliged him to develop the land as, and when, required by the government, he was given the option to surrender it to the government. To make it easier for him to do so, the government also provided that the Registrar of Lands would accept such surrenders without requiring the lessee to pay a surrender

267

fee!

The government claimed that it had a rational basis for its policy. It was anxious to develop the country's economy as fast as possible; land development was of fundamental importance in bringing about this transformation--ergo, it had a duty to use its newly acquired legislative and regulatory powers and require land owners either to develop the land or forfeit their rights to it. In strictly philosophical terms, it is difficult to disagree with the logic of this argument. Yet, when one looks at it from a practical point of view and in the context in which the policy became operative, it becomes evident that the government's efforts at "development" were directed against only that portion of the land that had been alienated to non-Africans. Land in worse condition held by Africans under native laws and customs was not converted into leaseholds, no new terms or conditions were placed on its development; nor were any of its owners or occupiers forced to improve production methods or to take other steps for more efficient use of the land. As Rutman has aptly observed, "It is difficult to believe that the development of the land was the real factor behind this policy. ..It appears that the real reason probably lies simply in the greater government control gained over the general operation of the foreign-owned estates."[57] A number of non-Africans, especially the Asians, the Greeks, and the Arabs, settled in Tanzania, believing government assertions that its only objective was development, demonstrated their confidence in the new African state by complying with the government's directives. Assuming that there was bound to be greater demand in the country for housing, they erected on their lands houses, offices, apartment complexes, warehouses, or other structures -- not only investing all their savings in the projects but also borrowing heavily from their friends, relatives, and other institutions in order to complete the development within the period stipulated by the government.

In a short time, Tanzania's capital, Dar-es-salaam, and other urban centers showed considerable improvement in their appearance. Landowners who failed to comply with the government's directives, of course, lost their properties, or, more accurately, had their rights of occupancy revoked by the government, as happened in the case of about thirty-five farms in November, 1964, when their owners were notified that the titles to their land (around 22,000 acres) had been revoked because of their failure to carry out development instructions. The same thing happened with regard to a number of pieces of land in the urban areas.

Within less than ten years, almost all these new structures were nationalized by the government. In 1968, the government had enacted the Urban Leaseholds (Acquisition and Re-Grant) Act which empowered the government to acquire private urban property "for public use." The term "public use" however was so defined that it included the right to take the property (as well as to revoke the right of occupancy for the land on which it stood) whenever it was believed that the lessee (or the owner) was exploiting the tenants by charging exorbitant rents. The government had the right to hand over such property, without charge, to the actual occupiers. By 1971, about four hundred such transfers had taken place; virtually all involving taking property away from non-Africans ("the local capitalists") and giving it to Africans ("the rightful owners").

In 1971, the government went even further and launched what was described as a "mopping up operation against exploitation." On April 22, 1971, it produced a new bill, had it briefly discussed and passed in the national legislature under a Certificate of Urgency, obtained the presidential consent as required by law, and promulgated into law (all within twenty-four hours) The Acquisition of Buildings Act, 1971. Its effect was to bring all rented buildings, valued at more than 100,000 shillings (approximately $15,000) automatically under government ownership;

the land on which they stood, it may be remembered, already belonged to the government under the provisions of the 1962 Acts. Even if only part of the building was rented, and the other part occupied by the owners, the whole building belonged to the government making the owner the government's tenant for that part of the building which was in his occupation and with the same obligation to pay rent to the government as the other tenants. If a person owned and rented more than one building but none exceeding the above sum in value, all belonged to the government if their cumulative value exceeded this sum.

Since the provisions of the Rent Restriction Decrees did not apply to government-owned housing, it was now open to the government to charge market rents to its tenants. Since the lands on which these buildings stood already belonged to the government, the only claim the owners had for compensation was in respect to the value of the buildings. For the purposes of computing this figure, however, the law empowered the government to take into account the actual or market value of the building at the time it was built, not its market value at the time of expropriation, thus disregarding the high rate of inflation and the equity. Furthermore, from this deflated figure the government was given, under the law, the right to deduct 1/120 of it for every month the build-ing had been available for rental. Therefore, if the building was ten or more years old the owner was not entitled to any compensation. If it was built in January, 1963, following government's notification of development covenants, and taken over by the government in April, 1971, the owner was entitled to receive in compensation only 1/6th or 16.7 per cent of the original cost. The cost of maintaining the building during these years, expenses of renting it, period during which it re-mained vacant, the five per cent Rent Tax charged by the government, income tax paid to the govern-ment on the rent received, and property taxes and other impositions were not to be taken into account. Compensation was paid in local currency and was generally subject to the strict exchange control regulations introduced by the government, thus making it difficult, if not impossible, for the owner to transfer these funds overseas or outside Tanzania. If an owner was dissatisfied with the way any of the discretionary powers had been exercised by the representatives of the government, he had the right of appeal to a specially established tribunal, called the Conciliation Board whose decision was final. To file an appeal, the appellant had to pay a filing fee of 10,000 Shillings (approximately $1500). If the applicant lost the appeal, he forfeited the filing fee; if he won it, only half the fee was returnable.

Within less than a month of passage of the Act the government took physical possession of more than a thousand buildings, most of them belonging to non-Africans. (Most of the African buildings were comparatively small in size and did not reach the specified figure in value--a figure, which, of course, had been carefully selected; the few that did fall within the Act were in fact built only recently thus qualifying the owners for at least some compensation). The Asians were the hardest hit. It was a common practice among them to build houses larger than were in fact needed with the view of renting part of the building. It was also regarded as a secure investment--a kind of security for widows and children. As a result of the implementation of this Act, a number of widows, therefore, instead of obtaining some income out of the houses left by their late husbands, found themselves liable to pay rent to the government. Many ended up petitioning the president in a most humiliating way. The president, it must be added, did make some exceptions in terms of implementing the law, a fact which those who emphasize the humanitarian nature of Tanzanian socialism, of course, never fail to mention. On the whole, however, the non-Africans failed to obtain even ten percent of the value of the property taken over by the government.

Although the Germans were the first ones to
devote money and efforts to develop plantation
agriculture in Tanzania (sisal, coffee, cotton,
rubber, tea, and other cash crops), by 1961,
most agricultural farms in the country were in
the hands of the British, Greeks, and Asians, and,
of course, a few Germans. Occupying a relatively
small percentage of Tanzania's agriculturally
productive land, non-African farms accounted for
about forty-five per cent of the value of the
country's total agricultural production. Not
only was their per acre production rate much
higher than that on the African farms held under
the customary tenure system, they also contributed in a significant way to Tanzania's foreign
exchange earnings, since most of them produced
export crops.

All freehold farms, as noted above, had been
converted in 1962 to government leaseholds. A
new law enacted in 1966 empowered the government
to take over agricultural land owned by a person
who was absent from Tanzania or who, while
present in the country, had allowed his land to
be occupied and developed by others and grant a
leasehold over it to the actual occupants. In a
sense, the law protected from eviction those who
had somehow managed to occupy the land. The law
proved particularly useful to the government
against those non-Africans who, for one reason
or another, found it necessary or expedient to
leave the country for an extended period of time.
The government also employed its power to expel
a non-citizen farmer from the country which was
followed by take over of his farm. In September,
1971, for example, Mr. Petrus Hedrik Hugo, who
had a 3170 acre farm in northern Tanzania, and
Mr. Carl Richard Lundgraen, who had a 652 acre
farm near Moshi, both of whom had been farming
in Tanzania at least since the early fifties,
were declared prohibited immigrants and their
rights of occupancy revoked on the argument
that "they cannot be allowed to continue to
hold rights of occupancy over our lands."[58]
No reason was specified for expulsion nor was any

compensation paid. (The device of individual expulsions followed by take over of their property is further discussed below).

When Tanzania became politically independent, sisal, coffee, and cotton accounted for over sixty per cent of its agricultural exports. Between 1954 and 1964, sisal production doubled, making Tanzania responsible for a third of the world's total output of sisal--almost all grown on non-African farms. Almost a quarter of Tanzania's foreign exchange earnings came from sisal. Its cultivation requires a large initial capital outlay; and the plants take several years to mature--facts which by themselves demonstrate the willingness of the non-Africans to continue investing in Tanzania.

In October, 1967, to ensure that it "will be in full control of the means of production of our country," the government declared that it would immediately take over six major sisal farms and acquire sixty per cent interest in thirty-three others. About this time, however, the world market price of sisal began to fall, and this considerably dampened the government's enthusiasm to take control of the country's means of production. Undisturbed by the government, several non-African farmers continued to operate their farms with a fairly high degree of efficiency even though they were not highly profitable. Some of the state farms had begun to deteriorate during the same period because of their non-profitability. In 1973, however, the market price rose sharply and the government found it necessary once again to move towards controlling the country's means of production. In early 1974, for example, twenty-two sisal farms, all belonging to Tanzanian Asian citizens were taken over. Their bank accounts were frozen and they were ejected from the farmhouses, their only homes. Today, virtually the whole sisal industry is in the hands of the government.

Other non-African farms (e.g. coffee) were

were much smaller in size than the sisal estates and were scattered all over the country. In the early 1960's the world bank reported that of the approximately 900 non-sisal farms (coffee, tea, and coconuts)

> about fifteen per cent had less than 100 acres. One sixth have a labor force of less than five.... There are several which are held by companies and run by paid managers. These have less serious financial, technical, and social problems than the second type. These are run by European or Asian yeomen farmers, very often pioneers on new land, many of them having settled after the first World War. [59]

In October, 1973, the government expropriated about fifty of the non-sisal farms owned by Greeks, Asians, Germans, Swiss, and the British. Tanzania's Vice President, Rashidi Kawawa, said: "We are nationalizing (these farms) because it is our policy to create a socialist state, and our land must be owned as farms by extended families or cooperative groups."[60] The owners received their first hint of the decision when representatives of TANU (the only political party in the country) called on their farms on October 22, 1973. They took immediate possession of not only the land but also the farmhouses, implements, machinery, and even private automobiles parked on the land. In one case, there were reliable reports that the take over of the farm and the owner's immediate eviction led to the theft of all his personal effects, including the family's clothes.

In the early 1970's, Tanzania inaugurated an ambitious program of "Ujamaaisation" (a cross between an Israeli Kibutz and a Chinese Commune) with the aim of converting all agricultural land (whether occupied individually or under the customary tenure system) into cooperatively cultivated land. A series of Ujamaa (brotherly or communal) villages were to be established so

274

that people could understand the benefits of
working for the common good of the villagers.
The well-looked after non-African farms provided
a convenient vehicle to make the Africans aware
of the possible benefits of communal living, since
there would be more incentive to join the village
in the first place if it could begin life with an
already efficiently managed farm.

From an examination of official documents and
the speeches and writings of Tanzanian leaders it
is easy to obtain an impression that although
Tanzania believes in socialism and communal ownership of land, it at least respects the right of an
individual to be compensated for value added to
the land before the land is given to an ujamaa
village. President Nyerere himself has declared:

> When I use my energy and talent to clear a
> piece of ground for my use it is clear that
> I am trying to transform this basic gift
> from God so that it can satisfy a human
> need.... By clearing that ground I have
> actually added to its value and have
> enabled it to be used to satisfy a human
> need. Whoever then takes this piece of
> ground must pay me for adding value to it
> through clearing it by my own labor.[61]

The TANU Creed (the operating documents of the
ruling party) recognizes this concept as do most
laws enacted by the government, at least in principle. The Preamble to the Constitution specifies
that enjoyment of property is one of the inherent
and inalienable rights of all individuals regardless of race or place of origin, subject only to
the rights and interests of others and of the
public interest. Virtually all statements
emanating from the president's offices, especially those likely to be picked up by foreign
reporters, contain statements respecting the
right of compensation. These, to put it bluntly,
belie actual practice. As noted above, the
concept has been considerably diluted in some of
the laws. The Acquisition of Buildings Act (1971)

regarded receipt of rent for ten or more years as totally relieving the government from any obligation to compensate the owners. Another law precluded compensation for improvements made on the land within the last five years of a thirty-three year lease (or the last ten years of a longer one). And yet another empowered the government to withhold compensation from absentee owners whose rights of occupancy were revoked or from individuals who had been declared prohibited immigrants. Even when the laws obliged the government to compensate, determination of its amount was generally left to specially appointed tribunals instead of to the ordinary courts. In those rare cases where access to the judicial system was allowed, it was necessary under the laws to obtain written permission from the Attorney General before any suit against the government could be filed in the courts. Ordinary non-Africans, generally dependent upon government officers for the issue of various types of licenses, permits, passports, and other documents felt it expedient to accept whatever meagre compensation, if any, they could obtain from the government rather than resort to the courts and antagonize the government.

They also knew that resorting to the courts did not guarantee respect for their rights. In some cases, the courts allowed a reduction in the amount of compensation on the theory that the benefits derived by the individual from the use of the land while it was occupied by him must be taken into account and balanced against any compensation that might be awarded to him.

Non-Africans also found that some of the practices of government officers, or informal arrangements made among them, often were sufficient to side-track the issues. For example, when the government nationalized the non-sisal farms so that they could be cooperatively owned by the village communities, the vice president conceded that the owners had not committed any crime or broken any rule or regulation. And yet, in this and similar cases, the government successfully avoided compensating the owners. It had correctly anticipated that most of those adversely affected would not be so bold as to pursue their claims in court or do more than send meaningless, polite petitions to the president.

Those who did file suit against the government found that there was little chance their cases would come to trial. The Chief Justice, Tanzania's highest judicial officer, issued verbal directives to all judges and magistrates of the lower courts transferring to his court all cases involving claims arising out of the government's attempt to establish Ujamaa villages. In one of his statements published in a government-controlled newspaper, he is reported to have said:

> Since Tanzania believed in Ujamaa then, the interest of many people in land cases should over-ride those of some few individuals. The judiciary could not be used as a tool to oppose ujamaa.... As citizens and TANU members, the courts are duty bound....to further ujamaa.[62]

In his view, while the courts were obliged to apply the laws as they stood, they also had a higher responsibility to interpret them in the correct political context. Not all members of the judiciary, of course, agreed with this view; but instead of confronting the Chief Justice and the government, some preferred to resign quietly, some to migrate overseas, and some, while expressing their disagreement, accepted the situation and hoped for change.

The result was that these were placed (and, as far as the authors are aware), remain on the docket, with little, or no chance, of ever being heard. The juridical issues, so important are they, should be of considerable interest to students of political science and law; but detailed treatment in scholarly publications (invariably quoting the writings of Presdient Nyerere) of the function of courts in a socialist society, are of

little use to non-Africans. Under the law, they
have the right to be compensated; but, in practice
their rights may not be exercised because the
court through this informal arrangement, has
virtually closed its doors to them. Of course, it
would make things much easier for the Chief Justice if the government were to enact a law which
would debar compensation in such cases. But,
doing this, would make it difficult for Tanzanian African leaders to have their cake and eat it
too. By following present practice the ujamaa
villages are more effectively, albeit unjustly
enriched, and Tanzania and President Nyerere's
reputation in the outside world remains untarnished
since laws providing for compensation remain on
the statute books with very few people knowing
of their inutility to non-Africans. And, Tanzania
continued to receive foreign aid--the highest in
terms of per capita in black Africa. In 1979, an
empty-handed Japanese delegation was taken to
task for trading with South Africa. In 1980, it
returned with $70 million and was spared being
castigated for its relations with South Africa.
Despite this, Tanzania has made only a modest
progress. In 1980, it is short of foreign exchange, its agricultural production is dropping,
its factories are running only at about 40% capacity, and its state-run organizations are generally
running at a loss.

Nationalizing the Medical, Legal, and Teaching Professions

Until April, 1974, when its military forces
overthrew the existing civilian government, Portugal regarded its African colonies as integral
parts of the homeland--"the overseas provinces,"
and insisted upon its right to maintain control
over and safeguard the territorial integrity
of the entire country. Its professed goal was
to have a multi-racial pluricultural society.
It discounted the importance of such facts as
the thousands of miles of distance between the
metropole, and the overseas provinces, and
that they contained population of a different

color. Portugal often bolstered its case by arguing that if the United States could regard Alaska (or Kenya the Somali populated areas in the North) as parts of their national territory then Portugal should be able to define Angola, Mozambique, and Portuguese Guinea as integral parts of the homeland. Such sophistic arguments, however, were insufficient to persuade African nationalists residing in or originating from these African areas, leaders of independent African states, or the vast majority of U.N. members who believed that these areas were Portuguese colonies, that Portugal had an obligation under Article 73(e) of the United Nations Charter to submit regular reports on conditions in these non-self governing territories, and that the peoples of these areas were entitled to self-determination and independence. They also believed that the same pressures as were exerted against other colonial powers in Africa should be mounted against the Portuguese and that the intensity of this pressure must increase in proportion to the Portuguese intransigence in moving away from its position regarding these areas as part and parcel of its national territory. Portugal refused to budge, though it did extend to provincial legislatures greater local autonomy and an increased share in the decision-making process. Such concessions, however, were summarily dismissed by advocates of self-determination. Africans called them window-dressing and contended that the members of these local legislatures, whatever their color, were in fact stooges of the Lisbon government.

Beginning in 1961, Africans embarked upon an ambitious program of guerilla warfare to force Portugal out of Africa. Initially, the guerillas were no real threat to Portugal. Their activities were uncoordinated, irregular, and haphazard. The various groups also had difficulty in getting along with each other and obtaining arms, ammunition, and other supplies. In time, however, with the active support of independent African states like Tanzania and Zambia, some of the communist countries-- the Soviet Union, China, and Cuba--and, a large number of non-governmental organizations, the

279

guerillas became a formidable problem for the Portuguese police and the armed forces. The World Council of Churches was among the private organizations supporting the guerilla movement. In early 1974, for example, it contributed $450,000 to eleven African liberation movements, including the National Front for the Liberation of Mozambique (Frelimo). In a report submitted by Rev. James Lawson to the council's twenty-fifth annual congress in late 1973, Frelimo was described as deserving the church's support because of its "efforts to humanize violence."[63] With its population of less than ten million, tiny Portugal found it more and more difficult to maintain large number of troops in its African provinces. It was obliged to draft new recruits at the young age of sixteen and increase the period of service to four years. Also, hanging on to the "provinces" was proving economically costly. Although accused of having exploited her colonies, Portugal had apparently realized no spectacular gain from having done so, for its own economy compared to other Western European countries remained undeveloped. Nor was it able to provide its armed forces in Africa with appropriate arms and equipment--a fact which contributed to the army's increasing disgust with the war. These and other factors led to the overthrow of the existing government and the rise to power in April, 1974, of General Spinola with the declared policy of seeking a political solution to the problem--the resolution of which was, in less than two years, independence for Portuguese Guinea (which promptly changed its name to Guinea-Bissau), Mozambique, and Angola.

When General Spinola assumed power there were some 200-220,000 Portuguese living in Mozambique, (total population 8-9 million). There were also 10-15,000 other non-Africans, especially Asians living in the country. Many non-Africans were born there, and some Portuguese familes had been living there for hundreds of years. Therefore, General Spinola, although willing to accommodate the aspirations of African nationalists, was also concerned with safeguarding legitimate interests of non-Afri-

cans, if only to prevent the emergence of a secessionist movement among the whites. His intention,
at least initially, was to promote self-determin-
tion through a political process which would include formation of political parties and a referendum through which the people of Mozambique
could decide for themselves between a loose federation with the metropole or independence. Should
they prefer independence, there would be a smooth
transition taking into account the legitimate
interests of all concerned. The general's ideas,
although commendable, were quickly modified by
events.

Frelimo, the leading African guerilla movement in Mozambique, insisted that the new Portuguese government recognize it as the only movement or party representing the people of Mozambique and transfer power directly to it without
delay. To persuade the Portuguese to do so, the
Frelimo leadership indicated its willingness to
undertake certain commitments. At a meeting held
in Lusaka, Zambia in September, 1974, with representatives of the Portuguese government, Frelimo
leaders pledged that it would protect the safety
and interests of non-Africans residing in Mozambique. They claimed to favor a multiracial
society. They pledged that whites had nothing to
fear from black rule. Partly influenced by such
assurances and partly because the Portuguese
representatives shared some of the leftist
leaning ideological stance of the Frelimo leaders,
Portugal agreed to grant political independence
to Mozambique in June, 1975, and agreed that until
then the country would be governed by an interim
government in which Frelimo was to be in the
majority. At the end of this conference, Mr.
Joaquim A. Chissano, one of the Frelimo leaders
who was expected to be the Premier of the Interim
Government, stated that whites in Mozambique had
no reason for worry or alarm--"we are working to
create a society in which all races can live."[64]

Soon after the Frelimo leaders had been installed and power transferred to the Interim

Government, this conciliatory tone underwent a subtle change. In a policy statement issued soon after this transfer, Frelimo called for a major transformation of the economic, cultural, and political life in Mozambique. The statement also assured the whites "tranquility and an atmosphere of confidence" in which "the majority (of the whites) would have a positive contribution to make to the national reconstruction of our country."65 To those with little background knowledge of contemporary black Africa, the change was unnoticeable. To some, it may have even sounded like a perfectly logical, rational statement consistent with Frelimo's previous declarations. Some of the frightening implications of the change, however, did not escape the non-African residents. Their suspicions were further aroused a few days later when Mr. Samora Machel (now President Machel) announced:

> "...our objective is to conquer complete
> independence, to install a people's power,
> to construct a new society without ex-
> ploitation, for the benefit of all those
> who feel themselves to be Mozambicans."66

Realizing that Mozambique had yet to become fully independent and that some Portuguese troops were still present in the country, Mr. Machel (as well as other Frelimo leaders) was, however, extremely careful not to make statements that might be construed as having racial implications. In January, 1975, for example, Mr. Machel said:

> "The righteousness of our line won all races
> and social classes to the cause of national
> independence. We do not think a nation, or
> a people can be defined on the basis of false,
> reactionary criteria such as skin color or
> tribal or regional origin."67

This statement was widely reported in the world under the heading "Machel Rejects Racism in New Nation."

Mozambique became independent in June, 1975.

Even before it celebrated its first anniversary, the new government, led by President Machel, had, inter alia--

a) renamed the country the People's Republic of Mozambique;

b) arrested and imprisoned, sometimes for months, without trial, thousands of non-Africans for "crimes against decolonization," or for "economic sabotage" or simply for "being white." A number of them were also held in communal farms (which were in fact more like concentration camps) for "mental decolonization;"

c) decreed that foreigners (interpreted in practice as non-Africans) could engage only in those economic activities which were needed by the country (thereby forcing thousands of unskilled or semi-skilled Portuguese workers out of their jobs;)

d) nationalized all rented homes (many Portuguese had invested their savings in second homes or apartments which they had rented to others);

e) ordered the troops and the police to take physical possession of all unoccupied houses in the name of the state as "abandoned property" (Portugal's claim that this was an unfriendly act which disregarded the spirit of the accord signed between the two countries in Lusaka, Zambia in September, 1974, was ignored); and

f) allowed the non-Africans to be regularly harrassed and blamed for all the evils, including some of the tribal and intraparty conflicts. On several occasions, President Machel himself made speeches attacking the whites, Asians, and mixed-blood Africans, partly, it must be added, to divert the people's attention from some of their economic problems.

During this period, Mozambique also nationalized the medical, teaching, and legal professions--

all of which were dominated by the non-Africans.
Private clinics and hospitals, including those
operated by church missionaries were nationalized.
All private medical practitioners were forbidden by
law to practice medicine except as government employees. The government's policy was to provide
health services to rural areas and most doctors
were assigned to practice in small villages where
most of the Africans lived. (Most found it difficult to adjust to the change and left the country.
Ten months after independence there remained
fewer than twenty doctors in the country). All
private schools, including mission schools, were
nationalized. All teachers became government
employees. To help "wash off" their old elitist
ideas derived from the colonial educational system,
all teachers were required to undergo reorientation
training. All private law offices were ordered
closed. It was illegal for anyone to practice
law, except as a government employee. And, in
February, 1976, the government announced that
"some people might have to work three years without pay (non-Africans) because of the country's
economic plight."[98] There were also rumors,
around this time, that President Machel was about
to declare nationalization of children, wives, and
private bank accounts.

By October, 1974, only about 10,000 non-
Africans had left the country, and it seemed that
the rest were prepared to stay or, at least, were
willing to wait and see. As an Indian businessman
residing in Mozambique's capital said:

> "I, for one, want very much to stay and to
> participate in the new country. If the
> rights of the minorities are protected,
> there should be no problems. The skills of
> the whites and Asians are needed and I am
> sure Frelimo leaders know this."[99]

But with the increase in Frelimo's rhetoric, denouncing colonial masters, economic saboteurs
and imperialist ideas and, in particular, with the
implementation of the ideology of "scientific

socialism" espoused by President Machel in the manner described above (of which in practical terms non-Africans were the only victims) more and more departed. By February, 1975, an additional 20,000 had left; by June, 1975, another 40-50,000 and so on. Today, there are about 15,000 non-Africans who were there prior to independence still living in Mozambique, less than ten percent of their population in 1974. As a result partly of the departure of the so called "old Portuguese" and partly of the new government's zeal and overindulgence in formulating and implementing socialist economic policies, Mozambique's economy has suffered considerable setback in the post-independence period. Recruitment by the new government of a large number of non-Portuguese speaking foreigners--Cubans, North Koreans, Chinese, Russian, and Eastern Europeans, through agreements with their governments and of a comparatively small number of Swedes, British, and Americans of socialist orientation through direct contacts--to work in the country on contractual basis as teachers, engineers, technicians, doctors, and civil servants was, after some bitter experiences, found to be an unworkable solution.

By 1980, President Samora Machel had been obliged to recognize the fact that the nationalized enterprises were simply not working at even marginally satisfactory levels. The "people's shops" established following the independence to distribute food and clothing were often empty with little effort being made by those entrusted to run them to replenish the goods. In March, 1980, Machel called on those industrialists and shopowners who had left the country to return. He promised them special incentives if they would come back and invest in farms, shops, restaurants, and other economic enterprises. He also added, however, that while private activity had an important role to play "in straightening out our country," Mozambique's socialist objectives will have to be recognized by those who return. It is questionable if many of the "old Portuguese," especially those with the right qualifications, experience, and entrepreneurial ability, will ever return after what they have gone through in the last few years.

It must be noted that they had decided to leave even though the decision was fraught with uncertainties. In the first place, under Mozambique laws most of them were not allowed to take out of the country anything except a suitcase of clothes and a maximum sum of $2,000. Everything else had to be left behind to be confiscated by the state as abandoned property. And yet most thought that it was a rational decision to make. As a fifty-eight year old office worker who entered Portugal with only two small plastic bags containing his clothes said: "There is no future for Portuguese in Mozambique only persecution, insults, and provocations." 70

Portugal itself had become saturated with refugees (or "retornados" as they were called there) from its "overseas provinces," especially from Angola where about 500,000 Portuguese had settled and most of whom had fled the civil war raging in that country. (To return to Angola, which became independent on November 11, 1975, they would need visas). At least the French who fled from Algeria had been allowed to take their belongings with them when they left for France in the early 1960's. But in the case of the Portuguese "retornados," they had been left with no alternative but to rely on hand-outs from the government at a time when Portugal itself was suffering from high unemployment rates, a shortage of investment capital, and political instability. Nevertheless, during 1975 and 1976 it was spending on an average about $30 million dollars a month to care for the retornados. (They were not entitled to any assistance from the United Nations refugee organizations because, it was argued, they were not strictly refugees but were simply returning to the country of their origin!)

It is quite conceivable that many Portuguese economists and intellectuals must now be thinking, in retrospect, that their former Prime Minister Marcello Caetano was prophetic when he said on

March 3, 1974:

"The guerillas and their allies...will accept
no political settlement save that of our
handing over power to the terrorist movements,
followed by the immediate or eventual expulsion of the whites residing in the country as
had happened all over Africa.... Even if they
came on stockinged feet to declare that the
whites could stay, there would sooner or
later be a move towards the Africanization
of foreign possessions...." [71]

Deportation of Selected Individuals Followed by Confiscation of Their Property

Malawi, formerly known as Nyasaland, a small
country about the size of Pennsylvania, located in
southeastern Africa with a population of about
five million, became politically independent on
July 6, 1964. A notice appearing in its April,
1970, Official Gazette read:

Government Notice No. 66

ORDER

Under powers conferred by section 2 of the
Forfeiture Act, President Hastings Banda being
satisfied that the person whose name is set
out hereunder has been acting in a manner
prejudicial to the economy of the State and
subversive to the lawfully established government, hereby declares such person to be subject
to forfeiture.

CHITUBHAI PREMA PATEL formerly of Plot No. TP
1153, Henderson Street, Blantyre.

Sd. H. BANDA [72]
PRESIDENT

The person subject to such a notice might be
imagined to be a fiery, dangerous subversive out to
destroy the new nation, who must be removed from the

country. Such an image would be far from accurate.
Mr. Patel is, in fact, about fifty-four years old,
mild-mannered, and operates a restaurant in Chicago.
He has a degree in chemistry and for a number of
years was a pharmacist in Malawi. He had always
been sympathetic to the African cause. When Dr.
Hastings Banda (who now likes to be known as H.
Kamuzu Banda) returned to Malawi in July, 1958,
after a long absence during which he resided in the
United States, the United Kingdom, and Ghana,
Mr. Patel was the first to receive him at the
Malawi airport. It was Mr. Patel's automobile
that was used to bring him into town. It was
Mr. Patel who over the years advised many African
leaders during their struggle for independence
and contributed over $30,000 to their cause.

        Mr. Patel was eventually prosecuted on a
charge of attempting to violate the exchange
control limit on the amount of Malawi currency
that could be taken out of the country. He was,
on appeal, found not guilty. On March 19, 1970,
the court also ordered that the currency notes
which the Malawi police had found in Mr. Patel's
house (in which the pharmacy occupied the first
floor) and which had been used as exhibits in the
case must be returned to Mr. Patel within thirty
days. Before this period could expire Mr. Patel
was served with the above notice and he and his
family were required to leave the country forthwith.
All their property, including the money which the
government was supposed to return to him, was
forfeited to the state.

        The Forfeiture Act referred to in the govern-
ment order empowers the president (who was acclaimed
president for life in 1970) to at any time declare
that the presence within Malawi of a non-citizen
(all but 200 of the twelve to fifteen thousand non-
Africans (Europeans and Asians) in the country were
non-citizens) was prejudical to the state or subversive to the government. Upon his declaration
the presence in the country of the named person became unlawful and all his assets in the country
were automatically forfeited to the state. In

theory, these powers were to be exercised only in extreme and rare circumstances. In practice, the situation was almost the reverse. And when the president declared an individual prejudicial or subversive, not only he, but all of his family, were deported from the country. Nearly anything non-citizens did which did not meet the approval of the president subjected them to the risk of deportation and confiscation of their property. And the demands made by the new African government on the non-Africans were by no means few or simple. All private doctors were required to volunteer at least two hours a day in the government hospital. If the president was about to pass through a street, all shops on that street had to close at least two hours before the scheduled time. At least twice a month they had to decorate their shops for one reason or another. Whenever the Malawi Congress Party (the only political party in the country) or its youth wing, the Young Pioneers, needed funds, Asian shopkeepers were asked for specified donations. No checks were accepted, only cash.

It is difficult to say exactly how many people were deported from the country in the same manner as Mr. Patel, because not all such orders were published in the Gazette. Estimates range between two to four hundred orders. Some of the well-known, documented instances are:

    ---Mr. Peter Moxon, a European, one time a
    member of the parliament, suspected of sup-
    porting African politicians who had dared
    challenge certain policies of Dr. Banda's;

    ---Mr. B. H. Patel, an Asian businessman,
    suspected of providing medication to Mr. Henry
    Chipembere, the leader of the African group
    opposed to Dr. Banda (diabetes pills, Mr.
    Patel's wife suffered from the disease, and
    unfortunately, so did Mr. Chipembere);

    ---The Yannakis Brothers, Greeks, accused of
    furnishing Mr. Chipembere's group with small
    fishing vessels which could have been used to

bring arms and equipment into the country.
The brothers were fish merchants;

---The proprietor of Lakhshmi Silk Store, an
Asian, one of the richest men in Malawi for
having in his possession at Nairobi airport,
Zambian currency notes. On his return to
Malawi he was arrested, detained in jail for
ninety days, and deported. His property,
worth at least $200,000 was forfeited to the
state;

---About seventy-five Goan (Asian) families.
In March, 1976, they were attending a dance
and reception following a wedding. It came
to the president's attention that at the
time he was addressing the people on television, the Goans had preferred dancing to
listening to the president's speech. All
were imprisoned for two weeks and then deported from the country.

There are fewer than 5,000 non-Africans in Malawi
today.

SOME CONCLUDING REMARKS

The employment of the devices described
above by Uganda, Kenya, Sierra Leone, Zaire, Ghana,
Nigeria, Tanzania, Mozambique, and Malawi respectively should be considered illustrative only.
Because a state has been described here as having
used a particular device should not be interpreted
to mean that it did not employ the other methods.
In fact, each of the nine states have engaged in
several of these practices. For example, Malawi
resorted not only to selective expulsion, but also
to removal of non-Africans from positions in the
public service, and to imposing restrictions on non-
African participation in retail trade, especially
in the rural areas; Kenya not only forced non-
Africans out of employment in the public and private
sectors, but also imposed restrictions on their

290

commercial activities. Tanzania expropriated non-African farms and buildings, forced professionals to work for the government, and placed restrictions on non-Africans participating in certain trading activities.

Moreover, it cannot be argued that these nine black African states are unrepresentative of all African countries under majority rule and that their actions are justified by the unique circumstances confronting them. Virtually all African states characterized by heavy foreign investment resorted to one or more of the same practices regardless of their official ideologies as soon as they were free to do so. There were differences in timing, intensity, and the extent to which non-African economic interests were harmed. But, it is abundantly clear that there has been a more or less identical sequence of events and results in all black African states following the end of colonial rule. An official commitment to achieve "total" or "genuine" independence was followed by a series of specific acts of implementation which by intention and design created severe economic and personal hardship for non-Africans.

It may be argued that use of such techniques was necessary to the achievement of national goals which transcend even the most important individual rights and certainly was more important than the preservation of the high economic status enjoyed by the non-Africans before independence. It may be claimed that while non-Africans suffered numerous economic losses there were compensating factors sufficient to enable them to continue life in their homelands had they really been committed to making the difficult transition from colonialism to independence a successful one in light of the need to establish true majority rule after decades of minority rule in all aspects of national life. The next two chapters will examine the political conditions of life in black Africa since independence. Only then may judgment about the viability of post-colonial life in black Africa for minorities be rendered.

CHAPTER IV: FOOTNOTES

[1]"Asian Migration," Bulletin of the Africa
Institute of South Africa, No. 5, 1974, p. 188.

[2]"From Racism to Genocide: Extracts from
Reports of the International Commission of Jurists,"
Transition, No. 49, p. 8. See also Richard Plender,
International Commission of Jurists Review, No. 9,
December, 1972, pp. 1-19.

[3]"Violations of Human Rights," A Study of the
International Commission of Jurists, S-3143, quo-
ting Mr. Gheevala, Honorary Secretary, Shri Brihad,
Bharatiya Samaj, p. 7.

[4]"From Racism to Genocide: Extracts from
Report of the International Commission of Jurists,"
op. cit., pp. 7-8.

[5]"Violations of Human Rights," A Study of the
International Commission of Jurists, op. cit., p. 6.

[6]"Search for Lost Baggage," Uganda Resettle-
ment Board, News Bulletin, (London,) No. 4, p. 3.

[7]Talk given by Gwen Cashmore, Director, CCWEU,
UKIAS Conference, London, April 7, 1973, (mimeo),
p. 1.

[8]Africa Recorder, No. 19, p. 3224.

[9]For full details, see K.C. Kotecha, "The
Shortchanged: Uganda Citizenship Laws and How They
Were Applied to Its Asian Minority," International
Lawyer, Vol. 9, No. 1, January, 1975, pp. 1-29.

[10]Ibid.

[11]Letter of January 11, 1973, from Mr. Dattani to the United Kingdom Immigrants Advisory Service, London.

[12]Personal Interview with members of the family, and examination of copies of some of the relevant letters.

[13]The Journal News, Rockland County, New York December 18, 1972.

[14]Africa Digest, March, 1973 and June, 1973.

[15]A. L. Ad , The Civil Service in New African States (New York: Praeger, 1965), p. 114.

[16]Ibid., p. 117.

[17]The Constitution of Kenya, December 12, 1963, Articles 2 (1), 4, and 5. Nairobi: Kenya Official Gazette, Legislative Supplement, No. 69.

[18]Richard Cox, Kenyatta's Country, (New York: Praeger, 1965), pp. 178-179.

[19]Ibid., p. 169.

[20]Ibid., p. 166.

[21]The Immigration Act, 1967, Act 25 of 1967, Kenya Gazette, Sections 18 and 19.

[22]H. L. van der Laan, The Lebanese Traders in Sierra Leone (The Hague: Mouton & Co., 1975), p. 6.

[23]The Sierra Leone (Constitution) Order in Council, Her Majesty's Stationery Office, Statutory Documents, 1961, No. 741, reprinted in Amos J. Peaslee (ed.), Constitutions of Nations, Vol. 1: Africa (3rd edition, The Hague: Martinus Nijhoff, 1965), pp. 715-771.

[24]The Sierra Leone Constitution (Amendment) Act, No. 11 of 1962; The Sierra Leone Constitution (Amendment) (No. 2) Act, No. 12 of 1962, Laws of Sierra Leone. See also The Constitution (Consolidation of Amendments) Act, No. 52 of 1965, reaffirming these amendments.

[25]See the explanation given by the Prime Minister to the Sierra Leone House of Representatives, Sierra Leone Parliamentary Debates 1965-1966, 2:299.

[26]Constitution (Amendment)(No. 2) Act, 1962, Art. 3.

[27]Sierra Leone Nationality and Citizenship Act, No. 10 of 1962, Laws of Sierra Leone.

[28]Sierra Leone Parliamentary Debates, House of Representatives, 1965-1966, 2:269.

[29]Personal interview, August, 1976 (name witheld).

[30]The Sierra Leone Citizenship Act, No. 4 of 1973 and The Sierra Leone Citizenship Regulations, 1973, Public Notice No. 62 of 1973, Rule 5, Laws of Sierra Leone.

[31]The Sierra Leone Citizenship (Amendment) Act, 1976, Art. 1.

[32]From an official tape recording of the proceedings of the Sierra Leone Parliament.

[33]U.S. Department of State, Background Notes: Republic of Zaire (Washington, D.C.:Department of State Publication 7793, February, 1972), p. 7.

[34]United Nations, Official Records of the General Assembly, Twenty-eighth Session, October 4, 1973, p. 53.

[35] Jean de la Gueriviere, "Zaire's Second Independence" Translations on Africa, (U.S. Department of Commerce, Washington, D.C., No. 1449, March 21, 1974), pp. 29-30.

[36] "Zaire Orders Expulsion of Foreigners" Portugal, Vol. 4, No. 1, January, 1974, p. 4.

[37] "Zairisation in Practice" Zaire-Africa, London: The E. D. O'Brien Organization, No. 160 March 31, 1974, p. 2.

[38] The London Times, March 28, 1962.

[39] Africa Digest, August, 1965, p. 15. See Also: West Africa, June 19, 1965.

[40] Africa Confidential, March 31, 1967.

[41] "Ghana's Military Beset by Economic Troubles, Looks to Civilian Aid." The New York Times, November 21, 1976.

[42] Monthly Economic Bulletin, Ghana Commercial Bank, Vol. 6, No. 2, April, 1975. et seq.

[43] A. N. Hakam, "Impediments to the Growth of Indigenous Industrial Entrepreneurship in Ghana," Economic Bulletin of Ghana, Vol. 2, No. 2, 1972, pp. 73-74.

[44] Ibid.

[45] "Ghana: More Indigenisation," Africa, No. 47, July, 1975, p. 45.

[46] Paul Collins, "The Political Economy of Indigenization," African Review, Vol. 4, No. 4, 1974, p. 492. See also: "The Second National Development Plan 1970-1974," Nigeria: Government Printing Press, 1970.

[47] Nigeria, Federal Military Government, Supplement to Official Gazette Extraordinary, Vol. 58, February 28, 1972, p. 289.

[48]For full details of this complex legislation, see Paul Collins, "The Policy of Indigenization: An Overall View," The Quarterly Journal of Administration, Nigeria, April, 1975, pp. 137-147. See also: I. Teribe, "Financing Indigenization," Quarterly Journal of Administration, January, 1975, pp. 160-164.

[49]"Nigerianization," African Development, March, 1974, p. 13.

[50]"Nigeria's Indigenization Policy Under Fire," New York Times, October 30, 1976.

[51]R. H. Jackson, "Political Stratification in Tropical Africa," Canadian Journal of African Studies, Vol. 7, No. 3, 1973, p. 395. See also: John P. Mackintosh, Nigerian Government and Politics, (London: George Allen & Unwin, Ltd., 1966), p. 617.

[52]"Ujamaa--The Basis of African Socialism," in Knud Erik Svendsen and Merete Tiesen (eds.,) Self-Reliant Tanzania (Daressalaam: Tanzania Publishing House, 1969), p. 160.

[53]African Recorder, May 7-20, 1967, p. 1640.

[54]"The Arusha Declaration and TANU's Policy On Socialism and Self-Reliance," in Martin Minogue and Judith Molloy (eds.) African Aims and Attitudes, Selected Documents (New York: Cambridge University Press, 1974), p. 77.

[55]African Recorder, September 10-23, 1968, p. 2034.

[56]International Bank for Reconstruction and Development, The Economic Development of Tanganyika, (Baltimore: John Hopkins Press, 1961), p. 87. For a detailed treatment of Tanzania's real property laws, see R. W. James, Land Tenure and Policy in Tanzania, (Toronto: University of Toronto Press, 1971), et seq.

[57]Gilbert L. Rutman, The Economy of Tanzania, (New York: Praeger Publishers, 1968), p. 87.

[58]African Recorder, November 24-December 6, 1971, p. 2974.

[59]International Bank Reconstruction Development, "The Economic Development of Tanganyika," loc. cit., p. 205.

[60]African Digest, October 22, 1973.

[61]Essay by President Nyerere entitled, "National Property," in Julius K. Nyerere, Uhuru Na Umoja (Freedom and Socialism), (London: Oxford University Press, 1968), pp. 53-54.

[62]"Put Ujamaa First," Daily News, Tanzania, September 26, 1972; also: "Tanzania: Ujamaa and the Law," Africa Confidential, Vol. 15, No. 9, May 3, 1976. See also: Rude W. James, "Implementing the Arusha Declaration: The Role of the Legal System," Africa Review, Vol. 3, No. 2, 1973, pp. 179-193.

[63]Report submitted by Rev. James Lawson at World Council of Churches, Twenty-fifth Annual Congress, 1973, Portugal, Vol. 4, No. 3, March, 1974, p. 3.

[64]"Mozambique Sets a Cautious Policy," New York Times, September 18, 1974.

[65]"Black Leaders are Installed in Mozambique and Call for Changes,"(New York Times, September 21, 1974, p. 3) quoting from statement issued upon the installation of an interim government dominated by the Front for the Liberation of Mozambique.

[66]"The Men Who Will Control Mozambique: Their Aim is More Than 'Black Power'," New York Times, September 21, 1974.

[67]"Mechel Rejects Racism in New Nation," Lisbon, Oseculo, January 13, 1975, p. 9.

[68]"Work Without Pay Set in Mozambique as Economy Falters," New York Times, February 4, 1976.

[69]"New Portuguese High Commissioner Begins Talks on Mozambique Freedom," New York Times, September 13, 1974.

[70]Portuguese Flee Mozambique and Tell of Persecution," New York Times, March 2, 1976.

[71]Address by Prime Minister Marcello Caetano of the Annual Conference of the National Popular Action Movement, Lisbon, Portugal, Vol. 4, No. 3, March, 1974. See also: Portugal, No. 9, Vol. 3, September, 1973, p. 1. For an illustration of how quickly and easily promises made by Tanzanian leaders were forgotten following independence, see Africa Confidential, April 19, 1962.

[72]Government Notice No. 66 of April 7, 1970 issued under the Forfeiture Act, (cap. 14.06), Laws of Malawi, 1970.

CHAPTER V

THE TYRANNY OF THE MAJORITY

The root principles of democracy are majority rule and minority rights. Without effective safeguards for the political rights of minorities the weight of majority power is likely to overwhelm the interests and perhaps endanger the existence of numerically inferior groups. True majority rule implies that today's minority, by exercising traditional political rights of free expression and organization, may become tomorrow's majority. For the better part of human history small, powerful elites or minorities oppressed the mass of people. But, with the spread of democratic ideas, in particular the notion of majority rule, the potential abuse of power by numerically superior groups has been recognized by acceptance of various institutional checks on majority power.

These checks may take the form of constitutional guarantees of individual rights and due process of law, institutional arrangements decentralizing governmental power or, less formally, toleration of organized political opposition in leadership selection processes.

With very few exceptions, black African states today fail to protect the legitimate political rights of the individual and, in fact, have moved in numerous ways to destroy the influence of politically unpopular minorities. With few

299

exceptions, a tyranny of the majority exists today in black Africa.

This was not always the case. Upon independence virtually all African states adopted constitutions including specific acknowledgment of the limits on governmental power over civil and political freedoms. Furthermore, judicial processes designed to support the rule of law and minimize political interference in the administration of justice were an integral part of the new constitutions.

Formal guarantees of basic political rights in the "independence constitutions" were buttressed in nearly every case by adoption of federal forms of government. Federalism divides and decentralizes governmental power by recognizing the relative autonomy of regionally based groups and interests. Federalism is a means of establishing union where no unity exists. Federal constitutions are particularly appropriate in societies divided by strongly felt, geographically defined differences in which numerically small or politically weak groups fear the superior power of homogeneous majorities. The regional governments and the territories over which they exercise semi-autonomous authority constitute separate, protected arenas of influence enabling sectional interests to co-exist.

Africa presents a particularly good example of how federalism may be an appropriate, perhaps necessary, response to conditions of great diversity. In nearly every case, the movement from colonial status to independence was accompanied by discussion of how to preserve the basic rights and political survival of important minorities. In nearly every case, the federal institutions were chosen as best answer to this question.

As we review the emergence and eventual dismantling of federal systems in black Africa, it should become clear that formal decentralization of governmental power was far closer to being a

necessary rather than merely a useful means of
protecting minority rights and preserving the
substance of democracy.

Cameroon

Cameroon is unique in Africa in that the
British and French shared occupation of its territory. The French-speaking area became independent
on January 1, 1960, and the remaining English-
speaking population only agreed to become part of
the new nation upon condition that it be organized as a federal republic. The constitution was
to recognize a semi-autonomous division between
French-speaking East Cameroon and the far smaller,
English-speaking, West Cameroon. These conditions
were met and, following a plebiscite, the English-
speaking population agreed to become part of a
new union known as the Federal Republic of Cameroon.

The people of West Cameroon were not only
seeking recognition of their cultural and language
differences but also protection against the greater
size and economic power of the French-speaking
people of East Cameroon. Also, under the British,
the people of West Cameroon had enjoyed the protection of a judicial system incorporating recognition of fundamental civil and political rights.
Their different tribal heritage and the resulting
potential for conflict between the two greatly
accentuated the value of a federal union in the
eyes of citizens in West Cameroon. In short, they
had reason to fear the consequences of a close
political merger with a partner having the capacity
and perhaps the desire to dominate them. A federal constitution, they assumed, would afford
protection against domination while extending
the benefits of cooperation. This assumption
was strengthened by frequent public assurance
from the leader of East Cameroon, President
Ahidjo, who had played a major role in negotiating terms of the federation between the two
groups. Mr. Ahidjo asserted his personal commitment to maintenance of a bilingual, pluralistic
nation.[1]

Analysis of the specific provisions of the constitution reveals that representatives of West Cameroon were willing to accept the principle of majority rule, and their consequential junior status in the federation in return for guarantees of political survival and formal recognition of their vital interests.

The federal president was to be chosen in a national election with no limitation on re-election to that office. Practically speaking, the chief executive in all likelihood would come from the East. The vice president could not be a native of the president's home area, but this would mean little since the office of vice president was powerless.

The federal legislature would also, in the normal course of events, primarily reflect the greater share of the new nation's population in the East since it was to be unicameral and be elected by a system of universal suffrage based on one deputy per 80,000 inhabitants. Eastern deputies would outnumber those from the West by about four to one.

Each state in the federation had its own legislature although they were vested with very limited powers. Many responsibilities normally entrusted to the states in a federal system, e.g. education, public health, prison administration, were placed with the national government although article six of the constitution specified that the states would exercise responsibility over these activities unless the national government deemed it necessary to assume control of them. [2] Thus, residual power in these matters lay technically with the states but, by design, the central government could preempt responsibility simply by legislative action. In effect, the dominant majority from the East retained the option of considerably reducing the role of the states in the union.

Further evidence of the unusually skewed

distribution of power between state and national
levels of government in Cameroon is found in the
president's powers to dissolve state legislatures
and refer state laws to the Federal Court of
Justice for constitutional validation.

Thus, the federal constitution of Cameroon
contained the seeds of its own destruction--an
outcome toward which the nation began to move
almost immediately following ratification.
Within a very few years the national legislature
had assumed responsibility over the area of state
control described in article six. Within ten
years the state legislature retained little more
power than that "apt to be vested in a local
government unit within a unitary system." [3] Also,
the federal administrative system had assumed
virtually complete control of all areas of
governmental activity, state and national, except
primary education.

In May, 1972, President Ahmadou Ahidjo declared his intention to abolish what vestiges of
federalism that remained and establish a unitary
state. In due course, a national plebiscite
approved the President's proposal. That is, the
political majority in the East for whom the President always spoke, achieved a predictable victory
which effectively abrogated previous "binding"
agreements between the dominant majority and
the far smaller, English-speaking minority
affirming the political integrity of each group.
In retrospect, the President's early opposition
to formation of alternative political parties
should have warned the minority of his intention
to consolidate power at the top as soon as
possible.

The present constitution, approved in the
1972 plebiscite, provides for a more powerful
presidency--vesting power over the armed forces
and the police in him besides making the president the head of state, chief administrative
officer and head of the cabinet. The state civil
service was abolished and merged with the federal

service but perhaps the most dramatic change was
in the method of electing the national legislature.
The entire country is designated as a single electoral district and the party with the most votes
wins all 120 seats in the National Assembly.
State legislatures were abolished altogether as
were the state courts. Theoretically, opposition
political parties may form and conduct their
affairs openly but, in practice, West Cameroon-
based parties have been harrassed by the police
and, of course, denied any real opportunity to
share power by the winner-take-all system of
legislative elections. The dominant party, the
Union Nationale Cameroonaise (UNC) is led by
President Ahidjo. He received 99.9% of the votes
cast in his 1975 reelection and UNC legislative
candidates also garnered 99.9% of the popular
vote. No great exercise in deduction is needed
to infer that the political power and integrity
of West Cameroon is completely destroyed.

In other ways, however, West Cameroon retains
its cultural identity. English is still spoken
in the western sections of the country and in
countless ways beyond the capacity of the
majority to extinguish, this distinctive but
politically impotent minority survives; visible
proof of the substantial and legitimate basis for
the original agreement on a federal constitution.

Nigeria

Nigeria became independent on October 1,
1960. Its constitution identified three states
united in a federal system. The total Nigerian
population accounted for one-sixth of Africa's
people. Nigeria consisted of over 290 tribes
but three major tribal units dominated Nigerian
society.

The Hausas living mainly in the north are
Muslim, they constitute between 50% to 60% of the
total population. They are relatively poor, uneducated but deeply proud of their cultural
heritage and history. The Hausas feared from the

304

beginning of independence that their comparative
poverty and lack of education would exclude them
from positions of leadership and responsibility
in the new nation.

The Ibos and Yorubas are Christian, well
educated by Western standards, and enjoy a stronger
economic position than the Hausas. These two
tribes both look down upon the Hausas as backward
and poor while the Hausas perceive their more
fortunate brothers as arrogant and domineering.
Politically, the two smaller tribes feared
the possible future domination of the numerically
superior Hausas.

Thus, in the years preceding independence,
Nigerian nationalist leaders generally agreed that
a federal constitution recognizing the distinctive
position of the three primary tribes was essential
to the stability of independent Nigeria. Colonial
government leaders shared this opinion, but it
should not be presumed that federalism was foisted
upon Nigerian independence leaders by the British.
As John P. Mackintosh has observed:

> But at this stage it was now up to the
> Nigerian leaders to decide which aspect they
> wished to emphasize. Dr. Azikiwe and the NCNC
> wanted a more decided move in the direction
> of federalism and in a Memorandum they pro-
> posed that the Central legislature should
> deal only with defence, foreign affairs, and
> the currency, all other matters being left
> to the Regional Councils. In 1947, Chief
> Awolwo had declared that 'Nigeria is not a
> nation. It is a mere geographical expression'
> ...The important point to note is that a
> federal constitution is the only thing suit-
> able for Nigeria. For the Northerners, there
> is no doubt that it was the regional aspect
> of the Constitution that was most welcome. [4]

With the exception of the National Independence
Party from the East, all political parties agreed
on the utility of a federal structure with as much

regional autonomy as possible. Leaders from each
region were concerned about safeguarding their
respective interests. During the negotiations
preceding independence, they mainly discussed the
distribution of power between the central and
regional governments, the allocation of resources,
and internal regional boundaries.

Therefore, the constitution adopted by the
new state on the day of its independence was
federal with residual powers assigned to the
regional governments. The central government's
powers included foreign affairs, defense, currency,
foreign trade, internal transportation, and the
postal and telegraphic system. Both the central
and regional governments exercised concurrent
powers over higher education, industrial development, labor relations, and the regulation of the
legal and medical professions. All remaining
services including education, health, public
works, and agriculture were to be administered by
the regional governments.

The process of centralization began almost as
soon as the colonial authorities relinquished
power. Almost immediately, the central government claimed the right to dissolve regional legislatures, assume full authority, and suspend the
regional constitutions. Central authorities even
asserted a right to alter regional boundaries,
to change the procedure for appointment to judicial
offices, and to probe the affairs of regional
political leaders through federal Commissions
of Inquiry. Some were prosecuted on charges of
treason, a federal crime.

Federal power in public finance and economic
planning also grew. The regions were responsible
for providing costly services--health, education,
public works, agriculture. They sought additional
revenues from federal sources. But instead of
making outright grants to the regions, federal
officials placed tight controls on how and where
money was spent. Most of the funds went to support
federal projects or to expand regional projects

favored by federal officials. Nigeria attracted numerous offers of foreign economic and technical aid which gave the federal government additional leverage in its relations with the regions, leverage often used in exasperating ways.

In the East, there was bitterness at delays in Lagos (the federal capital). When that region wanted pioneer certificates or tax concessions for new industries, when they asked for visas to allow foreign business-men to come and survey the situation, months passed without any response. But when the Federal Government was looking after its own interests, such delays, it was alleged, never occurred. The West decided to build a match factory, carried out a "feasibility study" and sent the proposal to the Economic Planning Unit and the Committee on External Aid in Lagos. Nothing was heard for some time and then the reply came that it would be better as a federal project. After further delay the West heard that a match factory was established in Ilorin in the Northern Region with the approval of the Federal Government. [5]

Internationally, Nigeria had acquired a reputation for moderation, statesmanship, and as "the stable and democratic star of independent black Africa." [6] In January, 1966, the first Commonwealth Conference to be held outside London was held in Lagos, where the great issue of the day was Rhodesia. For Nigerians, however, the far more important issue was the overthrow of civilian rule led by Ibo military officers that same month.

The new military regime suspended the federal constitution, dropped the word "Region" in favor of "Groups of Provinces," established a unified command with military governors in charge of each province. In May, 1966, the regime issued Decree No. 34 amalgamating the federal and regional civil services empowering the military to establish a

unified civil service with the power to transfer
federal and regional bureaucrats to all parts of
the country. This action virtually dissolved the
federal structure and predictably incurred the
wrath of the Hausa who feared Ibo and Yoruba domination. They rioted, rendering thousands of Ibos
homeless and were also instrumental in staging a
counter-coup which brought about the fall of the
Ibo army officers and the emergence of Lt. Col.
Yakubu Gowon as the new military head of state.
The Ibos, many of whom had settled in different
parts of the country, fearing further repression,
returned to their own Eastern Region. The
following account of the scene at the Port Harcourt
railway station illustrates their plight:

> What came out of that train is beyond des-
> cription. Some got out with severed limbs,
> others with broken heads. But the most
> chilling sight was a woman who came out
> completely naked, clutching in her hand the
> head of her child killed in the North. This
> particular sight aroused the crowds standing
> in the station to a frenzy. They began to
> beat up all the Northerners within sight and
> rampaged through the entire town of Enugu,
> attacking Northerners, and destroying and
> looting their property.[7]

A year later the Eastern Region seceded from
Nigeria and declared a separate independent state--
The Republic of Biafra. They had been prompted to
do so by the atrocities committed against them in
the North. They believed that secession was the
only way to safeguard the security of their persons and property. Civil war raged for two and
one half years, killing nearly a million people,
costing well over one billion dollars from 1966
until Nigeria's return to civilian rule in 1979.
Reconstruction costs added another half billion
dollars to the terrible price of this conflict.

During that period first General Gowon and
then General Obasenjo moved Nigeria toward an
essentially unitary system. The country was

reorganized into nineteen states, mainly for ease of administration by the central government. Most important decisions are made at the center, including jurisdiction over revenue measures, a unified educational system, commodity prices, wages, economic planning and investment of most public funds.

In 1979, Nigerians gave themselves another opportunity to demonstrate their capacity to implement federalism. Its new constitution borrows heavily from the U.S. Constitution and took four years of discussion to write. Under this new document, Nigeria consists of nineteen states instead of the original three. Each state has its own legislature and chief executive. The federal legislature is bicameral with the Senate containing ninety-five and the House of Representatives 449 members. An executive president heads the federal administration. After a series of elections, Nigeria, for the first time since 1966, reverted to civilian rule on October 1, 1979. The elections were marred by numerous allegations of fraud or precedural irregularities. Over one thousand candidates were disqualified by the Federal Elections Commission including Aminu Kano of the People's Redemption Party, the only party in the race having a leftist orientation.

Under the election rules, the federal president had to win a plurality of all votes cast and no less than twenty-nine percent of the vote in two-thirds of the country's states. The winner was Shehu Shagari, leader of the National Party of Nigeria who drew heavy support from the Muslim Hausa-Fulani and Nigerian businessmen. Shagari technically failed to satisfy the second requirement of twenty-nine percent in two-thirds or thirteen states, having only twenty percent in the thirteenth, but was still declared victorious by the Federal Elections Commission over Mr. Olafemi Awolwo, supported mainly by the Christian Yoruba tribe.

In the Senate, Mr. Shagari's party captured

thirty-six of ninety-five seats and 168 of 449
seats in the House of Representatives. Thus, he
needed support from other parties to gain a
legislative majority for his programs. His main
partner is the Nigerian People's Party led by
Nnamdi Azikwe, the party of the Catholic Ibos.
Whether this portends a return to the tribal based
politics of the pre-1966 period is still unknown.
An attempt to soften the tribal political
divisions has been made by the requirement of
twenty-five percent of the vote in two-thirds of
the states, forcing presidential candidates to
choose running mates from tribes other than their
own. Certainly, this is a recognition of the
existence of tribal politics in Nigeria while at
the same time, it is a positive step toward the
nationalization of party politics.

Kenya

The constitution adopted by Kenya upon independence was the result of prolonged negotiations
among diverse, well identified political groups.
European, Asian, and small African minority groups
sought guarantees of their political integrity in
the constitution. They feared domination by the
country's progressive and ambitious majority
tribes, the Kikuyu, the Luo, and the Kamba. To
protect their interests, the various small, rural,
and relatively backward tribes had formed appropriate organizations (e.g., the Masai United
Front, the Coast People's Union, the Kenya African
People's Party, etc.) and eventually, to increase
their effectiveness, united under the banner of
Kenya African Democratic Union (KADU), against
the Kenya African Natinal Union (KANU)--the
political party which mainly represented the
interests of the three major tribes, the Kikuyu,
Luo, and Kamba. Moreover, there were two
secession movements in the country, and each
directly or indirectly supported KADU's demands
for maximum regional autonomy. One movement
consisted of Muslims living in the Coastal
Region around the port of Mombasa. The other
separatist group was the Somalis in the North

Frontier District, racially, culturally, and
religiously distinct from the majority of Kenyans.
Linked by their mutual fear of Kikuyu-Luo domination, there was little chance these groups would
agree to Kenya's independence under a constitution
which did not reflect this basic concern.
According to KADU the best way to prevent Kikuyu-
Luo domination was to distribute power among the
regions. Its leader, R.G. Ngala had at one time
asserted:

> ...just how easily the Westminster pattern
> of government can be perverted into a ruth-
> less dictatorship. I assure you that the
> adoption of an orthodox Westminster pattern
> for Kenya would inevitably result in
> placing absolute power in the hands of a
> dictator. 8

Other leaders dared suggest that unless agreement
could be reached on a constitution based on
regionalism, KADU might ask for partitioning of
the country. KANU leaders, representing the
majority, grudgingly consented to a constitution
incorporating regional bodies through which
minorities could share political power.

Thus, the independence constitution contained several "federal"features. The country was
divided into seven regions. Each area had its own
Regional Assembly elected by people living within
the region, its own Regional President elected by
the Assembly, and its own civil service. There
were detailed provisions in the Constitution
dividing governmental powers between the central
and regional governments. In view of what follows,
we shall omit specific descriptions of these
complex provisions. Suffice it to say that KADU's
distrust of the central government was such that
during constitutional negotiations it insisted on
a provision that no regional assembly could
surrender its powers to the central government.
Its "fears could only be allayed by a detailed
allocation of functions--to the determination of
which legislature could provide for public

lavatories and refuse and effluent disposal, and which executive was responsible for implementing the law on these subjects."[9]

> The matters on which the Regional Assemblies alone could legislate included agricultural matters (elementary training centres, and branding of livestock), archives (other than records of the Government of Kenya), auction sales, primary, intermediate and secondary education (with the exception of certain important educational institutes and schools), housing, medical facilities and institutions (again with the exception of a list of important hospitals), the protection and control of nomadic people, common minerals, barbers and hair dressers....[10]

The Regions had exclusive authority not only over these subjects but also over those where the central government had been given concurrent legislative powers. The regional governments had also been given certain independent powers of taxation. To protect each regions' constitutional authority, KADU had also fought to make unilateral amendments to the Constitution difficult. The regional boundaries, for example, could not be changed unilaterally by the central government. Some provisions were especially well fortified against change by requirements for extraordinary majorities of seventy-five and in some cases ninety per cent of the legislators.

In the end, however, all constitutional precautions were fruitless. The KANU leaders who controlled the central government insisted on an extremely narrow interpretation of regionalism. They ridiculed the concept of regionalism as "only a dignified name for local authorities"[11] and belittled the constitutional powers of the regions. This attitude was reflected in their actions. KANU leaders made no serious attempt to implement the complex constitutional provisions. Instead of dealing with Regional Assemblies and Regional political leaders, the central government ministers insisted on continuing to use as their channel of communication the civil servants in the area. They denied the Regional Assemblies assistance in establishing their own civil services. They agreed to "Help them out" by transferring senior civil servants from the central government but made certain that these bureaucrats accepted instructions only from the central authorities including complying with a directive that all draft bills put before Regional Assemblies must first be submitted to the central government for appraisal. Regional finances were to be controlled, according to the constitution, by the Regional Assemblies, but central authorities deliberately delayed transmitting to the regions tax funds which technically belonged to them. Revenue-earning services were not immediately placed under regional government jurisdiction as called for in the constitution. Also delayed was access to appropriated funds necessary to operate the regional governments. It was clear to perceptive observers that the central government had no intention of promulgating the provisions of regionalism. Having thus delayed, the central government in August, 1964, proposed changes, the effect of which would have been to abolish, for all intents and purposes, regional autonomy. One of its arguments in justification of the new law was that regional politicians had failed to prove their capability to perform their functions satisfactorily and that it was, therefore, necessary to bring responsibilities which had initially been assigned to the regions directly under the jurisdiction of the central government.

The KANU-dominated government, through promises of appointments to official positions, managed to secure the support of some non-KANU legislators and in November, 1964, KADU itself was dissolved. The strict and elaborate requirements introduced in the independence constitution for amending its provisions now became almost totally meaningless. A series of

constitutional amendments were enacted which
resulted, within eighteen months of independence,
in the abolition of regionalism and creation of
a unitary state. The First Amendment, passed
in November, 1964, took away all but the most
essential (entrenched) powers of the Regional
Assemblies; the Second passed in December, 1964,
made the Regional Assemblies financially dependent upon the Central Government by ending
Regional powers of taxation, and empowered the
Central Government unilaterally to alter
regional boundaries; and the Third enacted in
June, 1965, (affecting entrenched constitutional
provisions) abolished executive powers of the
Regions, renamed Regional Assemblies Provincial
Councils, and placed all governmental powers
under the competence of the Central Government.
As Y. P. Ghai and J. P. McAuslan have remarked,
"all these changes reduced the regional system
to a purely nominal one; it became at best a
glorified system of local government, deriving
its legislative and executive authority...from
the Centre."[12] In April, 1968, the Provincial
Councils, which ceased performing any important
functions after 1965, were abolished altogether
and all references in the Constitution to
provincial or district boundaries were removed.
KADU leaders, weakened by defections and fearful
of imprisonment by the Central Government, could
only acquiesce to the total centralization of
power in the hands of the KANU.

In virtually all African states where
originally power was distributed broadly, the
course of events was similar. The Constitution
adopted by Ghana upon its independence in 1957,
provided for Regional Assemblies, with tribal
chiefs acting as heads of Regions. Some constitutional provisions were also entrenched and could
not be amended without approval of the Regional
Assemblies. Only three years later, on July 1,
1960, the Constitution was replaced by a new
Republican Constitution which declared Ghana a
sovereign unitary republic, abolished the Regional
Assemblies, and brought all regions directly

314

under the control and supervision of the Central
Government of Dr. Kwame Nkrumah and his political
party, the Convention People's Party. Within
three years of independence, regionalism was dead.

Zaire became independent on June 30, 1960,
following a Round Table Conference in Brussels at
which the provisions of Loi Fondamentale setting
out the Constitution for the new state were agreed
upon. It represented a compromise between those
African leaders like Joseph Kasavubu who favored
a federal structure and Patrice Lumumba, among
others, who preferred a highly centralized government. This Constitution was immediately overwhelmed by the trauma of civil war.

The army mutinied on July 5, 1960, a mere
five days after political independence. Katanga
announced its secession from the new state on July
12, 1960; and on July 14, the Security Council
authorized United Nations forces to intervene and
re-establish order in the country. It was not
until January, 1963, that the United Nations could
claim to have done so, although U.N. troops
remained in the country until June, 1964. Between
1962 and 1964, U.N. experts worked on a new
Constitution. Their proposals were considered by
a Commission established by the new African Government and a revised Constitution was promulgated into law in June, 1964. It was federal in
character and differed very little from the Loi
Fondamentale. It placed the federal government
in charge of foreign affairs, army, customs, and
immigration, the national economy, penal code,
higher education, and important communications.
The provincial governments were responsible for
the courts, primary and secondary education, and
a range of secondary functions. Each province
enjoyed a major local autonomy, with its own
Provincial Assembly and a Provincial President.
Specifically prohibited was the attachment of
Federal representatives to the Provinces. There
was also provision for a Constitutional Court to
settle jurisdictional disputes between the federal
and provincial governments. This revised

Constitution was given no opportunity to become
operative, either. In November, 1965, it was
suspended when President Kasavubu was deposed in
a coup led by Lt. Gen. Joseph Desire Mobutu,
commander-in-chief of the army. Through successive steps, he has since concentrated power in
his own hands.

Uganda became independent on October 9,
1962, after its African political leaders had
reached agreement at constitutional conferences,
held prior to independence under the auspices of
the colonial government, to adopt a federal system
with five component states: Baganda, Ankole, Bun-
yoro, Toro, and Busoga. The Constitution defined
the spheres of authority of the central and state
governments. It was also agreed that Sir Edward
Mutesa, the Kabaka, the leader and King of the
Baganda, should become the first President having
the status of a constitutional monarch. Within a
few years, the Prime Minister, Milton Obote,
actual leader of the country, dispelled any
illusions the Kabaka or leaders of the other
federal states may have had about the future of
federalism in Uganda. He declared a state of
emergency, pushed constitutional amendments
through the legislature, forced the Kabaka into
exile, deposed leaders of the other states, and
brought all parts of Uganda under direct control
of the central government. He divided the country
into administrative districts and acquired power
to suspend, dissolve, reinstate or constitute a
District Council or other local authority at any
time, for any period, and to dismiss or replace
members of local councils. Under newly enacted
laws, the Courts were precluded from entertaining
suits questioning the legality of such actions.
Sir Edward Mutesa, the former Kabaka, complained
fruitlessly to the Secretary-General of the
United Nations that Dr. Obote had acted in
violation of the Constitution. And while in exile,
Sir Edward wrote a book, appropriately entitled,
Desecration of My Kingdom.

In Zambia, too, not only was the dream of

the Lozis of a separate state of Barotseland
unrealized, but, inexorably, their exclusive
powers reserved under the independence constitution were circumscribed, undercut, and ignored
until Barotse Province was brought under direct
and complete control of the central government.

By now the point is well made that the concept of regional autonomy died within a few years
of independence, not only in states formerly under
British control, but also in Zaire, which was
under the Belgians, and the Cameroon, at least
part of which was under the French. Federal
constitutions were not forced upon the Africans.
In virtually all cases, Africans themselves
argued for regionalism as a protection for deeply
embedded preferences for self-determination among
many groups too small to constitute viable political entities alone. Regionalism through federal
constitutions was to be a compromise between
political fragmentation and the obliteration of
local interests. It is too easy to accuse the
British of drafting constitutions which were not
understood by Africans or which failed to take
into account the African environment. But, the
Zairian constitution was drafted not by British
administrators but by United Nations constitutional
experts, and it, too, was very much like its prede-
cessor and suffered the same fate. Nor is the
failure to operate federal institutions limited
to any particular geographic area. Cameroon
and Nigeria are in west Africa, Kenya and Uganda
in the east, Zaire in central Africa, and Zambia
in southern Africa. Regionalism ended in different ways in each country: in Nigeria through
civil war; in Zaire it was preceded by military
coup; in Uganda it was achieved through exercise
of emergency powers and the use of federal troops
against the Kabaka; and in Cameroon and Kenya it
was accomplished through gross political and
legal manipulation. In all, however, the result
was the same. Is it presumptuous to suggest that
it is a fundamental aversion to any notion of
power sharing which characterized these failures
to implement federalism? At a time when there is

increasing talk of African unity, it should be
instructive to evaluate this criticism by examination of African efforts to form political
unions and federations since independence.

EAST AFRICAN FEDERATION

The best example of independent Africa's
attempt at forming a federation of contiguous
states is the example of Kenya, Uganda, and
Tanzania. Prior to independence, these countries
enjoyed extremely close political, economic, and
cultural relations.

All three were British colonies. Their
progress towards independence was more or less
simultaneous; all became politically independent
within two years of each other--Tanzania, December 14, 1961; Uganda, October 9, 1962; and
Kenya, December 12, 1963. In all three Britain
tried to introduce basic parliamentary practices,
concepts of judicial independence, and other
ideas relating to the role of the civil service
and the military in the society. The legal system
and laws in these three states were so similar
that a New York University professor of law published a book in the early sixties entitled,
Unity Through Law. [13]

In addition, since 1948, cooperation between
the three states had become so formalized that
institutions arose which could easily have been
regarded as precursors of federal structures of
the future. The East African High Commission
(subsequently renamed East African Common Services
Organization) was responsible for developing
policies and implementing projects benefiting all
three countries. The policies of the Commission
were determined at regularly held meetings
attended by representatives from all participating
states--an organizational framework which could
easily have been converted into federal legislature. The Commission had its own civil service,
with prescribed rules and regulations for recruitment, promotion, and transfer from one country to

another. Its pool of experienced administrators
and technical personnel could have formed the
nucleus of the federal civil service. Finally,
there was the East African Court of Appeal
entitled to hear appeals from High Courts of all
three countries and whose decisions were binding
upon all other courts in East Africa--an arrangement which would have proved extremely useful in
the establishment and successful operation of the
Federal Supreme Court.

Under the above organizational framework,
the three countries had already been collaborating
prior to independence in various economic and
cultural matters--matters which under a federal
system would fall under the federal jurisdiction.
For example, the 3,760 mile railway which traversed
the three countries was operated by the Commission;
ports and harbors in all three countries, (along
the Indian Ocean as well as in Lake Victoria) were
under the Commission; and there were future plans
for building interstate roads. Interstate transportation was therefore already under federal
control. So was interstate commerce. All three
countries had common tariff rates for imported
goods. There was permitted free movement of goods
and people within and between all three. All used
the same currency controlled by the East African
Currency Board--which could easily have been turned
into an East African Reserve Bank acting as a
central bank for the federation. All three
countries had the same rates of income tax and
the machinery for collection of federal income
tax was already available in the East African
Income Tax Service operating under the policy
direction of the Commission which was responsible
for collecting taxes in behalf of the three
countries.

In all three, Swahili was at least understood
by most people; and English had been introduced in
schools and colleges. Most prospective new
leaders spoke it fluently and many had even been
educated in universities in English speaking
countries abroad. Geographic contiguity and

overlapping tribes provided additional argument
for cultural and social integration.

Instead of forging an East African Federation,
leaders of these countries have, in the post-
independence period, moved in exactly the opposite
direction. Today, these countries are farther
apart than they ever were before independence,
with each state increasingly insistent upon exercising its full sovereign rights. In July, 1976,
for example, Uganda's claim that large parts of
Kenyan territory (three-quarters of its most
fertile land) belonged to Uganda resulted in Kenya's
closing its port facilities at Mombasa to Ugandan
imports and exports. The armed forces of both
countries were ordered to the common border. In
1972, President Nyerere of Tanzania refused to sit
at the same table with President Idi Amin of
Uganda ("I am not going to sit at the same table
with murderers") thereby making it difficult to
hold meetings of the common organization and
endangering effective operation of an institution
which had the potential of becoming the federal
legislature. The nucleus of the federal civil
service was also jeopardized by events like those
in February, 1973, when the Director and Regional
Supplies Officer of the East African Railways and
other Kenyans working for the railway in Uganda
were reported missing. Kenyan authorities lost
confidence in the ability or will of Ugandan
government to protect the lives and property of
Kenyans working for railways and other East African projects. And the emphasis placed by each
state on regarding its own highest court as the
supreme judicial body signalled the death of the
East African Court of Appeal, or at least of its
right to issue judgments binding upon all three
states. Some of the old institutional structures
still remain, but the original vitality is gone.

The various areas in which the three had
successfully cooperated in the past also dimin-
ished. In the operation of the East African
Railways, for example, there were serious disputes
about the failure of the Ugandan and Tanzanian

branches to transfer funds to the headquarters in
Kenya. All three states following political independence had introduced separate currencies making
it necessary for the Ugandan and Tanzanian branches
to obtain permission from foreign exchange control
officials before they could transfer the funds to
Kenya. And the granting of permission was dependent upon the foreign exchange position of the
country at the time of the request. Once, the
head office in Kenya, in an attempt to force the
hands of the Uganda and Tanzania officials,
retaliated for the delay by withholding salaries
of employees. In 1975, trains leaving Kenya for
Tanzania and vice versa were regularly stopped at
the border and reloaded on those standing on the
other side. The rationale for this absurd exercise was the suspicion of each government that the
other would withhold or delay returning locomotives,
freight or rolling stock to the other side. Tanzania, which commissioned and continues to operate
the Tanzam railway outside the framework of East
African Railways accused Kenya of deliberately
allowing the operational capacity and efficiency
of the latter to suffer in order that the trucking
business, dominated by the Kenyans, could increase
profits. The Kenyans were also blamed for constructing and operating a pipeline through a
company in which the Kenyan Foreign Minister and
other officials had substantial interests resulting
in the loss of millions of dollars of business to
the East African Railways.

While the three countries indulged in
accusations and counter-accusations, the railway
deteriorated. There was a shortage of rolling
stock, spare parts, and maintenance engineers and
drivers willing to move freely throughout the
three countries. There is little doubt that by
1973, the railways were operating at drastically
less capacity and efficiency than before independence with even passenger service suspended on
several occasions. Other transportation and
communication services also suffered, including
the East African Airways, though not to the same
extent as the railroad. The East African Postal

Organization was simply dismantled. Each state began to issue and control the sale of its own stamps.

Interstate commerce was also adversely affected. Instead of the common tariffs each state introduced separate rates and even imposed tariffs, in some cases, on goods originating in or coming from the other East African states. Each state also set its own economic priorities and each, especially Tanzania, in an effort to promote industries located within its borders sought to protect its infant industries. Each also adopted its own pattern of foreign trade and its own systems of taxation. Not only could goods no longer move unrestricted from one East African country to another, but it was often easier to import from overseas than to trade with other East African countries. Nor were workers allowed to move freely from one country to another in search of jobs. New laws were introduced in each country which required citizens of other states to obtain work permits before they could lawfully take up employment in the country, although except in the case of non-Africans, these laws were irregularly implemented depending upon the state of the economy and political climate.

Ideological and foreign policy differences further aggravated the situation. Tanzania was unenthusiastic about cooperating with capitalistic Kenya which, it believed, was bogged down in a quagmire of corruption and individual greed. Kenya, in turn, disapproved of Tanzanian economic policies which were viewed as costly socialistic experiments, especially because of the way foreign investment was discouraged by Tanzanian nationalizations of foreign holdings. Both Kenya and Tanzania resented the unpredictable, although imaginative and flamboyant, General Idi Amin of Uganda. Uganda which had adopted a strong pro-Arab policy, in turn, suspected Kenya of collaborating with Israel, and Tanzania of harboring Ugandan exiles and even encouraging them to restore to power former President, Dr. Milton Obote, who shared Tanzanian President Nyerere's socialist ideas. In the circumstances, it was not surprising that, in 1975, Kenya's Attorney General, Mr. Charles Njonjo, led the call for dissolving whatever structures for cooperation among the East African countries that still remained. According to him, such cooperation had failed for lack of "political goodwill," that "the corpse should be thrown to the hyenas" and that the whole concept of political federation among the East African states should be "forgotten and buried."[14]

By 1980, not only had the East African community been disbanded but the three states had also acted as hyenas fighting over the corpse. Each wanted a larger share of the assets of the defunct community, especially of the regional bank that had been jointly owned by all three. All suffered as a result of the souring atmosphere. Each was obliged to increase its defense expenditures. Uganda's Idi Amin, anxious to maintain himself in power for an indefinite period and to effectively retaliate against threats by supporters of the former President Milton Obote from Tanzanian territory, felt that he had to build up and placate his armed forces. Kenya believed that it was being encircled by hostile regimes. In the North, Somalia made periodic claims against its northwestern territories. With the ouster of the former Emperor Haile Selassie, Ethiopia came under a new socialist regime friendly with the Tanzanians. In the West, President Idi Amin claimed that large areas of Kenya's most fertile territories belonged to Uganda. He was also chagrined by Kenya's open support of Israel. In the South, socialist Tanzania had closed its land border with Kenya. Even the islands in the East--Seychelles, Malagasy, and Zanzibar (Tanzania)--now had socialist regimes unfriendly to Kenya. It had little alternative but to increase its defense capabilities. This was also the case with Tanzania. President Idi Amin of landlocked Uganda had made little secret of his distaste of President Nyerere and of his ambition to obtain access to the Indian Ocean by taking over the Tanzanian port of Tanga. In 1978, he

attacked Tanzania in the areas west of Lake
Victoria and seized 710 square miles of Tanzanian
territory and offered to cease his aggressions only
if the diminutive Nyerere agreed to duel with him
(refereed by Muhammad Ali, the former world heavyweight boxing champion from the United States)!

In April, 1979, Ugandan exiles (who had by
then regrouped under the name of Uganda National
Liberation Front) and at least 30,000 Tanzanian
official troops marched into Uganda, forcing
President Idi Amin to flee to Libya, and installed
Prof. Yusuf Lule as Uganda's new president. Until
this time, economic cooperation between the two
countries had come almost to a standstill. In
addition to its indirect adverse impact upon the
economy in general, the war had cost the Tanzanians
at least $500,000,000.

In 1977, demonstrating its dissatisfaction
with Kenyan policies and in an effort to provide
an incentive to its infant industries, Tanzania
closed its land border with Kenya. It remains
sealed to trade, tourism, and private transport.
There were also times when all flights (except
charter) were prohibited, as was the use of the
Tanzanian ports by Kenyan vessels. The action
caused considerable reduction in Kenya's exports
not only to Tanzania but also to Zambia. In early
1980, even the resurrection of the community to a
level prevailing before independence seemed
exceedingly remote, not to mention the establishment
of genuine federation of these three states with
sharing of power.

To forestall the dominant Kenyan tribes from
controlling all government activities and believing
that the Federation could provide the minorities
in Kenya with additional protection, the KADU
leaders had, in 1964, insisted that the KANU-dominated Kenya government (led by Jomo Kenyatta) set
a specific date for the formation of the Federation.
Not only did the KADU fail to persuade the Kenya
government to do so, but as was noted above, instead
of full fledged Federation even   the elements of

324

cooperation between the East African countries that existed before independence are now in the process of disintegration. These developments have had an adverse effect on the minority tribes in Kenya as well as on non-African minorities residing in different parts of East Africa. For example:

a) With the removal of the right of appeal to the East African Court of Appeal, their capacity to protect their legal rights was considerably reduced. Instead of enjoying the additional protection of federal courts, they now find themselves totally dependent upon the judicial systems within their own state. Had there been a federal supreme court, perhaps the owners of farms that were nationalized by Tanzania for purposes of establishing the 'Ujamaa' villages might, for example, have stood a better chance of obtaining judicial redress.

b) Their persons and property became further insecure. Whenever there were riots or demonstrations in any part of East Africa which the local police found difficult to control, the British Colonial authorities brought reinforcements from one of the neighboring East African countries. This was also done in circumstances where for tribal or other reasons the authorities had reason to believe that the local police might be unwilling to take effective measures against the rioters or demonstrators. Any hope the minorities had of having federal troops available to protect them in such circumstances after independence faded away with the disintegration of the nascent East African Federation.

c) Instead of common East African citizenship laws, each state, after independence, enacted its own laws providing for circumstances in which local citizenship was to be granted. As was observed earlier, Kenya and Uganda enacted laws granting citizenship by birth to those who were born in their territories with at least one of their parents also born there. Prior to independence, there was relatively free movement of persons from one colony

325

to another. As a result of the new laws, a number of Asians who had lived in East Africa for decades found themselves in the position of being non-citizens simply because they were born in one East African country but their parents were born in another.

d) With each state introducing its own licensing and work permit laws restricting non-citizens from taking up employment or partici-pating in other economic activities, it became more and more difficult for minorities, especially those who were accustomed to do so prior to independence, to move from one country to another.

e) The increasing tension between East African countries made each one more aware of the need to protect its territorial integrity through building and maintaining defense forces. To finance their military establishments each country collected more taxes. Additional revenue was obtained either by imposing new taxes or making collection more efficient. A large propor-tion of income tax paid in East Africa was coming from non-African minorities. In many cases, Africans paid no income tax, especially those in agricultural jobs. New industries established in the post-independence period by non-residents often enjoyed tax relief as an incentive to foreign investors. The additional tax burden, therefore, fell mainly on resident minorities. With the end of income tax collection by one agency throughout East Africa, the separate states divided the task. And with increased efforts by local administrators to collect more revenue, it soon developed that non-African minorities were singled out for auditing or re-examination of past returns to locate addi-tional sources.

f) In any industry a minimum level of pro-duction is necessary before it can meet capital and production costs, or become profitable. East African countries as a whole constituted a market of well over thirty million people; separately, with restrictions on exports to the others, each constituted a much smaller market.

The case of the House of Manji provides a good
example of how minority businesses were adversely
affected as a result of the failure of the East
African Federation to materialize.

The House of Manji, a Kenyan corporation
controlled by Asians, operated a large plant in
Kenya manufacturing biscuits. A substantial
portion of its production was exported to neighboring Tanganyika. On the assumption that the
other East African markets were open to them, the
Directors of the House of Manji first decided to
expand operations in order to compete with biscuit
manufacturers in England. In 1965, however,
Tanzania concerned about its own industrialization,
imposed a selective licensing system on goods
entering its territory from Kenya. Simultaneously,
it sought to persuade Kenyan manufacturers to
establish plants in Tanzania. It banned importation of biscuits from Kenya, almost ruining the
House of Manji, and did not relax the ban until
the company agreed to build a new plant in Tanzania.
The company's Kenya operations were sufficient to
meet East African demand. But, it was obliged
to further expand production by establishing a new
plant in Tanzania which seriously jeopardized the
financial position of this very important domestic
business enterprise. Rational allocation of
economic resources was sacrificed to the over-
riding demands of short-sighted parochialism.

The Federation of Ethiopia and Eritrea

Ethiopia's history stretches over three
thousand years. Emperor Haile Selassie came to
power as regent for the Empress Zauditu in 1916
and remained as the Imperial Majesty until 1974,
when he was ousted by the military. The oldest
independent state of Africa, Ethiopia was admitted
to charter membership in the United Nations on
November 13, 1945.

Ethiopia, a term first used by Homer or Herodotus to refer to all the lands inhabited by black people, includes in its northeastern section the territory of Eritrea, the first Italian colony in Africa. Italian rule there, which began a century ago came to an end during the Second World War when the British invaded and and occupied the colony. When the war ended, Emperor Haile Selassie proposed that British occupation of Eritrea end and that the territory of Eritrea, in view of the close ties between Ethiopia and Eritrea, be annexed to Ethiopia. When Italy renounced all claim to its colonies in Africa, the Ethiopian government, which had taken an active role in the organization and operation of the United Nations since its inception, sought to have the United Nations decide the fate of the former Italian colony. Britain did not object. Accordingly, a United Nations Commission for Eritrea composed of representatives of five member states was established to examine the situation and report to the General Assembly. In its report to the Assembly, the Commission did not make a unanimous recommendation but provided sufficient background material to enable the Assembly to reach its own decision.

During discussion in the Assembly, the Ethiopian representative informed the world body that "the problem of minorities did not complicate the issue in the case of Eritrea" and that "in view of Ethiopia's profound affinities with Arab countries, the Moslems of Eritrea had nothing to fear from a union with Ethiopia."[15] Nevertheless, the United Nations, seeking to safeguard the ethnic and social characteristics of the Eritreans as well as their economic interests, recommended that Eritrea should be linked to the Ethiopian Empire in a loose federation--"an autonomous unit federated with Ethiopia under the sovereignty of the Ethiopian crown."[16] In the resolution incorporating this recommendation, the Assembly expressed the desire that this association should "assure to the inhabitants of Eritrea the fullest respect and safeguards for their institution, traditions,

328

religions and languages, as well as the widest possible measure of self-government."[17] The resolution also outlined how power should be distributed between the federal (i.e. the Ethiopian Imperial Government) and the Eritreans. In one section it specifically decreed that "The Eritrean Government shall possess legislative, executive, and judicial powers in the field of domestic affairs."[18] Ethiopia accepted these conditions and reassured all indigenous and foreign minorities in Eritrea that it would respect their rights and privileges. To assist Ethiopia and to insure that this was done, the General Assembly appointed a United Nations Commissioner to help Ethiopia establish the federation. With the help of a panel of legal consultants appointed by the secretary-general, and the cooperation of the Ethiopian government, the commissioner completed all preliminary arrangements and on September 15, the Federation of Ethiopia and Eritrea became a reality.

In his report to the Assembly, the Commissioner emphasized that the United Nations had placed considerable confidence in the Ethiopian Government and that it was now Ethiopia's responsibility to ensure continued and effective operation of the federal structure. In reply, the Ethiopian Foreign Minister informed the Assembly that Ethiopia wished to promote the well-being of Eritrea in full accordance with the provisions of the federal constitution; that the constitution provided for protection of human rights; that Ethiopia had already demonstrated by action its desire to allow the minority parties to participate in the decision-making process and that it was Ethiopia's wish that all Eritreans should enjoy all the privileges of Ethiopian citizenship with no obligations other than those resulting from the Federation. On December 17, 1952, the General Assembly ratified the proposed federal constitution, welcomed the establishment of the Federation of Eritrea with Ethiopia and noted, with satisfaction, Ethiopia's "expression of determination scrupulously to execute the

329

provisions of the Federal Act."19

On November 15, 1962, less than ten years later, Ethiopia abolished the federation and "after the Assembly of Eritrea, which some observers regarded as having been packed by the Addis Ababa government, went through the necessary parliamentary motions" annexed Eritrea.20Eritrea became a province of Ethiopia, with a Provincial Governor appointed by the Emperor to act as his personal representative, exercising absolute power over people. The annexation was no surprise. In a sense, it was the culmination of a policy of progressive "Ethiopianization" which the Emperor had put into effect soon after the 1952 General Assembly resolution. Between 1952 and 1962, Eritreans were required to learn Amharic, the Ethiopian official language. The Emperor had refused permission to have any of his decrees translated into any other language. He had sought to spread Christian religion in the area, and generally to increase the Amhara influence, even by encouraging the settlement of the Amhara in the Eritrean area. Although in theory the area and its people were to enjoy autonomy in most matters, in practice the Emperor treated Eritrea like any other province of Ethiopia. The Eritrean Assembly had its authority reduced in several important ways and gradually became little else than an extension of the Ethiopian Government. Not only the Muslim Eritreans but also the Christian Eritreans resented the forced spread of Amhara influence and became especially critical of the Ethiopian government in 1962 when it prohibited formation of political parties in the country.

The Eritrean leaders protested the Ethiopian take-over to the United Nations claiming that the annexation decree violated resolutions of the United Nations and violated the right of Eritreans to self-determination. They also appealed to the Organization of African Unity. All to no avail. In the end, a substantial number of Eritreans who could not accept Amhara domination fled to Saudi Arabia, Egypt, and Somalia. Others, including a

330

number of militants among them, formed the
Eritrean Liberation Front. In the words of
one of its leaders:

> The Emperor broke up the federation created
> by the United Nations and simply annexed us.
> We had a local parliament. He abolished it.
> There was a local government. He abolished
> it. All our rights were suppressed.
> Occupation has turned us into a colony. We
> are struggling for independence.[21]

The Front waged intermittent guerilla warfare
against the Ethiopian government which was
unrelenting in its policy of centralization after
the military take-over. Ethiopian counter-
insurgency forces were brutal in suppressing the
guerillas. They bombarded Eritrean villages,
burned crops, and forced thousands of refugees
into neighboring countries. In 1976, it even
went so far as to organize a human march of the
Amhara into the Eritrean areas to force Eritreans
into submission. According to Eritrean leaders,
Ethiopian policy was to force out the Eritreans and
settle the Amhara and other supporters of the
government in the area. The Government's claim
was that it was acting against the rebels and in
the interest of re-establishing law and order.
In 1977, the Eritrean People's Liberation Front
took advantage of the preoccupation of Ethiopian
forces with Somalia, and occupied over ninety
per cent of Eritrea with the government controlling
only three major population centers--the capital
city of Asmara, Massawa and Barentu. However, in
1978, approximately 30,000 Ethiopian troops,
strengthened by a massive introduction of Russian
weapons, equipment, and advisors, bombed the
Eritrean-held areas into submission. They
regained control over most of the territory,
forcing the EPLF to revert once again to low-
level guerilla warfare.

Since 1974, under the leadership of Col.
Mengistu Haile Mariam, Ethiopia has developed
close ties with the Soviet Union, entered into a

treaty of friendship and cooperation with the
Russians, and embraced a Marxist orientation. The
Square of the Holy Cross in its capital city of
Addis Ababa has been renamed Red Square and
portraits of Marx, Engels and Lenin have replaced
those of the former Emperor. Like the previous
regime, the government of Col. Mengistu is
unalterably opposed to regional autonomy for the
Eritreans, at least until the EPLF has been
militarily defeated and a communist party
consolidates its power throughout Ethiopia. The
Russians, following their goal of a Marxist
Federation of Horn (composed of Ethiopia, Somalia,
and South Yemen), have sought to persuade Col.
Mengistu to make a public offer of regional
autonomy to the Eritreans. But, Col. Mengistu has
so far been unwilling to do this. At the same
time, his own efforts to offer a limited and
largely undefined degree of autonomy to the
Eritreans have met with only a lukewarm response
from them.

    The Ethiopian move against Eritrea cannot be
explained as an inevitable conflict of Christians
versus Moslems. In 1950, the total number of
inhabitants of Eritrea, according to the United
Nations Commission on Eritrea, was 1,067,000, of
which 524,000 were Moslem, 506,000 were Christian,
and 8,000 were pagan. Since then it is possible
that the percentage of Moslems has increased.
But, it was and remains true that nearly half of
all Eritreans profess Christianity. This fact is
far more relevant than the political tactic of
Eritrean Liberation leaders stressing religious
ties with the Arab states in order to gain their
support. As in previous examples, the irresistable
opportunity to expand power and domain at the
expense of weaker groups is a better general
explanation for the Ethiopian annexation of
Eritrea.

The United Republic of Tanzania

On April 22, 1964, the Republic of Tanganyika
and the Peoples' Republic of Zanzibar "being
mindful of the long association of the peoples
of these lands and of their ties of kinship and
amity, and being desirous of furthering that
association and of strengthening these ties and
of furthering the unity of African peoples"
agreed to be united in one sovereign republic to
be known, it was later declared, as the United
Republic of Tanzania.[22] The Articles of Union
specifically provided that the following matters
shall be reserved for the Union government
which will have exclusive authority in such
matters throughout the United Republic:

a) The Constitution and Government of the
   United Republic
b) External Affairs
c) Defence
d) Police
e) Emergency Powers
f) Citizenship
g) Immigration
h) External Trade and Borrowing
i) The Public Service of the United Republic
j) Income tax, corporation tax, customs and
   excise
k) Harbors, civil aviation, posts and
   telegraphs. [23]

It was also provided that a separate government in
and for Zanzibar should have exclusive authority
within Zanzibar for matters other than those
covered by a) to k) above. On July 3, 1964, the
Tanzanian Foreign Minister referred to the Union
in the following terms:

We are not interested in a federation which

333

is not a genuine political federation. A genuine political federation is one in which the constituent states merge their sovereignty in the larger federal unit. That is the meaning of our union with Zanzibar. Our brothers in Zanzibar understood our purpose and we have forged with them a link which no one can break....24

The union still survives, but the association can hardly be described as a genuine political federation. The "brothers" in Zanzibar have not only insisted upon freely and independently exercising most residual powers, but on various occasions they have encroached upon the powers of the Union government. Many such encroachments went unreported, but there is little doubt of the accuracy of the following examples:

*** Although Defence and Police (items c) and d) above were reserved exclusively for the Union government, Zanzibar insisted on having its own police force and its separate armed forces. In fact, in terms of overall military strength, it might even be more powerful than the United Republic;

*** Although Citizenship (item f) above) is a Union matter, Zanzibar has successfully required all persons claiming local citizenship on the basis of their birth or residence on the islands of Zanzibar and Pemba to submit their applications in Zanzibar, thereby forcing all Zanzibaris who, for political or other reasons, may be afraid to return to the islands, to either remain stateless or risk detention at the hands of the Zanzibari leaders.

*** Although Immigration (item g) above) is a Union matter, Zanzibar has effectively controlled admission to and exit from the islands. In fact, it is known that at least on one occasion Tanzanian or the Union Republic's immigration officers were them-

334

selves required to obtain visas from Zanzibar
authorities before they were allowed to
enter the islands.

***Although External Trade and Borrowing
(item h) above) are Union matters, as are
External.Affairs (item b) Zanzibar entered
into direct negotiations with foreign private and state trading corporations. It
even entered into economic agreements with
other states. It maintains its own foreign
bank accounts, depositing its earnings from
the sale of cloves, and although the Union
Government was often in desperate need of
foreign exchange, steadfastly refused to
merge its foreign exchange reserves with
those of the Union Republic.

***Although Customs and Excise (see item j)
above) were made Union matters thereby
creating an impression that goods would move
freely within different parts of the Republic, this has not been the case. In practice, Zanzibar imposed its own customs and
excise duties on goods entering or leaving
Zanzibar whenever it felt like doing so.

***Under item k) above, posts and tele-
graphs were reserved as Union matters. But
this did not prevent Zanzibar from censoring
all incoming and outgoing mail and from inter-
cepting or listening in all telegraphic or
telephonic messages or conversations.

The United Republic operated under an
Interim Constitution adopted in 1965, which
provided that there shall be only one party.
However, this provision was qualified by stating
that "until the union of Tanganyika African
National Union (TANU) with Afro-Shirazi Party
(ASP) of Zanzibar, which united party shall
constitute the one political party, the party shall
in and for Tanganyika be TANU, and in and for
Zanzibar be the ASP."[25] But for the next decade or
so, the two parties continued to remain separate,

335

with each dominating the politics and government
of the area under its control. It was not until
the end of 1976 that the two parties agreed to
merge with the new united party to be named Chama
Cha Mapinduzi (the Revolutionary Party of Tanzania), to be known in its abbreviated form as
CHAMA, and not until introduction of an amended
constitution in 1977 was Zanzibar entitled to
elect representatives to a national assembly.

In general, during the period the Union has
been in existence, Zanzibar has functioned in the
manner of a sovereign state. The Union Agreement
and the Interim Constitution left extensive powers
in the hands of the Zanzibaris. The constitution
guaranteed no fundamental rights; Zanzibar was
entitled to its own system of courts; the Union
Judicial Service Commission had no disciplinary
powers or control over judicial officers in
Zanzibar; there was no federal supreme court to
which appeals could be taken; and the President
had only a restricted right to grant pardons or
remit sentences imposed by the Zanzibar authorities. The Union also had no right to investigate
any person in office in Zanzibar even if there
were allegations of misconduct or abuse of
office. There were, therefore, few formal limitations upon the exercise of power by the Zanzibar authorities.

The example of the United Republic of Tanzania
differs from others in that it reflects the capacity of a constituent member of a federation to
resist the central government rather than the
inexorable trend toward domination of the federation from the center. What is dramatically
illustrated, however, is the recurring political
incapacity for real power sharing in most black
African states. Zanzibar and the Union government, in reality, co-exist as virtually separate
political entities with the Zanaibari jealously
guarding their near-complete independence.

The Federation of Mali
French colonial rule in West and Equatorial

Africa produced two large federations--the
Afrique Occidentale Francaise (AOF) and Afrique
Equatoriale Francaise (AEF). Until 1946, most
laws, decrees, or ordinances applicable to the
territories in French West or Equatorial Africa
originated in metropolitan France. Usually, it
was the local representative of the French Government, who, upon instructions from Paris, caused to
be published in the local journal officiel whatever
law, decree, or ordinance that had been made
applicable. The local representatives had no power
to make any alterations in the laws before promulgating them. The 1946 French Constitution authorized establishment of federal assemblies--one for
AOF and one for AEF. It also established Territorial Assemblies in each of the Constituent
territories, but their powers were limited. Increased pressure for independence led, in 1956, to
the enactment of Loi-Cadre which increased the
powers of the territorial assemblies while de-
creasing those of the federal assemblies. The
Territorial Assembly of each colony became the main
organ for enacting laws and administering them in
matters like agriculture, forestry, fisheries, public health, education, internal trade, etc., while
the Federal Assemblies became coordinating agencies
with no specific legislative powers. The powers
of the territorial assemblies were further extended
in 1958 and again in 1960.

    In a referendum held in September 1958, the
people of territories comprised in the AOF and AEF
were asked to decide whether they wished to
participate in the French Community of Nations.
Under this proposal, the territories were to
become autonomous republics with full legislative
competence in most internal matters. Jurisdiction
over certain matters, however, including foreign
policy, defense, currency, common economic and
financial policy, and policy on strategic raw
materials, was reserved to the Community, which was
to be headed by the French President. Guinea was
the only French colony (territory) that refused
to join the proposed community. This was interpreted by France as constituting secession.

The French sovereignty over Guinean territory was therefore deemed by the French Republic to have terminated effective September 30, 1958. On October 2, 1958, Guinea's Territorial Assembly issued a proclamation declaring the independent Republic of Guinea and transforming the Territorial Assembly into the National Constituent Assembly. Following this a Constitution was hastily drafted and promulgated on November 10, 1958. All other territories, however, decided to join the Community. But within a few years, they too became independent sovereign states when the competences reserved to the Community were finally transferred to the Territorial Assemblies. French black Africa became independent, not as two Federations composed of several territorial component units, but as the sovereign states of Guinea, Ivory Coast, Dahomey, Senegal, Upper Volta, Gabon, Central African Republic, etc., the individual territories. Most students of African politics were and remain very critical of France for adopting this procedure, calling it a policy of "Balkanization." But despite the experience they gained in operating federal structures and inter-territorial parties, post-independence African leaders of former French Africa have had little success in forging political federations of their own, although their record of economic cooperation is undoubtedly much better than that of the East African states.

The Mali Federation was originally conceived in January, 1959, and was expected to include Senegal, the Sudan, Dahomey, and Upper Volta. The proposed Federation constitution contained sixty-two articles. There was to be an Executive President assisted by two Ministers from each component state and a Federal Legislature with twelve members nominated from each of the four Territorial Assemblies. But it never reached the implementation stage. The Federation proposal was defeated in referendums held in Dahomey and Upper Volta; the Federation, left with only two states, Senegal and the Soudan (now Mali) broke up within a year. Among the reasons for the Federation of

of Mali's failure: the deep-seated conflict between the policies of the UPS (Union Progressiste
Senegalaise, Dr. Senghor's governing party) and
the Union Soudanaise (M. Modeiba Keita's governing
party); between gradualism and radicalism in
matters of economic and social policy; between a
broadly pro-French and a strongly Pan-African
orientation; between the conception of Mali as a
loose federal system and as a centralized unitary
state.   Or, in short, the inability to share
political power.   And since then, regional or
territorial federations have eluded the French
speaking African states.

The Union of African States

At the Sixth Pan-African Congress held in
Manchester, England in 1945, Dr. Kwame Nkrumah
organized the West African National Secretariat
which, in August, 1946, pledged itself to promote
the concept of a West African Federation to be
used as a stepping stone for the eventual organization of the United States of Africa.   After
Ghana became independent in 1957, Dr. Nkrumah
immediately moved to implement his goal.   On
May 1, 1959, Ghana and Guinea issued a declaration
entitled Basic Principles of the Union of Independent African States.   Both leaders, Kwame Nkrumah
and Sekou Toure solemnly agreed to work towards
establishing the Union and envisaged the Ghana-
Guinea link as a forerunner of a Union of Independent African States.   Although the two leaders
had used the word "union" to describe the relationship, careful reading of the Basic Principles
reveals their intention to create a federal
structure.   For example, the declaration provided
that each member of the Union "shall preserve its
own individuality and structure"; that the member
states "will decide in common what portion of
sovereignty shall be surrendered to the Union...";
that each state "will have its own army"; that
"apart from their own citizenship, the nationals
of the state members of the Union will have a
Union citizenship"; and that, like the Union, each
member state will have "its flag, anthem and motto

distinct from the flag, anthem and motto of the Union."[26]

In December, 1960, the State of Mali agreed to join the Union and the Presidents of Ghana, Guinea, and Mali issued a declaration of intention to establish a union of their three states and set up two special committees to examine practical methods of achieving this objective. They also condemned "all forms of African regroupment based on languages of the colonial powers" and appealed to African leaders to follow "a higher and more healthy conception of African unity."[27] In early 1961, Dr. Nkrumah tried without success to persuade Upper Volta, a former French colony, to join the Union.

Following a report from the special committees, the three states issued in July, 1961, a charter the first two articles of which read:

Article 1. There shall be established between the Republic of Ghana, Guinea, and Mali a Union to be known as "The Union of African States" (UAS).

Article 2. The Union of African States (UAS) shall be regarded as the nucleus of the United States of Africa....[28]

The conference of the heads of state of the union was to meet every three months. It was designed to be the supreme executive organ of the Union of African States and its resolutions were to take effect immediately. The charter called for establishment of political bodies to coordinate trade union, women's and youth movements in the member states, for coordination through frequent consultation and for sending directives to the diplomatic missions of the member states, for organizinga common system of defense, for coordinating and harmonizing economic policies, and, for relentlessly pursuing "rehabilitation of African culture and the development of African civilization."[29] If the intention was to unite the three under a unitary or even a federal government, this was not entirely clear in the charter; though the use of the term Member States suggests that at most, the drafters have had a federal union in mind.

On June 3, 1963, President Sekou Toure formally announced the dissolution of the Ghana-Guinea-Mali Union. In fact, it had never reached an advanced stage of implementation. No common political institutions existed and even the modest proposal that each country should have a Resident Minister serving in each of the other cabinets did not really work. Each member state continued to pursue its own political, economic, and social policies independently, without reference to the others. Neither Upper Volta nor any other African state joined the Union of African States. Nor have there been subsequent attempts by West African states to act on the resolutions of the Sixth Pan-Africanist Congress. In West Africa federalism was a dead issue.

Senegambia

Gambia is a small country of less than 4,000 square miles and a population of less than a half million, literally surrounded by Senegal which has a land area of approximately 76,000 square miles.

Even before it became fully independent on February 18, 1965, the British colonial government was concerned about the capacity of this small state to survive on its own. It was with British cooperation, therefore, that in 1963, a visiting team of United Nations experts fully explored the situation and set out three alternatives for the Gambians: a) to integrate into Senegal as a unitary state; b) to enter into a federation with Senegal; and c) to establish close and cordial treaty relations with Senegal. The first alternative was unacceptable to the Gambians who felt that this would negate their separate cultural and political identity. The

341

second was rejected by Senegal which, after the dismal failure of the Federation of Mali, had no interest in this relationship with another state. The third alternative was chosen to be implemented after independence. In 1967, the Senegal-Gambia Interstate Committee met on several occasions to work out the terms of an agreement for economic cooperation. But although every now and then there is talk of establishing the federation of Senegambia, there has not been much progress towards that end. Since then, even economic cooperation has often led to difficulties, particularly in relation to each nation's failure to prevent large scale smuggling of goods across the border from both sides.

What, in summary, is the record of African attempts at political cooperation and power sharing? In review: 1) The East African Federation which would have consisted of territories formerly under the same colonial rule and which shared important historical, political, legal, economic, and cultural similarities failed to materialize; 2) The Federation of Mali consisting of territories formerly part of the French community, which had had some experience in federalism, lasted only briefly; 3) The Union of African states, if it can be described as an attempted federation of states whose leaders, Kwame Nkrumah, Sekou Toure, and Modeibo Keita, shared the same ideological inclinations, also failed; 4) The patently clear geographic and economic need for the federation of Gambia and Senegal has gone unfulfilled; 5) The Federation of Eritrea and Ethiopia, midwifed by the United Nations, survived only long enough to be regarded by the international community as a preparation stage before the inevitable infanticide; 6) Zanzibar became independent on December 12, 1963. Both before and after independence, its Arab Sultan was and continued to function as a constitutional monarch. In the pre-independence elections held on July 8, 1963, the Zanzibar Nationalist Party,

generally characterized as the Arab party, won
47,943 votes and twelve seats in the national
legislature; the Afro-Shirazi Party, composed
primarily of Africans who had migrated from the
mainland and which throughout the period preceding
independence had the support of President Nyerere,
won 87,402 votes and thirteen seats; and the
Zanzibar and Pemba Peoples' Party won 25,610 votes
and six seats. It was this third party, composed
mainly of those Africans who had through a long
process of acculturation come to profess Islamic
religion and culture, that had held the balance
of power and had decided to form a coalition
government with the Zanzibar Nationalist Party.
It was the leader of this third party who was the
Prime Minister. In his Cabinet of ten, there were
only three persons who were full Arabs. In the
thirty-one member national legislature, only five
were full Arabs. Only one-sixth of the total
population of the islands was Arabic, many of whom
had settled on the islands long before the Afrikaans migrated to South Africa. This lawfully
constituted government fell victim to a military
coup within a month of independence which brought
to power Abeid Amani Karume, the leader of the
Afro-Shirazi Party until his assassination in
1977. Not only did President Nyerere unhesi-
tatingly recognize the new revolutionary regime
but declared in justification of his action that
the "Zanzibar coup would not have occurred if the
British had not allowed the un-African government
to come into power." Suddenly, the Arabs and Afro-
Arabs became "non-Africans." Many were killed or
forced to leave the country. But, as was seen above,
even a federation based to a substantial degree on
racial ties has not been consummated.

The record of post-independence African
attempts to establish and operate federal institutions reflects a series of hopeful attempts but
clear failures of black African leaders to share
political power. It is in this context that we
shall look at the Organization of African Unity.

The Organization of African Unity

The charter of the Organization of African
Unity agreed upon by the heads of thirty-two
independent African states on May 25, 1963,
concealed the differences among its members on
the central question of political unification.
Dr. Kwame Nkrumah of Ghana had advocated a political union of all independent African states
"along the lines of the USA or the USSR." He
favored the establishment of a United States of
Africa with a "Central Political Organisation"
comprising a bicameral legislature. It would
control foreign policy, defense, currency, and
economic planning of the union of Africa. He
published a book entitled, Africa Must Unite,
in which his proposal and the arguments for it
were fully described.[30] However, he failed to
persuade other African states to agree to his
proposal and, in the end, had to accept a charter
which, in essence, paid lipservice only to the
concept of the political unification of Africa
along federal lines, even though the charter does
contain several references to the concept of
political union. The preamble to the charter,
for example, includes statements to the effect
that the leaders had agreed to the terms of the
charter because they were "inspired by a common
determination to promote understanding and
collaboration among our States...in a larger
unity transcending ethnic and national differences" and also because they were "desirous
that all African and Malagasy States should
henceforth unite so that the welfare and
well-being of their peoples can be assured.[31] But
it also states almost in contradiction that they
were "determined to safeguard and consolidate
the hard-won independence as well as the sovereignty and territorial integrity of our States...."[32]
Similarly, one of the purposes of the Organization as set out in Article 2 was "to promote
unity and solidarity of the African and Malagasy
States" but another purpose set out in the same
article was "to defend their sovereignty, their
territorial integrity and independence." Even

344

more important were some of the operative articles
in which the member states in pursuing the purposes
of the Organization pledged themselves to observe
scrupulously the principles of a) sovereign
equality of all States; b) non-interference in the
internal affairs of States; and c) respect for the
sovereignty and territorial integrity of each
State and for its inalienable right to independent
existence. Each member State had one vote and the
resolutions of the Organization required only a
two-thirds majority of those present and voting.
However, the Charter was totally silent on
whether these resolutions were binding upon those
who were absent, non-voting, or who had voted
against the resolution. The word "unity" in the
title to the Organization had been used to placate
Dr. Nkrumah and his supporters. In reality, the
Charter showed the desire of African states to
refrain from surrendering any of their soverign
powers to the Organization of African Unity. In
this respect it was less important than the United
Nations Charter where, in matters relating to
international peace and security, the decisions of
the Security Council are binding upon all states
and to that extent all members, with the exception
of the Big Five, by implication have surrendered
part of their sovereignty to the world body.

Attempts made since 1963 to move the
Organization in the direction of political
unification have not met with success. In
July, 1964, for example, Ghana once again introduced a resolution calling for the establishment
of a "continental union government" but its
proposal was met with little interest or support
from the other states and was kept alive only by
referring it to committees for further study--out
of respect for Dr. Nkrumah. It is interesting to
note some of the reasons advanced by other African
states for so doing, most of whom at the same
time though expressed their commitment to the
ideal of African unity:

We are not yet ready to form an African government...to speak at the present time of a union

government for Africa seems to me to be premature. (Tunisia)

This ideal, toward which all our efforts tend, must be the final step in the development of African unity...a union government of Africa on a continental scale must be prepared in successive stages, by degrees, by successive relays. (Senegal)

Ghanaian proposal seems to be somewhat incomplete. We must define...how it will function, what are to be its relations with the governments whose independence must be preserved...will have to have substantiating documentation. (Cameroon)

The Republic of Mali has provided in its constitution for the possibility of a partial or total surrender of sovereignty in favor of an African whole, when objective conditions have been fulfilled. (These) objective conditions not having been fulfilled...(Mali)

There are African territories which are not yet independent...wise to wait for these states to gain independence, so that their representatives could air their views... (Cameroon)

...it will not sound serious...If...it becomes known that we are going to study the possibility of forming a government for the whole continent, I believe this would hurt the prestige of the Organization of African Unity (Tunisia)

Before any unity is put into effect, there must first be a unity of thought. (Egypt)[33]

Only in very exceptional cases did any African leaders openly express what was in the back of the minds of most of them. But during this particular debate, Nigeria's president said:

I think this idea of an African government is
a dream. It is a dream or a nightmare. As
far as Nigeria is concerned, I must make it
absolutely clear that we, on our own free
will, shall never surrender our sovereignty
to any organization.[34]

And, presumably, it was this blunt language which
led Madagascar's president, who had already spoken
earlier to add:

...I completely associate myself with the
President of Nigeria...We must be frank.
There are many here among us who do not want,
under the present circumstances, to lose
their sovereignty. We Malagasy people have
just achieved our independence. We are jea-
lous of this independence. If we are replaced
tomorrow by a world government or even by a
continental government, the Malagasy people
will refuse.[35]

The crux of the matter was the unwillingness of
the states to surrender any of their newly acquired
sovereign powers. And the same still holds true
today. A respected African intellectual, now
living in exile, stated in an editorial entitled
"Confederation--Not Conferences"

What we need is not ad hoc conferences of
our leaders to pass resolutions. We have had
enough of that. We have had just that for the
past ten years. Now we need a union government for Africa--a government with specific
and exclusive powers over a list of subjects
that have an African common denominator, in
foreign policy, continental defense, the
liberation struggle, and external struggle.[36]

In the same editorial he argued that if African
leaders within each state could, for the benefit
of their countries, claim to exercise power over
all their citizens regardless of their individual
views in the name of the nation, then there was no
reason why the same leaders could not accept

347

limitations upon their powers imposed at the continental level in the interests of the people of Africa as a whole. African national leaders, however, have not and are unlikely to accept such logic. In their quest for unlimited power, most leaders of African states have been extremely reluctant not only to surrender any part of their power to the Organization of African Unity but, also, to permit such organizations to criticize actions taken by them within their own territorial boundaries. They have sought to achieve the latter by insisting on strict organizational adherence to the principle of non-interference in the internal affairs of member states incorporated in Article III of the Charter of the Organization of African Unity. Accordingly, the organization has refrained from even discussing let alone doing anything about the genocide in Burundi, the massacre of thousands of Africans in Uganda, the expulsion of Asians from East Africa, and the gross violations of human rights in a number of other countries. Even in the Nigerian-Biafran War which resulted in massive loss of life and destruction of property, and in which a number of other non-African states became involved, the Organization continued basically to accept the thesis that it had no right to interfere in Nigeria's internal affairs. Simultaneously, of course, it has felt no compunction about issuing pronouncements on the internal affairs of South Africa condemning its policies of racial separation. To the O.A.U. only white racism mattered.

It was not until July, 1979, that the Organization was, for the first time in its history prepared to discuss and adopt a resolution addressing the question of human rights in the rest of Africa. During its sixteenth conference held in Monrovia, Liberia, July 27, 1979, Liberian President William R. Tolbert, Jr. (who was himself killed in April, 1980, following a successful military takeover by Master Sgt. Samuel K. Doe) contended that in the African context, sovereignty had become an excuse for not speaking out against inhuman actions taken against fellow Africans by

Africans themselves. He was supported by the new
President of Uganda, Godfrey Binaisa, who denounced
former President Amin as a "primitive fascist with
an insatiable appetite for blood" and called for a
resolution condemning violations of human rights
at that time taking place in Equatorial Guinea and
Central African Empire. As a result of objections
from several countries, including President Sekou
Toure of Guinea, the remarks of President Binaisa
were ordered stricken from the record as constituting interference in the internal affairs of
the two named countries. However, the Organization did adopt a resolution directing its
Secretary General to organize a meeting for purposes of preparing a preliminary draft of an
African Charter of Human Rights. The draft, of
course, will have to be discussed and approved by
the Organization. As a result, minorities and
others living in different states of Africa can
only dream of the day when troops of the O.A.U.
march into their country to prevent its leaders
from violating people's constitutional rights.

In addition to the unwillingness of African
leaders to relinquish any part of their sovereignty there are, of course, other substantial
reasons why it has been difficult for African
states to establish a continent-wide federation.
Until South Africa comes under black majority
rule, there is no prospect of a continental span
of the projected federation. The Arab countries
of North Africa are unlikely in the near future to
detach themselves from the politics of the Middle
East and the Arab League. Also the prospect that
the all-African federation would be dominated by
black African states of sub-Saharan Africa dampens
their desire to move more rapidly toward unification. The differences between the Arabs and
the Africans over the location of the headquarters
of the O.A.U. and over the selection of the
Secretary-General of the Organization are a sign
of the problems likely to arise between them over
federal institutions and processes. Among the
black African states, too, account must be taken
of the differences between the Anglophone and the

Francophone states, between the various geographical regions and the demographic, tribal, ethnic, linguistic, and religious differences among the peoples of the continent. The paucity of interstate transportation and the economic differences between the states, including minerals and other natural resources, stages of industrialization, the competitive character of agricultural products, also present barriers to creation of a political union which would allow freedom of movement, trade, and currency across the whole continent. Nevertheless, these problems are secondary in comparison to the reluctance of all African states, displayed by their actions (in contrast to their rhetoric) to surrender any part of their sovereignty. As Doudou Thiam pointed out in his book, <u>Le Federalisme Africain</u> <u>ses</u> <u>Principes</u> <u>et</u> <u>Ses</u> <u>Regles</u>:

> In Africa, nationalism no longer tends to fight for national independence, but for its preservation. Each state wants to preserve all the attributes of sovereignty. The result is a serious obstacle to political integration and sometimes even to simple cooperation.[37]

Political cooperation among diverse peoples and nations is never easily achieved--and may be impossible except in a very limited way. One need only review the history of European attempts to develop effective joint political, economic and military relations since 1945. With all of their historic animosities and national jealousies, European nations still faced a less troublesome challenge than the post-independence black African states. But, until African political leaders feel secure enough in their leadership to break the equation between personal power and national strength, pan-Africanism or even limited cooperation will have only rhetorical significance.

350

FOOTNOTES: CHAPTER V

[1]Jos Blaise Alima, "Cameroun: La Nouvelle Republique," La Jeune Afrique, June 10, 1972, p. 22.

[2]Constitution of the Federal Republic of Cameroon in Amos J. Peaslee, Constitutions of Nations, Vol. I, Africa (The Hague, Netherlands: Martinus Nijhoff, 1965, pp. 34-46.

[3]Handbook of Cameroon, American University, Washington, D.C., 1976, p. 135.

[4]John P. Mackintosh, Nigerian Government and Politics (Evanston, Illinois: Northwestern University Press, 1966), p. 23.

[5]For details, see John de St. Jorre, The Nigerian Civil War, (London: Hodder and Stoughton, 1972), p. 112 and et seq.

[6]For an example of this attitude, see Africa Confidential, April 29, 1960.

[7]Ntieyong U. Akpan, The Struggle for Secession, 1966-1970: A Personal Account of the Nigerian Civil War (London: Frank Cass, 1971), p. xii.

[8]Donald Rothchild, "Majimbo Schemes in Kenya and Uganda," in Jeffrey Butler and A. A. Castagno, Boston University Papers on Africa (New York: Frederick A. Praeger, 1967), p. 294.

[9]Peter J. H. Okondo, "Prospects of Federalism in East Africa," in David P. Currie, Federalism and the New Nations of Africa, (Chicago: The University of Chicago Press, 1964), pp. 29-38.

[10]Y. P. Ghai and J. P. W. B. McAuslane, Public Law and Political Change in Kenya, (London: Oxford University Press, 1970), p. 197.

[11]Ibid., p. 210.

[12]Y. P. Ghai and J. P. W. B. McAuslan, Public Law and Political Change in Kenya (London: Oxford University Press, 1970), p. 213.

[13]Donald Rothchild, Toward Unity in Africa: A Study of Federalism in British Africa (Washington, D.C.: Public Affairs Press, 1960); Thomas M. Franck,"East African Federation," in Thomas Franck (ed.,) Why Federations Fail (New York: New York University Press, 1968).

[14]"East African Community," Africa, No. 49, September, 1975, p. 26.

[15]Handbook for Ethiopia, (Washington, D.C.: American University, 1971).

[16]United Nations General Assembly Resolution 390, December 2, 1950, Fifth Session, Para. 1, United Nations Yearbook, 1950, p. 369.

[17]Ibid.

[18]Ibid.

[19]U.N. General Assembly Resolution 617, Seventh Session, United Nations Yearbook, 1952, p. 265-6.

[20]Robert L. Hess, Ethiopia: The Modernization of Autocracy (Ithaca, New York: Cornell University Press, 1970), p. 121.

[21]"Croissance Des Jeunes Nations," _Paris_, July-August, 1975, pp. 31-32.

[22]"The Articles of Union Between the Republic of Tanganyika and the Peoples' Republic of Zanzibar Preamble, Reproduced in Amos J. Peaslee, "Constitutions of Nations," Vol. I, _Africa_ (The Hague, Netherlands: Martinus Nijhoff, 1965), p. 1106.

[23]_Ibid._, p. 1107.

[24]_East Africa Reporter_, July 3, 1964.

[25]"An Interim Constitution of Tanzania,"Chapter I, Part 1, Section 3A, and the Constitution of Tanganyika African National Union Annexed as First Schedule to the Act to declare Interim Constitution, reproduced in William Tordoff, _The Government and Politics of Tanzania_ (Nairobi: East Africa Publishing House, 1967), pp. 205-251. See also: "Report of the Presidential Commission on the Establishment of a Democratic One-Party State," (Dar-es-salaam: Government Printers, 1965).

[26]Declaration of the Ghana-Guinea Union, Accra, May 1, 1959.

[27]Declaration by Ghana-Guinea-Mali, Conakry, December 24, 1960.

[28]Charter for "The Union of African States," Accra, July 1, 1961.

[29]_Ibid._, Article 4.

[30]Kwame Nkrumah, _Africa Must Unite_ (London: Heinemann Educational Books, 1963.)

[31]Charter of the Organization of African Unity, May 25, 1963, reproduced in Basic Documents and Resolutions, (Addis Ababa: OAU Secretariat, no date).

[32]_Ibid._

[33]W. Scott Thompson and I. William Zartman, "The Development of Norms in the African System," in Yassin El-ayouty, (ed.,) The Organization of African Unity After Ten Years, Comparative Perspectives (New York: Praeger Publishers, 1975), pp. 7-20. (The Pre-Eminence of National Independence as a Norm.)

[34]Ibid., p. 17.

[35]Ibid.

[36]Raph Uwechue, "Confederations Not Conferences," Africa, London, No. 23, July, 1973, p. 8. See also: Raph Uwechue, "Moment of Choice," Africa, London, No. 34, June, 1974, p. 6.

[37]Doudou Thiam, Le Federelisme Africain Ses Principles et Ses Regles (Translated) (New York: Praeger Publishers, 1972), Introduction.

CHAPTER VI

INSTITUTIONS OF PERSONAL POWER

We shall now examine the primary governing
institutions within modern African states. This
will reveal the extent to which the political party
systems, courts, and legislatures have been trans-
formed into vehicles for the political aggrandizement of African leaders jockeying for supremacy
in the rough and tumble of contemporary African
politics.

The Courts: Justice Denied

Peter H. Merkl has observed: It is no
accident that the protection afforded the
accused in a criminal trial often forms part of
the acid test of constitutional rule, considering
that no other form of governmental action can so
stringently interfere with the life and liberty
of a person as can a criminal court.[1]

Upon independence most African states inherited or wrote constitutions establishing strong,
independent judicial systems capable of limiting
the power and scope of authority of governmental
leaders. Today very few may boast of independent, impartial judiciaries able to restrain
political leaders from routing abuse of their
authority. In large part the current weaknesses
of the courts and the judicial process stem from
the penchant of African governments for quasi-

judicial forms of administering justice in place
of the regular court systems. In addition the regular courts remaining have witnessed the reduction
of their substantive powers. Finally, there has
been widespread interference by political leaders in
the personnel selection and other procedures of the
courts.

a) Alternative Forms of Judicial Administration

It is common practice for nations to create
special courts and a variety of quasi-judicial
bodies to perform specialized tasks in response to
changing needs. For example, the independent regulatory agencies of the Federal government in the
United States and the administrative court system
in many European countries were created to supplement and to improve the quality of justice in the
legal systems of those nations.

In many African states, however, the establishment of special tribunals has had the effect and
often the purpose of enhancing opportunities for
political leaders to intervene in or circumvent
judicial processes for political reasons. For
example, military courts have frequently been
imposed to reach well beyond their expected jurisdiction in black Africa into totally unrelated,
non-military subjects. Furthermore, these courts
have accorded to defendants few if any of the
normal safeguards of individual rights present in
regular courts. In Uganda, according to a former
government minister:

> The setting up of military tribunals to try
> offences known to the Uganda penal code, with
> powers to pronounce sentence of death has
> eroded the powers and prestige of the ordin-
> ary courts of law almost to extinction. The
> accused (in military courts) is not repre-
> sented by counsel of his own choice, indeed,
> he is not represented by anyone, because, in
> the eyes of the regime, lawyers are a nui-
> sance that will not be tolerated. The
> taking of evidence by the tribunals is an

abominable abuse of legal procedure and a
denial of justice that ought to be condemned
in the strongest possible terms. Several
people have been executed by firing squads
on false evidence...[2]

In Ghana the subversion decree enacted while
the country was under civilian rule empowered
military tribunals to try persons accused of
"subversive offenses." In 1972, four civilians
and five soldiers were tried before a military
court, accused of attempting to overthrow the
government and conspiring to assassinate leading
government officials--including a member of the
tribunal hearing the charges. The defense plea
that the tribunal member should remove himself
from the trial in order to insure a fair hearing
for the defendants was summarily rejected. To no
one's great surprise, all the defendants were
found guilty and either sentenced to death or long
terms in prison.

In Cameroon a military court sentenced the
Roman Catholic Bishop of Nkonsamba, Monsignor Albert
Ndongmo, to death along with five others accused of
"rebellion." In Zaire, in 1972, after a ninety
minute trial by a military court, four political
leaders were hanged in a public square before a
crowd of 100,000. The accused had allegedly
threatened the life of President Mobutu but no
prosecution witnesses were called, and the testimony of the accused former premier, Evariste Kimba,
and two ex-cabinet ministers was ignored.

Other African states have used State
Security Courts to achieve similar results. For
example, in Togo, in 1970, twenty-five persons
were sentenced to prison for ten years by a
State Security Court which convicted them of
conspiring to stage a coup. Ivory Coast in
December, 1964, employed a State Security Court
in sentencing six people to death for their part
in a plot against the regime. In April, 1974,
in Zaire government authorities moved against
the leaders of a religious sect, the Nzambi a

Mpungu. In Tanzania the same year, persons
accused of trying to assassinate Vice-President
Karume were dealt with by State Security Courts.

Numerous other examples of irregular judicial
procedures which largely excluded recognition of
the rights of those accused, mainly of political
crimes, could be cited, but examination of how
African judicial systems have treated non-political
cases is even more critical to an understanding of
the extent to which justice has been denied.

The practice of administering justice through
alternative forms has had even wider use in more
conventional situations. For example, commissions
of inquiry ordinarily refer to a small investi-
gatory body charged by the government to gather
information and file a recommendation on a
specified matter. Such bodies are not designed
for evaluation of evidence and determining of
individual guilt or innocence. But all across
Africa since independence, commissions of inquiry
have been created to adjudicate criminal cases
and have been vested with broad powers of investigation and punishment. For example in 1972,
Ghana was operating commissions of inquiry separate
from the regular system of courts with jurisdiction
over cases of bribery and government corruption,
tax evasion, and cases involving registration of
lands and titles and the abuse of government
licensing powers. Ghana used commissions of
inquiry to enforce the Investigation and Forfeiture
of Assets Decree of 1972. Regular judicial procedures including the right to appeal were completely
circumvented in cases arising under this decree.
Most important, the usual presumption of innocence
was suspended in commissions of inquiry proceedings.
Defendants bore the burden of proving they were
not guilty. Neither were the commissions limited
by normal rules of evidence and practice followed
by the regular courts. Obviously, the government's
task is made far easier by such expediencies.

Another common practice in modern judicial
systems is the use of so-called ministerial

justice in which department heads and other high level administrators are entrusted with specified judicial functions. But it is customary to require administrators to justify in advance their departure from ordinary judicial processes and to allow appeal of their decisions to the regular courts. However, in Malagasy in 1975, the government amended a law against actions by voluntary associations which were "contrary to the imperatives of public order and which constituted a threat to public order and safety, good morals, or national unity." The revised law provided that cases arising under this ambiguous statute could be decided by the minister of the interior instead of the courts. The minister was unfettered by rules of evidence or procedure, and his decisions could not be appealed to any other body. In effect, all voluntary groups in the country became dependent for their very existence on the unchallengeable, unchecked judgment of one official. Many other African governments have resorted to ministerial justice for a variety of purposes.

In many instances, the substantive powers of regular courts have been reduced primarily through drastic reduction or outright elimination of constitutional guarantees of basic civil rights. In Ghana for one example, the original 1957 constitution was replaced in 1960 by a document which relegated detailed, separate provisions for civil rights to mere passing, unspecific references within the preamble to the revised constitution. Soon after approval of the new constitution, the government successfully argued in court that the preamble was not part of the constitution and that the language describing certain individual rights was only an expression of intention or hope, and therefore, not binding.

Another example of this method of reducing judicial power is the 1965 Tanzanian Constitutional revision. Here again, the revised fundamental law excluded previous language clearly establishing and precisely defining a broad range of civil and political rights in favor of platitudes having no legal force or effect. Thus, courts are deprived of a vital function--guarding the fundamental rights of citizenship in both political and civil terms. When this duty ends, courts tend to regard their function as mainly being the application of law as written by legislative bodies rather than the maintenance of transcendant principles of individual rights.

An alternative technique of gutting constitutional guarantees of individual rights and shrinking the authority of the courts is reflected in Sierra Leone's constitution. A separate provision for basic civil and political rights exists, but so many exceptions are included that the presumed intent of the rights section is rendered unenforceable in the courts. But far less subtle means of weakening the courts have been developed. Many African countries grant heads of state or governments stand-by power to declare a state of emergency which effectively excludes the courts from jurisdiction over many cases during the supposed emergency. Nearly all former French colonies have constitutional provisions for declarations of emergency, the conditions for which are extremely vague. But whatever the colonial background the use of emergency power is a far too easy expedient enabling many African political leaders to rule by decree for long periods without fear of judicial challenge. In Uganda, for example, a state of emergency existed in one area for over seven years, 1964-70, at which time the declaration was extended to include the rest of the country.

Preventive detention laws have been another means to circumvent conventional judicial processes. In most African states such laws were enacted after independence enabling political leaders to arrest persons even in "non-emergency" times who are deemed a threat to "public safety or public order" and hold them indefinitely without need to provide a trial. Malawi authorized its Prime Minister in 1964 to use preventive detention powers. Uganda and Zambia incorporated this power into their laws in 1971. Zambian authorities have used such laws to arrest and detain hundreds of Asians for "pursuing only selfish political aims and causing both anarchy and political instability." And in Tanzania, in January 1977, there were more persons in jail under preventive detention laws than in South Africa!

Few threats to basic principles of fairness and individual rights are more odious than ex post facto laws. Yet many African leaders have resorted to retroactive legislation on numerous occasions. Uganda, Sierra Leone, Nigeria, and Sudan have all used ex post facto statutes for obvious political purposes.

Blatant political interference in judicial personnel selection and procedure is common today in Africa. Two examples will suffice.

In 1963, in Ghana five persons were tried on treason charges before the Ghana High Court; composed of three judges including the Chief Justice, Sir Arku Korsah. Two of the accused were convicted; the others acquitted. The trial drew much attention since it was regarded as a major test of judicial independence, a test the court was recognized as having passed when it freed three of the five defendants. Displeased with the court's display of autonomy, President Nkrumah removed the Chief Justice from office, declared the trial null and void and had all five defendants retried before another court. (None had been released after the first trial but were held under preventive detention laws). The second trial soon resulted in a verdict of guilty for all five of the accused.

In Zambia the political attack on the Chief Justice was only slightly less flagrant. In the summer of 1969, two Portuguese soldiers had been convicted by a Magistrates' Court of unlawfully entering Zambian territory from neighboring

361

Mozambique, then under Portuguese control. They
were sentenced to two years' imprisonment. Under
the law, the maximum punishment a Magistrates'
Court was empowered to impose for the offense was
nine months. The soldiers had entered Zambia in
broad daylight, unarmed, and showed no signs of
sinister intent. It appeared as if they had been
invited by Zambian border guards to "walk over."
In this circumstance, the verdict was appealed
and the Zambia High Court reduced the sentences
to the period already served, about three weeks,
and ordered the soldiers released from jail.
Immediately, the Portuguese soldiers were re-
arrested and placed under "protective custody."
Thereupon, President Kenneth Kaunda publicly
castigated the judges for their actions.

Retribution against the Chief Justice, James
Skinner, took the form of student attacks on his
office which forced him to barricade himself in
his office. The attacks were greeted with
expressions of praise and gratitude by President
Kaunda. Chief Justice Skinner fled the country
shortly thereafter, never to return.

In many less dramatic, often petty ways, the
institutions of justice are subverted widely in
modern Africa. Lawyers in some countries are
often denied access to their arrested clients or
are afraid to take cases with high political risks
attached. Attorneys have themselves been arrested
for defending too vigorously "controversial"
defendants. Once accused, defendants often find
themselves continually harrassed and re-charged
with other crimes even if initially exonerated.
The politicizing of judicial processes threaten
to destroy completely any semblance of independence or integrity among African judges. Until
the courts are restored to their former status and
protected from political retribution, due process
of law in black Africa will remain more the
exception than the rule.

362

The Legislatures: Executive Intimidation and One Partyism

In March, 1967, Sierra Leone for the first time came under military rule. The new leaders immediately issued a proclamation entitled, "Administration of Sierra Leone," empowering the military regime to issue laws binding upon all the people of Sierra Leone. The proclamation in part read:

(1) All the provisions of the Constitution of Sierra Leone, 1961, which came into force on the 27 April, 1961, which are inconsistent or in conflict with this Proclamation or any law made hereunder shall be deemed to have been suspended with effect from the 23rd day of March, 1967.

(2) In addition to and without derogation from the generality of the foregoing sub-paragraph--
    (a) the House of Representatives elected under the said Constitution of Sierra Leone is dissolved; and
    (b) all political parties are dissolved and membership of political parties is prohibited with effect from the 23rd day of March, 1967. [3]

Today, approximately half the African states are under military rule. In these states, functioning legislatures do not exist although the physical forms remain. In every case military rulers claim that their leadership is only temporary and that after an unspecified period of time, the legislatures in a reorganized form will be restored to true governing status.

In democratic legislative bodies, the major burden of criticizing the administration falls upon legislators organized into opposing political parties. Today, with increased governmental involvement in all areas of life, it is impossible for individual legislators to command sufficient

knowledge and expertise to limit executive power.
Only through combination with others, sharing
resources, and distributing the workload can
legislators effectively monitor and oppose modern
executives. Thus is their ability to organize
opposition parties indispensable to their role as
watchdogs of the executive. In most of Africa,
this role is not and may not be performed. For
example:

Zambia: When Zambia achieved independence in
1964,there were two major political parties in the
country--Kenneth Kaunda's United National Independence Party (UNIP) which was in power and Harry
Nkumbula's African National Congress (ANC), the
main opposition party. In 1968, as a result of
the split within the governing UNIP, Nalumino
Mundia, a former government minister, formed the
United Party (UP). However, this new party was
banned by government order soon after its formation. So, too, was the United Progressive
Party (UPP) formed in 1971 by Simon Kapwepwe,
another UNIP leader, who had served as vice-
president of the country. The ANC was allowed
to continue in operation, although not without
government harrassment. After the 1968 elections,
the ANC claimed twenty-three seats in the national
legislature, compared to eighty-one captured by
the governing UNIP. Yet, the ANC was refused
recognition in legislature as the official
Opposition Party on the ground that it had failed
to win twenty-five per cent of the seats. The
ANC leader was denied access to government
documents which he would have been entitled to
as leader of the official Opposition Party. He
was also denied the salary which the government
was by law to pay the leader of the opposition.
In 1970, attempts were made to deny the ANC
recognition even as a parliamentary party. And in
early 1972, Kenneth Kaunda, the leader of the
ruling UNIP and president of the country, announced
his intention to convert Zambia into a one-party
state. He established a commission to study and
recommend the changes that should be made in the
constitutions of the Republic of Zambia and of the

UNIP to implement the decision. Mr. Kaunda
asserted that it was neither necessary for the
commission to consider the constitutional validity
of such a radical change nor was it essential that
it should be decided by the people in a referendum.
He claimed that there was sufficient evidence of
popular support for his goal and that he had
received hundreds of messages and letters from
organizations and individuals all over the
country exhorting him to take this extraordinary
action.

In a State of the Nation speech delivered in
June, 1972, President Kaunda said that the purpose
of one-arty state was to insure that power was
vested in the people and that the institutions
that would be created in implementing participatory
democracy within a one-party framework would
increase freedom not limit it. Before the year
was over, Zambia had become, de jure, a one-party
state. On December 8, 1972, the governing UNIP
introduced a constitutional amendment to establish
the UNIP as the only legal political party in the
country and preclude anyone not UNIP member running
for election to the national legislature. Not only
was formation of rival political parties and
organizations to be banned, but expression of
opinion or sympathy with other parties or organizations would be illegal. In the course of his
long speech in support of the change, President
Kaunda said that the old foreign system which was
based on foreign values and foreign experiences
was now replaced with Zambia's own brand of
participatory democracy based on Humanism.

Malawi: Two years after winning independence
in 1964, Malawi amended its constitution to make
President Kamuzu Banda's party--the Malawi Congress
Party (MCP), the only legal party in the country.
There was no referendum. Previously, the MCP
leaders had openly signalled their objectives.
They had portrayed opposition parties and leaders
as sinister forces from whom it was necessary to
protect the fledgling state. Dr. Banda said:

"...this government and the public must be
protected from ambitious politicians like
Chipembere, Chirwa, Chisiza, Bwanausi, Chokani
and their dupes....We are new, our government,
our constitution, our independence have to be
protected by drastic measures...." [4]

In the national legislature too, the MCP leaders
had often expressed their distaste for opposition
parties. A leading member of the MCP, A.W. Chip-
ungo, who was also the Parliamentary Secretary of
Health, had at one time declared:

"There is no opposition in heaven. God
himself does not want opposition. That
is why he chased Satan away. Why should
Kamuzu (Dr. Banda) have opposition?" [5]

Zaire: In 1972, President Mobutu of Zaire
proclaimed a political concept called "Authenticity." He claimed that it was "a dictate of
conscience for the people of Zaire that they
should return to their beginnings and search for
the values of their ancestors." [6] Although the
concept was vague, actions taken by Mr. Mobutu
to implement it were not. He declared his own
political party, the Mouvement Populair de la
Revolution (MPR), the supreme political authority
in the country. All other parties were banned.
The principle of "authenticity" was effectively
used to discredit opposition parties. Political
partisanship was declared to have been imported
from abroad. It was unauthentic and therefore,
had no place in Zaire. Under the new one-party
system, every Zairian became a member of the
MPR at birth. His expulsion from it made him the
equivalent of a non-person. All candidates for
the National Assembly had to be nominees of the
MPR. The MPR and its political bureau would
function as a supra legislative body. All other
political organizations, including the National
Assembly, would be subordinate to the MPR.

Kenya: Immediately prior to independence
in 1963, there were three main political parties

in the country--the Kenya African National Union
(KANU), the Kenya African Democratic Union (KADU),
and the African Peoples' Party (APP). KANU, which
commanded sixty-four seats in the national legislature, was the ruling party with Jomo Kenyatta as
its leader. KADU and the APP shared approximately
forty seats and represented the opposition.
Within less than a year of independence, however,
the APP was dissolved, KADU merged with KANU, and
Kenya became, de facto, a single party state.
Commenting upon whether the merger of KANU and
KADU was voluntary, B. O. Nwabueze has said:

> Clearly it was forced upon KADU by the mass
> defection of many of its parliamentary
> members. Nor were the defections voluntary.
> They were procured by pressure exerted on
> the members by the chiefs and elders. The
> technique has been to make life as intolerable
> as possible for the opposition members by
> various forms of discrimination and victimi-
> zation ranging from denial of amenities to
> physical molestation, and even lynching and
> death, until, their will broken, they are
> obliged to join the ruling party....[7]

Although under the Kenya Constitution, opposition parties are not prohibited, in practice, (as
the example of Oginga Odinga's unsuccessful efforts
to form Kenya Peoples' Union in late sixties clearly
demonstrates) it is virtually impossible in contemporary Kenya for an effective opposition party to
emerge. Occasionally, individuals in the Kenyan
legislature seek to perform this function. But
their number is insignificant. More important
they suffer from the disadvantage of operating as
individuals without the collective, open support
of any organized political party or coalition.

It serves no purpose to cite more examples
of African states in which new leaders have either
overtly or in practice prevented organized
opposition from emerging in their national
legislatures. Suffice it to say that of the
African states under civilian rule, although

national legislatures exist in all but three,
organized opposition is either forbidden by law
or is, in practice, prevented from emerging.
These three exceptions are only peripheral to
Africa. One is Mauritius, a group of islands
located in the Indian Ocean hundreds of miles
from the African coastline with more than seventy-
five per cent of the population composed of
Indians, Europeans, Chinese, and Creoles (of
mixed French stock, approximately 20,000). The
other two are tiny Gambia and landlocked Botswana,
economically dependent to a large extent on
South Africa. The three combined represent
 less than one-half per cent of total African
population. Since 1976, Senegal, following a
period of one-party government during which
President Senghor's Union Progressiste
Senegalaise (UPS) was the only legal party in
the country, permits those members of the
national legislature who are opposed to the UPS
to organize into political parties provided they
are parties of "contribution, not of opposition."

     African leaders whose parties have thus been
entrenched in power have gone to great lengths
to explain their support of the one-party system.
Some of the more popular explanations are:

     1) Political parties, as they exist in
Western societies, represent class interests.
Classless societies do not need organized
opposition in the form of political parties. There
are no classes among Africans and it is undesirable to create them. It is best, therefore, for
Africans to prohibit organized opposition parties.
     2) Upon independence, new states are confronted
with numerous political, economic, and social
problems just as massive as those confronting
Western Europe after World War II. Just as some
Western European societies found it necessary
to establish broad coalition governments, it is
necessary for the new African states to do the
same in order to prevent the dissipation of
 national will and energy. Opposition political
 parties, therefore, would be detrimental at this

stage of African national development.

3) Only within the context of a single party system is it possible to effect the social and economic transformation of African states. Since these new states are desperately short of qualified manpower, it is necessary to harness every qualified person to the task of nation-building. To allow educated, skilled persons to occupy positions in opposition to the ruling party would be merely wasting their talents.

4) The people of Africa seek genuinely democratic systems. National political systems dominated by single mass parties whose leaders are popularly elected and which allow full and complete freedom of discussion within the parties would, in fact, be more democratic than some Western democracies where legislators are subjected to strict party discipline.

5) To liberate the rest of Africa from foreign rule and to liberate the whole continent from the clutches of imperialists and neo-colonialists it is necessary to mobilize all African people. Allowing opposition parties will not only divert popular energies but will also provide an opportunity for sinister foreign forces to divide Africans.

6) In pre-colonial Africa, the villagers or their elders would sit under a big tree and talk until they reached a consensus. This is the African traditional way of governing. Permanent, institutionalized opposition parties are unnecessary in Africa as long as expression of differing viewpoints is permitted within the single party.

7) There is unity of purpose among the people of the new states. There is a universal, primary desire to eradicate poverty, ignorance, and disease from their midst. In these circumstances it is not necessary to have opposition parties since alternative programs are irrelevant under existing conditions.

8) In the international arena, it is necessary that the people of comparatively weak states present a solid and united front to the world. This can best be done under a single party system.

If there arise differences among the people, they
may be best reconciled within the moderating
context of the mass single party.

These theories include fragments of pure
speculation and logic. But none reflects the
underlying reason for the popularity of single-
party systems in Africa. The emergence of a
single party state in Sierra Leone suggests the
political realities of the growth of one partyism
in Africa and dramatically shows how shifting
personal interests may override political principle.

Upon independence, two major political parties
were represented in Sierra Leone's legislature.
One was the ruling party, the Sierra Leone Peoples'
Party (SLPP), supported mainly by the people of the
Mende tribe. The other was the All Peoples'
Congress (APC) headed by Siaka Stevens and supported
mainly by the Temne tribe. In February, 1966,
(less than five years after independence) Albert
Margai, the leader of the ruling SLPP and also
the Prime Minister of Sierra Leone charged the
two-party system with responsibility for all the
country's ills. He named a special committee to
consider the feasibility of changing to a one-
party system. Margai prevailed upon the national
legislature to adopt a resolution supporting such
a change. In addition, he embarked upon a
well-organized propaganda campaign to persuade
the people that such a system was necessary to
unify the country because this was the traditional
African way of government. In these efforts, he
was opposed by Siaka Stevens, the leader of the
APC, who claimed that the change would inexorably
lead towards dictatorship, as it had in Ghana.
These two antagonists were a study in role reversal.
Margai, who favored return to African traditional
ways, was a full-fledged English barrister
trained to respect and protect the rule of law and
the freedom to organize while Stevens, who posed
himself as the main supporter of Western democratic systems, was a rough spoken trade union
leader with little formal Western education.

In March, 1967, Sierra Leone came under
military rule. One coup followed another. In
the end, in April, 1968, a group of army officers
belonging to the Temne tribe turned over political
power to the civilians, with Siaka Stevens as the
head. Under his leadership Sierra Leone became a
republic in April, 1971. Stevens immediately
launched a campaign of political attrition against
the opposing SLPP resorting to questionable
electoral practices and trumped up charges against
SLPP leaders among other devices. By the end of
1974, Sierra Leone had become a single party
system de facto, and in August, 1975, the
parliament of Sierra Leone unanimously adopted the
following resolution:

> Be it resolved that this House hereby agrees
> to implement the wishes of the people of
> Sierra Leone to transform this country into
> a one party state and for this purpose calls
> upon Government to introduce a new one party
> Republican Constitution under Section 42 of
> the 1971 Constitution.[8]

In the course of the debate on this resolution,
members of Siaka Stevens's Cabinet argued that a
one party state would eliminate political conflict,
and petty jealousies, the same argument which they
had denigrated only a few years before while
members of the opposition party. Sorie Koroma,
Vice-President of Sierra Leone, and second only
in rank and political power to President Stevens
supporting the resolution stated that

> "...of all nations in the world only about
> fifteen still practised the multi-party
> system. Of OAU states, just four retained
> the two party system and two of those were
> monarchies--Morocco and Swaziland...."[9]

Supported by President Stevens, APC supporters
demonstrated in the streets of the capital city
of Freetown carrying huge banners stating "Pa
Sheki (a nickname for Siaka Stevens), We Demand
that You Declare One Party State Forthwith."

371

People visited his office with requests "to avoid a waste of money and time by declaring a one party state without a referendum." And similar appeals were made in resolutions adopted at meetings of various voluntary agencies. A bulletin issued by the Sierra Leone High Commission in London and distributed to other countries around the world described the events in the following terms:

> "...the jubilant crowds of women marched through the streets of Freetown on Friday, singing and dancing, in a public display of solidarity with the Government and public support for the motion calling for a one-party system of Government for Sierra Leone...."[10]

Although better organized, the propaganda campaign led by Stevens and the APC was like the one waged a few years earlier by Margai. Ironically, leadership opposing the change, rests with Albert Margai, living in exile in England.

In August, 1976, Sierra Leone's Attorney General drafted a new single party constitution at the direction of President Stevens. The tables have turned. But the scenario is basically the same, and the motives of competing leaders were and remain more political than theoretical.

According to Ruth Morgenthau "the number of parties is far too simple a criterion upon which to decide whether or not a system is democratic."[11] But if we assume that it would be possible in African one-party states for the legislature to limit and control executive power, this could occur only if it can be shown that legislators do have the capacity and, in fact, openly and routinely criticize executive leaders.

To freely challenge the actions of executives, legislators should feel confident that the executive may not impose sanctions so severe as to destroy their independence and power. They should also enjoy immunity from criminal or civil process for statements made in the performance of their legislative duties. The laws of most African one-party states grant immunity to their legislators. However, to regard these laws as evidence of African legislators' freedom to criticize executive behavior would be wrong. For there also exists in nearly all African one-party states, laws empowering executives to place any person under preventive detention whenever the executive believes it to be in the national interest. Legislators are not really exempt from the operation of the preventive detention laws and the most that can be said is that they cannot be placed under preventive detention for anything said or done in the course of their legislative activities. This protection, however, is empty. Under most preventive detention laws, the executive is under no obligation to provide any information regarding much less reasons for detention of anyone. Neither the legislature nor the courts can force the executive to do so. In practice, therefore, it is very easy for the executive to remove from the political scene a critical legislator by placing him under preventive detention and claim that the action is unrelated to anything said or done in the legislature. Preventive detention may also be used to drive a legislator out of office and to destroy his political career altogether. Under the preventive detention laws of Zambia and Tanzania, for example, a legislator placed under preventive detention, after the expiration of a certain period, loses his seat in the national legislature and is disqualified from running for political office in the future. Under the laws of several other countries, exceeding a maximum number of absences from the legislature means expulsion. In these states, the executive merely has to place the legislator under preventive detention long enough to strip him of his seat automatically. African executives have also taken other measures, short of preventive detention, which effectively silence critics of the government. These, as Nwabueze has noted, include "unwarranted prosecutions, often on trumped-up charges, destruction of property or

business, beating or lynching, and denial of
facilities for business activities. The aim
here is to make life as intolerable as possible
for them and thereby, subdue their will to oppose
and criticize."12

All African single parties retain the right
of expulsion from the party. On the principle
that once a legislator has been expelled from the
party, he may not again represent that party in
the national legislature, his seat (for example,
in Kenya, Ghana, Zambia, and Malawi) is deemed to
have been automatically vacated. A legislator who
has been critical of the government and antici-
pates expulsion from the party cannot retain his
seat by resigning from the party before he can be
expelled. Resignation from the party also entails
the loss of the seat in the national legislature.

Executive control over a legislator's income
is always a significant factor in determining how
free he is in criticizing the government. This
is particularly so in African states where election
to the legislature almost invariably results in a
substantial improvement in the legislators'
social and economic status. As a legislator, he
receives a monthly salary. Expulsion would mean
loss of this income, as well as of other perquisites that come with the office. Moreover, it is
common in many African one-party states to make a
number of legislators directly responsible to the
executive through appointing them as ministers or
assistant ministers. For example, in the government of Western Nigeria in 1965, out of the total
of ninety-four legislators, as many as forty-nine
were also ministers; in Zambia in 1974, the figure
was fifty-three out of one hundred nine; in Kenya
in 1969, it was fifty-two out of 171, and by 1979,
it had increased to seventy-eight out of 172--a
majority. Fifty-eight were ministers or assistant ministers, all entitled to the use of a
chauffeured Mercedes limousine and government
housing. In Tanzania, President Nyerere often
has appointed potential critics of his government to posts as assistant ministers and even

obliged them to lead the debate in the national legislature on certain bills to which they, as ordinary legislators, might otherwise have been opposed. In several single party states it is possible for the executive to make the legislators directly or indirectly accountable to the government by appointing them district governors, managers of state corporation, members or chairmen of special commissions or as top administrators in parastatal bodies. The fear of losing these positions is a danger all legislators must consider before they criticize their benefactors. In most African one-party states political independents who might have adequate private means to absorb such financial losses are not allowed to run for office. This is the case in both Tanzania, a de jure single party system, and Kenya, a de facto one-party state.

The freedom to criticize is of little value unless there is an opportunity to exercise this freedom. Over time there has been a major reduction in such opportunities in all African one-party states. The constitutions of most former French colonies (e.g., Ivory Coast, Gabon, Senegal) provide that the legislatures shall enact laws and "consent to taxes." Immediately following this general provision giving broad powers to the national legislature, specific lists of responsibilities are included which may be dealt with by legislative action. All other matters are explicitly or implicitly excluded from their jurisdiction. They fall within the administrative purview of the executive and are usually dealt with by decree or issuance of regulations. In the former British colonies, too, (except Gambia and Zimbabwe which have yet to declare themselves republics), there has been an increase in the independently exercisable powers of executives. This is particularly evident in periods of emergency when the executive enjoys wide-ranging powers to enact permanent laws without reference to the legislature. Often, the declaration of the state of emergency itself is left solely in the discretion of the executive. Legislative

approval, even where necessary, is usually only
ex post facto. In strictly theoretical terms, it
may be desirable to provide for such exercise of
power by the executive in circumstances of
impending disaster. In Africa, however, the
executives have not resisted the temptation to
declare states of emergencies in circumstances
which could hardly constitute such a danger.
And once assumed, emergency powers are seldom
relinquished. Zambia, for example, has been
under emergency rule since 1969. Parts of
Kenya were under emergency rule from 1963 to
1971.

Even during non-emergency periods, legislators' opportunities to criticize the executive
have often been drastically curtailed. Although
erratic, the overall pattern of parliamentary
activity in most African one-party states has been
one of decline in the frequency of meetings.[13]
Moreover, often the general rule that government
business should have priority over all private
bills has enabled the executive to dominate the
proceedings even on those days on which the
legislatures meet. A related technique, frequently
resorted to by executives on matters that are
likely to lead to criticism, is to withhold prior
publication of the intended bill, introduce it at
the last minute in the national legislature under
a Certificate of Urgency, have the Standing Rules
of procedure suspended, and push it through within
a single day. Such a procedure not only takes
prospective critics by surprise (who find the bill
enacted into law even before they have had a
chance to study it) but also makes it impossible
for them to consult with each other to map out
strategies for opposing it. In Tanzania there
have been periods when over half the bills proposed
by the government were enacted by the legislature
following this procedure. As Nwabueze has
pointed out, this technique has also been successfully adopted in Kenya on crucial issues.[14]

In addition to the corruption of procedures
described above, there are many forms of harrassment

and petty indignities employed by the government to discourage criticism. Frequent interruptions, gestures ridiculing the legislator speaking against the executive, open displays of disinterestedness, cynical stares (all observed by one of the authors in parliaments of some of the single party African states) and other such methods are often more than adequate to discourage all but a few extremely thick-skinned legislators from taking advantage of the few opportunities they might have to criticize the leadership or the government. Criticism is also not very easy to make when the executives have a tendency to take it as if it was directed personally against them. Note, for example, the following exchange between a legislator and the Vice-President (Prime Minister) of Sierra Leone in November, 1974.

> Mr. A. Y. Komeh: Mr. Speaker, I read through the objects and reasons of the Bill (The Passport (Amendment) Bill, 1974) which say "The objects and reasons of the bill is to empower the President to make any Order or Rules for the further carrying into effect the provisions of this Act of 1964." As the amendment now stands, it is going through parliament. After this we are going to empower the President with general powers to make orders or rules. The point is we do not know what these orders are going to be. Then the other fact is, these orders and rules are going to be brought to us and laid on the table in Parliament after the bill has gone through the House.
>
> What power do we then have? Suppose the rules and orders are detrimental to us, what powers do we have to amend them? This is my worry because just now we know that we have a very generous President who we all know is the father of the State. We do not know what will happen in the future. Suppose we get a President who says "nobody is going to get a passport to get out?" What power do we have over the orders? This is my worry, Mr. Speaker.[15]

This was a legitimate concern expressed in extremely guarded language demonstrating dissatisfaction with the increasing tendency of the executive to have the legislature enact framework laws which do little more than delegate the powers in relation to the subject matter of the bill to the executive. The government's reply to it, reproduced below, was a thinly disguised attempt to silence Mr. Komeh. It did not answer the legitimate concern expressed by the legislator.

> The Vice-President and Prime Minister: This is the last nail, sir, to the coffin. The Member for Tonkolili Central (Mr. Komeh) when making his contribution mentioned that the President might make orders and regulations which are detrimental to the state....
>
> We, the people and the state are the same. It is the word detrimental that I am against. Before I say anything, I would ask the honourable member for Tonkolili Central kindly to withdraw that word because in my opinion, it is casting aspersion on the integrity of the President. He is the embodiment of the State, the Fountain of Honour--the embodiment of the State. He cannot therefore make regulations which can be detrimental to the State. I would ask him to withdraw the word "detrimental" from his statement or substitute a better word.
>
> Mr. A.Y. Komeh: With respect, I withdraw the word "detrimental."[16]

Freedom to criticize is not of much use in practice unless the legislators have adequate data available to effectively monitor and constructively criticize the activities of the executive. Otherwise they will merely be wasting the few opportunities they do get to express their dissatisfaction. That would also make it that much easier for the government leaders to ignore, ridicule, or claim as irrelevant whatever criticisms the

legislator may have made. African executives
have been notoriously prone to secrecy and have
sought on many occasions to keep the legislators
ignorant by making it impossible for them to
obtain or have access to relevant documentation.
Note the following examples drawn after only a
cursory examination of two volumes of Sierra
Leone's parliamentary records:

> MR. FILLIE FABOE: I rise to support the bill
> entitled....What I want the Government to
> know is that it is unfortunate that some of
> us are not even fortunate to possess the
> original act (which the bill under consid-
> eration sought to amend); but nevertheless....

> I want to quote from the report of the Gov-
> ernor to the Board of Governors of the Bank
> of Sierra Leone....I will be quoting what
> the report stated but my only regret is that
> as Members of Parliament, we are not privi-
> leged in getting the annual report, we are
> Members of Parliament, we are the law makers
> here....

> MR. S. G. M. FANIA:...this Bill (The Chiefdom
> Councils (Amendment) Bill, 1974) got to us
> last night...This has been the practice of
> government or the ministers concerned; each
> time they bring Bills to this House they are
> only sent to us overnight. The parent act
> is not available; we are frustrated by that
> and when we make complaints here, we are told
> to go to the library. How can we go to the
> library, when the Bill gets to us in the
> morning? We are a little bit bored with this
> type of thing. Each time...the bills are sent
> to us in the middle of the night. Sometimes
> we are not in our houses. Sometimes we do not
> have enough time to look at it in the morning,
> and we come to this House, and do not even
> know what to say.

> MR. S. R. FILLIE FABOE: The Minister is going
> away,Sir. This is how they treat us, when we

are bringing important questions they should
listen to us. We get our Gazettes very late
and even the Bills are received only the
night before they are to be debated. I would
like this practice to stop. At times the
blame is put on the Law Officers' Department
and at other times it is on the Printers....

MR. A. T. KOMEH: Mr. Chairman, our Consti⌐.
tution is not up to date yet still they have
given us another version. We do not know
which one we should go by. The man who
made the Constitution is reading from one.
This is why we always say that these papers
should be given to all Members of Parliament.
Some of us here are still without copies.

ALHAJI S. H. O. GBORIE:....We are now going
to amend something which we do not know
much about and so this is one point that is
of great concern to me....So Mr. Speaker, I
must on behalf of my colleagues, make this
plain that we need the volumes of the Laws
of Sierra Leone. If they are not coming into
this House and we just sit down with open
mouths because we do not know what, in fact,
we should know.

MR. H. T. T. WILLIAMS:...I would like to know
why it is that irrespective of the fact that
there are 1001 questions which have been
submitted to this House by Members, they
still remain unanswered and uncared for, and
we have come here to be given answer s to
only two questions?....I for one have sent
questions over four months ago which have
nothing to do with the personal character of
anyone (the Vice-President and Prime Minister
had claimed that this was so) I sent questions
about Delco, the mining industries, etc.[17]

If a legislature is to effectively perform
its task of limiting the executive, its members
must possess the capacity to have their views
publicized. In the United States Congress,

members not only have their views but other
supporting documents inserted in the Congressional
Record and the proceedings of standing committees
available to the public. American legislators
issue reports to their constituents, give interviews on national media, issue press releases all
in the expectation that citing their views in
public will remind the President that his powers
are not unlimited and that his activities are being
scrutinized by the voters in the light of the
criticisms emanating from the legislative branch. In
most African one-party states, the legislators do
not enjoy this capacity to publicize their criticisms of the executive. Elsewhere in this book,
we have dealt at some length with the problems of
news media in Africa. Suffice it to say, that "if
we define freedom of the press as the right to
fully report and criticize the conduct of government without fear of official recriminations, then
there is precious little of that kind of freedom
anywhere in Africa.[18]To a very large extent, it is
African executives who are responsible for its
absence.

By and large, African legislators operate
under objective conditions which are not conducive
to limiting the government or the leadership.
They have the capacity neither to organize, nor
to publicize and the restraints upon their capacity to criticize are such that they have little
alternative but to indulge in spurious criticisms
but otherwise act simply as listening bodies. If
the executive is the motor, and the legislature
the brakes, the braking mechanisms in African
political systems can only be considered useful
for decorative or ornamental purposes.

In recent years, Tanzania has acquired a
reputation among some observers as a one-party
democracy. It is instructive to describe the
restrictions under which Tanzanian legislators
operate today. A Tanzanian legislator is permitted
to oppose or criticize government policy only on
practical grounds, not on principle. Also, he is
not entitled to oppose publicly a policy decision

381

made by the Party's National Executive Committee.
Within the confines of the legislative chambers,
he can only oppose a policy on practical grounds
before it has received legislative approval. Once
the legislature has passed a bill into law, he has
the obligation to support it. This does not mean
mere passive support. He must actively work and
explain government policy to his constituents. For
him to distinguish between some of these potentially conflicting demands by the Party leadership
is not easy. Is he, for example, entitled to
oppose on practical grounds in the national legislature a measure already approved by the Party's
National Executive Committee? Or is he entitled
to oppose a matter on practical grounds which
might be construed to be a criticism of the Party's
ideology? If he does answer such questions in the
affirmative, can he be sure that for broadly
interpreting his functions he would not be expelled
from the Party--which would automatically deprive
him of his seat? The legislators offer no simple
solutions to such issues. And the leadership has
no reason to clearly answer such questions. The
understandable result is that most legislators do
not actively criticize the government on a
regular basis even on practical grounds. Virtually
all decisions in the Tanzanian legislature are
made by voice vote. In the debates preceding these
votes, the legislators scrupulously avoid sensitive
issues. Most of the speeches are either supportive
of the government or deal with mundane local
matters.[19] Only in rare circumstances is a piece of
legislation supported by the government altered in
the legislature in any substantial manner. As
Raymond F. Hopkins noted in 1970:

> On balance, the legislative arena is still a
> forum in which the government's ideas and
> proposals are largely praised or defended
> and criticism is not systematic, let alone
> organized. Among those M.P.'s who were
> most critical according to the analysis of
> speeches in the 1965/66 period (Tanzania
> introduced a single party system in 1965),
> nine had lost their Assembly seats for

political reasons by December, 1968, either
by virtue of having been expelled from the
Party or due to political detention or exile.[20]

In view of the fact that the leadership has the
power to place legislators under preventive
detention and that this power has actually been
exercised on several occasions it is not surprising that most legislators remain silent. And
even on the rare occasions when they dare to
criticize the government, they do so with extreme
circumspection, in oblique terms, and on comparatively minor issues. No Tanzanian legislator, for
example, has ever dared question a military
appropriation. The legislators are afraid to talk
to foreign reporters. And the local media is
exclusively controlled by the government. If the
Tanzanian legislators are free to express opinions
contrary to those of the leadership, they certainly
do not do so in the legislature. This is quite
evident even from a cursory look at the parliamentary records. Whether they do so at Party
meetings is unclear. These take place in secret.

It is clear from our survey of legislative-
executive relations in modern African states that
legislative capacity to limit executive abuse of
power is very weak. Legislative bodies are
essentially unorganized for effective use of
political power. They operate mainly through one-
party systems where leadership resides in the
executive branch. The threat of retribution from
executives enjoying virtually unchecked access to
loose preventive detention laws would intimidate
even the bravest African legislator. African
parliaments lack even the rudiments of legislative power--information, participation in
preparation of bills, and even their personal
integrity and independence is compromised through
the widespread practice of dual administrative/
legislative service. Until major alterations are
made in this imbalance of power between the two key
policy making bodies, representative government
in Africa will remain at best a possibility for
the future, at worst a corruption of the very

concept. We turn now, however, to an examination of the electoral process in modern Africa.

The Selection of Political Leaders

Democratic theory relies heavily on the assumption that the people are the best judges of their own government. All democratic political systems, therefore, provide for election of those who govern by qualified voters for limited or terminable periods of time. To hold officials accountable to the people who elect them and to ensure popular control, most democratic political systems also provide for circumstances in which elected officials can be removed from office even before the expiration of their terms of office.

Elections are imperfect mechanisms of popular control. Thomas R. Dye and L. Harmon Zeigler for example suggest that elections cannot be effective instruments of control unless four conditions are met. 1) Parties, or their candidates, must offer clear policy alternatives to the voters; 2) Voters must recognize and care about policy choices; 3) Majority preferences on issues must be identifiable through selections; and finally 4) Elected officials must be bound by their campaign pledges.[21] They have also contended that, despite the existence of two political parties, vibrant and relatively free news media, and comparatively well educated electorate, people in the United States do not exercise real control over the policies of their government. They concede, however, that the American elections perform the function of "giving the masses an opportunity to express themselves about the conduct of the public officials who have been in power. Elections do not permit the masses to direct future events, but they do permit the masses to render judgment about past political conduct" and that while "elections do not permit masses to decide what should be done in their interests, they do encourage governing elites to consider the welfare of the masses. Knowing that a day of reckoning will

come on election day, elected officials strive to
make a good impression on the voters in the meantime."[22] In other words, aware of the fact that
voter dissatisfaction might spell disadvantage
or even disaster for him in the next election, a
rational official will regulate his conduct,
during the current term, in an appropriate fashion.
And, to that extent, at least the American masses
through their power to vote can be deemed to
exercise a limiting influence upon their leaders.
As Gerald Pomper has noted:

> The existence of the vote does not make
> politicians better as individuals; it simply
> forces them to give greater consideration to
> demands of enfranchised and sizeable groups,
> who hold a weapon of potentially great
> force....The ability to punish politicians
> is probably the most important weapon avail-
> able to citizens.[23]

This weapon, however, must be credible. The
elected official must be distinctly made to
feel that he can ignore the day of reckoning only
at his peril. For him to be genuinely frightened
into behaving himself there must be the clear
possibility that he could lose the next election.

Whether or not in African states the electoral
process encourages elected leaders to feel
limited is a question which demands careful
examination. At first, however, it is necessary
to provide brief descriptions of electoral
processes in   selected African nations.

Zaire: Under the third Constitution of the
Democratic Republic of Zaire adopted on June 24,
1967, the President of the Republic is elected for
a term of seven years on the basis of universal
adult suffrage. Deputies to the national legislature called the National Assembly are also
similarly elected for a term of five years.

Zaire is a de facto single party state. The
Constitution provides that there can be no more

than two political parties in the country. In practice, however, President Mobutu, who is in power, has made it abundantly clear, by words and deeds, that he will not tolerate the formation of a second political party in the country, let alone allow it to operate freely and run candidates for election to national office. In the presidential elections on November 1, 1970, President Mobutu was the only candidate and was elected for a term of seven years by a popular vote of near one hundred percent. Two weeks later, elections to the 420-member National Assembly were held. The Political Bureau of the MPR, the only political party in the country, chaired by President Mobutu had nominated exactly 420 candidates to run for office in the name of the MPR. There were no other candidates. All 420 were elected by over-whelming majorities. None, at any time, had reason to feel threatened that they might lose the election. In December, 1977, Mobutu once again was the sole candidate and re-elected for another seven year term by a vote of 98.16 per cent. In October of the same year, People's Commissioners were elected to a new legislative assembly. The results did not vary much from the earlier elections.

Ivory Coast: There is no provision in Ivory Coast's constitution restricting the number of political parties that can exist in the country. Ivory Coast, however, is also a de facto single party state. The electoral laws enacted by the government of President Houphoet Boigny, in accordance with the powers conferred upon the government under the Constitution, and the policies and practices of the government as well as of the PDCI (Parti Democratique Coute de Ivoirie), the only political party in the country, headed by President Boigny, are such that it has been impossible for an opposition party to emerge and survive. In February, 1971, President Boigny was re-elected for another term of office by a vote of 99.97 per cent and again in November, 1975, by 99 per cent. In the 1971 National Assembly elections, too, all the candidates nominated by the PDCI were returned into office with 99.98 per cent of the total votes cast supporting the PDCI slate. There was little possibility of a PDCI nominee losing an election. The 1975 elections produced nearly identical results.

Malawi: In Africa, there is generally no limit on the number of times a political leader can be re-elected. Malawi, a de jure single party state, is an exception. There the President does not have to run for re-election at regular intervals. By a constitutional amendment enacted in 1970, its President, Dr. Kamuzu Banda is entitled to "hold the office of the President for his lifetime." The first post-independence elections to its National Assembly were held in April, 1971. All candidates had to be members of the Malawi Congress Party (MCP) headed by Dr. Banda. Prior to the elections, he had asked his regional ministers to visit all fifty-eight constituencies in the country and submit to him names of five candidates that had been proposed for nomination by MCP members in each constituency. It was from these that Dr. Banda selected fifty-eight who were nominated for election. All fifty-eight were elected by overwhelming majorities. There was no chance of any one of them ever losing the election. In May, 1976, following a dissolution of the National Assembly by President Banda, eighty-five members were elected to the Assembly. Exactly eighty-five candidates had been nominated by the Malawi Congress Party. All were elected by overwhelming votes.

Kenya: Following the 1968 constitutional amendments the President is elected by universal adult suffrage as are members of the approximately 170 seat National Assembly. Presidential and parliamentary elections take place at the same time. The Constitution and the electoral laws do not prohibit formation of political parties; on the contrary these contain complicated provisions for a second ballot which may be necessary in certain

387

circumstances. In practice, however, Kenya is a
de facto single party state. Such circumstances
are never likely to arise. These provisions are
therefore, most unlikely to become operative, at
least in the near future. Consistent with
Kenya's practices in many other aspects, this
result has been achieved with certain amount of
guile. According to the electoral laws and regulations, candidates for the office of the presidency can only be nominated by political parties
which have been registered with the appropriate
governmental authorities. No person is allowed
to run as an independent candidate. And so far,
the authorities have been extremely cautious
about accepting registration of new political
parties formed in opposition to the ruling
Kenya African National Union (KANU). The same
applies to candidates running for election to the
National Assembly. Their candidacy must be
supported by the leader of a registered political
party. KANU, the only registered party in the
country, has adopted its own rules governing
circumstances in which its leader would sponsor
the nominations. These require submission to
the Party of a written application accompanied
by a duly signed and witnessed statement entitled
Pledge of Loyalty. It should read as follows:

"I,_____, wishing to seek the nomination
of KANU as a candidate in the forthcoming
parliamentary election for the _____Consti-
tuency, hereby make a solemn pledge that if
I am elected a member of the National Assembly
and so long as I continue as such member on
behalf of the KANU, I Will

a) remain loyal to the President and Party;
b) give my full support to the constitution
and manifesto of the Union (i.e. the Party);
c) give my full support to the policies of
the KANU government, and....

And I undertake to make this pledge public in
the said Constituency."

The rules also require that the applicant must be
a KANU member. It is not incumbent upon the party
or the president to accept an application, even
when there is nothing wrong with it in principle.
In the 1974 elections, for example, all applications made by those KANU members who formerly
belonged to the Kenya People's Union (KPU) and
who had, at any time in the past, been placed
under preventive detention on suspicion of engaging
in subversive activities were rejected. In the
November, 1979, elections held following the death
of President Jomo Kenyatta, Mr. Daniel Arap Moi
was the only candidate for the presidency. In
the elections to the National Assembly, Mr. Oginga
Odinga and several other members of the former
Kenya People's Union were arbitrarily barred by
KANU from running. So was George Anyona, a
well-known critic of the government. Nevertheless,
it is not uncommon for the Party to allow more than
one KANU member to run for election from any
particular constituency; though in most cases, the
Party makes it clear which one is its favorite.
In the 1979 elections, a number of National Assembly
members, including a few members of the cabinet,
failed to obtain reelection. In part, this
occurred because of the willingness of the
people to vote against politicians who had been
close to Kenyatta (now that he was gone it was
safe to do so) and partly because of a protest
vote by the second largest tribe in the country--
Luo--against the government's decision to dis-
allow Mr. Odinga's bid for a seat in the national
legislature. On the whole, therefore, except in
rare cases, the candidate favored by the Party
can be reasonably sure of winning the election.
In any event, he never has to face opposition
from an independent or from a candidate of another
party.

It may be noted here, that a thirty-two page
newsletter issued by the Kenyan Embassy in
Washington, D.C. and widely distributed in the
United States government included a twenty-two
page long list entitled "Results of the General
Elections held in Kenya on October 24, 1974."[24]

It carried the names and constituencies of all candidates and their vote totals. There was no mention of the Party or Parties to which the candidates belonged. But the list was prepared in such a style that only the most critical observer would note the lack of partisan differences among them. In fact, each candidate was a KANU member and had pledged his loyalty in writing to the President in the manner described above.

Tanzania: A leading article in the August, 1975, issue of News Review, issued by the government controlled Tanzania Information Services in Daressalaam, Tanzania began with the following two paragraphs:

> "The general elections are with us, and polling day is October 26, 1975. October 26, this year, is election day. More than eight million Tanzanians will go to the polls on that day to vote into office their President, members of parliament, and District Development Council representatives for a term of five years.
>
> The whole country is in election mood. The mass media are being fully used throughout the country to explain to the electorate the importance of the coming general elections. TANU's ability to penetrate into the country-side is being demonstrated this year by the number of citizens rushing in hundreds to election centres for registration. FOR RESPONSIBILITY CAST YOUR VOTE. Just after two weeks of registration, the Electoral Commission announced confidently that the number of voters was expected to be more than eight million, as compared to only five million in the 1970 elections."[25]

But in these elections only one candidate was allowed to run for the presidency of the country, TANU's leader Dr. Julius Nyerere, who was re-elected by an overwhelming majority. This was

also the case in October, 1975, when President
Nyerere was once again re-elected (to his fourth
five-year term) by a vote of 91.5 per cent. In
elections to the National Assembly, Tanzania has
within the framework of a de jure single party
system admittedly made it possible, to a limited
extent, for the voters to make the elected
officials feel afraid that they might lose in the
election. This has been achieved by allowing
voters in each constituency to choose between two
candidates both belonging to TANU. Both campaign
at meetings organized and chaired by local party
officials. The expenses of the campaign come out
of the Party funds. The party is said strictly to
adhere to the principle that both candidates are
equally acceptable to the Party and that it is
up to the voters to decide which candidate they
want to represent their constituency in the
national legislature. This gives the people an
element of choice and makes it possible for
them at least to express their discontent with
one of the candidates. It is this innovation
that has made the Tanzaniaphiles characterize
the country as a One Party Democracy but many of
them, however, either fail to realize or will not
admit to the narrow application of the dual choice
principle in Tanzania. It must be noted, for
example, that 1) elections following the above
procedure have been held only in the part of the
country formerly known as Tanganyika, not on the
islands of Zanzibar and Pemba; 2) it is the Party's
National Executive Committee that homes the two
candidates from each constituency. To qualify to
run from a particular constituency, one needs the
signatures of only twenty-five registered voters.
Very often, therefore, there are more than two
candidates vying for nomination from a constituency.
In such cases, the obligation of the Party's
district representatives is to select their top
two choices by secret ballot. The party's
National Executive Committee, which makes the
final selection, however, is not bound by the
choices of the District representatives. All that
the District representatives do is to report the
results of the secret ballot to the National

391

Executive Committee. In practice, the National
Executive Committee has not always accepted the
candidates of the District representatives; 3) It
is the option of the National Executive Committee
to select for any particular constituency only one
candidate instead of two. In the 1965 elections,
for example, six persons were declared elected
unopposed from six different constituencies. They
happened to be the Vice-President and Prime
Minister, Rashidi Kawawa, four Cabinet members and
one junior minister of state; 4) Only a little
more than half of the members of the National
Assembly are elected according to the above
procedure, 107 to be exact. The rest, which can
number as many as 97 are appointed by the President (32 from the Zanzibar Revolutionary Council,
20 other Zanzibaris; 20 Regional Commissioners, and
15 "National" representatives). With the merger
of TANU and the Zanzibari ASP this distribution
may change; 5) Although the candidates are
allowed to campaign at meetings organized by the
Party in each constituency, they are bound not to
raise certain issues upon which there is agreement
by the Party's National Executive Committee. Other
forbidden topics are tribalism, race, or religion
which could generate tension among the people; and
6) The President may appoint to the National
Assembly a defeated candidate. In one such
election, for example, Mr. Paul Bomani, the
Minister of Finance, rejected by the voters from
the district of Mwanza (East) was appointed to the
legislature by the President and made the Minister
of Economic Affairs and Development Planning. The
President claimed that he had the right to do so
because Mr. Bomani had "fulfilled his national
responsibilities in an exemplary fashion and
because his particular services were badly needed
in the immediate future."

    The electoral processes of Zaire, Ivory Coast,
Malawi, and Kenya described above are not unique.
Detailed examinations of elections elsewhere in
Africa would reveal similar facts. There is
adequate evidence to justify the conclusion that
African voters exercise no control over the

policies of their governments. In all but three where elections are held it is impossible to present clear policy alternatives to the voters through the medium of political parties. With increased "democratic centralism" in the internal operations of the single parties in power, it is difficult if not impossible, for a candidate even where more than one person is allowed to run from each constituency, to offer voters clear policy alternatives and to compete for votes on the basis of contrasting programs. It might be recalled that even in Tanzania the real weeding out of candidates takes place <u>sub</u> <u>rosa</u> so that both approved candidates are likely to share the same ideological perspective. Also, both are bound to support the major direction of public policy already determined by the National Executive Committee. They are also dependent to a considerable extent on the government or the party controlled media for bringing their views to the attention of the voters. In the circumstances, competition between them usually is manifested only on relatively insignificant local issues and in the image presented to the people. A significant proportion of African voters are illiterate and therefore beyond the reach of any political discourse. And with the government controlled media the main source of information for the educated few, their level of knowledge is also very limited. The large number of votes cast in support of candidates of the single parties in power cannot be interpreted as support for any particular set of policies. Nor can it be argued that African electorates are capable of holding elected officials to campaign promises. In fact, voters lack the capacity to perform even the limited function of controlling official behavior by the fear that unless they respond to voter preferences they may be replaced by their rivals at the next election. On the contrary, from the perspective of political leaders, elections in Africa only perform the function of entrenching them in power by making it possible for them to proclaim that their policies and performance enjoy widespread popular support.

393

With little possibility of effecting change through the ballot box, those inclined to challenge such claims become increasingly reluctant to initiate or respond to any reformist movements. Would-be challengers decline in number and spirit. Incumbents become unbeatable. And elections become primarily symbolic exercises tying the peoples to the established order by making them feel they are participating in the electoral processes.

Thus, the traditional mechanism controlling executive power in democracies are largely absent or exist in a very weakened form in modern Africa. Moreover, virtually no political interest group actively exists to provide informal buffers against government abuse of power. No trade unions, business groups, professional associations or other continuously organized bodies of people seeking goals through political action exist in Africa in sufficient number or effective enough to counterbalance executive power. Students, who might be expected to play a liberalizing role and be capable of organized political action, are neutralized by their frequent dependence on government scholarships or threats of expulsion from the universities. Occasionally, transitory protest groups of urban workers or students arise to pursue a specific grievance, but they are quickly dispatched by government action, and thus deprived of the opportunity to consolidate and expand their bases of power.

FOOTNOTES: CHAPTER VI

[1]Peter H. Merkl, Political Continuity and
Change (New York: Harper & Row Publishers,
1967), pp. 191-192.

[2]"From Racism to Genocide: Extracts from
Reports of the International Commission of
Jurists," Transition, No. 49, p. 10.

[3]National Reformation Council Proclamation,
1972, Article 2.   Public Notice No. 28 of 1967,
Sierra Leone Gazette Extraordinary, Vol. XCVIII,
No. 29, June 25, 1967.

[4]Philip Short, Banda (Boston: Routledge &
Kegan Paul, 1974), p. 162-163.

[5]Ibid., pp. 52-53.   See also: T. David
Williams, Malawi, The Politics of Despair,
(Ithaca: Cornell University Press, 1978), pp.
196-230.

[6]United Nations, Official Records of the
General Assembly, Twenty-eighth Session, Speech by
President Mobutu before the General Assembly, October 4, 1973, p. 51.   See also: "Le Regime
Presidentiel Au Zaire," Centre de Researche et
d'Information Socio-politique, TA 144, December
20, 1972.

[7]B. O. Nwabueze, Presidentialism in
Commonwealth Africa (New York: St. Martin's Press,
1974), pp. 218-219.

[8]"Sierra Leone News," Sierra Leone High Commission, London, July, 1975, p. 8. See also: "Sierra Leona: One Party Moves," Africa, London, No. 50, October, 1975, p. 40.

[9]Ibid.

[10]For details, see "Sierra Leone News," Sierra Leone High Commission, London, August, 1975, p. 7.

[11]Ruth Morgenthau, "Single Party Systems in West Africa," American Political Science Review, June, 1961, No. 2, p. 294.

[12]B. O. Nwabueze, Presidentialism in Commonwealth Africa (New York: St. Martin's Press, 1974), p. 294.

[13]Jay E. Hakes, "The Weakness of Parliamentary Institutions As a Prelude to Military Coups in Africa: A Study in Regime Instability," Paper presented at Annual Meeting, Southern Political Science Association, November 11-13, 1971, p. 13.

[14]Raymond F. Hopkins, "The Role of the M.P. in Tanzania," The American Political Science Review, Vol. LXIV, No. 3, September, 1970, p. 756. See also: B.O. Nwabueze, Presidentialism in Commonwealth Africa (New York: St. Martin's Press, 1975), p. 286, and 268.

[15]Parliamentary Debates, Official Report, Vol. XVIII, No. 45, Proceedings of the Meetings of the House, November 22 - December 6, 1974, p. 155.

[16]Ibid., pp. 158-159.

[17]Parliamentary Debates, Official Report, Vol. XVI, No. 43, Republic of Sierra Leone, p. 87, (October 16, 1976);Vol. XIV, No. 41; P. 911,(August 13, 1974); P. 143, (June 27, 1974); P. 895; (August 6, 1974); P. 911, (August 13, 1974).

[18]William A. Hachten, Muffled Drums: The News Media in Africa (Ames: Iowa State University, 1971), p. 47.

[19]For details see: J.H. Proctor, "The National Members of the Tanzania Parliament: A Study of Legislative Behavior," The African Review, Vol. 3, No. 1, 1973, pp. 1-20. See also: Raymond F. Hopkins, "The Role of M.P. in Tanzania," American Political Science Review, Vol. LXIV, No. 3, September, 1970, p. 755.

[20]Raymond F. Hopkins, "The Role of the M.P. in Tanzania," American Political Science Review, Vol. LXIV, No. 3, September, 1970, p. 758.

[21]Thomas R. Dye and L. Harmon Ziegler, The Irony of Democracy, An Uncommon Introduction to American Politics (Belmont, California: Wadsworth Publishing Company, Inc., 1970), pp. 149-175.

[22]Ibid., p. 153.

[23]Gerald Pomper, Elections in America: Control and Influence in Democratic Politics (New York: Dodd, Mead & Co., 1968), pp. 254-255.

[24]"Kenya Newsletter," Embassy of the Republic of Kenya, Washington, D.C., Vol. 3, No. 5, October-November, 1974.

[25]"News Review," Tanzania Information Services, Daressalaam, Tanzania, No. 64, August, 1975, p. 1.

CHAPTER VII

AFRICA: THE VEILED CONTINENT

At one time Africa existed mainly in the imaginations of Europeans and Americans. Geographers and anthropologists knew something of this giant land, but most people relied on tales told by missionaries, sea captains, adventurers, and slavers. Black Americans, of course, carried within them the fragments of their personal history before enslavement. But, until recently, Africa was an object of popular speculation, unlimited by knowledge, fed by a fascination for the unknown. Truly, it was the dark continent.

Today, the speed of technological and political change, especially since 1945, has illuminated every corner of this once impenetrable vast continent. But another kind of darkness now limits our ability to learn the truth about modern African life. A veil of political expediency, social romanticism, and intellectual partisanship has obscured our vision of conditions and events.

Since the early 1960's, hundreds of books, monographs, and articles from American and European presses purport to describe different aspects of African life, society, and politics. Though many such works make useful contributions to our knowledge of modern African life, a large number lack depth of information about and understanding of African realities. If this book appears more critical of African post-independence political evolution than some, it is because it includes material that has been either left unexamined or underemphasized, or only discussed among scholars. There are several reasons for this. The more important ones are discussed below.

The approach and assumptions adopted by writers inevitably influence their scholarship. A basic problem confronting all students of African politics has been to identify the scope of their studies. And, in this respect, even the simplest organizing device--that of viewing Africa in terms of physical geography and limiting the scope of the work to the countries and peoples located physically on the African continent--is risky. As we have observed, the continent consists of over fifty different jurisdictions grouped into several different regions. The advisability of lumping together the study of the politics of states in Southern Africa with the rest of Africa may be legitimately questioned. Some may question the wisdom of including the Arab states of North Africa (Morocco, Algeria, Tunisia, Libya, and Egypt) in a study of African politics. The U.S.Department of State, for example, has an organizational framework which places them within the purview of the Bureau of the Middle East and South Asia. It feels that the national and international policies of these states can be better monitored and evaluated by regarding them as parts of the Middle East and not Africa. Once a writer commits himself to a particular scope, his views are affected by it. A book on the politics or history of Africa, limited basically to sub-Saharan Africa, for example, would exclude any detailed treatment of the role of the Arabs in the historical or political development of the continent and its peoples. It may also exclude the politics of states in the periphery--Sudan, Somalia, Chad, Mauritania--where, as was observed in the preceding pages, the relations between the Arabs and the Africans may be crucial to the

course of national politics. Little or no attention
would be drawn to the dichotomy between the
interests of the Arabs and the Africans and the
various areas of conflict between them. Similarly,
a book on sub-Saharan Africa which excludes from
its scope the political and economic system and
process of South Africa will tend to ignore not
only questions relating to majority rule and the
future of over four million non-Africans residing
there, but will also tend to underemphasize the
heavy dependency of black African states like
Lesotho, Botswana, Malawi, and Mauritius on
benefits directly or indirectly derived from the
modernized economy of South Africa.

The problem of identifying the appropriate
boundaries becomes further complicated when a
writer seeks to delineate the scope of his study
in human instead of physical dimensions. Under
this view, the study of Africa encompasses an
examination of the cultures and activities of
peoples of African origin, regardless of where
they may presently be physically located. In
strict logic, this approach should include Afro-
Americans in the United States, as well as others
of African origin presently living in the Caribbean
area and Latin America. It should also include
those among two million "Coloreds" residing
in the United Kingdom who are of African origin.
Simultaneously, it should exclude except perhaps
in a peripheral manner, consideration of the role
of whites in Southern African and of peoples of
Indian, Lebanese, and Syrian descent. Such
writers face the issue of whether to include two
to three million people of "mixed race" with
some African blood found in South Africa or the
millions of other such people found in Brazil,
Argentina, and other parts of the world. These
examples suffice to alert the reader to the
complex methodological problems writers who see
Africa in human geographical terms must resolve.
These issues are of such magnitude that they can
never be satisfactorily and consistently resolved.
In these circumstances, it is not surprising that
most writers who adopted this approach have

concentrated on the cultures of black sub-Saharan African states, Afro-Americans in the United States, and, in perfunctory fashion, on the people of African origin in the Caribbean area. In their writings they seek to draw attention to elements that are believed to be common to peoples of African origin residing in those parts of the world. In varying degrees of intensity they endorse the ideologies of black Negritude, black solidarity or pan-Africanism. In virtually all cases, the tone is militant, the contents anti-imperialist, replete with condemnations of non-blacks for their exploitation of the sons of African soil.

There are writers who take a triadic view and seek to describe and explain the global interaction and inter-penetration of economic, social, and political power by dividing it into three separate "worlds." They define the "First World" as comprising mainly the modern capitalistic democracies of North America and Western Europe. The economically advanced and organizationally sophisticated Communist countries (the Soviet Union and most of the countries in Eastern Europe) are described as the "Second World." And the economically under-developed and organizationally weak countries, located mostly in Asia, Africa, the Middle East, and Latin America, are the "Third World." The great majority of these Third World countries are viewed as facing basically similar problems of economic, political, and social development and their political leaders are generally viewed as engrossed in the task of selecting and implementing the appropriate strategies and techniques of modernization. In short, those who adopt the triadic view believe that there is a sufficient degree of commonality among the Third World countries in the ways in which they came into their present position (all were former colonies and were exploited by the colonizing powers), in how they compete with the economically advanced countries of the First and Second Worlds, and in their tendency to see themselves as a distinct group of countries, to justify their treatment as a single focus of study. They regard Africa as a necessary, important, and integral part of the Third World to be studied in conjunction with and not separated from the rest.

One of the major difficulties of this approach is that it is far easier to define the broad outlines of the Third World than its precise limits. While most African countries acquired their independence after World War II, the Latin American states achieved their sovereignty over a century ago. Their predominant culture is Latin and not indigenous. Their dominant groups are usually European in origin. And their relations with the United States are unique in world affairs, and unparalleled in the experiences of the Asian and African states. Moreover, their field of international concern has been generally limited to the hemisphere and their intercourse with Afro-Asian countries (with few exceptions) has been minimal. Similarly, the interests of nuclear or near-nuclear powers like the Peoples' Republic of China (with a population twice that of all African states put together), India and Brazil cannot possibly be identical with the rest of the Asian and African states.

Perhaps the clearest approach to defining the Third World is to stress its poverty and economic underdevelopment. Certainly, poverty is a great source of unity in bargaining and negotiating with the rich countries, especially if the results are likely to benefit all and help promote common goals. However, upon further examination, this perception appears overly simplistic, even deceptive. Poverty also can lead to disunity through increased competition for limited foreign aid or capital investment from the First World. Further, some Third World countries are poorer than the others, with the relatively rich among them unwilling to share their resources with the others. The Organization of Petroleum Exporting Countries

(OPEC) is composed exclusively of states from the Third World and since October, 1973, has success- fully asserted its monopolistic control over this vital source of energy and more than quintupled the price of crude oil. As a result, the oil ex- porting countries have enjoyed considerable influx of foreign capital into their countries-- funds that have so far largely been used developing their domestic economies, building up their armed forces, and to invest in major countries of the First World.

The triadic approach to the study of Africa may provide a broad general outline of the common bonds between the countries of Asia, Africa, and Latin America, and some insight into the common- alities in their goals, strategies, and tech- niques of development, and the instances where they sought to create a united front against the rich countries of the First and Second Worlds. But the study will, of necessity, be superficial because it is impossible to delve at any length into the num- erous political, economic, social, religious, and regional issues which divide the states and peoples of the Third World. In particular, all such studies avoid discussing the deep differences that exist between the Arabs and the Africans. The assumption that there is great commonality within the Third World tends to inhibit them from drawing attention to issues which divide the states and peoples of the Third World. Neither do they wish to accentuate the problems of tribalism which, as we have seen, affect politics throughout black Africa.

Following the practice adopted for other countries or continents, those scholars who specialize in studying Africa are known as "Africanists." Who are they and what is their background? For the sake of brevity, we have restricted ourselves to the United States in volume, one of the leading countries producing publications on Africa. Prior to World War II, scholarly interest in Africa among Americans was limited to anthropologists and other social scientists in predominantly black colleges. The anthropologists showed neither the desire nor the capacity to make use of their headstart and broaden their horizons to include post-World War II Africa. Nor did the faculty of black colleges--many of whom either were overworked and/or too old to make research trips to Africa and even to keep up with the rapid changes taking place there. Consequently, the task of carrying out major research on Africa fell to the younger generation of post-World War II graduates. They had the necessary training, time, and physical capacity to do so. They were understandably fascinated by new developments on the African continent and were interested in learning more. The late fifties and early sixties were also the years of successes in the civil rights movement in the United States and of high optimism over the future of race relations in the United States. A preponderant majority of those who were engaged in African studies during this period were hopeful, indeed euphoric about the prospect of democracy, economic development, and racial justice in independent Africa. They were politically liberal and humanistic in outlook. When they visited Africa or did extensive research work on the continent, they easily identified themselves with the ideas, hopes, and aspirations of African nationalist leaders. The charges of exploitation and repression made by these leaders against the colonial powers struck a familiar chord and they unquestioningly supported demands for total liberation of the continent from the clutches of the imperialistic and racist Europeans. The end of the fifties and the beginning of the sixties brought a large number of new books and articles on Africa into American universities, libraries, and homes in which, with few exceptions, the authors favored rapid decolonization, and while recognizing possible problems, they expressed confidence in the ability of the new African leaders to lead their countries and peoples out of the miseries of colonial repression and economic exploitation.

For example, in a book entitled <u>Africa: The Politics of Independence</u> published in 1961,

Immanuel Wallerstein contended that "though originally supported by the majority," the view that "Africans were incapable or not yet capable of exercising responsible self-rule and creating modern democratic societies" had "rapidly declined in acceptance, while a small group of impertinent settlers (European) still cling to it." [1] He then proceeded to explain that, despite the dominance of single parties, enactment of preventive detention laws, interference with the independence of the judiciary, and restrictions on formation of voluntary organizations in some independent African states (Ghana and Guinea provided examples in those days), it was incorrect to assume that African political systems would inevitably degenerate into dictatorships. According to him, "the one-party system in the African context is often a significant step toward the liberal state, not the first step away from it." [2] Subsequent events on the continent have demonstrated that such statements were premature. The rapid political and economic progress which they thought would inevitably follow independence has, as we have seen, not come about. However, just as it is difficult for an alcoholic to reform, this type of Africanist, accustomed to the influence of too much optimism and emboldened by detailed knowledge gained from limited residence in Africa, has also found intellectual sobriety an elusive goal. No better example exists of the intellectual blinders many Africanists wear than their treatment of the fall of the Emperor Haille Selassie of Ethiopia.

He was often described as an excellent example of charismatic African leadership, but on September 12, 1974, he was ousted from power by a Provisional Military Administrative Committee, which within less than three months, began to remake Ethiopia's political, social, and economic institutions. In doing so, on November 24, 1974, it executed, without trial, over sixty Ethiopians, including two former prime ministers, and other well-known government civil servants, military officers, and land owners. Hundreds others were arrested and put into prison. These actions were described by one such Africanist as merely "a political attempt to neutralise the tremendous power of the landowning class that could be expected to try and destroy socialism at its very birth." According to him, "the regime of Haille Selassie represented an oppressive feudal order which violated the human rights of peasants on a massive scale"[3] and that the acts of the new regime were necessary if they were to succeed in bringing about a fundamental transformation of the social system. Of course, no such transformation has in fact been brought about in Ethiopia; but we presume that most Africanists will leave any criticism of the existing Ethiopian regime until a new one comes into power and there is a need to rationalize the actions of this new regime. Emperor Selassie's regime was in fact oppressive. It did violate the rights of the workers and peasants. But it was rarely, if ever, criticized by these Africanists at the time the Emperor was in power. Initially, they ignored events and actions that did not fit their theories and expectations. When these became outmoded, they tried to explain away events as seen as exceptions to the rule.

The year 1979, witnessed a series of important changes in Africa. In Uganda, President Idi Amin was removed from power after the Tanzanian invasion. In the now renamed Central African Republic, Emperor Jean-Bedel Bokassa was replaced by the former President Mr. David Dacko, following elaborate arrangements made by France to ensure the change. And in Equatorial Guinea, President Francisco Macias Nguema fell victim of a coup engineered by his cousin. These events removed from the African scene some of the most violent and repressive regimes on the continent. During 1979, as we have noted, the Nigerian military leader, General Olusegun Obasanjo voluntarily handed over power to a civilian government headed by President Shehu Shagari. In September, 1979, the Ghanaian military leader Flight Lieutenant Jerry Rawlings,

407

who had come into power through a counter-coup a
few months earlier killing three former heads of
state, returned power to a civilian government
headed by President Dr. Hilla Limann promising
to return to the barracks. And in Upper Volta,
elections for the new President and legislature
were held.

All these events were sufficient to prompt
several Africanists to assert the beginning of a
new trend. The events, they claimed, justified
an attitude of guarded optimism, portended movement away from self-perpetuating single-party
and military regimes. Since the Tanzanian
invasion, there has been little indication of any
genuine movement towards democratic rule in
Uganda. In the Central African Republic, President
Dacko's actions, while he was in power prior to
the emergence of Emperor Bokassa, must speak
better than his words. He had, at that time,
ordered dissolution of all opposition parties and
banned all political parties except his own. In
January, 1980, the new Ghanaian President was
himself reported to have said, "Since June 4,
1979, I have been holding a time bomb in my hand.
Everyday before I go to bed, I hear there will be
a coup, but let anybody try and he will be
starved." In the circumstances, it would seem
presumptuous to suggest that the winds of democracy and human rights are blowing in Africa as
obviously as some Africanists like to believe.

Twenty years ago only a handful of black
Americans identified with Africa and the Africans;
today, however, despite their inadequate knowledge
of the diversity of this vast continent, a
majority of American blacks emphasize the kinship
and deep emotional attachment between themselves
and their "brothers and sisters" in Africa. As a
result, a new breed of Africanists have come into
being which demarcates the boundaries of African
studies in human terms. They have succeeded in
establishing departments offering courses in black
studies at many American universities and colleges.
Black Americans could acquire psychological identity

and cultural pride through associating themselves with independent Africa. They see the historical glories of Africa reflecting their own distinctive history and culture. The portrayal of Africa by this new breed of Africanists as an independent, resource rich, and vibrant continent with an exciting future is a source of pride and a glimpse of their own future. They perceive the African past and present as beyond reproach. They emphasize the wealth, glory, and civilization of the empires or kingdoms of Ghana, Mali, Songhay, Kitwara, and Zimbabwe which existed at various times in African history. In their writings, speeches, classrooms, and interviews, they portray a dazzling picture of contemporary Africa as a dynamic, progressive, and a humanistic society and, of course, favor an immediate end to white rule in South Africa. Moreover, with a view to regarding such an Africa as strictly their own, they adopted an exclusionist policy--manifested, for example, in demands that only those of African origin should be allowed to teach courses on Africa and/or that there be separate classes in black (including Afro-American) history and culture exclusively for black students. In an effort to limit the whites' interest in Africa, they enshroud their approaches in words, rituals, or modes of dress that are foreign to the Westerners by for example, selecting fairly common words from relatively obscure African languages and giving them a different twist, adopting a method of shaking hands novel to the Westerners (though quite common among the Muslims all over the world, including those of non-African origin), or by wearing "Afro" hairstyles and West African "dashikis." Le Roi Jones, an articulate and dynamic Afro-American artist has insisted, whenever invited by American university groups to speak, that he will accept the engagement only on condition that he be provided with black escorts, that blacks would sit in the front rows and the whites in the rear, and that, while at the university he would converse only with black students and professors.

To the extent that the writings and behavior of Afro-American Africanists help provide black Americans with a much-needed sense of identity and confidence, they, of course, perform a very useful purpose. But the distortions of African history and politics that intrude into their writings and speeches make a mockery of scholarly integrity and objectivity. They rarely, for example, discuss arbitrary exercises of power, nepotism, and triba ism in African politics. In a sense, from their point of view, total silence on such matters is the best strategy.

It must be added that it is not only the Afro-Americans who have succumbed to the temptation to achieve their objectives with one neat stroke. There are also quite a few African Africanists (mostly from Nigeria, Ghana, and Kenya) now permanently settled in the United States who have found it convenient to join this movement. Taking advantage of the increased interest in African culture among Afro-Americans, of demands by black students that only blacks teach courses on Africa, and of the extraordinary interest shown by university administrators in recruiting black faculty members (partly to comply with Federal government Affirmative Action requirements), many black Africans have succeeded in obtaining employment at American universities and research centers, often at salaries far in excess of what they would command at home. A number have also found it profitable to make rounds of American universities as guest speakers, with stipends paid out of appropriations for operation of local black studies centers or student or faculty organizations. They usually tell their audiences what those who organized their speeches (usually the directors or leaders of black studies groups) expect them to say. In private conversations, especially with those who know a good deal about Africa, they may express very different views.

The most indefensible obstacle to research in modern Africa is the deliberate policy of governments to obstruct any scholarship which might be critical of them. African governments have become increasingly restrictive granting visas to researchers. This is particularly true of sensitive disciplines like politics. The visa applicants are required, among other things, to disclose the topics of their research, sources of funds, and names of local contacts, to affiliate with a university in the host country, and to specify whether or not the research findings will be made available to the host government before publication. Often it takes as long as a year to obtain a visa. At times, it is simply denied with no explanation. This is, of course, the right of every sovereign government. But it is undeniable that such actions on the part of the African governments and the restrictions imposed by them on researchers to whom they would issue visas are designed directly or indirectly, to force scholars either to abandon field research altogether or frame their projects and conclusions to meet the preferences of leaders in power. Whatever the case, free pursuit of scholarship, especially in sensitive areas like tribalism, nepotism, and, arbitrary exercise of power is almost impossible. Scholars however are not the only ones refused visas. The same is true for those representing international agencies who may seek to enter an African state to investigate an incident or complaint. In a letter to the Daily Telegraph (January 19, 1971) a fiance of one of the Zanzibari girls who had been forced to marry African members of the Revolutionary Council wrote:

> "We have appealed for help for the kidnapped girls to various international bodies including the United Nations, also to various Heads of State of Africa and the Commonwealth and also to the Pope, but so far everyone seems to be quiet."[4]

One reason why everyone was quiet was Tanzania's conception and exercise of its sovereign power to refuse entry visa to any person without assigning any reason. Officials of the International Red Cross were thus unable to visit Zanzibar and

411

question the various parties involved in this
situation. Meanwhile, of course, it was open
to the Tanzanian government to tell the world
its version of the story. In August, 1972, for
example, a high ranking Zanzibari official told
visiting members of the press (who had been carefully selected and their movements controlled)
that it was untrue that the girls had attempted
to run away, that they were living happily with
their husbands, and that Zanzibar was going to be
an example of racial integration and harmony in
Africa.

For many researchers, newspapers, both local
and foreign, constitute an important and primary
source of raw data. Several foreign newspapers
and their reporters (e.g. <u>Christian Science
Monitor</u>, <u>La Monde</u>, the <u>London Times</u>, the <u>New York
Times</u>, and <u>The Observer</u>) have acquired a well-
deserved reputation for objective reporting of
events in Africa. But, partly because of
obstacles placed by African governments upon their
activities, their in depth coverage of black
African politics has reduced to almost a trickle.
Restrictions on the issue of visas, censorship
laws and regulations, arbitrary and frequent exercise of powers of deportation have all made it
very difficult for them to critically report on a
consistent basis over a reasonably long period
of time on black Africa. In a piece which for the
first time drew attention to instances which had
taken place long ago of abuses of power by Kenya
government leaders, (<u>Washington Post</u>, September 28,
1974) David B. Ottaway included the following
astute observation:

"Practically nothing has been written in the
Western press about the widespread abuse of
power and office (in Kenya) because foreign
journalists residing in Nairobi, Kenya say
they are under constant threat of expulsion
for any criticism of the government and
particularly of President Kenyatta. This
reporter was repeatedly warned by his
colleagues that the price for breaking this

story almost certainly was expulsion from
Kenya and from the two other countries in
the East African Federation, (there is not
a Federation in the strict sense though
there is apparently an understanding that
if one expels a reporter, the other two
will not harbor him) Tanzania and Uganda.
The government's way of dealing with unwanted
journalists and businessmen is to declare
them "prohibited immigrants" which means
they cannot re-enter the country."[5]

At one time or another virtually all African
states have exercised this power, often on
spurious grounds. For example, in March, 1974,
Lord Chalfont, a BBC reporter, was banned from
Kenya for producing a documentary which referred
to "the somewhat intolerant attitudes of the
present regime." In Tanzania, in June, 1974,
David Martin who had been reporting about Africa
from Tanzania for the previous ten years was
summarily expelled on twenty-four hours' notice
for, of all things, reporting of a purge that
was then taking place in Uganda. In 1976 and
1977, Zaire expelled dozens of journalists for
unfavorable reporting on civil war in the country;
Ethiopia asked all resident western correspondents
in the country to leave, Nigeria threw out the
bureau Chief of Reuters by putting him, his wife,
and eight-year old child in a canoe headed for
Benin, and Ghana expelled from the country
journalists bent on reporting hunger and star-
vation in its rural areas. In practice, with a
few exceptions, resident foreign reporters refrain
from being overly critical of the governments in
black Africa and even when they do so they are
extremely cautious of what and how they say it.

A number of African governments are also
known to use a variety of techniques to dissuade
foreign reporters from sending out derogatory
reports. Some of these were vividly brought to the
world's attention by a journalist covering Muhammed
Ali's celebrated championship fight against George
Foreman (in this respect sports reporters seem to

be more willing and daring) in Zaire working for
The Sun (Chicago):

> "If they do not like some things you have
> written, your story has a way of getting
> lost. In a crisis, they simply pull the
> plug. Then you cannot phone it in either.
> I tried RCA Telex. No luck; they were not
> getting through. I tried ITT Telex. Same.
> Then, I tried my last resort, and usually
> best--the telephone. Usually it took 20
> minutes to get through to New York. One
> hour passed. Two. I kept nudging the
> French-speaking operator. "Problem" said
> the male voice. Then "general breakdown,"
> then a giggling laughter which annoyed the
> hell out of me.
>   It gets to you. They begin crossing
> out of the story references to the big
> beetles and lizards one British newsman
> found in his shower, and the descriptive
> passages about how the native women walk
> for miles with wood piled atop their head.
> The government wants to be known as pro-
> gressive, sophisticated, but it is not."6

In 1979, Senegal enacted a new law applicable
to the press. Under its provisions, all publications must be submitted for approval to the
Minister of Interior, the Minister of Justice,
and the Solicitor General. It also created
a commission, presided over by a magistrate, which
would have the power to refuse to renew or revoke
a journalist's press card if he has proved himself
to be "irresponsible." A number of African governments also require that before entering the
country, a foreign correspondent must submit a
full itinerary of what he wishes to do, who he
wishes to see, and what questions he proposes to
ask. Deviations are discouraged.

The situation at the local level is far worse.
In the first place, the total number of newspapers
in Africa ironically has been on the decline--there
were 220 in 1964, and only 179 in 1975. Second,

and more important, is the fact that "African newspapers which were vigorously in the vanguard of the
nationalist struggle for independence now have
relatively less freedom to publish under indigenous
African governments they helped to found than they
did under white colonialists."[7]

Some African governments have taken over all
privately owned newspapers; some have established
their own newspapers under Ministries of Information;
some have strict censorship requiring, in practice,
submission of all articles to the government cen-
sors before publication; some control the editorial
policies of local newspapers by controlling the
appointments of editors-in-chief; some have enacted
laws and issued guidelines which the local journalists are expected to adhere to; and some are known
to have used a variety of physical, psychological
and other pressures (including in quite a few cases
murder and preventive detention) to dissuade them
from publishing material unacceptable to those in
power. And in this respect, despite their pious
proclamations of belief in humanism and the freedom of the press, even leaders like Dr. Kenneth
Kaunda and Dr. Boigny are not blameless. Kaunda,
for example, had no qualms firing the editor of
the Zambian Mining Mirror for criticizing his
government and appointing a person of his own
choice in that position. He also appointed his
former United Nations representative as the
editor-in-chief of the Times of Zambia. In the
Ivory Coast, President Boigny is empowered by law
to ban "any publication which brings about a disregard of the laws of the country or injures the
morals of the population or casts discredit on the
political institutions or their working" and uses
it to discourage criticism against his government.

The result is that even in those countries
where privately owned newspapers still exist,
because of the conditions under which they must
operate, African newspapermen have become experts
at self-censorship. A number of them, knowing that
otherwise it would be difficult for them to survive,
print only what they know would be acceptable

to the government. Others, who still have some
pride left in them, refrain from publishing anything that can even remotely be interpreted as
critical of the policies and practices of the
existing regime. Such newspapers, if any of the
readers would like to discover for themselves,
usually contain columns and columns on beauty
contests held all over the world, however distant
from the African continent with large pictures of
the various participants. Editorial comments
would be few and far between, often written after
discreet consultations with the appropriate
government officials (e.g. Senegal, Cameroon).
In these circumstances, it is not surprising that
most African newspapers contain considerable
material on racism in Southern Africa, but little,
if anything, on tribalism, corruption, and black
racism. As a result, such topics cannot easily
be researched and documented by using newspapers,
foreign or local, as the primary sources.

     All Africanists, regardless of their
orientation and research topics, face the general
problem of a lack of resources that are often
taken for granted in Western societies. For
example, there are only a few African countries
which produce verbatim reports of the proceedings
of their legislative assemblies and, those that do,
rarely if ever produce them within a reasonably
short time. Not a single African country produces
documents on foreign policy as the United States
does.

     In recent years, one of the most important
methodological innovations in the social sciences
has been the development of survey research
techniques. In contemporary Africa, to discover
scientific truths through the application of
quantitative survey research concepts and techniques is far more difficult than is the case in
the West. Great distances and poor communications; difficulty of operationally defining and
translating vital terms and concepts in African
languages; unwillingness of respondents to convey
their ideas honestly and truthfully, are only

some of the problems encountered.

Demographic data are often relied upon by researchers in selecting samples and in relating findings in a village or a small town to the whole country. The utility of a survey depends on the validity, reliability, and general appropriateness of available data. In this case, the validity of the findings of the survey would depend, to a very great extent, on the accuracy of the basic data on total population. And these can rarely be relied upon. As a Ghanaian graduate student once said, "It does not matter what the interviewers say. My mother will never give them a correct answer as to how many children she has." In 1972, a group of Africanists produced a five hundred page handbook entitled <u>Black Africa</u>: <u>A Comparative Handbook</u> which sought to incorporate the latest statistical information available for thirty-two independent black African states.[8] Relying on the latest United Nations estimate, it indicated the total population of Nigeria in 1970 as 55,070,000. The 1975 census held by the Nigerian government found the total population of the country to be over eighty million. This would represent an annual increase of nine per cent per year, a rate which, even for a country like Nigeria, is so disproportionately high as to justify our questioning of at least one, if not both, of these figures. Often, even when documents or figures are known to be in existence, it is not easy to obtain access to them, even when they do not relate to aspects that could reasonably be considered to be involving national security. In a comment on the research difficulties of scholars interested in African states, Mr. El-Erian, a well-known Egyptian international lawyer, once observed that:

"...The O.A.U. (Organization of African Unity) documents, some of which you will be surprised to note, are not available, even in Addis Ababa. You write to the Secretariat for documents which are vital to your research when you are studying some aspects of the O.A.U. and you want to make a reference...

417

you get no reply for six or nine months...
and eventually if you run elsewhere into a
member of the Secretariat he will say, Oh,
it is with somebody, I will check up when I
get back to Addis....If at O.A.U. level we
meet with difficulties looking for O.A.U.
materials, how much more when we are looking
for other documents."[9]

Ev n when the figures are available, it does not
necessarily mean that they would be made available
to researchers, especially when the research
involves aspects that might prove embarrassing to
those in power. One of the authors was confronted
with several ingenious obstacles when he tried to
obtain figures relating to citizenship applications
in Sierra Leone.

African leaders have been acutely aware of the
usefulness of the United Nations both as a source
of aid (througl its specialized agencies) and as
an instrument to cultivate world public opinion in
their favor. They have cleverly, if not craftily,
exploited the differences prevailing among the
world powers and made exceedingly sophisticated
use of their voting strengths both in having
resolutions of their liking adopted and in suppressing even the discussion of those that were
likely to result in damage to their prestige or
interests. In lengthy speeches before various organs of this international body, they have vigorously presented their point of view. They have
managed to have the international organization regard the question of civil, political, and human
rights in Southern Africa as a priority issue
and have helped stimulate a U.N. obsession for
questions of the illegal and immoral exercise of
power by a racist minority, 'and for the liberation
of the unlawfully occupied Portuguese territories
of Angola, Mozambique, and Guinea-Bissau (until
their eventual acquisition of sovereign status
in the early seventies). Simultaneously, they
have managed to prevent the organization from
even discussing allegations of gross violations of
human rights in black African states. For example,

418

the whole Nigerian/Biafran War (in which several foreign states were directly or indirectly involved) was accepted by the United Nations as a matter which was essentially within the domestic jurisdiction of the Federation of Nigeria, and was not even fully discussed in the world body. The expulsion by the government of Uganda of over 50,000 Asians residing there, regardless of whether they were Ugandan citizens, on three months' notice and confiscation of all their assets as "abandoned property," was similarly ignored in the world body. When a British representative on the United Nations Human Rights Sub-Commission on the Prevention of Discrimination and Protection of Minorities, Mr. Robert Rhodes-James, proposed that a telegram of protest be sent to President Amin, he was defeated by a vote of fourteen to one with six abstentions. The Nigerian representative raised strong objection even to its being placed on the agenda because he did not feel "the matter was related to human rights," although the International Commission of Jurists has had no difficulty in ruling that the expulsions did violate article two of the Universal Declaration of Human Rights. Since 1967, an international Ad Hoc Working Group of Experts on South African prisoners and detainees has been collecting information from all sources, including non-governmental organizations, to expose violations by the government of South Africa. But no attempt has been tolerated by the African states to carry out similar activities with regard to hundreds of political and other prisoners languishing in the jails in states under black African rule. As Warren Warrenstein has noted:

> According to news accounts, the Sub-Commission on the Prevention of Discrimination and Protection of Minorities, since 1972, has drawn the attention of the Commission to cases other than violations in southern Africa, Israeli Occupied Territories, and Chile. These other cases have included gross violations of human rights in Burundi and Uganda and much more minor violations in Tanzania. However,

419

none of these cases has ever been discussed in public.....This has amounted, at the Commission level, to a continuation of the pernicious double standard which has characterized African policy on human rights at the UN. [10]

The course of post-World War II international politics has been characterized by increasing competition between the United States and the Soviet Union, and the Peoples' Republic of China. Each of these world powers has been heavily involved in a continuous struggle and competition to win friends and increase its influence among the new states of Africa. The result has been that each has been very selective in its criticisms of African states. In particular, none has been willing to be critical of the actions of those African leaders that are "friendly" to it. President Mobutu of Zaire and the United States perhaps provide an excellent example. Despite the large number of violations of international law and human rights described in the preceding pages, the United States has so far refrained from levelling any criticism whatsoever against the regime of Sese Seko Mobutu. He has, on the contrary, often been lavishly praised.[11] To a limited extent this is also true of the Western European countries. There has been intense and sometimes brutal competition between France, Britain, Germany, and Italy, constituting almost a new scramble for Africa, for establishing investment spheres, export and import markets, and for political and ideological influence in these new states.[12] Not all Western countries have therefore been equally willing to criticize black African states, only those whose oxes were being gored. African leaders have been opportunistic in taking advantage of these "inter-imperialist contradictions" just as they have of the triangular competition between the three (or two and a half) superpowers.

Most Africanists in the United States prefer to ignore, especially in their writings, the less pleasant aspects of African rule. A number of them seem to think that to do otherwise would not be in good taste. They are willing to take their own government to task for the simplest violations, but judge the actions of the Africans with a more flexible standard. In their eyes, the historically downtrodden Africans have acquired an aura of martyrdom. They still share the image of the "innocent" African who can never do anything wrong. We have sought to explain the behavior of at least two major groups of Africanists. It is difficult to pinpoint the reasons for almost similar behavior on the part of majority of the rest. One cannot help but wonder whether feelings of guilt for the past misdoings of their fore-fathers--slavery, imperialism, and racism--have something to do with their present behavior.

Upon independence African states and their leaders were confronted with massive problems. To a large extent, these emanated from the continent's physical, social, economic, and political geographies.

Physiographical and climatic factors have had considerable influence upon the history and development of this immense continent. In general, the major landscape features of Africa can be classi- fied into plains, plateaus, and mountains. It has no extensive plains or lowlands, especially alluvial plains such as those of the Ganges in India or the Mississippi in the United States. A narrow and discontinuous "coastal plain," aver- aging a width of only twenty miles rims the con- tinent with the ground rising up fairly quickly to the plateau. In fact in no other continent does the area of the plain below six hundred feet represent so small a proportion of the total area. With the exception of isolated ranges of mountains, the African plateau, which dominates the interior of the continent, ranges between one to five thousand feet. However, very often a plateau at one level changes rapidly to one at a different level with a sharp "step" between the two. Most African rivers, though fairly long, flow in gorges and are frequently interrupted by falls, rapids, and cataracts, especially nearer the coast when they drop into the coastal plain. African rivers are not only long but also broad. The River Gambia, a comparatively small river in West Africa, is between six to ten miles wide, thus making the erection of bridges a monumental task. Africa's coastline, which measures 16,000 miles, is mostly without deep penetrating indentations or well defined peninsulas. There are coastal stretches of as long as a thousand miles with virtually no sheltered, natural harbors. Moreover, the sea near the shores is often shallow, forcing ocean-going ships to lay anchor and remain some distance from shore, making it necessary for passengers as well as cargo to be taken to and from the ships in small motorboats, tugboats, or even canoes. Africa's lakes, rivers, coastline, are, therefore, of only marginal utility as routes of communication. It would of course be possible to counteract these natural barriers by building bridges across these broad rivers, interconnecting railway lines which would enable river traffic to avoid rapids, falls, and cataracts, and by constructing deepwater ports or artificial harbors. Many of these problems could also be remedied by expansion of air transportation. Today, African air transport accounts for less than five per cent of the world's total air traffic. The situation could, of course, be radically changed by African airlines' (several now exist--Air Afrique, Air Zaire, Ghana Airways, Nigeria Airways, Ethiopian Airline, Air Malawi, etc.) developing sufficient capital and technical resources to expand internal services, though the low level of passenger load factor may force them to keep their operating costs as low as possible.

Deserts cover two-fifths of the continent. The Sahara, which divides the Arab north from the rest of Africa and where temperatures reach into the hundreds, has never been an attractive trade route. Except in the oases, the deserts lack significant vegetation. Another twenty per cent of Africa is covered by dense equatorial forests stretching across the whole of the West Coast to the center of the continent. Mosquitoes, tsetse flies, crocodiles, and hippos make crossing the forests on a regular and permanent basis a hazardous proposition.

The prevalence of dense, luxuriant forests, along with long, broad rivers and lakes might lead one to think that these constitute the most fertile parts of Africa. The reality is almost the opposite. Of all continents, Africa has the greatest percentage of land area in the tropics. Fully seventy-five per cent of Africa lies between the Tropic of Cancer and the Tropic Capricorn holding the world's largest desert and the most impenetrable swamps. The desert areas, with very little rainfall, demand artificial irrigation. In the equatorial areas, persistent and heavy rainfall often accompanied by violent thunderstorms creates floods, destroys crops, and more importantly, washes away fertilizing minerals such as potash and lime, which, at high temperatures, are soluble in water. Leaves, twigs, and branches fallen from trees, decaying grass and roots, all contribute to the presence of humus which provides fertility to the soil. Unfortunately, under warm conditions this humus is easily destroyed by further decay. The hot tropical afternoon sun rapidly destroys this valuable substance, particularly in those areas where the forest cover has been removed. In the steppelands, which constitute another one-fifth of the continent, the problem of finding adequate moisture is also prevalent. In these arid or semi-arid regions, evaporation causes certain salts to accumulate in the upperlayers of the soil making it even more complex than usual to provide artificial irrigation. In the mountain areas, the floor of mountain valleys carry dense forest but it usually thins out with increasing altitude until there is almost no vegetation at the highest levels. Water in the agricultural sense is therefore scarce over much of Africa--it is a case of either too little or too much. Although Africans occupy almost a quarter of the world's land surface, it is by no means an unmitigated advantage. However, through the use of modern science and technology it would be possible to make the physical environment increasingly permissive and the land more productive, make the desert fit for agricultural production, introduce perennial irrigation schemes to counter seasonality of rainfall, build dams and reservoirs to prevent flooding, implement reafforestation programs, and adopt various other schemes to assure effective use of the soils.

No book on Africa can be complete without some reference to wildlife. Undoubtedly, the continent has the greatest and the most varied reserves of wildlife on earth. It is mandatory for the human race to preserve this unique heritage. Some of the species are already rare. The sights of wildlife in their natural habitat--animals grazing across vast grasslands, in the valleys of the mighty rifts, on the slopes of mountains are indeed beautiful and worthy of our affection and tenderness. But there is also another side to this haunting beauty of African wildlife--a side which rarely enters the minds of most non-Africans. The wild game are also carriers of disease. The fur, feathers, and hides of these animals communicate diseases not only to other animals but also to human beings. As it is, the continent is already plagued with diseases like sleeping sickness, malaria, yaws, leprosy, bilharziasis, and yellow fever and this only adds one more constraint imposed by nature on African development. The wandering untamed animals damage farmland; marauding trampling elephants tear up the land, often destroying crops ready for harvesting; the rhinos, lions, and other animals eat up the livestock; and the baboons and monkeys constitute a permanent menace. It is possible for the Africans to protect themselves, their crops, their lands, and their livestock while at the same time preserving this unique heritage. It is possible for humans to live and flourish side by side with the wildlife. It would entail setting up reserves where the animals can live unrestricted and unmolested by poachers and hunters, maintaining strict control over conditions of sanitation and health, and keeping a watchful persistent eye on their rates of reproduction. Not only in East Africa but also in other parts of Africa such game parks could also be developed and effectively used to promote tourism, provided adequate hotels and other services usually expected by tourists all around the world are made available and are satisfactorily operated.

It is virtually impossible to give an accurate figure of the total population of Africa, though, one can safely say that it is somewhere between 425 and 475 million. Africa, occupying almost a quarter of the world's land surface, accommodates only about ten per cent of the global population. Its average density works out to be lower than that of any other continent except Australia. This leads some (and especially those who tend to look at the continent as if it were a single homogeneous entity with plenty of fertile land, rivers, lakes, and forests) to conclude that sparsely populated Africa does not have a population problem, or that a substantial increase in population might even by advantageous for economic progress. In reality, the African population is unevenly distributed across the continent.13 In some states (Rwanda, Burundi, Zanzibar (Tanzania), Mauritius, and parts of Nigeria and Egypt) the population density is almost as high as in parts of Asia and Latin America, while in others (Mali, Sudan, Botswana, Chad) it is even less than ten persons per kilometer. Within most states, too, the population is unevenly distributed. The density is uniformly high in the coastal plains, and low in the deserts and semi-arid grasslands. In view of the continent's physical geography, such uneven distribution is understandable. What is irrational, however, is the tendency of some to place heavy emphasis on average national and continental figures instead of on the actual carrying capacity of the land. As William A. Hance has correctly pointed out:

"Of what use is an average density figure for

Tanzania, for example, where one fifth of the population lives on less than two per cent of the area and two-thirds on ten percent while about two-thirds of the country is virtually uninhabited? Or how relevant in Kenya, where 36 percent of the population lives at densities of over 400 per square mile on less than two percent of the area?" [14]

According to him, "it is meaningless to compare the densities on Africa's leaches latosols with densities on the rich alluvials of monsoon Asia and conclude that Africa does not suffer from population problems."[15] He reaches the conclusion that forty-seven per cent of the African land and forty-five per cent of the population are in fact presently experiencing population pressure. In 1979, the population of Kenya was 15.8 million (with 80 per cent of the people living on 17 per cent of the land considered cultivable); and its population growth rate, at about 3.4 per cent per year, will, unless effective population control measures are taken in the meantime, result in at least doubling of its total population by the year 2000. It is expected to level off at 121 million in 2120. Other parts of Africa--Nangodi in Northeast Ghana, the Eastern Nigeria, Bukoba district in Tanzania, and the Sokoto area in Northern Nigeria--are also in a situation not too unlike the one in the cultivable areas of Kenya.

At present, the rate of population growth in Africa is second only to Latin America. Effective 1980, population growth rates are expected to decline in all continents except Africa. Between 1980 and 1985, its population is expected to rise at the rate of 2.96 percent a year. In the future, development of new drugs, successful eradication of malaria and yellow fever and other diseases, and improvements in sanitation and health services are bound to bring about a reduction in the death rate (especially infant mortality rates which are still high) as well as an increase in life expectancy (which is still about 45 compared to over 65 in the West), so that the rate of population growth is likely to increase, even if the fertility rates remain at the same level. According to many studies, African populations will not stabilize until late twenty-second century. Ethiopia, at 29 million in 1976, is not expected to stabilize until it reaches 184 million in 2175. Zaire at 25 million in 1979 will stabilize at 157 million in 2165, and Tanzania will level off from 15 million in 1976 at 113 million in 2160. Nigeria will stabilize in 2155 at 478 million. By contrast, the populations for developed countries are expected to stabilize early in the twenty-first century at levels only slightly higher than in 1979.

Of course, the situation and seriousness of the problem will vary among African states. In order to absorb this increase, most countries will need to undertake massive efforts and to find additional capital to educate children, provide adequate food (by increasing productivity per acre through the use of fertilizers, insecticides, artificial irrigation, hydro-electric power or other sources of energy, or by finding ways of cultivating areas that are now untillable through prevention of soil damage caused by overstocking, overgrazing, and excessive cultivation), remedy problems of unemployment and under-employment in both urban and rural areas, promote growth in non-agricultural sectors of their economies and seek to maintain minimum services and existing rates of per capita income. Alternatively, African leaders will be forced to recognize the existence of the problem and to adopt policies designed to reduce population pressure through family planning and birth control. Even then progress towards controlling the growth can neither be assured nor will the path be simple, inexpensive, or short in duration. The adoption of programs designed to curb population growth also brings African leaders in direct confrontation with those who believe that the white man has a Machiavellian motive in advocating and supporting family planning for the blacks and who may view establishment of

427

family planning clinics as simply a part of the
white man's conspiracy aimed at elimination of the
black race and those African leaders implementing
such policies as stooges of the imperialists and
neo-colonists.

Almost eighty percent of people in Africa live
in rural areas, making it the least urbanized of
all the continents. Under these circumstances
it is easy to rush to the conclustion that Africa
does not have the kind of urban problems which
seem to be the scourge of most of the cities
in the Western world. Nothing could be less
true. In most African states, one city dominates
the scene. The population of Tanzania's capital--
Daressalaam--is approximately seven times that of
its second largest city, Tanga. Uganda's second
largest city, Jinja, has only one-fifth of the
population of its capital, Kampala. African
capitals are not only seats of government but are
also focal poirts of industry, commerce, education,
and entertainment. They provide the best available means of communication, easy access to government offices and banking institutions, and contain
the largest consumers' market in the country.
Consequently, most of the industrial and commercial
enterprises are reluctant to establish anywhere
except in the capital or in the areas within its
immediate vicinity. To persuade them to relocate
is even more difficult. People seem to be flock-
ing into the capitals. For example, over sixteen
percent of Senegal's population lives in the
capital city of Dakar, consuming two-thirds of the
country's total production of electricity. Over
forty-five percent of Ghana's college graduates
live in the capital city of Accra. Between 1952
and 1963 the population of Lagos, Nigeria, grew at
a rate of over 8.6 percent per annum, the metropolitan population at 11.5 percent per annum and
the fringe population beyond the greater city
limits grew by no less than 19.2 percent per annum.
In Zambia, the population of the capital city of
Lusaka virtually doubled between 1963 and 1969.
The situation is the same in other African capitals.

Surveys carried out in the Ashanti areas of Ghana have revealed that fully 95 per cent of students expected to leave for the city upon completion of their primary education. The situation is similar in Malawi. The lure of the cities is irresistible. For the young, the cities provide a hope (however misplaced) of escaping rural poverty, avoiding social controls, obtaining education, and making enough money to live in relative security. It is not at all uncommon for Africans, both educated and uneducated, to explain their actions in terms like "In my village, people do not even have electricity, and there is nothing to do at night"; "In Lagos, there are lively entertainments and girls and cinemas"; "Freedom--Make I go Freetown, make I go free"; or as one of the young women migrants put it "To eat in fashionable hotels, to have men who wear white collars to their jobs as lovers, men who could spend."[16] Perhaps there is nothing intrinsically wrong in moving to the cities for such reasons. But such migrants do aggravate the problems of unemployment and impose heavy strains on available housing and related services like street lighting, road construction, water supply and sewage. They come to the cities expecting heaven on earth, but, in most cases, find only hopelessness and poverty worse than what they left behind in the villages. Most live in urban slums (called shantytowns, compounds). It is only a question of time before they are disenchanted, move to easier ways of making money, and swell the city's rates of crime, prostitution, and drunkenness. In Lagos, Nigeria (characterized by the World Health Organization as one of the unhealthiest cities in the world), at one time armed robbery became so prevalent that the government introduced capital punishment as a penalty for such offenses. In Nairobi, Kenya, in order to curb growing urban unemployment, the government ordered employers to increase their personnel by ten per cent regardless of whether they needed additional workers. Simplistic policies like these may serve as stop-gap measures but are unlikely to lead to permanent solutions to Africa's problems of urbanization and urbanism, many of which are not too unlike those faced by cities in other countries and can only be effectively solved through application of appropriate techniques and methodologies of urban and regional planning and/or rural development. These, of course, are expensive and time-consuming propositions.

The overall illiteracy rate among the Africans is in the region of 70 to 75 per cent. The rate, of course, differs from country to country, with some of the advanced coastal states having an edge over the others. The rate is invariably higher among women than among men. Most of the education, especially at higher levels, is in one of the foreign languages--English, French, or Arabic--if only because most indigenous languages--and there are over six hundred of them--have very little literature, or as in the case of a number of them, not even a written script. At the same time, not all persons residing within any particular country speak the same indigenous language, and the fact that a small percentage of the people can read and write or possess a working knowledge of one of the foreign languages to a certain extent sets them apart from the preponderant illiterate majority. Prior to independence, the major burden of educating the sub-Saharan Africans was borne by Christian missionary schools. While not minimizing their contributions to African education, it should be remembered that the primary task of the missionaries was to spread Christianity. One of the authors can assert from his personal experiences that the missionary schools in Africa were not averse to giving preferential treatment, in terms of education and grants, to Africans who embraced the Christian faith. Nor was it uncommon for Africans to convert to Christianity to obtain access to education or jobs, both at home and overseas. The net result is that most educated sub-Saharan Africans, especially those who received their education in the pre-independence period, are Christians, and that among them there are many whose conversion to Christianity was based more on expediency than

any real change in beliefs or values. The
"nationalization" of missionary schools which, as
we have noted, took place in several African states
has merely increased the obligations of the government to provide the necessary educational facilities and services.

The majority of sub-Saharan Africans profess
faiths and beliefs traditional to their own tribe.
Many attribute spiritual personality not only to
men but also to animals (and consequently came to
be referred to, especially in the West, as
Animists). The tendency among the Western
missionaries to disparage and discount African tribal religious practices as entirely irrational
and/or undesirable has resulted in christianized
Africans playing a dualist role--that of a Christian for some purposes and of a traditionalist for
others, one played openly, and the other quietly
and surreptitiously.

Most of the people in Northern Africa
(the conventional Muslim line being 10° above
the Equator) believe in Islam. The Islamic
religion, strictly adhered to, demands kneeling
before Allah facing Mecca at least four or five
times a day, abstention from alcoholic beverages or other intoxicants, having no more than
four wives at a time, treating all of them
equally, and fasting from dawn to dusk every year
during the holy month of Ramadhan. Although
Islam has spread south of the 10° line to as far
as Mozambique in the east and Senegal in the
west, it too has been accepted only partially by
the Sub-Saharan Africans. Many Negroid Muslims
are indifferent to prayer, consume liquor, take
the daily fasts of Ramadhan lightly, and either
tolerate continuation of tribal customs allowing
more than four wives at a time or insist on
monogamy on the grounds of progress and modernity. At the same time, however, they do regard
themselves as Muslims, celebrate the festivals
of Idd, and comply at least with the Islamic
religious requirements of death and burial
ceremonies. The religious, linguistic, educational,

and, of course, tribal differences prevailing among the people of most African states cannot help but affect politics and make the task of the African leaders that much more difficult.

Africa is one of the least developed continents in the world. It occupies almost a quarter of the world's land surface and contains approximately ten per cent of the global population, but it produces only about two to three per cent of the world's output.

In terms of mineral production, it is important not to exaggerate the importance of the continent. Africa contributes less than twenty per cent of the world's total mineral production. Not all Africa is rich in minerals. These are very unevenly distributed over the continent. Minerals contribute less than one per cent of the gross national product of at least twenty African states. On the other hand, a handful of states-- Libya, South Africa, Zaire, Algeria, Zambia and more recently Nigeria--are responsible for over eighty per cent of the continent's total mineral production. Another commonly held misconception is that Africa is equally endowed with all types of minerals. So far, five minerals (oil, copper, gold, diamonds, and iron) have constituted no less than ninety per cent of the continent's total mineral exports. The continent may, as some contend, be richly endowed with natural resources. But any substantial increase in mineral production in the near future seems doubtful. Some of the easily accessible minerals have by now already been thoroughly mined and it is unrealistic to expect to discover new rich deposits which can be exploited without taking into account questions of economic feasibility. Nor can it be assumed that the deposits presently being mined will continue in the future to remain unexhausted. Even if we were to assume that Africa is indeed a reservoir of increasingly scarce natural resources and these are bound to be discovered in the near future, the problems of finance and technology associated with the exploitation and marketing of these minerals

would still need to be surmounted. There is
inevitably a certain amount of lag between
discovery and actual exploitation with at least a
possibility, however remote, of newly invented
synthetics or substitutes taking the place of
minerals in short supply in the world today. And
there is always the possibility that deep ocean
mining and exploitation of minerals that lie
under the seas may, in the near future, begin to
compete with the African products.

Industry is perhaps the weakest sector of
African economies. In over thirty African states,
manufacturing constitutes less than ten per cent
of overall production. Only in three African
states, (South Africa, Zimbabwe, and Egypt), does
it exceed twenty-five per cent. Ten states
provide no less than seventy-five per cent of
total African manufacturing, and a large percentage of this is in respect to value added to
foodstuffs, beverages, and tobacco instead of in
production of machines, tools, and other capital
goods. Overall, only about one per cent of the
world's industrial production takes place in Africa.

At present, only about fifteen per cent of
Africa's land surface is considered suitable for
intensive agricultural cultivation. About three-
fifths of this fifteen per cent is devoted to
subsistence agriculture practised by over half of
Africa's total adult population. Through traditional means of cultivation, they produce barely
sufficient food to feed themselves and members of
their families. Their techniques have evolved
over centuries and the crops they produce are
those that have been proven capable of withstanding the ravages of climate, physical environment, and disease. As the tropical African soil
is generally poor in nitrogenous constituents,
their products (corn, plaintains, cassava, yams,
etc.) are usually rich in carbohydrates but
relatively poor in protein.

Other African farmers, mainly because of
European interest, have become involved in

production of cash crops (i.e., crops that are produced not for consumption in Africa but for exports
overseas). Though few in number (cocoa, coffee,
peanuts, cotton, lumber, tobacco, tea, sisal, rubber) these constitute approximately two-thirds of
Africa's total exports. Several African states
are in fact dependent upon the export of a single
cash crop, though in recent years some have made
an effort to diversify their agricultural production. Nevertheless, the overall productivity
of African farmers is comparatively low; about
a third of the food produced is lost to diseases
and pests, either in the field or in storage;
rapidly rising rates of urbanization have led
to a greater demand for food crops for sale
locally; and recurrent drought and substantial
increases in the price of oil and fertilizers have
all resulted in Africa's having to import
increasing supplies of food from overseas at a
considerable cost and the consequential adverse
effects upon balance of payments. As has been
noted:

> Statistics of the UN Food and Agriculture
> Organization show that in 1960, when Africa
> needed 34 million tons of cereal to feed
> its population, it produced 32 million. In
> 1973, however, when it required 45 million
> tons, it produced only 38 million. With an
> overall population growth rate of around
> 2.5 per cent a year, the gap continues to
> widen. Grave famines have become common
> predictions.[17]

Between 1970 and 1980, Africa's population has
grown by about twenty-one per cent, while its
output of food has declined by about ten per cent.
Nigeria, which has the largest population on the
continent, used to be an exporter of food. By
1980, it had already become a net importer of
food. It has been claimed, perhaps on legitimate
grounds, that Africa cannot only become self-
sufficient in food production, but in time can
also become the world's leading food exporter.
There has also been talk, for example that Sudan

alone can within the near future meet forty per cent of the world's food needs. (However, in 1980 as a result of ambitious plans designed to exploit its agricultural potential which had gone sour, Sudan finds itself unable to repay its $3 billion debt and has had to seek rescheduling. Its exports have dropped from $650 million to $450 million, and the deficit in its balance of payments increased to $700 million. It now spends nearly a third of its total export earnings merely to repay debt installments.) Some of these claims may be unduly optimistic but there can be little doubt that Africa's overall agricultural production can be substantially improved. To do so, however, would require determining, through research and experimentation, crops and techniques appropriate to the actual physical environment; selecting and promoting prevalence of appropriate sized farms; introducing and supervising administration of relevant programs, cooperatives, communes, and marketing facilities; changing the work habits of farmers including better discipline in timing; training them through extension courses and demonstration projects to make correct decisions; and providing the necessary infrastructure for transportation of food from one part of the country to another--all tasks which cannot be easily or inexpensively accomplished.

As we have indicated earlier, real economic progress has so far eluded most black African states. Most of the problems outlined above still remain.

The African political history involving slavery, colonial subjugation, struggles for independence, and, finally acquisition of statehood with artificial boundaries has further added to the constraints imposed by physical, social, and economic geographies on rapid development and progress of the continent. To achieve even minimum progress, African states require long-term and effective planning that takes into account all these conditions, honest efficient management, political direction and access

to additional capital and skilled manpower. Even
then success could not be assured. In these
circumstances, it is understandable that some
people might feel that we should not be too harsh
judging the leaders of these comparatively new
and immature states. It might even be understandable if they felt we must not only refrain
from exaggerating but should actively seek to
overlook the actions of African leaders who,
instead of creating game parks, themselves indulge
in poaching and smuggling of ivory, rhino horns and
leopard skins or when they fail to implement
reforestation programs while contributing to
desertification by participating in the lucrative
lumber export trade, or, for that matter, when
they indulge in the hosts of other indiscretions
that we have referred to in the preceding pages,
if only because their problems are so massive. It
would be relatively easy for people to adopt such
a charitable attitude, especially if they themselves stand to lose little from such errors and
indiscretions. And they can always rationalize
their positions by arguing that, after all,
African leaders are not the only ones in history
who have performed badly--an argument which
certainly has much truth in it. However, it is
much more difficult, if not impossible, for a
white living in South Africa or Zimbabwe to be so
sanguine and generous and adopt a similar stance.
It may be understandable if it is difficult for the
black Africans to see this (and many of them may
not want to see this): but it is a fact that in
the back of the minds of most non-Africans in
South Africa apartheid is not the only, or even
the biggest issue. The real issue is that of
political power and how it is going to be exercised in the future. Black African states, whatever their leaders may claim, cannot possibly be
against South Africa because it is not a genuine
democracy. As we have seen, with a handful of
exceptions, all African states themselves are
either under single party or military rule. They
are against the present South African government
because it is white. Similarly, they are not
against South Africa because it has adopted the

policy of apartheid or separate development which discriminates against people on the basis of their racial origins. As we have seen in the preceding pages, black Africans have themselves not been averse to adopting policies which discriminated against the Europeans, Asians, and Arabs on the basis of race and color. What they want is the transfer of power from the white minority to the black majority. Before conceding this power, it is only natural that the whites should be concerned about what place, if any, they would have and what rights if any, they would enjoy under the new order. After all, many of them were born in Africa, have spent their whole lives there, have invested all their savings there, and would like to remain. Contemporary African leaders, as part of their strategy to have the world exert as much pressure as possible upon the South African whites to transfer political power, have often made statements to the effect that the whites have nothing to fear from black rule in Africa. In the Lusaka Manifesto, published following a conference held in Zambia in 1969, leaders of the East and Central African states affirmed:

> We believe all peoples who have made their homes in the countries of Southern Africa (referring to South Africa, Rhodesia, and the parts of Africa which were then under Portuguese control, especially Angola and Mozambique) are Africans, regardless of the color of their skins; and we would oppose a racialist majority which adopted a philosophy of deliberate and permanent discrimination between its citizens on grounds of racial origin. (emphasis added)[18]

Even if this statement is followed to the word, it would still allow the new black order to "differentiate" between the whites and non-whites temporarily to redress existing imbalances in the standards of living of the whites and the blacks. (As might be recalled, this was the exact argument used by Kenya when it introduced a host of new measures discriminating between Africans and non-

437

Africans and which rendered thousands of Asians unable to earn a living in the country in which they were born and gainfully employed until the introduction of "t emporary" measures designed to correct the imbalances.)

Leaders of Zimbabwe's liberation movements have made similar statements. For example, the Rev. Sithole, one of the aspiring leaders of Zimbabwe (Rhodesia) has said "African leaders accept the basic proposition that Zimbabwe is as much the white man's home as it is that of the black man"; and Mr. Nkomo, another such leader, has said "The future of whites in a black-ruled Zimbabwe is assured. No one, but no one, wants to throw the white man out."[19]Bishop Muzorewa had made similar statements. In the elections held in early 1980, however, it was Mr. Robert Mugabe, the leader of the Zimbabwe African National Union (ZANU), who won an absolute majority in the National Assembly--57 seats out of 100, 20 of which were reserved for 230,000 whites residing in the country. Mr. Joshua Nkomo of the Patriotic Front won 20, and Bishop Muzorewa won three. With the merger of Mugabe and Nkomo's forces into a Patriotic Front, the coalition has sufficient seats in the Assembly to permit enactment of any laws, including amendments to the constitution without the agreement of the whites.

Prior to the elections, Mr. Mugabe, a self-styled Marxist and a guerilla leader, had the reputation of being one of the most radical African liberation leaders. He had been jailed by Ian Smith's regime and thoroughly hated that regime. In the negotiations that had preceded the elections, he had strongly favored elimination of any special representation for the whites and made no secret of his desire to institute radical changes in the economy of the country once he came into power.

However, soon after assuming the responsi-bility of leading this country of over 4 million people, he seemed to moderate his views. At different times, within one week of coming into power, he assured the whites that they had no reason to fear black rule. He promised not to seize white properties, accepting the realities of the situation and taking cognizance of the fact that his socialist principles, at least for the time being, will have to take second place to ensuring that the country's economy is not dis- rupted. He vowed not to interfere with private property. He specifically indicated that only unused farmland would be redistributed to the Africans and that even this will be done only after payment of adequate compensation to the owners. He flatly denied any intention to nationalize any of the properties including farms and the mines indicating at the same time that any such changes in the economy can only take place in a gradual manner. He claimed that "there is no intention on our part to use the advantage of the majority we have secured to victimize the minority. That will not happen. We will insure that there is a place for everybody in this country." [20] He promised that private enterprise would remain the basis of the country's economy and even guaranteed pensions for white civil servants.

Are his words empty or will Zimbabwe prove to be different from the other African states? Some would like to see Mugabe's Zimbabwe develop along the lines of Kenyatta's Kenya or Houphouet-Boigny's Ivory Coast instead of Tanzania, Zambia, Uganda, Zaire, Ghana, and Sierra Leone.

Since coming into power, Mr. Mugabe has moved quickly to consolidate his power. In the new Senate, he has conceded only one seat to the Patriotic Front, reserving nineteen for his own party. In the Cabinet, only four of the twenty-three positions have been given to the Patriotic Front, three of which are comparatively minor positions. The fourth one--given to Mr. Nkomo-- the Ministry of Home Affairs has had some of its powers reduced through a governmental reorgan- ization. The membership of his party's Central

Committee has been kept intact and powerful. The party has also been distributing applications for positions in the government on forms imprinted with party slogans. Prospective applicants are required to obtain recommendations from local party officials before they can be seriously considered for appointment. Mr. Mugabe has promised not to institute one-party system "unless the voters approve the move in a referendum." His Minister of Finance, Mr. Enos Nkala, continues to talk in terms of vast redistribution of wealth, but carefully avoids any timetable.

The question most white South Africans have in their minds: Are such verbal assurances credible? Over the last two decades, many of them have been watching, hearing, and reading, with considerable interest, about events in those parts of Africa which are now under black rule. Partly because of their geographic proximity, partly because their historical and cultural relations and partly because of their press (which is sensitive to and does pick up, though not without much difficulty events in black Africa that often go unpublicized), most Southern African whites know about what has happened and is happening in black African countries, especially those which were under British rule. Bearing this in mind, we have in the preceding pages tended to emphasize the events in Anglophone Africa while not ignoring the others. At least the bare outlines of African political, economic, and cultural nationalism, their manifestations, and their implications on the non-blacks that we have described in this book are indelibly stamped on the minds of every white South African. It should be understandable if under black rule therefore, most feel that in the long run, if not in the immediate period, their interests, political, economic, and cultural, would be so adversely affected by measures taken by the black governments in the name of "self-determination" that they would have little alternative but to leave Africa. There have been exceptions (e.g., Ivory Coast), but it would not be a gross exaggeration of the facts to assert that if black majority rule were to come in South Africa today, the chances are heavily in favor of their fears being proved correct.

FOOTNOTES: CHAPTER VII

[1]Immanuel Wallerstein, The Politics of Independence (New York: Random House, 1961), p. 153.

[2]Ibid., p. 163.

[3]Peter Schwab, "Human Rights in Ethiopia," Journal of Modern African Studies, Vol. 14, No. 1, 1976, pp. 156-157. See also: Africa, London, No. 52, December, 1975, p. 28.

[4]The Daily Telegraph, London, January 19, 1971.

[5]Washington Post, Washington, D.C., September 28, 1974.

[6]The Sun, Chicago.

[7]Alhaji Babatunde Jose, "Press Freedom in Africa," African Affairs, July, 1975, p. 256.

[8]Donald George Morrison, et al., (eds.), Black Africa: A Comparative Handbook (New York: Free Press, 1972, note especially pp. 410-414 on data reliability. See also: William M. O'Barr, David H. Spain, and Mark A. Tessler, Survey Research in Africa: Its Applications and Limits (Evanston, Illinois: Northwestern University Press, 1973).

[9]Conference on International Law and African Problems, Meeting of the Standing Committee, O.A.U., June 27-29, 1968, p. 7 (mimeo).

[10] Warren Weinstein, "Africa's Approach to Human Rights at the United Nations," Paper, Annual Convention African Studies Association, 1975, p. 10.

[11] U.S. Department of State, Background Notes; Republic of Zaire, Washington, D.C.: Department of State, Publication 7793, February, 1972, p. 7.

[12] For specific examples, see E.A. Tarabrin, The New Scramble for Africa (Moscow: Progress Publishers, 1974), et seq.

[13] Aderanti Adepoju, "Population Policies in Africa: Problems and Prospects," African Affairs, Vol. 74, 1975, pp. 462-3.

[14] William A. Hance, The Geography of Modern Africa (New York: Columbia University Press, 1975,) p. 378.

[15] Ibid.

[16] William John Hanna and Judith Lynne Hanna, Urban Dynamics in Black Africa (Chicago: Aldine-Atherton, 1971), p. 42.

[17] Special Correspondent, "West Africa: Rural Development," Africa, London, No. 45, May, 1975, p. 29.

[18] H. Adam, Modernizing Racial Domination: South Africa's Political Dynamics (Berkeley: University of California Press, 1971), p. 10.

[19] "Rhodesia: A Matter of Assurance," Africa Confidential, London, Vol. 16, No. 25, December 19, 1975, p. 6.

[20] New York Times, March 5, 1980. Also see: The Christian Science Monitor, March 5, 1980 and Business Week, March 17, 1980.

AUTHORS' PROFILES

Ken C. Kotecha is a practicing attorney in Ohio. He is a member of the U. S. Supreme Court, Ohio, and English Bars. He has the Barrister-at-Law degree from the Middle Temple, England and has a doctorate in Law and Diplomacy, Tufts University, Massachusetts. His background includes over twenty-five years of residence in Africa and teaching and research in African affairs in the United States for several years. He is also Director of Legal Affairs and Associate Professor of Political Science at Wright State University, Dayton, Ohio.

Robert W. Adams is Associate Professor and former Department Chairman of Political Science at Wright State University, Dayton, Ohio. His academic fields of interest are American party politics, public opinion and interest groups. Thus, his contributions to this book are exclusively as editor and writer for an original manuscript produced by Ken C. Kotecha. Adams earned advanced degrees from Syracuse University (M.A. history) and The Ohio State University (Ph. D. political science).

INDEX

Alien, 136-137
All African People's Conference, 56
All Peoples' Congress (APC), 370, 372
Alves, Jean Baptiste, 142
American Committee on Africa, 20
Amhara, 330, 331
Amin, Idi, 58, 63, 73, 111, 126, 127, 132, 150,
    155, 162, 177, 179-180, 183 (fn), 186 (fn),
    188-189, 191, 194, 195, 198, 199, 320, 322,
    323, 324, 349, 407, 419
Amnesty International, 123, 131, 183 (fn)
Anamy, Jerome, 123
Andoh, A.Y.S., 83 (fn)
Andre, Pierre (Kaynga, Pierre), 142
Andreski, Stanislav, 86, 181 (fn)
Angola, 32, 39, 46, 49, 50, 279, 280, 286, 418,
    437
Animist, 431
Ankole, 316
Anti-Apartheid News, 8
Anyona, George, 389
Apartheid, 4, 9, 12, 14, 23, 24, 28, 29, 30, 31,
    32, 35, 36, 39, 59, 41 (fn), 42 (fn), 436,
    437
Arabic, 430
Arab, 47, 136, 148, 149, 200, 201, 203, 213-
    234, 243, 247, 248, 249, 251, 254, 264,
    268, 322, 328, 332, 342, 343, 349, 400,
    401, 404, 437
Argentina, 22, 401
Argentine Sports Federation, 22
Army, 65-67, 72-73, 82 (fn), 83 (fn), 100, 206, 210
Arusha Declaration, 117, 185 (fn), 264, 296 (fn),
    297 (fn)
Asare, 115
Ashanti, 93, 429
Asian, 46, 47, 53, 111, 112, 146, 149, 150, 159,
    160, 162, 164, 165, 172, 179, 180, 185 (fn),
    188-199, 200, 201, 202, 203, 204, 205, 206,
    207, 208, 209, 213, 214, 215, 236, 243, 249,
    251, 254, 257, 264, 265, 268, 271, 272, 273,
    274, 280, 283, 284, 289, 290, 292 (fn), 310,
    327, 348, 361, 402, 404, 419, 425, 437

Currie, David P., 352 (fn)
Cypriots, 236

Dahomey, 338
The Daily Nation (Kenya), 135
Daily News of Tanzania, 149
Dakar, Senegal, 428
Dale, Richard, 43 (fn)
Danquah, Joseph B. (Dr), 52, 131
Dar-es-salaam, Tanzania, 269, 390, 428
Dacko, David, 407, 408
Dattani, 293 (fn)
Dave, L.S., 194
Davies, Constance, 124
de St. Jorre, John, 351 (fn)
Decalo, Samuel, 66, 83 (fn)
Declaration on Southern Africa, 31
Democracy, 60-61, 158, 299, 301, 365, 369, 370,
    381, 384, 391, 394, 397 (fn), 402, 405, 408
Democratic Movement for the Chadian Revolution in
    the Southern Provinces, 146
Denmark, 25
Dentention, 128-137
Department of Bantu Administration, 33
Deportation, 137-139, 179, 188-197
Deutsch, Karl, 57, 80 (fn), 81 (fn)
Dictatorship, 60, 311, 406
Diefenbaker, 3
Diop, Allioune, 185 (fn)
Discretionary Powers, 105-120, 160, 244, 271
Disequilibrium, 65
Distribution of Income, 177-178
Djibouti, 50
Doe, Samuel K. (Master Sgt.), 348
Doro, M.E., 181 (fn)
Draughtsmen's and Allied Technicians' Association,
    20
Dublin, 20
DuBois, Victor D., 145, 184 (fn)
Due, Jean M. 186 (fn)
Duggan, William Redman, 41 (fn)
Dunlop (Nigeria) Ltd., 258

Dutch Reformed Churches, 33
Dutch Trade Union Movement, 8
Dye, Thomas R., 384, 397 (fn)

Europeans, 46, 53, 136, 143, 146, 153, 154, 155,
    157, 172, 196, 198, 200, 201, 202, 203, 205,
    208, 209, 210, 213, 214, 215, 234, 243, 247,
    248, 252, 254, 260, 264, 265, 274, 280, 285,
    289, 310, 356, 368, 399, 402, 403, 405, 406,
    420, 433, 437
Expatriate Quota Allocation Board, 255
Eyadema, 77

Faboe, Fillie, 379
Fania, S.G.M., 379-380
Fanon, Frantz, 52, 57, 81 (fn)
Federalism, 300, 303, 309, 311, 316, 317, 341,
    352 (fn)
Federation of Ethiopia and Eritrea, 329-330, 342
Federation of Horn, 332
Feudalism, 83 (fn)
Fine Arts, 23
Finer, Samuel, 82 (fn)
Finland, 25
First National City Corporation, 17
First World, 402-403, 404
Foltz, William J., 80 (fn)
Food and Agricultural Organization (FAO), 11, 12
Foreign Service, 98-99
Foreman, George, 413
Forfeiture Act, 288
Fornah, Mohamed (Dr), 124
Fort Lamy, Chad (N'Djamena), 145
France, 12, 25, 39, 46, 49, 52, 53, 58, 60, 61, 99,
    125, 153, 210, 255, 286, 301, 317, 336-339,
    360, 375, 407, 420
Franck, Thomas M., 352 (fn)
Freetown, Sierra Leone, 124, 159, 216, 230, 371,
    372, 429
Frelimo, 280, 281-282, 283
French Community of Nations, 337- 338
FROLINAT, 146
Fula, 125
Fulani, 55, 309
Furedi, Frank, 185 (fn)

Gabon, 50, 129, 338, 375
Gaiger, Michael, 196
Gambia, 47, 50, 60, 63, 85, 116, 227, 341, 342, 368, 375
Ganges, 421
Garlick, P.C., 169
Gborie, Alhaji S.H.O., 380
General Assembly, 9, 12, 13, 14, 15, 20, 24, 54, 58, 328, 329, 352 (fn), 395 (fn)
General Electric Corporation, 17
General Motors, 16-17, 18, 67
Genocide, 125-128
Geography, 45-48, 421-424, 443 (fn)
Germans, 125, 272, 274
Germany, 49, 420
Ghai, Y.P., 314, 352 (fn)
Ghana, 4, 47, 50, 52, 54-55, 56, 60, 63, 64, 72, 73, 83 (fn), 89, 93, 99, 102, 106-107, 109, 110, 113, 115, 116, 118, 121-122, 131, 138, 153, 169-170, 175, 182 (fn), 183 (fn), 186 (fn), 199, 227, 242-254, 288, 290, 295 (fn), 314-315, 339, 340, 341, 344, 345, 346, 353 (fn), 357, 358, 359, 361, 370, 374, 406, 407, 408, 409, 410, 413, 426, 428, 429, 439
Ghana Agricultural Development Corporation, 245
Ghana Airways, 422
Ghana Cocoa Marketing Board, 245
Ghana Crafts Corporation, 245
Ghana Diamond Marketing Board, 245
Ghana Enterprises Decree, 249, 252
Ghana Fishing Corporation, 245
Ghana Match Corporation, 245
Ghana National Trading Corporation, 246
Ghana Paint Corporation, 245
Ghana Plastics Products Corporation, 245
Ghana Timber Marketing Board, 245
Ghanaian Business Promotion Act, 1970, 250
Gold Coast (Ghana), 47, 52, 81 (fn)
Gowon, Yakubu (Lt. Col.), 93, 308
Gower, (Dr), 104
Great Britain, 9, 12, 14, 20, 22, 25, 34, 35, 39, 42 (fn), 46, 47, 49, 52, 53, 60, 61, 64, 80 (fn), 86, 104, 110, 123, 126, 139, 146, 153,

455

Kakwa, 73
Kalenji, 101
Kamaliza, Michael, 130
Kamba, 310
Kampala Club, 198
Kampala, Roman Catholic Archbishop of, 196
Kampala, Uganda, 111, 190, 191, 428
Kano, Aminu, 309
Kansella-bantu, Joseph, 130
Ka.uri, 91
Kapwepwe, Simon, 147, 364
Karamoja, Uganda, 194
Karume, Abeid Amani, 136-137, 148-149, 155, 343,
    358
Kásavubu, Joseph, 123, 315-316
Katanga, 315
Katoria, Darmi Ranchod, 189
Kaunda, Kenneth, 49, 62, 80 (fn), 97, 103, 114,
    118, 132, 134, 147, 362, 364-365, 415
Kawawa, Rashidi, 274, 392
Keita, Medibo, 64, 339, 342
Kennecot, 240
Kenya, 4, 22, 39, 47, 50, 53, 62, 63, 90, 97,
    100, 103, 112, 113, 116, 131, 133, 135, 138,
    139, 146, 156, 157, 159, 160, 162, 164, 165,
    172, 179, 185 (fn), 190, 199, 201-215, 240,
    279, 290, 293 (fn), 310-314, 317, 318, 320,
    321, 322, 323, 324, 325, 327, 351 (fn), 352
    (fn) 366-367, 374, 375, 376, 387-390, 392,
    397 (fn), 410, 412, 413, 426, 429, 437, 439
Kenya African Democratic Union (KADU), 159, 310-
    314, 324, 367
Kenya African National Union (KANU), 63, 159, 310-
    314, 324, 367, 388-390
Kenya African Regiment, 101
Kenya Peoples' Union, 367, 389
Kenyan Public Service Commission, 205
Kenyanization, 208
Kenyatta, Jomo, 63, 90, 97, 133, 134, 146, 160,
    179, 185 (fn), 324, 367, 389, 412, 439
Kerekou, 113
Key, V.O., 84 (fn)

458

Kibedi, 183 (fn), 186 (fn)
Kikuyu, 97, 100-101, 103, 146, 160, 310, 311
Kimba, Euariste, 123, 357
Kinshasa, Roman Catholic Archbishop of, 143
Kisii, 63
Kitwara, 409
Kleptocracy, 86
Komeh, A.Y., 377, 378, 380
Kondo, 178
Koroma, Sorie, 371
Korsha, Arku, 361
Kotecha, K.C., 292 (fn)

Lagos, Nigeria, 307, 428, 429
Lake Albert (Lake Mobutu Sese Seko), 141
Lake Edward (Lake Idi Amin Dada), 141
Lake Victoria, 319, 324
La Monde, 412
Land Development (Protection) Act, 1962, 230
Langis, 58, 73, 126, 127
Latin America, 401, 402, 402, 404, 425, 426
La Tribune Africaine (Elombe), 142
Lausanne, 90
Lawson, James (Rev.), 280, 297 (fn)
Leadership Code, 118
Lebanese, 47, 122, 125, 145, 160, 162, 215, 216,
    234, 238, 243, 244, 250, 251, 253, 255, 258,
    293 (fn), 401
Le Courrier d'Afrique (Elima), 142
Legg, Keith, 83 (fn)
Legislatures, 99, 363-384
Legum, Colin, 41 (fn), 80 (fn)
Legum, Margaret, 41 (fn)
Lemarchand, Rene, 67, 80 (fn), 83 (fn), 127
Lemn, 332
Leopold II, 141
Le Progress (Salongo), 142
Lesotho, 28, 37, 50, 92, 401
L'Etoile (Myoto), 142
Levantines, 238
Levantis Motors, 258
Lever Brothers, 258

Levy, Marion J., 66, 82 (fn)
Leys, Colin, 76, 84 (fn)
Liberation Movements, 24-25
Liberia, 50, 68, 89, 227, 348
Libya, 199, 324, 400, 432
Licencing, 170-171, 172
Limann, Hilla (Dr), 254, 408
Lloyd, Selwyn, 80 (fn)
Loans, 171-173
Loi-Cadre, 337
Loi Fondamentale, 315
London, 90, 99, 149, 209, 241, 307
London Times, 412
Lozi, 97, 317
Lüle, Yusufu K., 199, 324
Lumumba, Patrice, 315
Lumumbashi, 238, 239
Lundgraen, Carl Richard, 272
Lusaka, Zambia, 428
Lusaka Manifesto, 437
Luo, 55, 97, 133, 134, 139, 160, 310, 311, 389
Lupembe, 210
Lusaka, Zambia, 281, 283

Machel, Samora, 282, 283-285, 297 (fn)
Macias, 58
Mackintosh, John P., 296 (fn), 305, 351 (fn)
Madagascar, 50, 64, 347
Mahamba, Alexandre, 123
Majority Rule, 27, 36, 39, 59-79, 205, 233, 263,
     291, 299-350, 401, 437, 441
Malagasy, 323, 344, 347, 359
Malawi, 26, 28, 45, 50, 63, 89, 98-99, 114, 129,
     131, 138, 159, 287-290, 298 (fn), 360-361,
     365-366, 374, 387, 392, 395 (fn), 401, 429
Malawi Congress Party, 138, 159, 289, 365, 387
Malays, 47
Mali, 50, 64, 68, 110, 338-339, 340, 341, 342,
     346, 353 (fn), 409, 425
Malloum, Felix (General), 77-98
Mamdani, Mahmood, 179, 186 (fn)
Mange, James Daniel, 30
Manufacturing Industries Act, 1971, 250-251

Marabouts, 74
Margai, Albert, 90, 370, 372
Marquard, Leopold, 35, 43 (fn)
Martin, David, 111, 127, 183 (fn), 413
Martine-Cisse, Jeanne, 41 (fn), 43 (fn)
Marxism, 29, 98, 157, 332, 438
Masai United Front, 310
Massawa, 331
Mauritania, 50, 400
Mauritius, 50, 368, 401, 425
Mazrui, Ali, 103-104, 182 (fn)
McAuslane, J.P., 314
McKean, Dayton, 84 (fn)
McMullan, M., 86, 87, 181 (fn)
Mecca, 431
Mediterranean, 47
Melson, 91
Mende, 73, 370
Mengistu Haile Mariam, 67, 331-332
Merkl, Peter H., 355, 395 (fn)
Mettle, M.A., 110, 182 (fn)
Mexico, 22
Mexico City, 90
Micombero, 127
Middle East 46, 47, 90, 349, 400, 402
Militarism, 25-26, 30, 64-67, 69, 71-73, 82 (fn),
      83 (fn), 92, 93, 102, 104, 112, 118, 132, 158,
      182 (fn), 190, 317, 363, 371, 396 (fn)
Military Isolation, 12-15
Miller, Norman H., 62, 82 (fn)
Mills, C. Wright, 151, 184 (fn)
Mineral Production, 432-433
Ministerial Justice, 358-359
Minogue, Martin, 80 (fn), 185 (fn), 296 (fn)
Minority Rights, 299, 301
Minority Rights Group, 127
Mississippi, 421
Mixed Marriages Act, 34
Mobutu, Joseph Desire (Lt. Gen.), 316
Mobutu, Sese Seko, 77, 85, 90, 123-124, 130-131,
      132, 140-145, 184 (fn), 234-236, 238, 241,
      357, 366, 386, 395 (fn), 420
Mohammed, Bibi Titi, 130

461

National Community, 54-57, 61
National Development Cooperative, 245
National Front for the Liberation of Mozambique
    (Frelimo), 280, 281-282, 283
National Independence Party, 305
National Language, 93
National Liberation Council, 249
National Party (of Nigeria), 309
National Party (S. Afr.), 4, 25, 35, 39
National Recovery Plan, 241
National Redemption Council, 113
National Security, 201
National Union of Mineworkers, 20
Nationalism, African, 49, 52, 57, 92, 129, 168-
    170, 181 (fn), 182 (fn), 350
Ndegwa, Duncan, 202
Ndongmo, Albert (Monsignor), 357
Negritude, 152-153, 185 (fn), 402
Negroid, 46, 47
Nehru, 3
Nelson, R., 181 (fn)
Neogy, Rajat, 131
Netherlands, 19, 46, 49
New York Times, 412, 443 (fn)
New Zealand, 3, 18, 21
News Media, 3, 7, 8, 9, 20-21, 130, 133, 135-
    136, 149, 151, 226, 381, 390, 397 (fn), 412-
    416, 442 (fn)
Ngala,R.G., 311
Nguema, Francisco Macias, 128, 407
Niger, 50
Nigeria, 4, 50, 52, 57, 60, 64, 68, 72, 73, 78, 91,
    93, 96, 99, 102, 103-104, 115, 116, 119, 120,
    128, 133, 135, 139, 173, 176, 181 (fn), 183
    (fn), 186 (fn), 254-263, 265, 290, 296 (fn),
    304-310, 317, 346-347, 351 (fn), 361, 374,
    407, 410, 413, 417, 419, 425, 426, 427, 428,
    429, 432, 433
Nigeria Airways, 422
Nigerian-Biafran War, 348, 419
Nigerian Enterprises Promotion Decree (NEPD), 256-
    261
Nigerian People's Party, 310

Oman, 47
O'Meara, Patrick, 81 (fn)
Open Door Policy, 255-256
Organization of African Trade Unity, 19-20
Organization of African Unity, 11, 18, 42 (fn), 154,
    330, 343-349, 354 (fn), 371, 417-418, 442 (fn)
Organization of Petroleum Exporting Countries
    (OPEC), 263, 403-404
Orange Free State, 34
Ottaway, David B., 412
Ouko, Robert, 202

Pademba Road Prison, 124
Pakistan, 22, 265
Pakistanis, 47, 145, 191, 234, 236, 237, 239, 240,
    243
Pan-Africanism, 151-152, 153-155, 255, 339-341, 402
Pan-Africanist Congress, 2, 4
Paper Conversion Corporation, 245
Pardhan, 164
Paris, 90
Parti Democratique du Cote d'Ivoire (PDCI), 68,
    78, 98, 386-387
Pass Laws, 34
Passport (Amendment) Bill, 1974, 377
Patel, B.H., 289
Patel, Chitubhai Prema, 287-288
Paternalism, 33, 35
Patriotic Front, 438, 439
Pax Americana, 72
Payroll Tax Act, 1972 (Sierra Leone), 226-227, 228
Peaslee, Amos J., 351 (fn), 353 (fn)
Pemba Peoples' Party, 343, 391
Penal Code (Guinea), 122
Pentagon, 67
People's Redemption Party, 309
People's Republic of China, 25
Petroleum, 16
Philippines, 22
Pienär, Lt. Col, 2
Police, 107-109, 115-116, 163, 206, 210
Political Machines, 76-78, 87

Political Rights, 37-40
Polynesians, 47
Pomper, Gerald, 385, 397 (fn)
Population, 20, 39, 46, 50-51, 165, 215, 417, 425-430, 443 (fn)
Port Harcourt Railway Station, 308
Portugal, 32, 39, 46, 48, 49, 57, 144-145, 234, 237, 240, 278-282, 285, 286, 298 (fn), 361, 362, 437
Potholm, Christian P., 43 (fn), 91, 181 (fn)
Pretoria, 3, 6, 22
Preventive Detention Act (Tanzania), 130
Price, Major, 196
Price, Robert M., 83 (fn)
Proctor, J.H., 397 (fn)
Progressive Federal Party, 29
Prohibition of Mixed Marriages Act, 28
Public Service Commission, 103
Pye, L.W., 82 (fn)
Pygmies, 47

Racism, 3-4, 5, 8, 9, 10, 14, 23, 34, 36, 59, 152, 156, 204, 282, 292 (fn), 348, 395 (fn), 405, 416, 418, 421, 437
Radford, Henry, 196
Ramadhan, 431
Rawlings, Jerry, 407-408
Refugees, 139, 286
Regional Assemblies Provincial Councils, 314
Rent Restriction Decrees, 270
Representation, 52, 63
Reynolds, 240
Rhodes, Cecil, 33
Rhodes-James, Robert, 419
Rhodesia (Zimbabwe), 4, 18, 32, 39, 53, 307, 437, 438, 443 (fn)
Riker, William, 75, 84 (fn)
Rio de Janeiro, 3, 21
Riordan, William L., 84 (fn), 181 (fn)
River Gambia, 422
River Niger, 45
River Zaire (Congo), 45
Rothchild, Donald, 351 (fn), 352 (fn)

Russians, 285, 331, 332
Rutman, 268
Rwanda, 47, 51, 129, 425

Sahara, 47, 422
Sao Tome and Principe, 51
Saras, 98, 145, 146
Saudi Arabia, 47, 330
Schwab, Peter, 442 (fn)
Scotland, 46
Second National Development Plan (Nigeria, 1970-
    1974), 256
Second World, 402-403, 404
Security Council, 12, 315, 345
Selassie, Haille, 90, 323, 327, 406-407
Self-Determination, 54-59, 108, 139, 152, 161, 165,
    178, 279, 281, 317, 330, 440
Semites, 46, 47
Senegal, 46, 51, 74, 101, 116, 152, 338, 341, 342,
    346, 368, 375, 414, 416, 428
Senegal-Gambia Interstate Committee, 342
Senegambia, 342
Senghor, Leopold, 152-153, 185 (fn), 339, 368
Separate Universities Act, 34
Seychelles, 51, 89, 323
Shagari, Shehu, 309, 407
Sharpeville, 1, 2, 5, 10, 41 (fn)
Sharpeville Demonstration, 1-5
Shils, E.A., 82 (fn)
Shikuku, 182 (fn)
Short, Philip, 395 (fn)
Sibeko, David M., 41 (fn)
Sierra Leone, 47, 51, 62, 72, 73, 90, 93, 96, 122,
    124, 138, 159, 160, 162, 182 (fn), 215-234,
    290, 293 (fn), 294 (fn), 360, 361, 363, 370-
    372, 377, 379-380, 395 (fn), 396 (fn), 418,
    439
Sierra Leone Citizenship (Amendment) Act, 1976,
    225-226, 233
Sierra Leone Citizenship Act, 1973, 224-225
Sierra Leone Nationality and Citizenship Act, 222
Sierra Leone Peoples' Party (SLPP), 370-371

Single-Party System, 61-64, 82 (fn), 84 (fn), 93,
    98, 158,   364-394, 406, 408
Sithole, (Rev), 438
Six Year Development Plan (Nigeria, 1962-1968), 255
Skinner, James, 362
Slave Trade, 49
Smith, Ian, 32, 438
Smock, David R., 92, 182 (fn)
Smuts, J.C., 43 (fn)
Societe Commerciale d'Afrique de l'Ouest, 258
Sokoto, 426
Somalia, 23, 47, 51, 92, 121, 279, 323, 330, 331,
    332, 400
Somalis, 310
Sónghay, 409
Sore, Fola, 183 (fn)
Soremkun, Fole, 184 (fn)
South Africa, 1-40, 46, 47, 48, 51, 78, 129, 196,
    262, 278, 343, 348, 349, 361, 368, 400, 401,
    419, 432, 433, 436, 437, 443 (fn)
South Asia, 400
South West Africa (Namibia), 32, 49
South Yemen, 332
Southern Rhodesia, 51
Soviet Union, 9, 25, 89
Soweto, 5-6, 27
Spain, 49
Spain, David H., 442 (fn)
Special Committee on Apartheid (U.N.), 9-10, 23,
    31
Spinola, (General), 280
Sports, 21-23 .
Standard, The (Kenya), 135
Stanley, Henry Morton, 141
State Furniture and Joinery Corporation, 245
State Security Courts, 357-358
Stevens, Siaka, 90, 222, 223, 370, 371, 372
Strayer, Joseph, 80 (fn)
Stultz, N.M., 181 (fn)
Sudan, 47, 51, 338, 361, 400, 425, 434-435
Sullivan, Leon F., Rev., 18, 42 (fn)
Sullivan Code, 18
Sun, The, (Chicago), 414, 442 (fn)

Supreme Council for Sport, 22
Supreme Revolutionary Tribunal, 125
Svendsen, Knud Erik, 296 (fn)
Swahili, 93, 148, 319
Swaziland, 51, 92, 371
Sweden, 25
Swedes, 285
Swiss, 274
Switzerland, 255
Syrians, 47, 122, 162, 215, 216, 234, 238, 243,
    244, 258, 401

Tanga, 323, 428
Tanganyika, 149, 263, 296 (fn), 297 (fn), 327,
    333, 335, 353 (fn), 391
Tanganyika African National Union (TANU), 62, 64,
    117, 130, 159, 274, 275, 277, 296 (fn), 335,
    353 (fn), 390-392
Tanzam Railway, 321
Tanzania, 9, 39, 45, 47, 51, 58, 61, 62, 64, 71,
    82 (fn), 88, 93, 99, 117-118, 129-130, 131,
    134, 135-136, 137, 138, 139, 148-150, 156,
    159, 161, 164, 184 (fn), 185 (fn), 224, 229,
    263-278, 279, 290, 291, 296 (fn), 297 (fn),
    298 (fn), 318, 320, 321, 322, 323, 324, 325,
    327, 333-336, 353 (fn), 358, 359, 361, 373,
    374, 375, 376, 381-383, 390-393, 396 (fn),
    397 (fn), 407, 408, 411, 412, 413, 419, 425,
    426, 427, 428, 439
Tanzania Information Services, 390, 397
Tanzanian Constitutional Revision, 1965, 359
Tanzanian Women's League, 130
Taqi, Ibrahim, 124
Tarabrin, E.A., 443 (fn)
Tate, John, 22
Tate & Lyle (Nigeria) Ltd., 258
Teamsters Union, 67
Temne, 73, 370, 371
Teribe, I., 173, 186 (fn)
Tessler, Mark A., 442 (fn)
Thiam, Doudou, 350, 354 (fn)
Third World, 9, 11, 83 (fn), 87, 402-404

Thompson, W. Scott, 354 (fn)
Tiesen, Merete, 296 (fn)
Times, (Zambia), 415
Tiv, 91
Togo, 51, 57, 67, 71, 357
Tolbert, William R. (Jr.), 348
Tolstoy Foundation, 195
Tombalaye, Francois (N'Garta), 98, 145-146
Tongo, 97
Tordoff, William, 353 (fn)
Toro, 316
Toure, Ishmael, 125
Toure, Sekou, 58, 69, 89, 98, 124-125, 183 (fn),
    339, 341, 342, 349
Trades Union Congress, 20
Transition, 131
Transport and General Workers' Union, 20
Transvaal, 34
Treason Act (Sierra Leone), 122
Tribalism, 91-105, 135, 158-159, 404, 410, 411, 416,
    431
Tribe, 48, 74, 126
Tropic of Cancer, 423
Tropic of Capricorn, 423
Tunisia, 346, 400
Tutsi, 47, 127-128

Udoji Commission, 102
Uganda, 39, 51, 58, 63, 73, 93, 111, 112, 125-127,
    131, 132, 139, 141, 155, 162, 177, 178, 179,
    183 (fn), 187, 188-199, 290, 292 (fn), 316,
    317, 318, 320, 321, 322, 323, 324, 325, 348,
    349, 351 (fn), 356, 360, 361, 407, 408, 413,
    419, 428, 439
Uganda Immigration Office, 179
Uganda Lint Marketing Board, 194
Uganda National Liberation Front, 324
Uganda People's Congress, 63
Ujamaa, 134, 156, 274-275, 277, 296 (fn), 297 (fn),
    325
Ujamaaisation, 274
Ukongo Prison (Tanzania), 129

University of California Regents, 17
University of Lagos, 104
University of Nairobi, 133, 135
Upper Volta, 51, 90, 338, 340, 341, 408
Urban Leaseholds (Acquisition and Re-Grant) Act,
    1968, 269
Urhobo, 91
Uwechue, Raph, 354 (fn)

Van der Laan, H.L., 293 (fn)
Venezuela, 265
Vorster, John, 6
Vyas, H.J., 194

Wallerstein, Immanuel, 91, 181 (fn), 406, 442 (fn)
Washington, D.C. City Council, 19
Washington Post, 412, 442 (fn)
Weinstein, Warren, 419-420, 443 (fn)
Welch, C.E., Jr., 82 (fn)
West African National Secretariat, 339
West Germany, 209
Widgery, Cyril, 196
Wildlife, 424-425
Williams, H.T.T., 380
Williams, T. David, 395 (fn)
Wilson, James Q., 84 (fn), 181 (fn)
Wilson, Woodrow, 54
Wolpe, H., 91, 181 (fn)
Woodcock, George, 42 (fn), 80 (fn)
World Bank, 254, 265, 274
World Council of Churches, 16, 20, 280, 297 (fn)
World Fencing Federation, 21
World Health Organization (WHO), 12, 429
Worrall, Denis J., 36, 43 (fn)

Yameogo, Maurice, 90
Yondo Rotes, 145
Yorubas, 73, 91, 104, 305, 308
Young, Andrew, 32, 43 (fn)